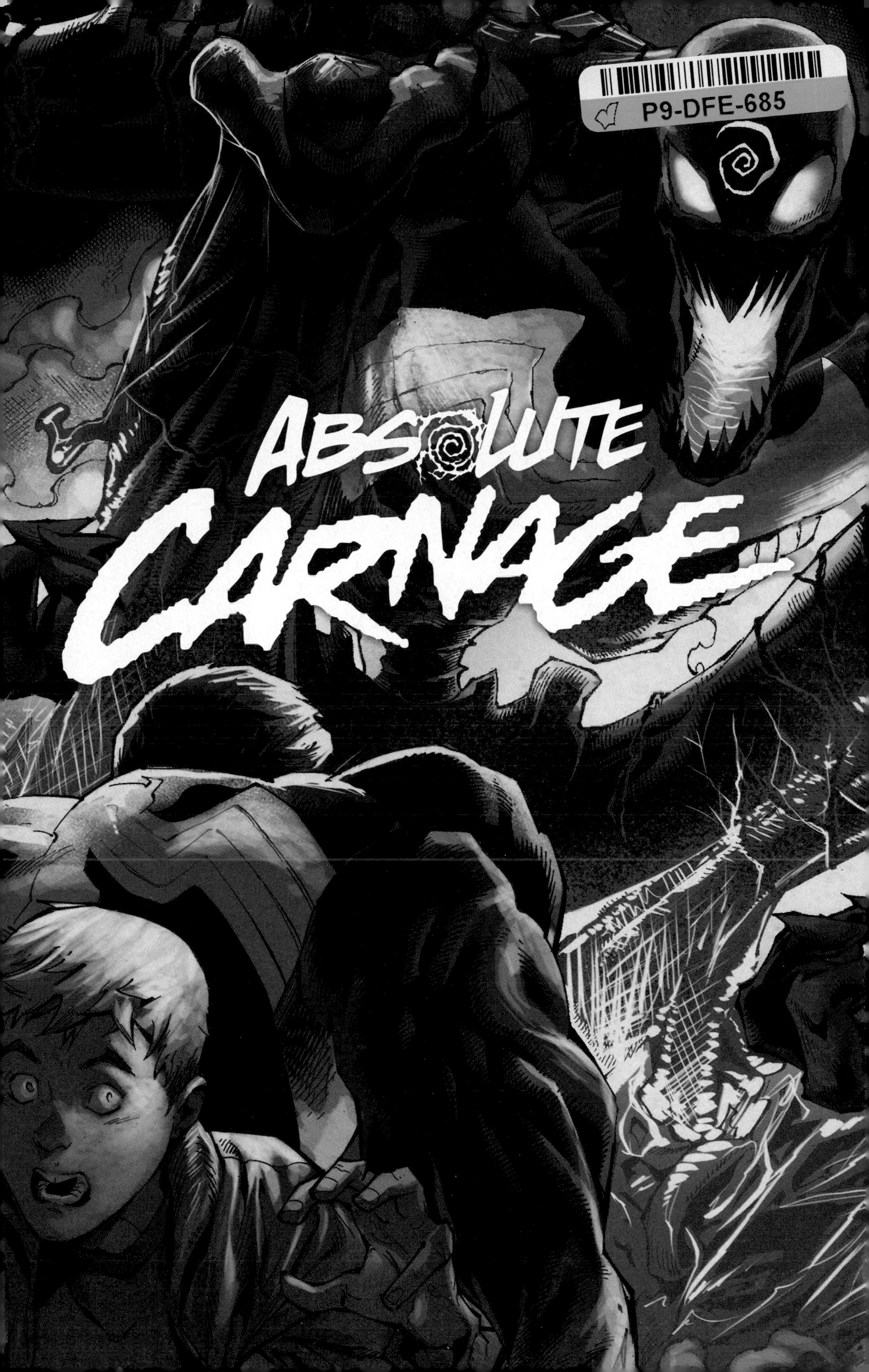
ABSOLUTE
CARNAGE

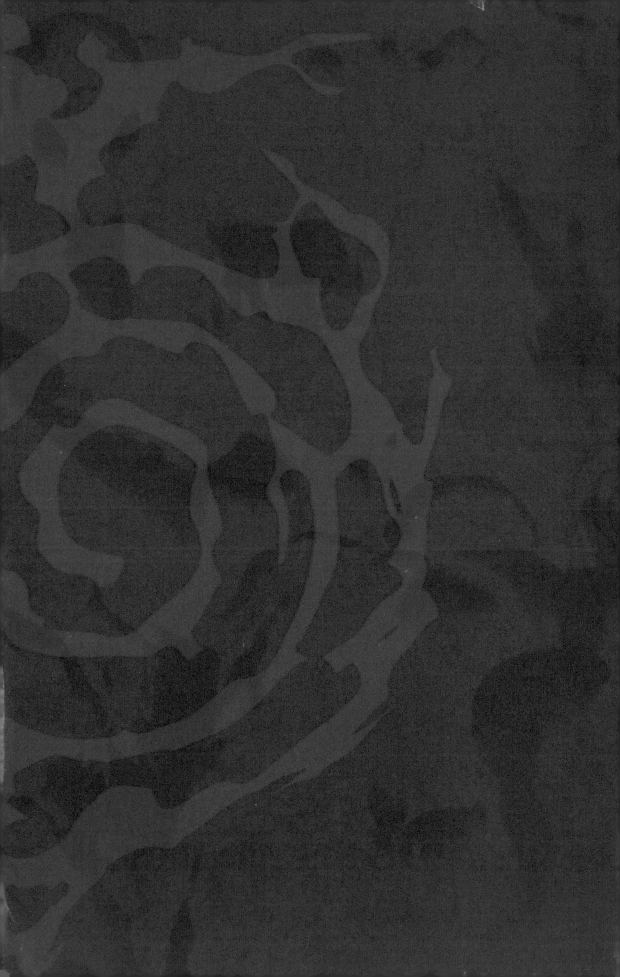

At one of the lowest points of his life, disgraced reporter Eddie Brock came into contact with an aggressive and parasitic alien organism called a symbiote. Sensing Brock's anger, the creature bonded with him, and their union granted him powers similar to those of the Amazing Spider-Man, as well as a number of unique abilities, and the **two fought crime as Venom**.

But Brock and **the symbiote are separated now**, driven apart after Eddie learned it had been tampering with his memories prior to the War of the Realms. He also learned that he has a son named Dylan, who has been led to believe that Eddie is his older brother.

All this while a familiar evil has been at work on the periphery of Eddie's world, with Eddie and everyone he cares about dead in its sights.

Somehow, Brock will need to keep himself and his son alive through **the coming storm**...

ABSOLUTE CARNAGE

Donny Cates
WRITER

Ryan Stegman
PENCILER

JP Mayer
with **Jay Leisten** (#4-5) & **Ryan Stegman** (#5)
INKERS

Frank Martin
COLOR ARTIST

Mark Bagley & **John Dell**
FLASHBACK ARTISTS, #5

VC's Clayton Cowles
LETTERER

Ryan Stegman & Frank Martin (*Free Comic Book Day 2019*) and
Ryan Stegman, JP Mayer & Frank Martin (#1-5)
COVER ART

Danny Khazem
ASSISTANT EDITOR

Devin Lewis
EDITOR

Nick Lowe
EXECUTIVE EDITOR

Collection Editor **Jennifer Grünwald**
Assistant Editor **Caitlin O'Connell**
Associate Managing Editor **Kateri Woody**
Editor, Special Projects **Mark D. Beazley**

VP Production & Special Projects **Jeff Youngquist**
Book Designer **Adam Del Re**
SVP Print, Sales & Marketing **David Gabriel**
Director, Licensed Publishing **Sven Larsen**

Editor in Chief **C.B. Cebulski**
Chief Creative Officer **Joe Quesada**
President **Dan Buckley**
Executive Producer **Alan Fine**

ABSOLUTE CARNAGE. Contains material originally published in magazine form as ABSOLUTE CARNAGE (2019) #1-5 and FREE COMIC BOOK DAY 2019 (SPIDER-MAN/VENOM) #1. First printing 2019. ISBN 978-1-302-91908-5. Published by MARVEL WORLDWIDE, INC., a subsidiary of MARVEL ENTERTAINMENT, LLC. OFFICE OF PUBLICATION: 135 West 50th Street, New York, NY 10020.

Printed in the U.S.A. DAN BUCKLEY, President, Marvel Entertainment; JOHN NEE, Publisher; JOE QUESADA, Chief Creative Officer; TOM BREVOORT, SVP of Publishing; DAVID BOGART, Associate Publisher & SVP of Talent Affairs; DAVID GABRIEL, VP of Print & Digital Publishing; JEFF YOUNGQUIST, VP of Production & Special Projects; DAN CARR, Executive Director of Publishing Technology; ALEX MORALES, Director of Publishing Operations; DAN EDINGTON, Managing Editor; SUSAN CRESPI, Production Manager; STAN LEE, Chairman Emeritus. For information regarding advertising in Marvel Comics or on Marvel.com, please contact Vit DeBellis, Custom Solutions & Integrated Advertising Manager, at vdebellis@marvel.com. For Marvel subscription inquiries, please call 888-511-5480. **Manufactured between 11/15/2019 and 12/17/2019 by LSC COMMUNICATIONS INC., KENDALLVILLE, IN, USA.**

10 9 8 7 6 5 4 3 2 1

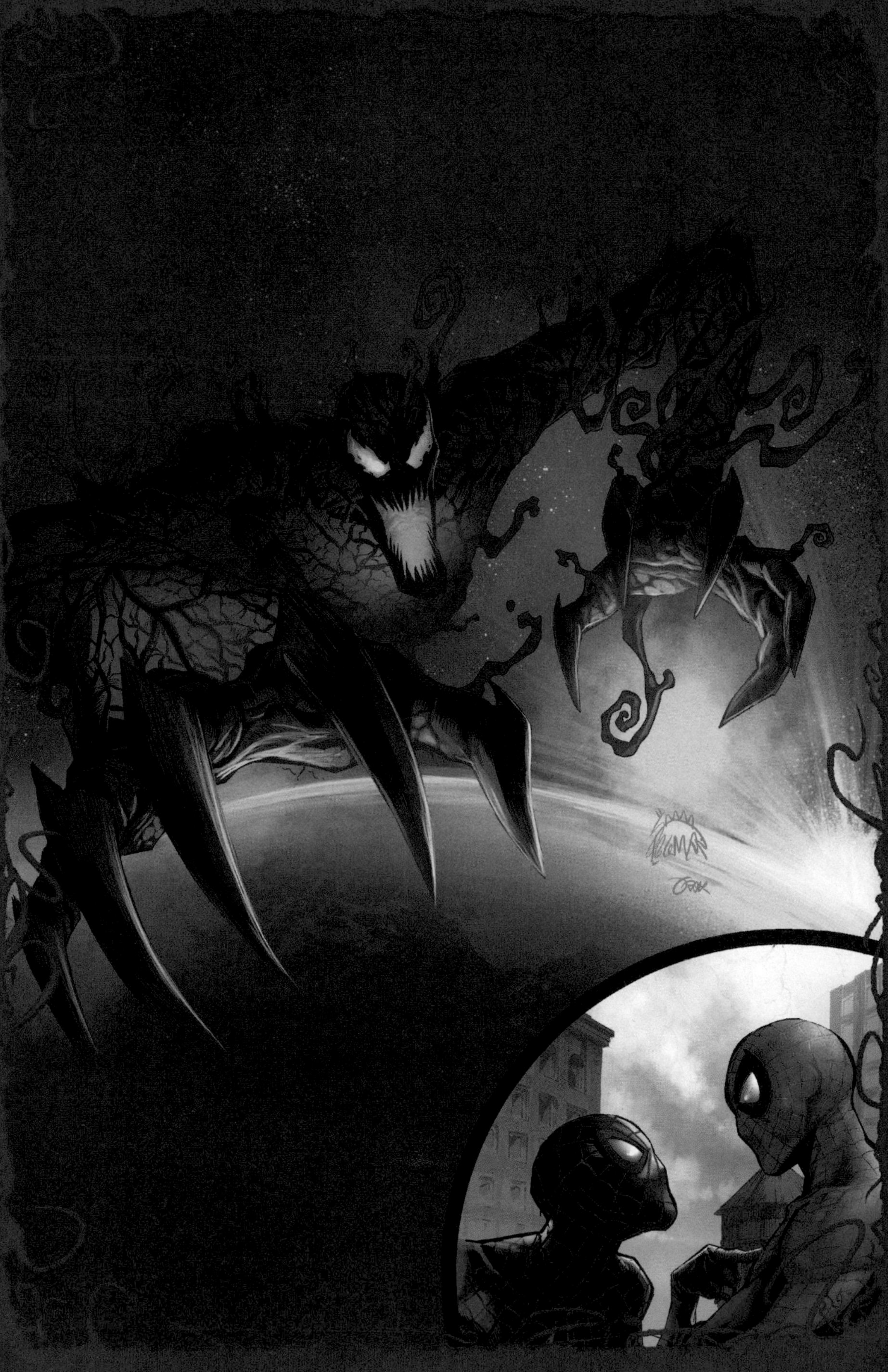

FREE COMIC BOOK DAY 2019

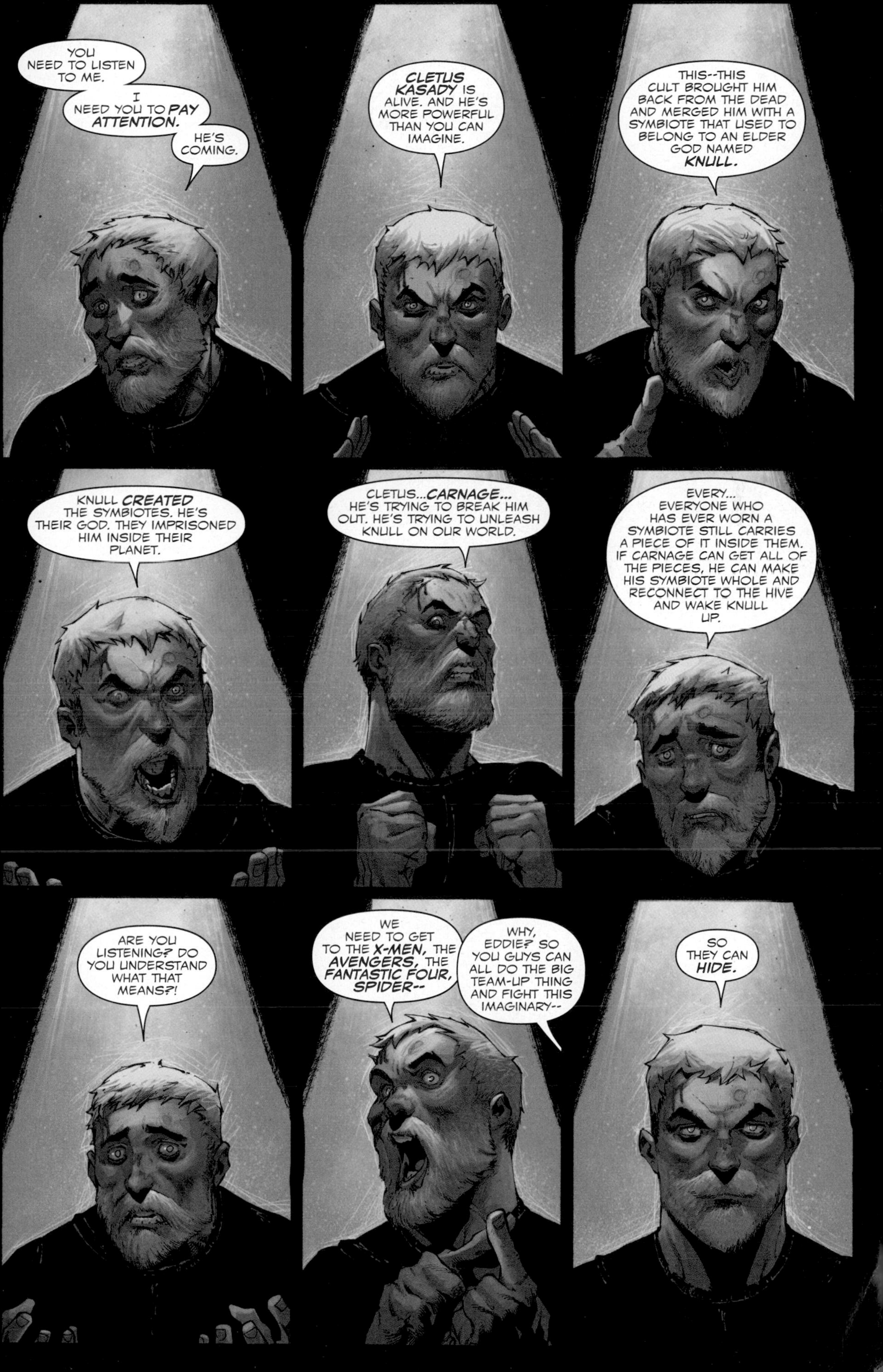
YOU NEED TO LISTEN TO ME.
I NEED YOU TO PAY ATTENTION.
HE'S COMING.
CLETUS KASADY IS ALIVE. AND HE'S MORE POWERFUL THAN YOU CAN IMAGINE.
THIS--THIS CULT BROUGHT HIM BACK FROM THE DEAD AND MERGED HIM WITH A SYMBIOTE THAT USED TO BELONG TO AN ELDER GOD NAMED KNULL.
KNULL CREATED THE SYMBIOTES. HE'S THEIR GOD. THEY IMPRISONED HIM INSIDE THEIR PLANET.
CLETUS...CARNAGE... HE'S TRYING TO BREAK HIM OUT. HE'S TRYING TO UNLEASH KNULL ON OUR WORLD.
EVERY... EVERYONE WHO HAS EVER WORN A SYMBIOTE STILL CARRIES A PIECE OF IT INSIDE THEM. IF CARNAGE CAN GET ALL OF THE PIECES, HE CAN MAKE HIS SYMBIOTE WHOLE AND RECONNECT TO THE HIVE AND WAKE KNULL UP.
ARE YOU LISTENING? DO YOU UNDERSTAND WHAT THAT MEANS?!
WE NEED TO GET TO THE X-MEN, THE AVENGERS, THE FANTASTIC FOUR, SPIDER--
WHY, EDDIE? SO YOU GUYS CAN ALL DO THE BIG TEAM-UP THING AND FIGHT THIS IMAGINARY--
SO THEY CAN HIDE.

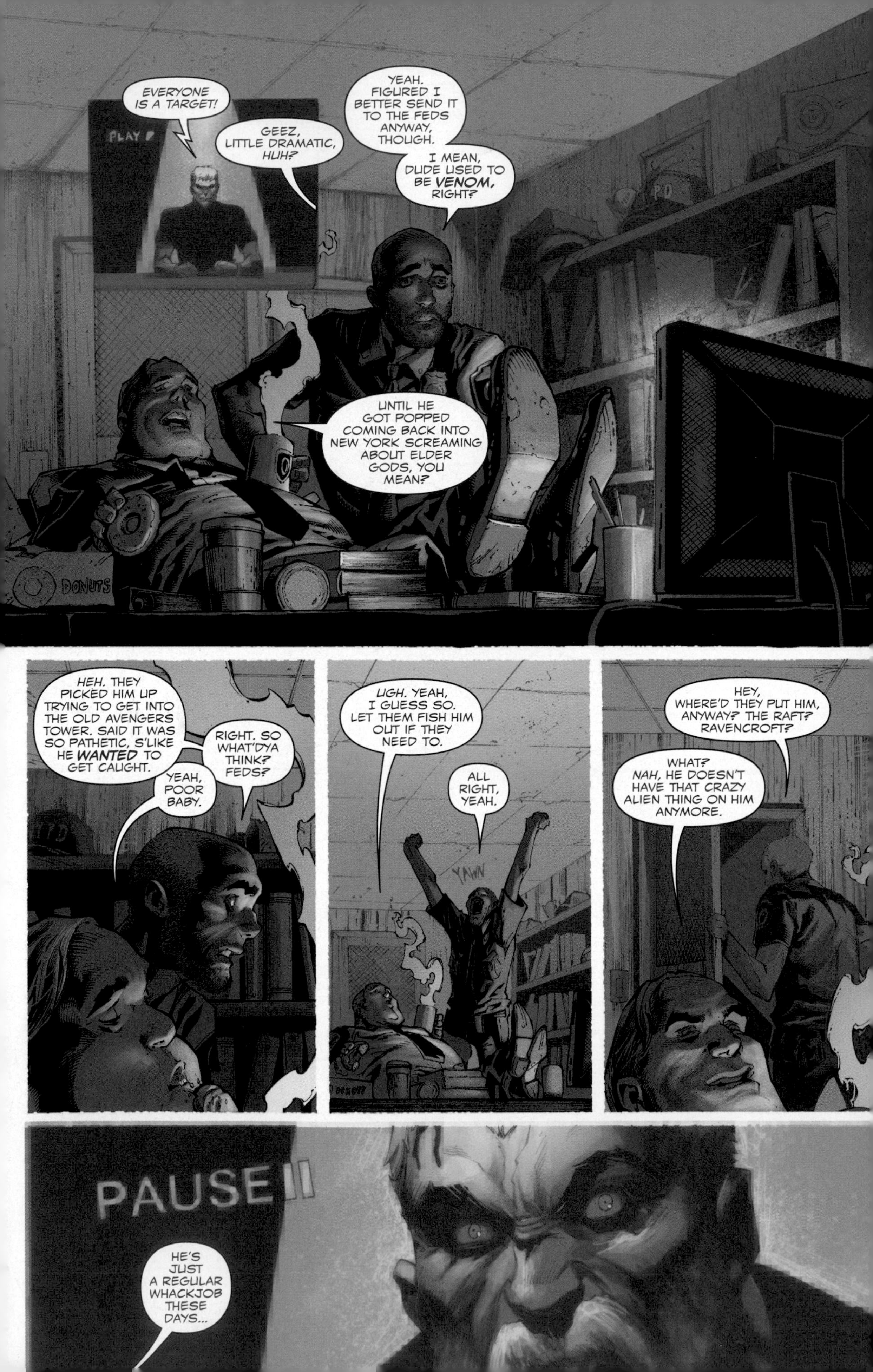
EVERYONE IS A TARGET!
PLAY
GEEZ, LITTLE DRAMATIC, HUH?
YEAH. FIGURED I BETTER SEND IT TO THE FEDS ANYWAY, THOUGH.
I MEAN, DUDE USED TO BE VENOM, RIGHT?
UNTIL HE GOT POPPED COMING BACK INTO NEW YORK SCREAMING ABOUT ELDER GODS, YOU MEAN?
DONUTS
HEH. THEY PICKED HIM UP TRYING TO GET INTO THE OLD AVENGERS TOWER. SAID IT WAS SO PATHETIC, S'LIKE HE WANTED TO GET CAUGHT.
RIGHT. SO WHAT'DYA THINK? FEDS?
YEAH, POOR BABY.
UGH. YEAH, I GUESS SO. LET THEM FISH HIM OUT IF THEY NEED TO.
ALL RIGHT, YEAH.
YAWN
HEY, WHERE'D THEY PUT HIM, ANYWAY? THE RAFT? RAVENCROFT?
WHAT? NAH, HE DOESN'T HAVE THAT CRAZY ALIEN THING ON HIM ANYMORE.
PAUSE II
HE'S JUST A REGULAR WHACKJOB THESE DAYS...

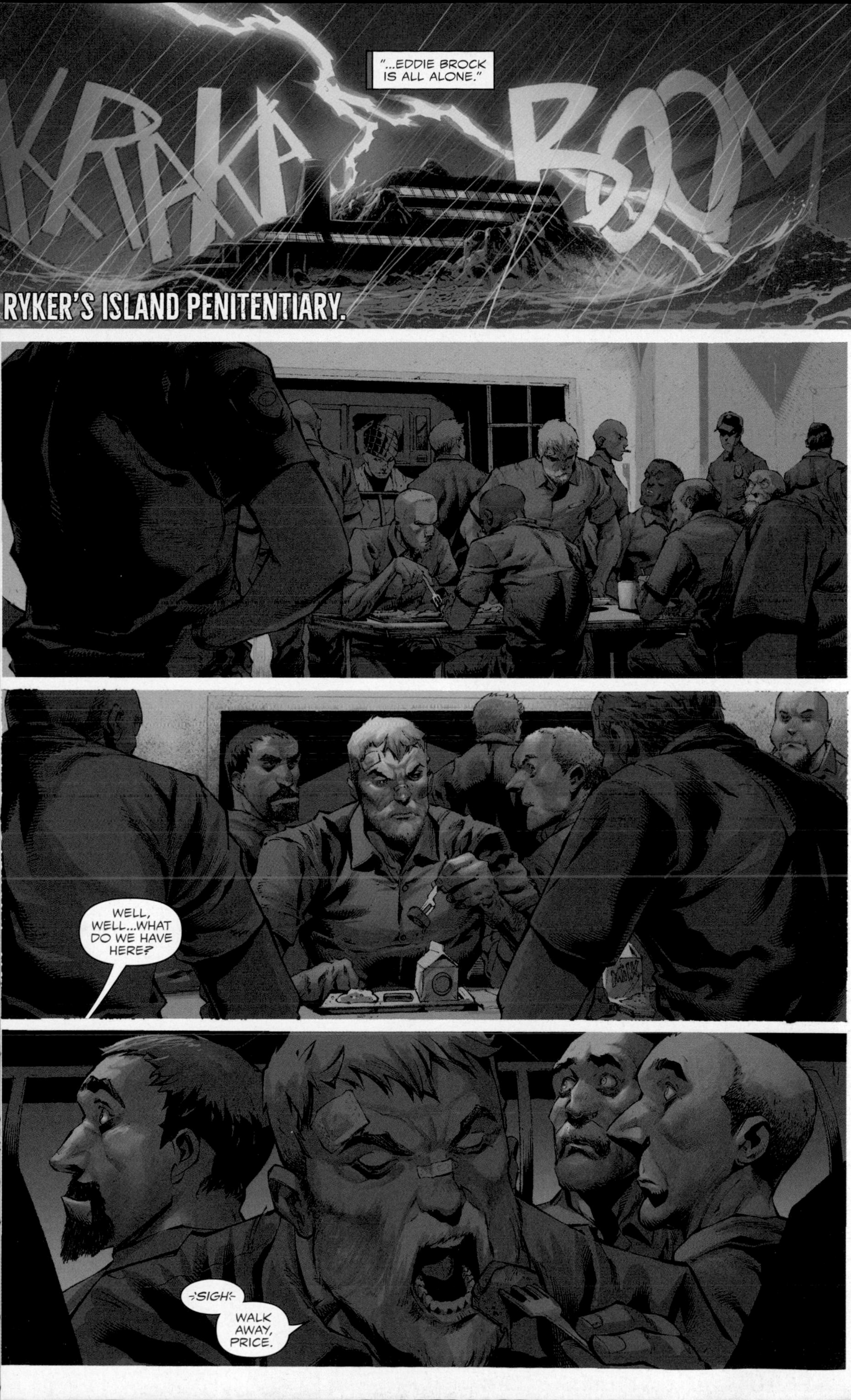
"...EDDIE BROCK IS ALL ALONE."
KRAKKA-BOOM
RYKER'S ISLAND PENITENTIARY.
WELL, WELL...WHAT DO WE HAVE HERE?
-SIGH-
WALK AWAY, PRICE.

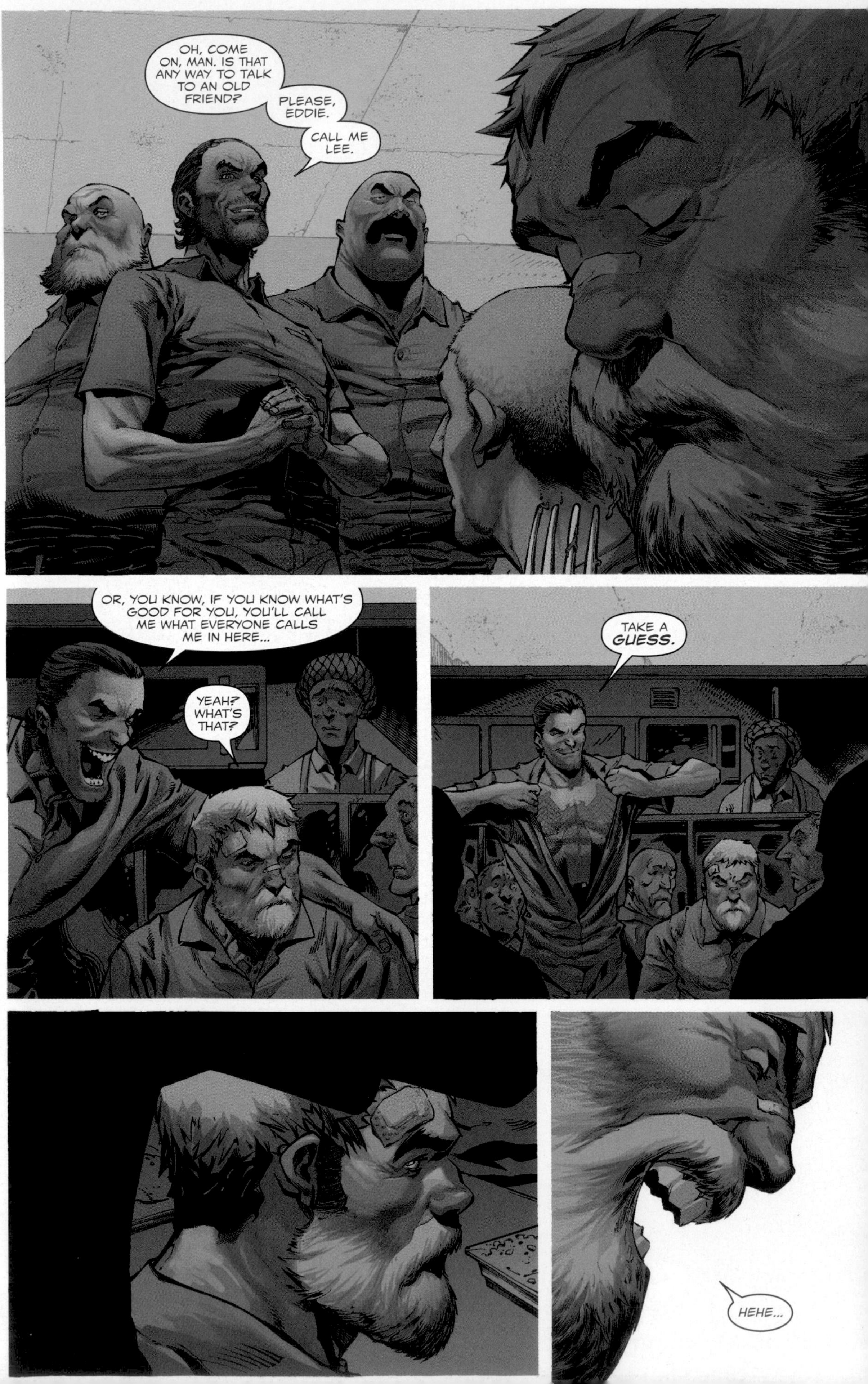
OH, COME ON, MAN. IS THAT ANY WAY TO TALK TO AN OLD FRIEND?
PLEASE, EDDIE.
CALL ME LEE.
OR, YOU KNOW, IF YOU KNOW WHAT'S GOOD FOR YOU, YOU'LL CALL ME WHAT EVERYONE CALLS ME IN HERE...
YEAH? WHAT'S THAT?
TAKE A GUESS.
HEHE...

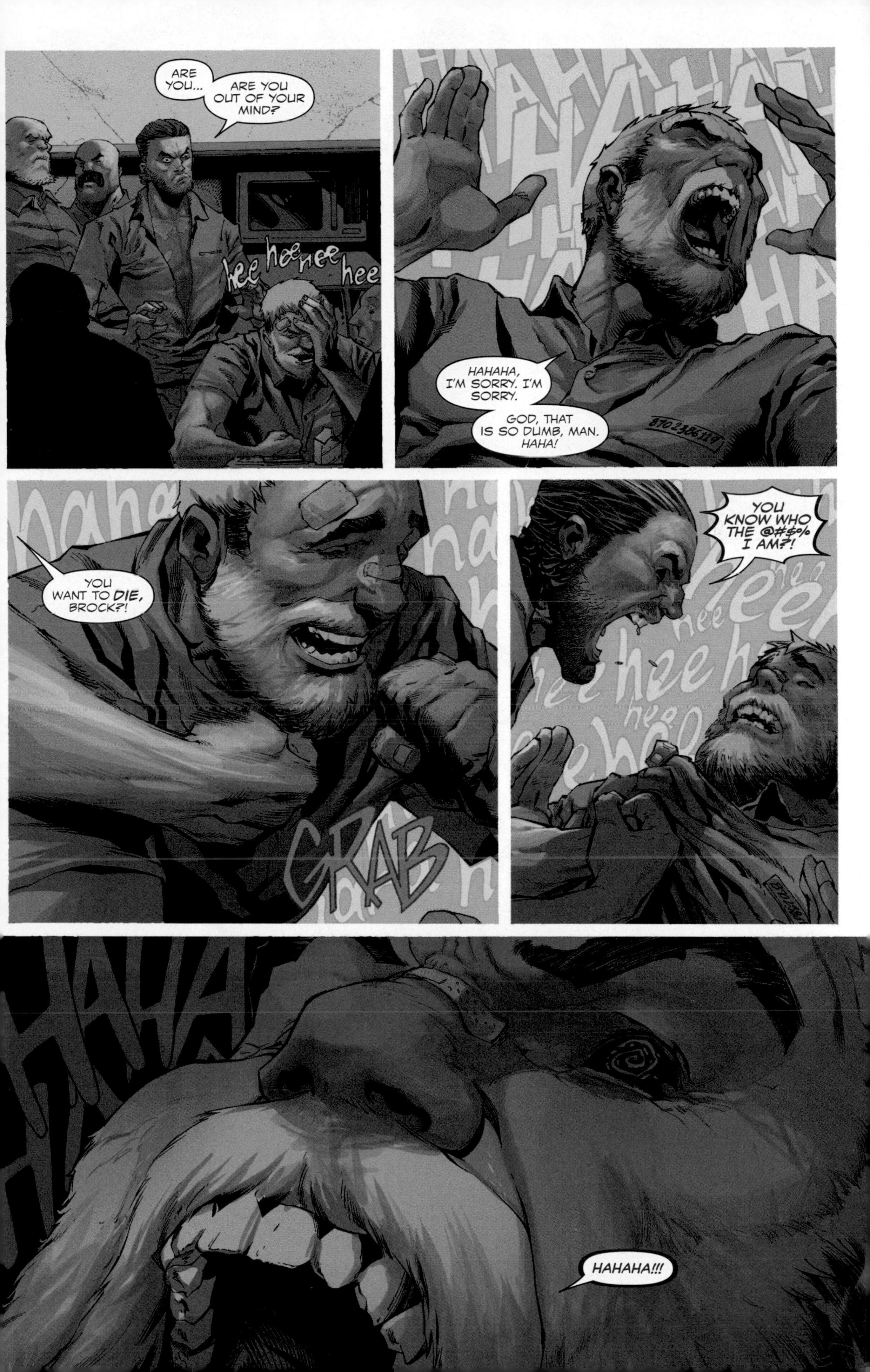
ARE YOU...
ARE YOU OUT OF YOUR MIND?
hee hee hee hee
HAHAHA, I'M SORRY. I'M SORRY.
GOD, THAT IS SO DUMB, MAN. HAHA!
YOU WANT TO DIE, BROCK?!
GRAB
YOU KNOW WHO THE @#$% I AM?!
HAHAHA!!!

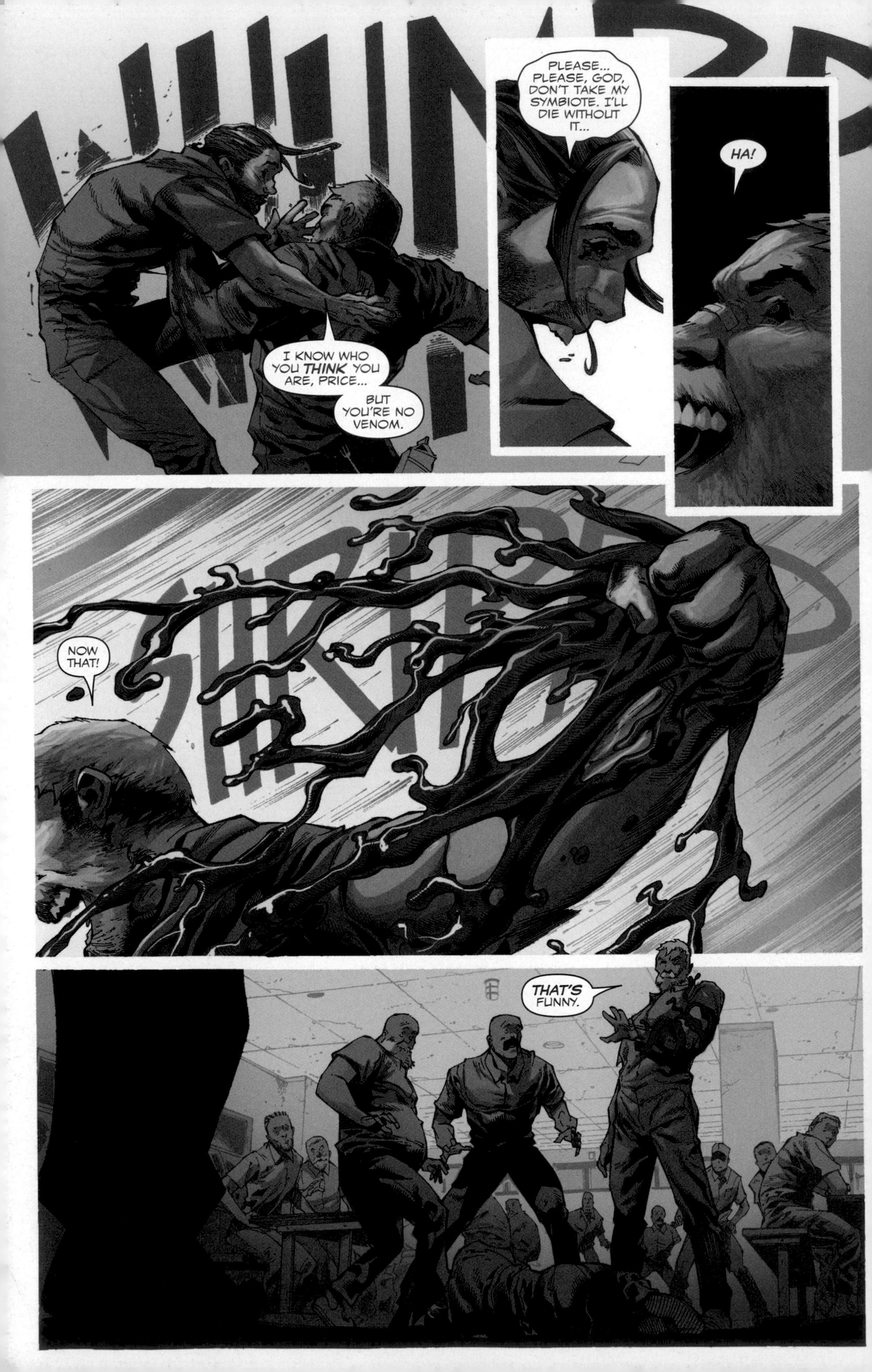
I KNOW WHO YOU THINK YOU ARE, PRICE...
BUT YOU'RE NO VENOM.
PLEASE... PLEASE, GOD, DON'T TAKE MY SYMBIOTE. I'LL DIE WITHOUT IT...
HA!
NOW THAT!
THAT'S FUNNY.

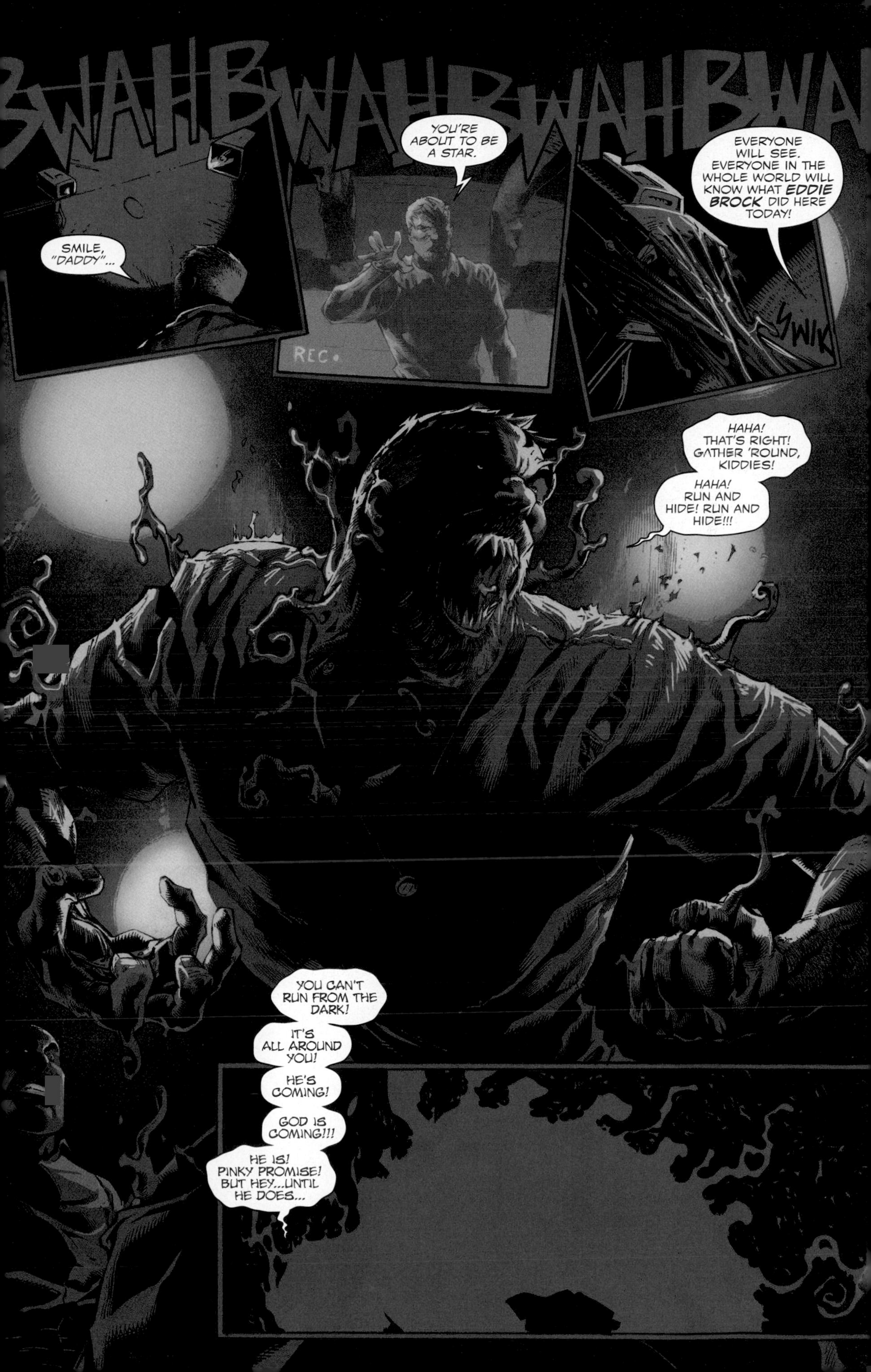
BWAHBWAHBWAHBWA
SMILE, "DADDY"...
YOU'RE ABOUT TO BE A STAR.
REC.
EVERYONE WILL SEE. EVERYONE IN THE WHOLE WORLD WILL KNOW WHAT EDDIE BROCK DID HERE TODAY!
SWIK
HAHA! THAT'S RIGHT! GATHER 'ROUND, KIDDIES!
HAHA! RUN AND HIDE! RUN AND HIDE!!!
YOU CAN'T RUN FROM THE DARK!
IT'S ALL AROUND YOU!
HE'S COMING!
GOD IS COMING!!!
HE IS! PINKY PROMISE! BUT HEY...UNTIL HE DOES...

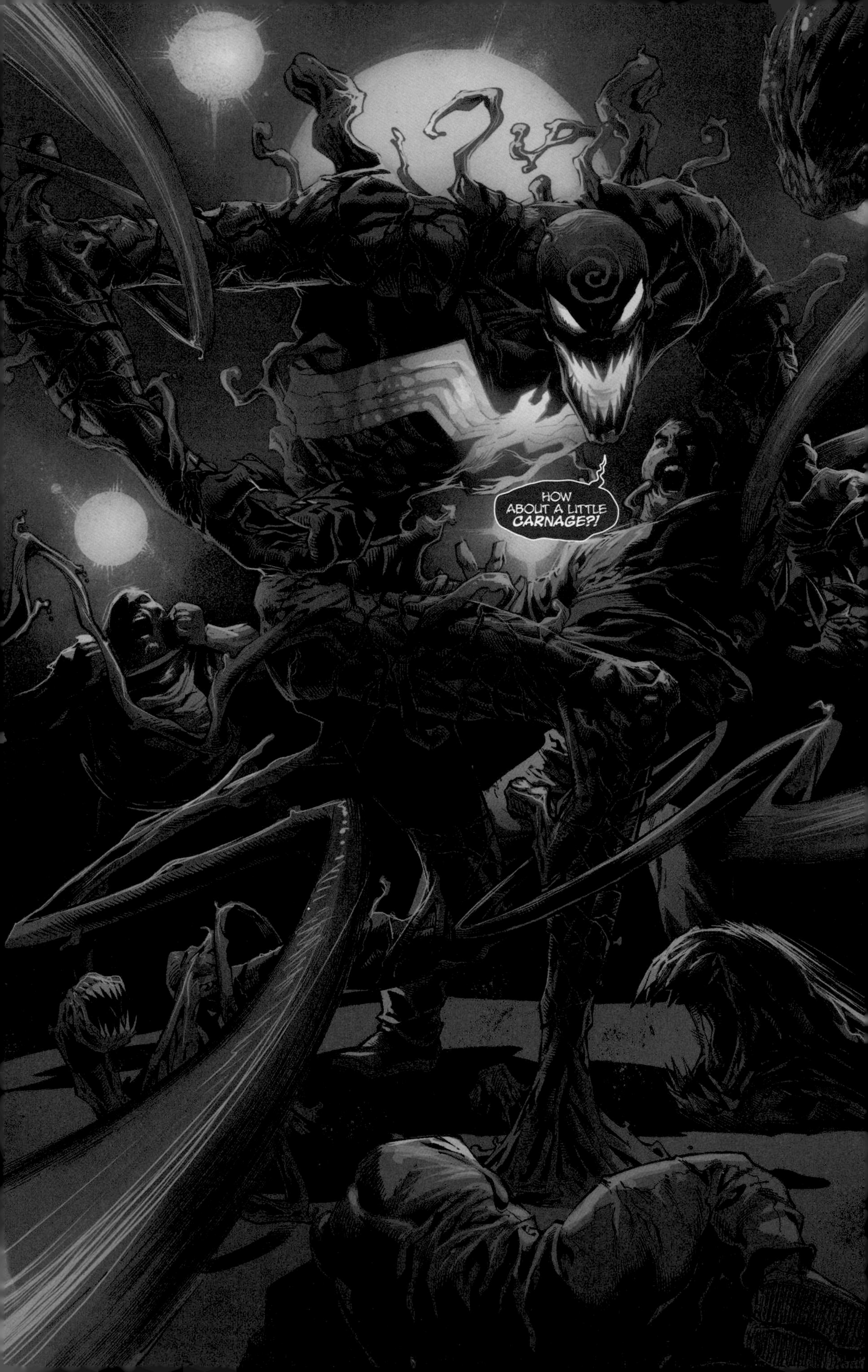
HOW ABOUT A LITTLE CARNAGE?!

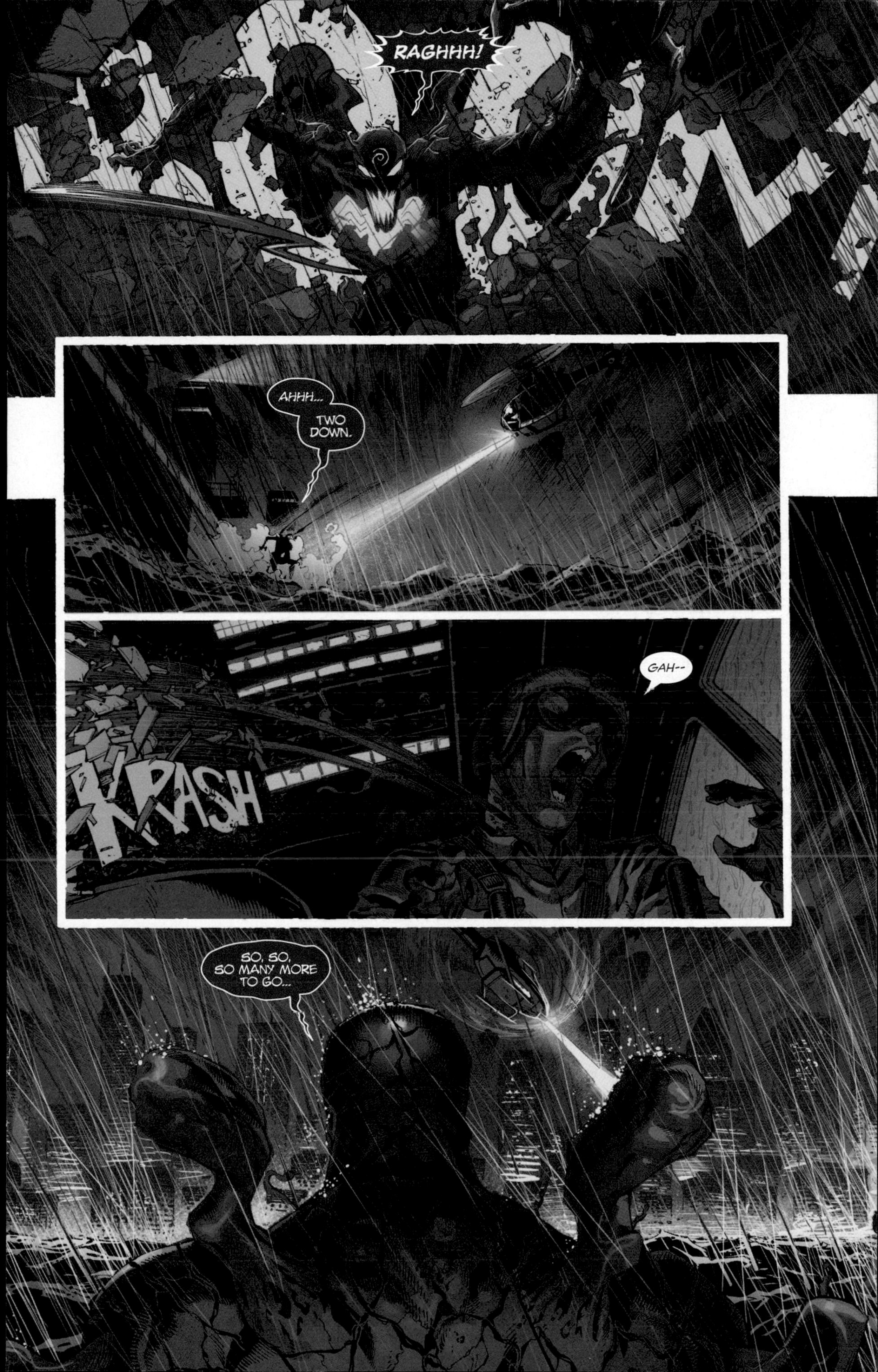
RAGHHH!
AHHH... TWO DOWN.
KRASH
GAH--
SO, SO, SO MANY MORE TO GO...

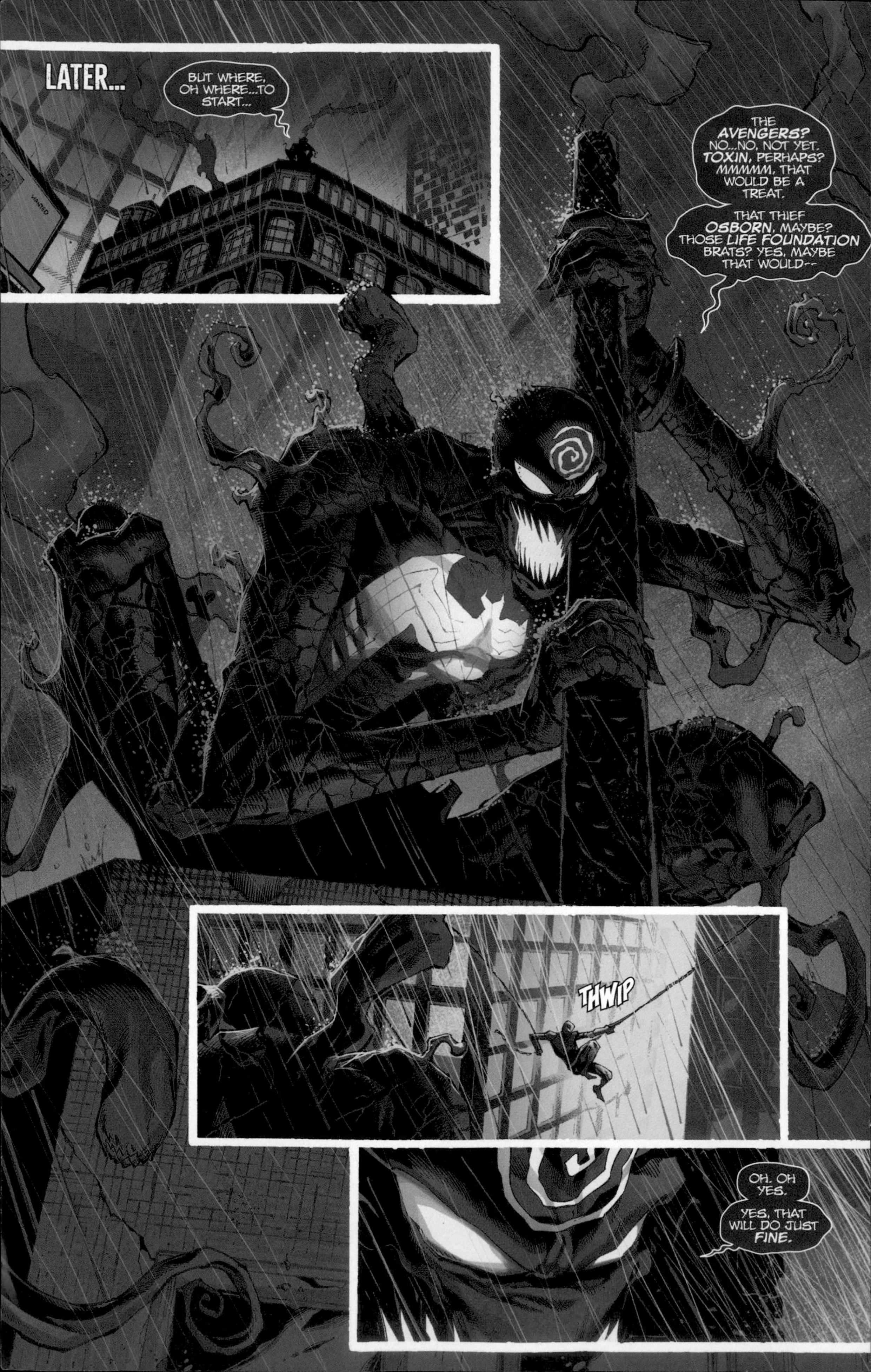
LATER...
BUT WHERE, OH WHERE...TO START...
THE AVENGERS? NO...NO, NOT YET. TOXIN, PERHAPS? MMMMM, THAT WOULD BE A TREAT.
THAT THIEF OSBORN, MAYBE? THOSE LIFE FOUNDATION BRATS? YES, MAYBE THAT WOULD--
THWIP
OH. OH YES.
YES, THAT WILL DO JUST FINE.

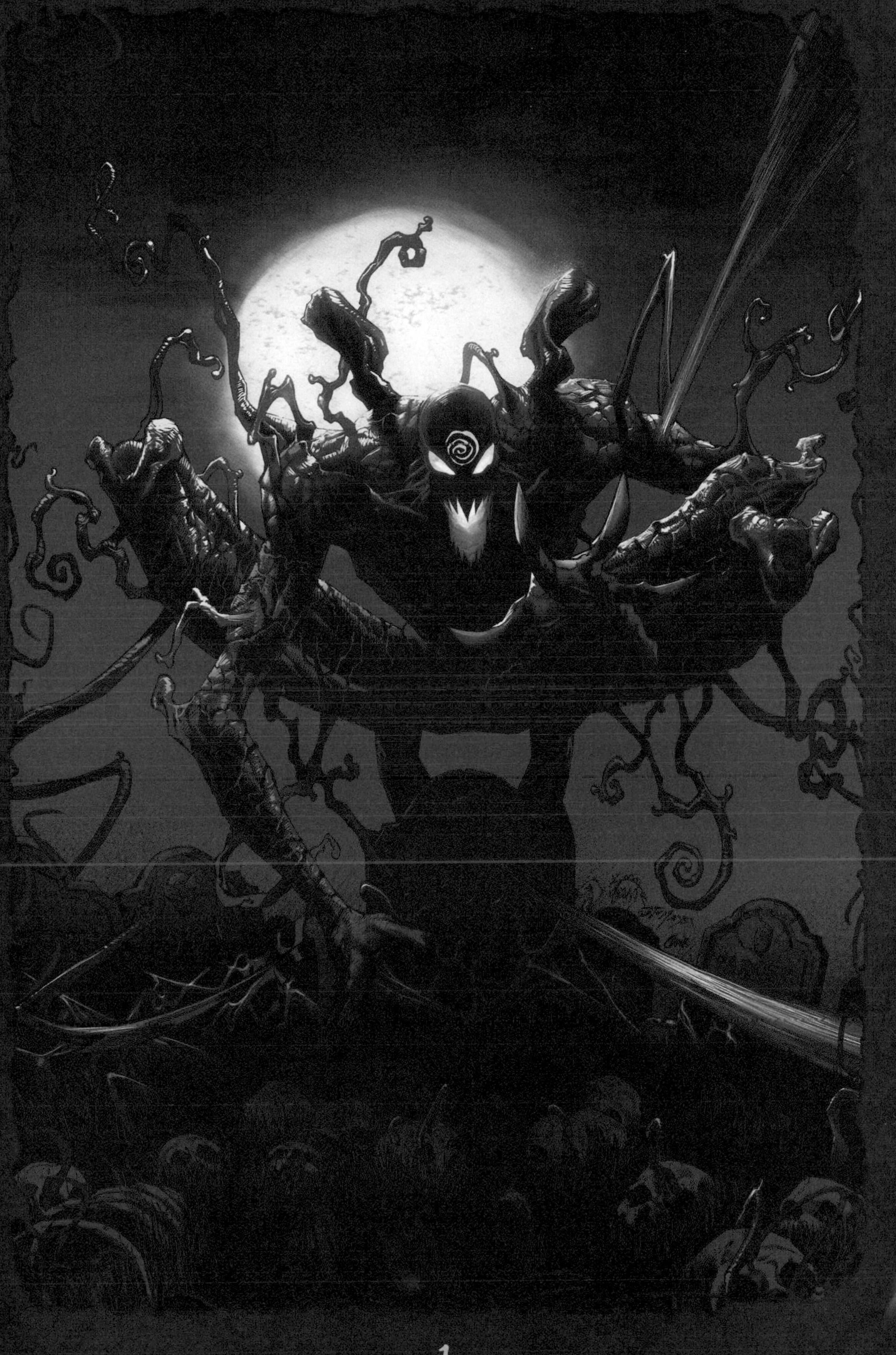

CHAPTER ONE:

THE BLEEDING KING

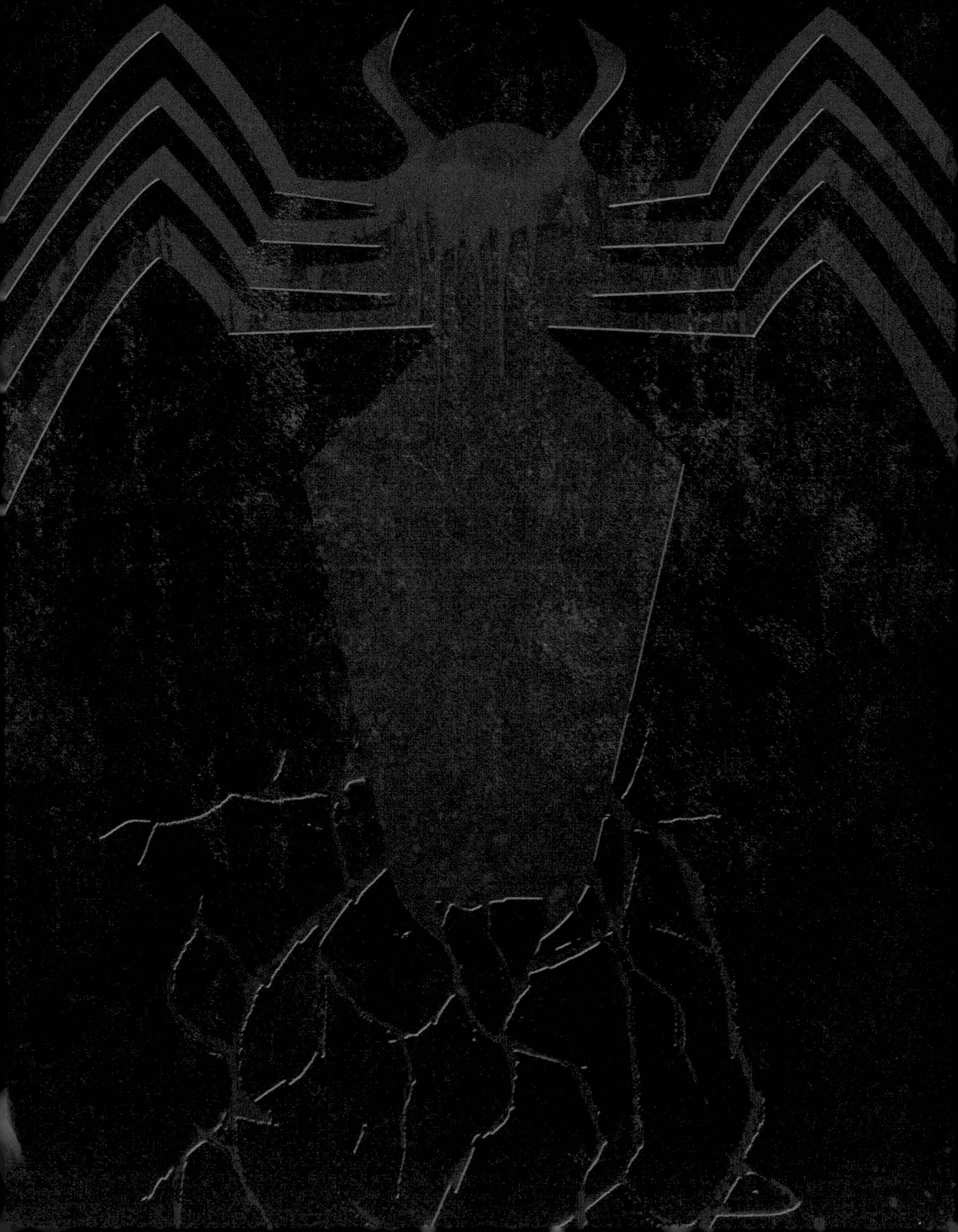

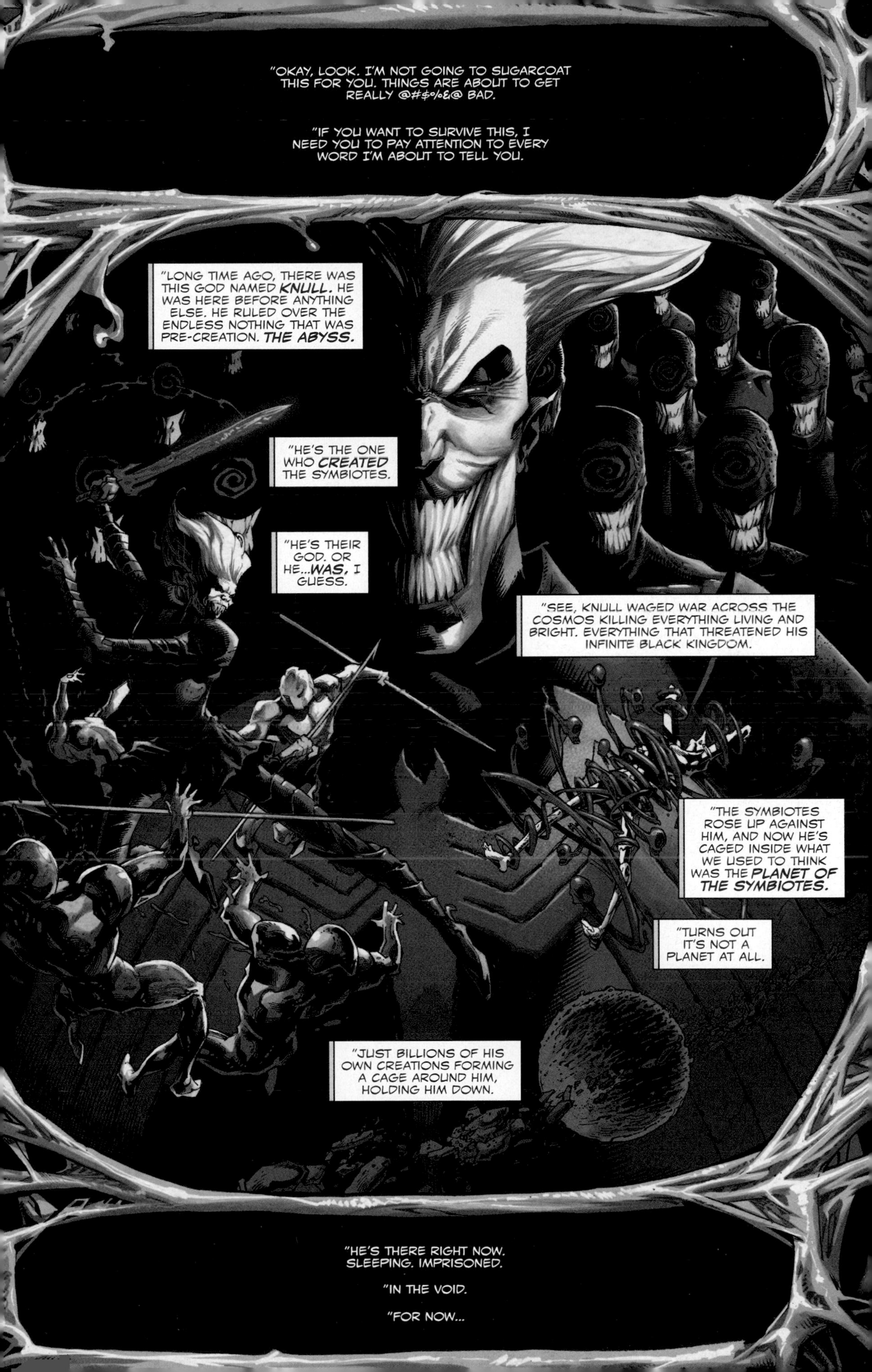
"OKAY, LOOK. I'M NOT GOING TO SUGARCOAT THIS FOR YOU. THINGS ARE ABOUT TO GET REALLY @#$%&@ BAD.
"IF YOU WANT TO SURVIVE THIS, I NEED YOU TO PAY ATTENTION TO EVERY WORD I'M ABOUT TO TELL YOU.
"LONG TIME AGO, THERE WAS THIS GOD NAMED KNULL. HE WAS HERE BEFORE ANYTHING ELSE. HE RULED OVER THE ENDLESS NOTHING THAT WAS PRE-CREATION. THE ABYSS.
"HE'S THE ONE WHO CREATED THE SYMBIOTES.
"HE'S THEIR GOD. OR HE...WAS, I GUESS.
"SEE, KNULL WAGED WAR ACROSS THE COSMOS KILLING EVERYTHING LIVING AND BRIGHT. EVERYTHING THAT THREATENED HIS INFINITE BLACK KINGDOM.
"THE SYMBIOTES ROSE UP AGAINST HIM, AND NOW HE'S CAGED INSIDE WHAT WE USED TO THINK WAS THE PLANET OF THE SYMBIOTES.
"TURNS OUT IT'S NOT A PLANET AT ALL.
"JUST BILLIONS OF HIS OWN CREATIONS FORMING A CAGE AROUND HIM, HOLDING HIM DOWN.
"HE'S THERE RIGHT NOW. SLEEPING. IMPRISONED.
"IN THE VOID.
"FOR NOW...

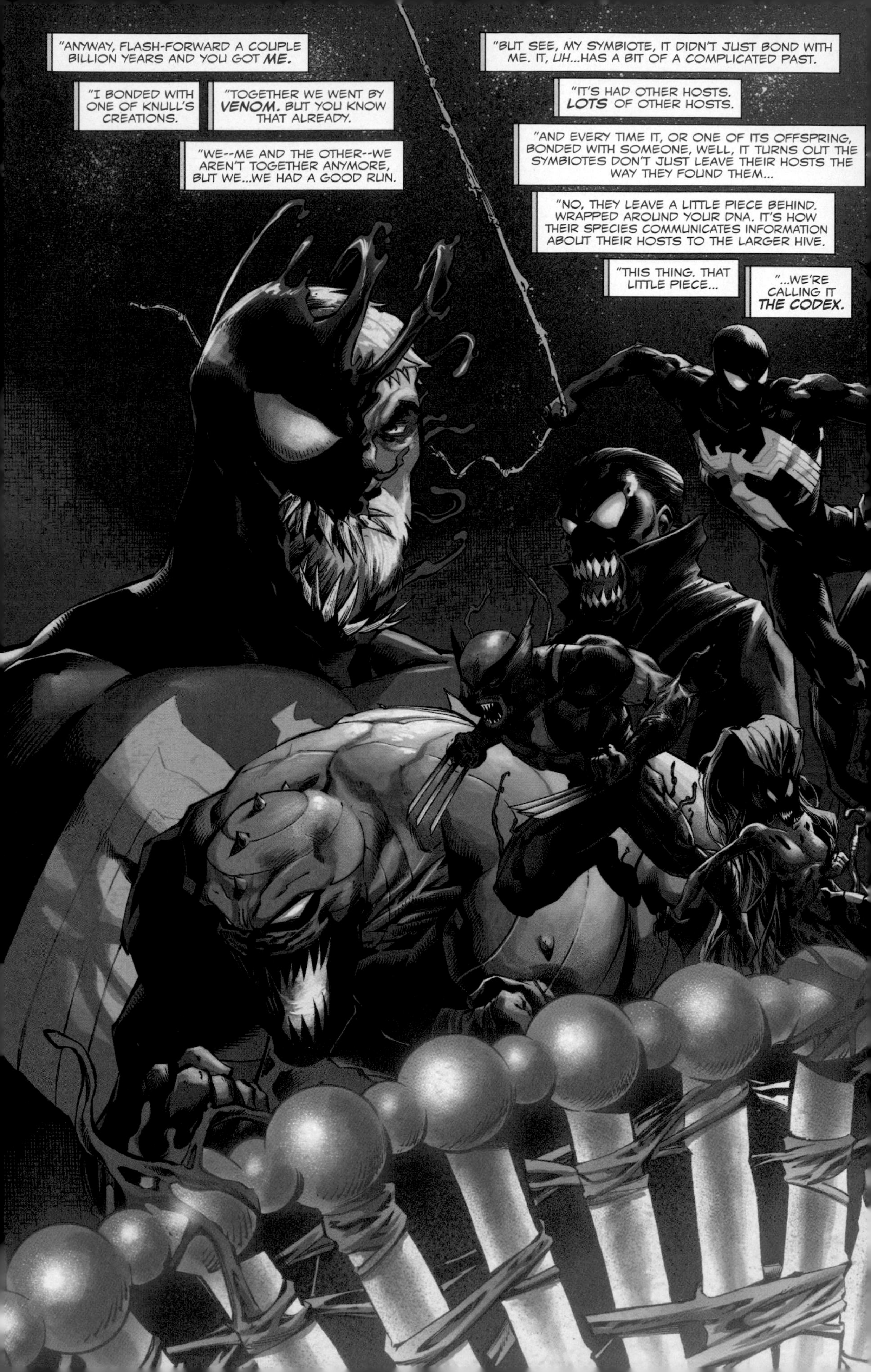
"ANYWAY, FLASH-FORWARD A COUPLE BILLION YEARS AND YOU GOT ME.
"I BONDED WITH ONE OF KNULL'S CREATIONS.
"TOGETHER WE WENT BY VENOM. BUT YOU KNOW THAT ALREADY.
"WE--ME AND THE OTHER--WE AREN'T TOGETHER ANYMORE, BUT WE...WE HAD A GOOD RUN.
"BUT SEE, MY SYMBIOTE, IT DIDN'T JUST BOND WITH ME. IT, UH...HAS A BIT OF A COMPLICATED PAST.
"IT'S HAD OTHER HOSTS. LOTS OF OTHER HOSTS.
"AND EVERY TIME IT, OR ONE OF ITS OFFSPRING, BONDED WITH SOMEONE, WELL, IT TURNS OUT THE SYMBIOTES DON'T JUST LEAVE THEIR HOSTS THE WAY THEY FOUND THEM...
"NO, THEY LEAVE A LITTLE PIECE BEHIND. WRAPPED AROUND YOUR DNA. IT'S HOW THEIR SPECIES COMMUNICATES INFORMATION ABOUT THEIR HOSTS TO THE LARGER HIVE.
"THIS THING. THAT LITTLE PIECE...
"...WE'RE CALLING IT THE CODEX.

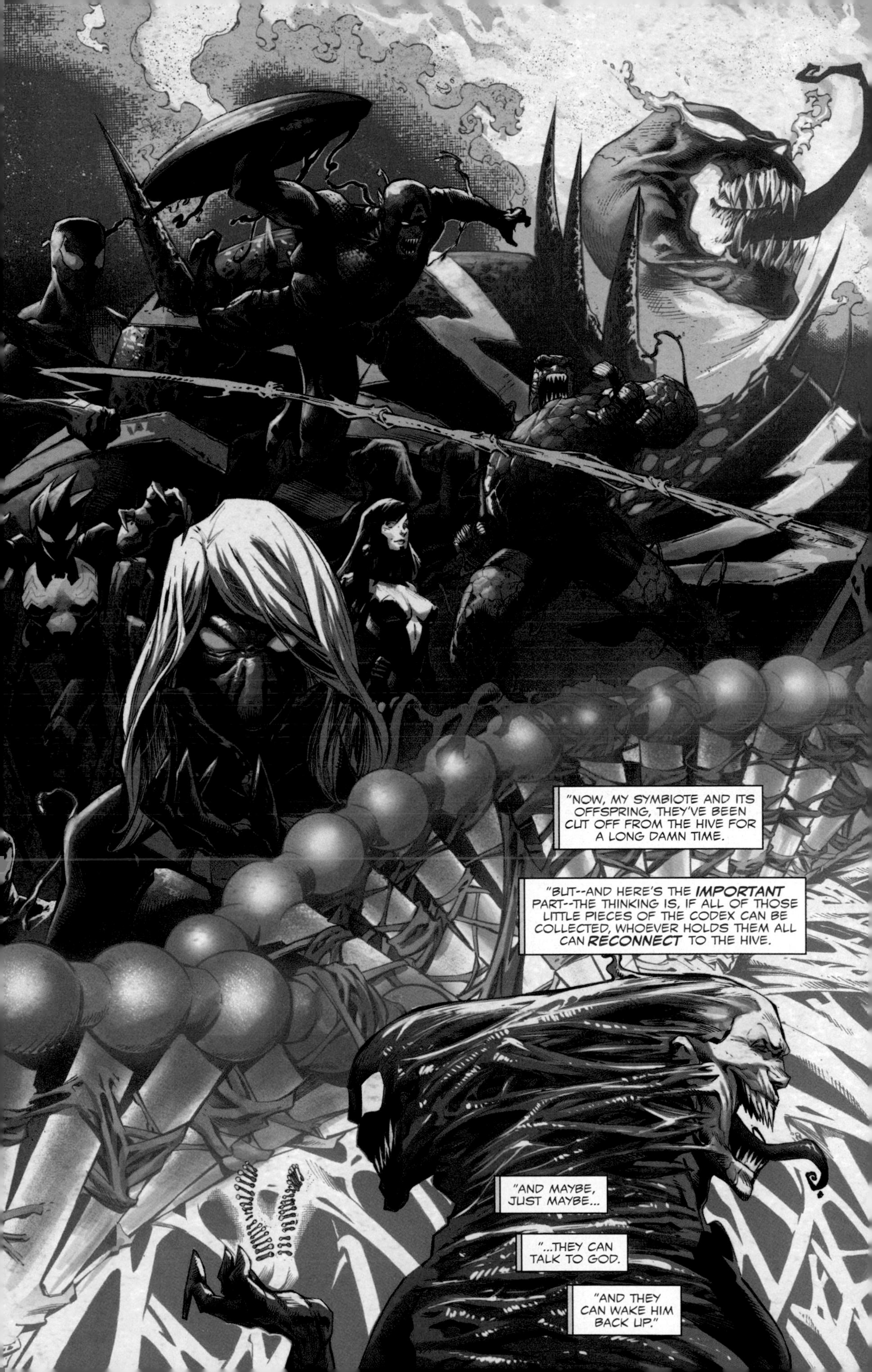
"NOW, MY SYMBIOTE AND ITS OFFSPRING, THEY'VE BEEN CUT OFF FROM THE HIVE FOR A LONG DAMN TIME.
"BUT--AND HERE'S THE IMPORTANT PART--THE THINKING IS, IF ALL OF THOSE LITTLE PIECES OF THE CODEX CAN BE COLLECTED, WHOEVER HOLDS THEM ALL CAN RECONNECT TO THE HIVE.
"AND MAYBE, JUST MAYBE...
"...THEY CAN TALK TO GOD.
"AND THEY CAN WAKE HIM BACK UP."

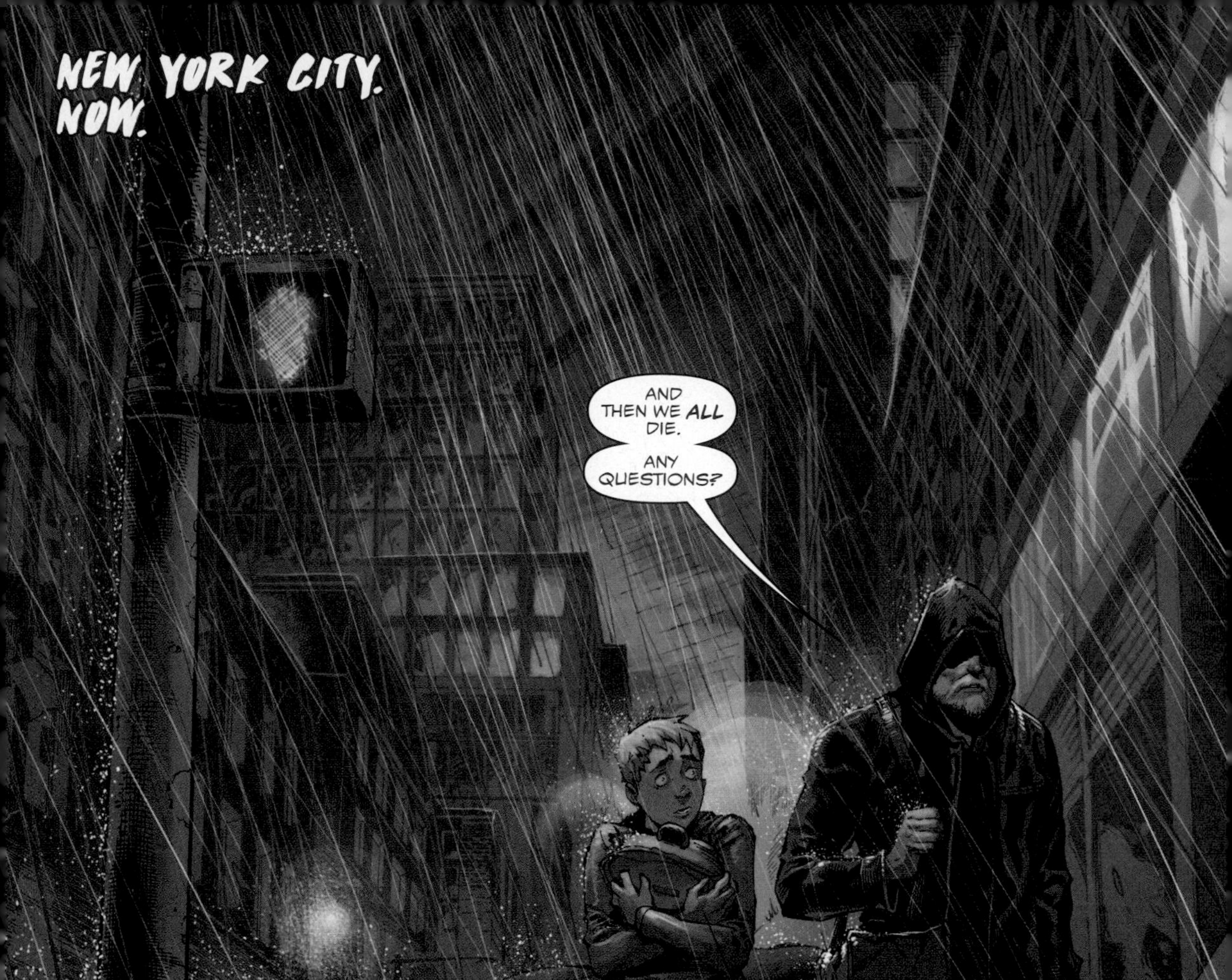
NEW YORK CITY.
NOW.
AND THEN WE ALL DIE.
ANY QUESTIONS?
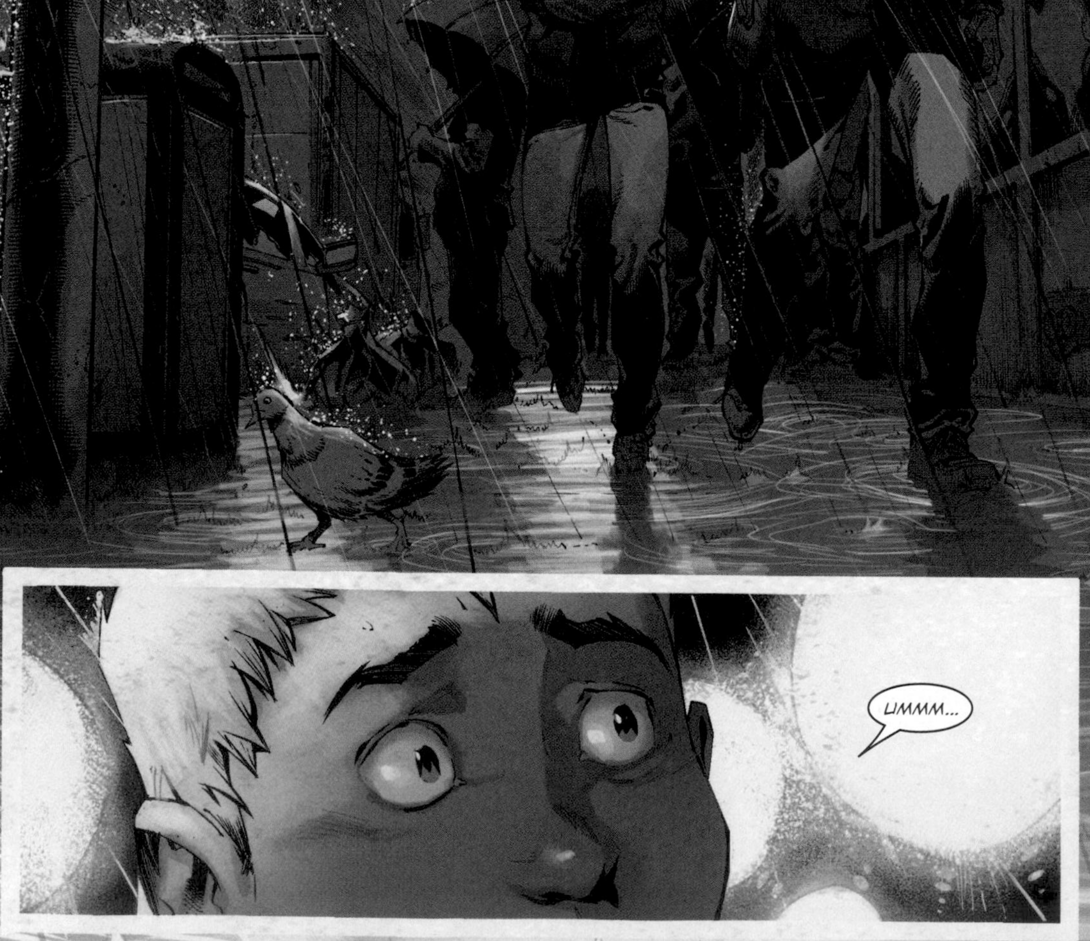
UMMM...

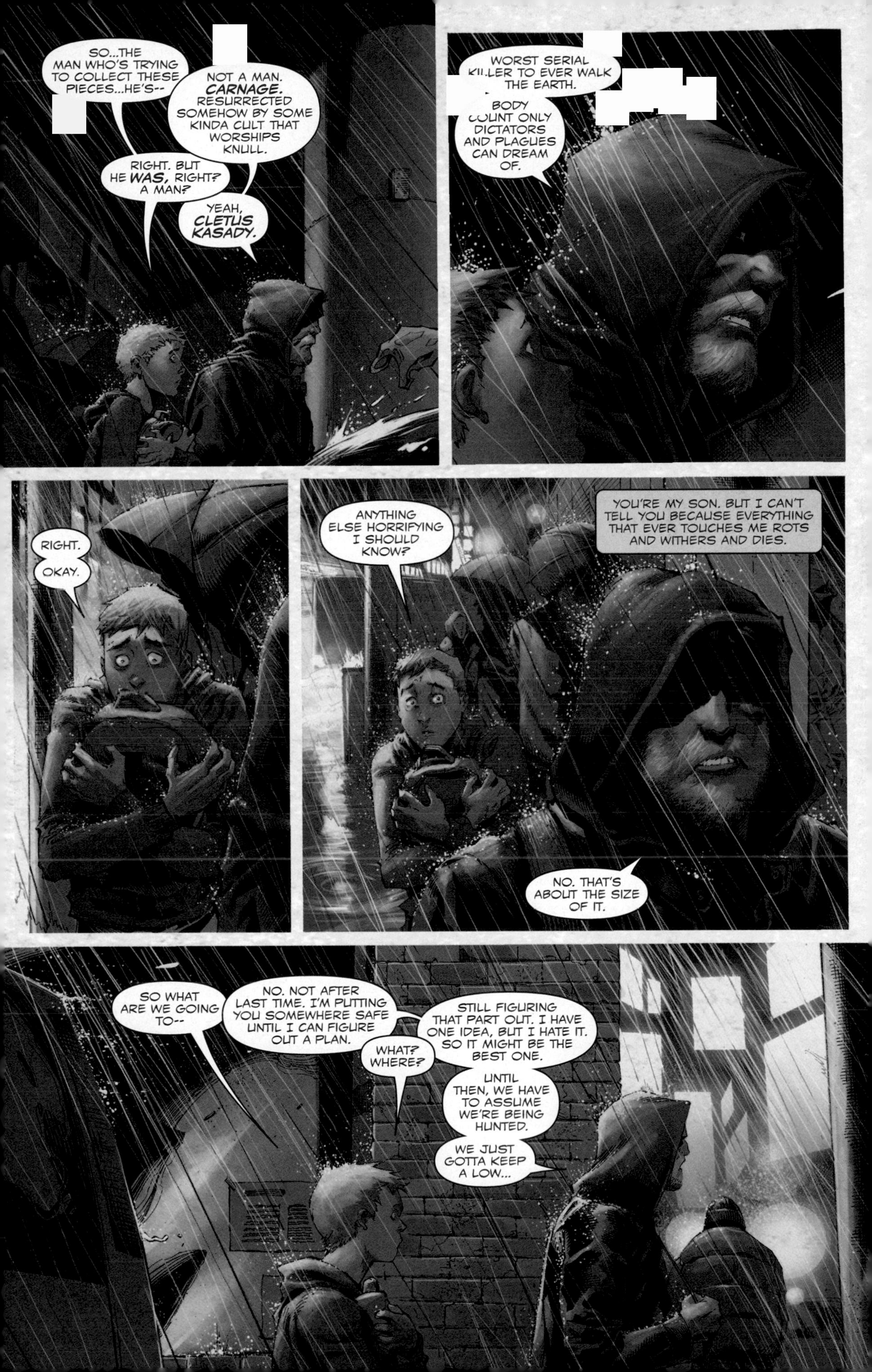

SO...THE MAN WHO'S TRYING TO COLLECT THESE PIECES...HE'S--
NOT A MAN. CARNAGE. RESURRECTED SOMEHOW BY SOME KINDA CULT THAT WORSHIPS KNULL.
RIGHT. BUT HE WAS, RIGHT? A MAN?
YEAH, CLETUS KASADY.
WORST SERIAL KILLER TO EVER WALK THE EARTH.
BODY COUNT ONLY DICTATORS AND PLAGUES CAN DREAM OF.
RIGHT.
OKAY.
ANYTHING ELSE HORRIFYING I SHOULD KNOW?
YOU'RE MY SON. BUT I CAN'T TELL YOU BECAUSE EVERYTHING THAT EVER TOUCHES ME ROTS AND WITHERS AND DIES.
NO. THAT'S ABOUT THE SIZE OF IT.
SO WHAT ARE WE GOING TO--
NO. NOT AFTER LAST TIME. I'M PUTTING YOU SOMEWHERE SAFE UNTIL I CAN FIGURE OUT A PLAN.
WHAT? WHERE?
STILL FIGURING THAT PART OUT. I HAVE ONE IDEA, BUT I HATE IT. SO IT MIGHT BE THE BEST ONE.
UNTIL THEN, WE HAVE TO ASSUME WE'RE BEING HUNTED.
WE JUST GOTTA KEEP A LOW...

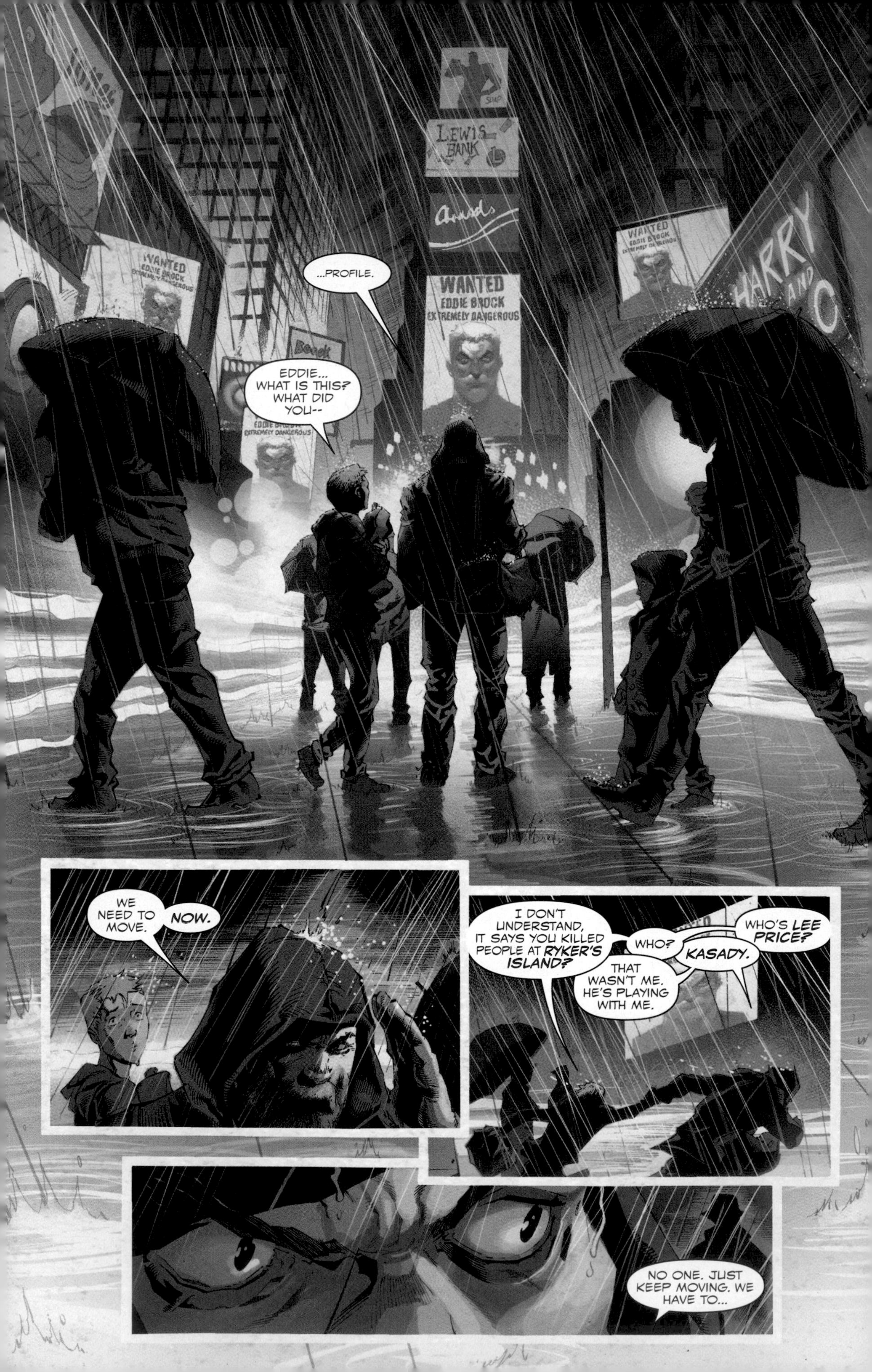

...PROFILE.
EDDIE... WHAT IS THIS? WHAT DID YOU--
WANTED EDDIE BROCK EXTREMELY DANGEROUS
LEWIS BANK
HARRY
WE NEED TO MOVE.
NOW.
I DON'T UNDERSTAND, IT SAYS YOU KILLED PEOPLE AT RYKER'S ISLAND?
THAT WASN'T ME. HE'S PLAYING WITH ME.
WHO?
KASADY.
WHO'S LEE PRICE?
NO ONE. JUST KEEP MOVING. WE HAVE TO...

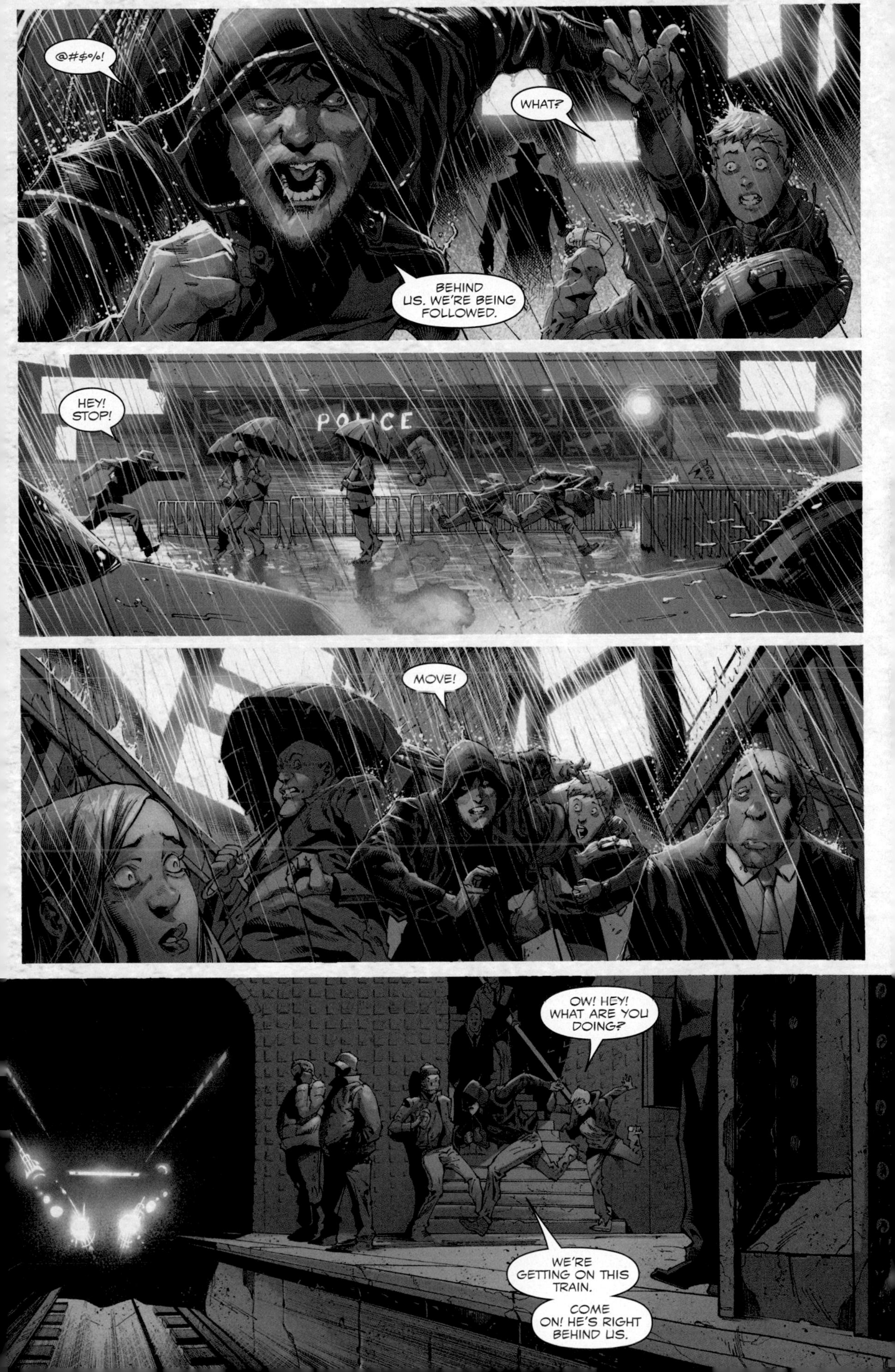
@#$%!
WHAT?
BEHIND US. WE'RE BEING FOLLOWED.
HEY! STOP!
POLICE
MOVE!
OW! HEY! WHAT ARE YOU DOING?
WE'RE GETTING ON THIS TRAIN.
COME ON! HE'S RIGHT BEHIND US.

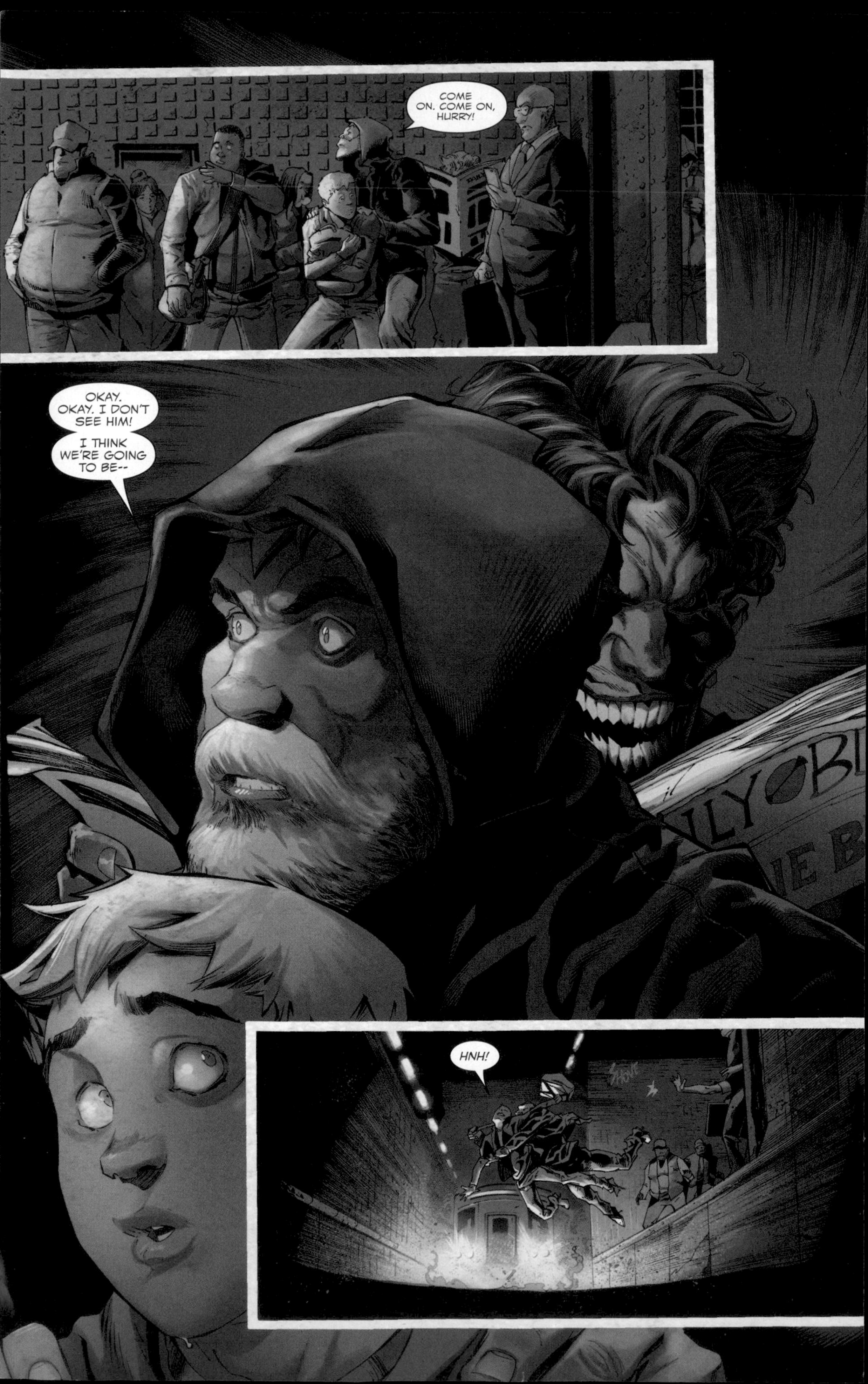
COME ON. COME ON, HURRY!
OKAY. OKAY. I DON'T SEE HIM!
I THINK WE'RE GOING TO BE--
HNH!

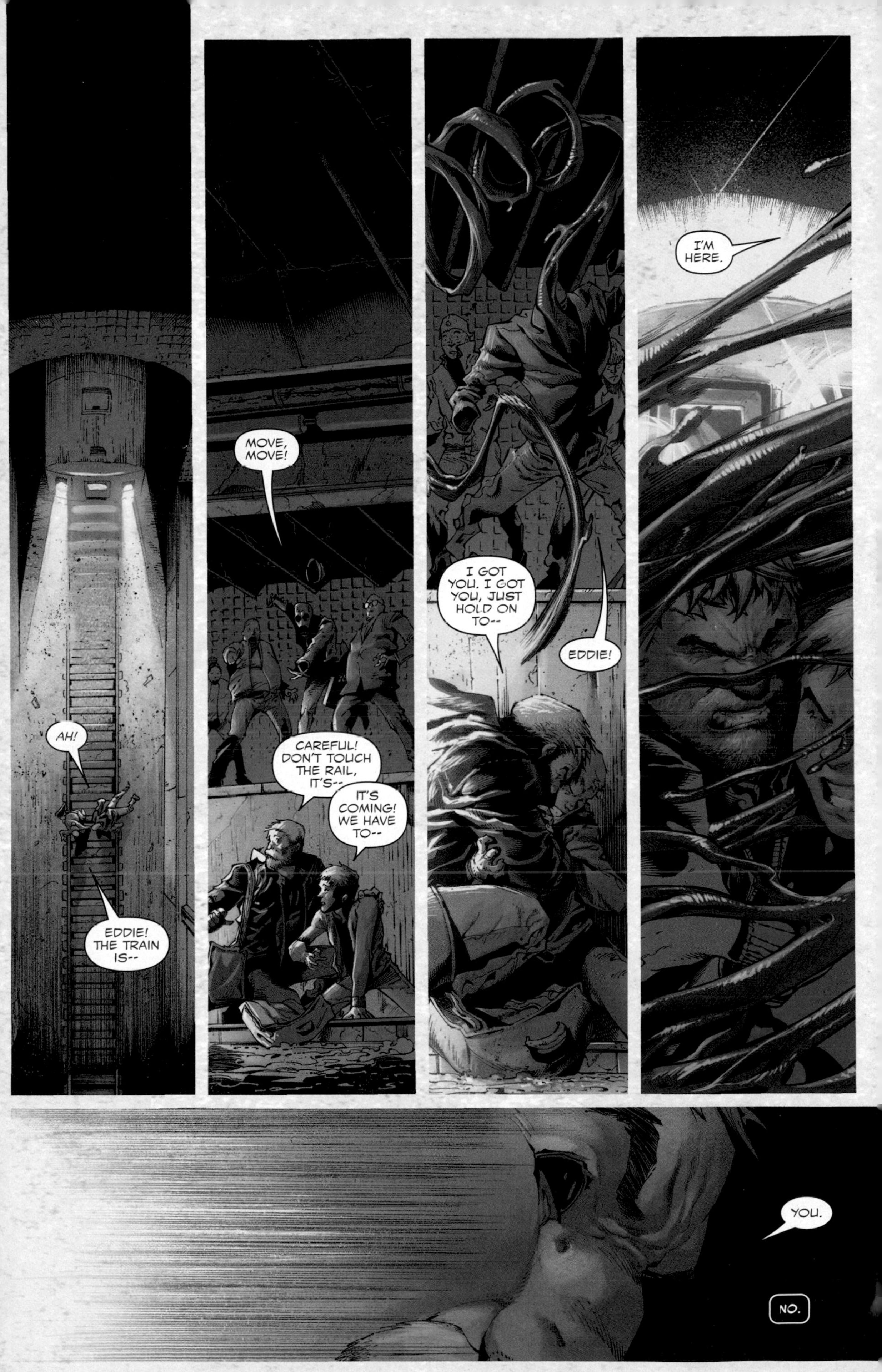
AH!
EDDIE! THE TRAIN IS--
MOVE, MOVE!
CAREFUL! DON'T TOUCH THE RAIL, IT'S--
IT'S COMING! WE HAVE TO--
I GOT YOU. I GOT YOU, JUST HOLD ON TO--
EDDIE!
I'M HERE.
YOU.
NO.

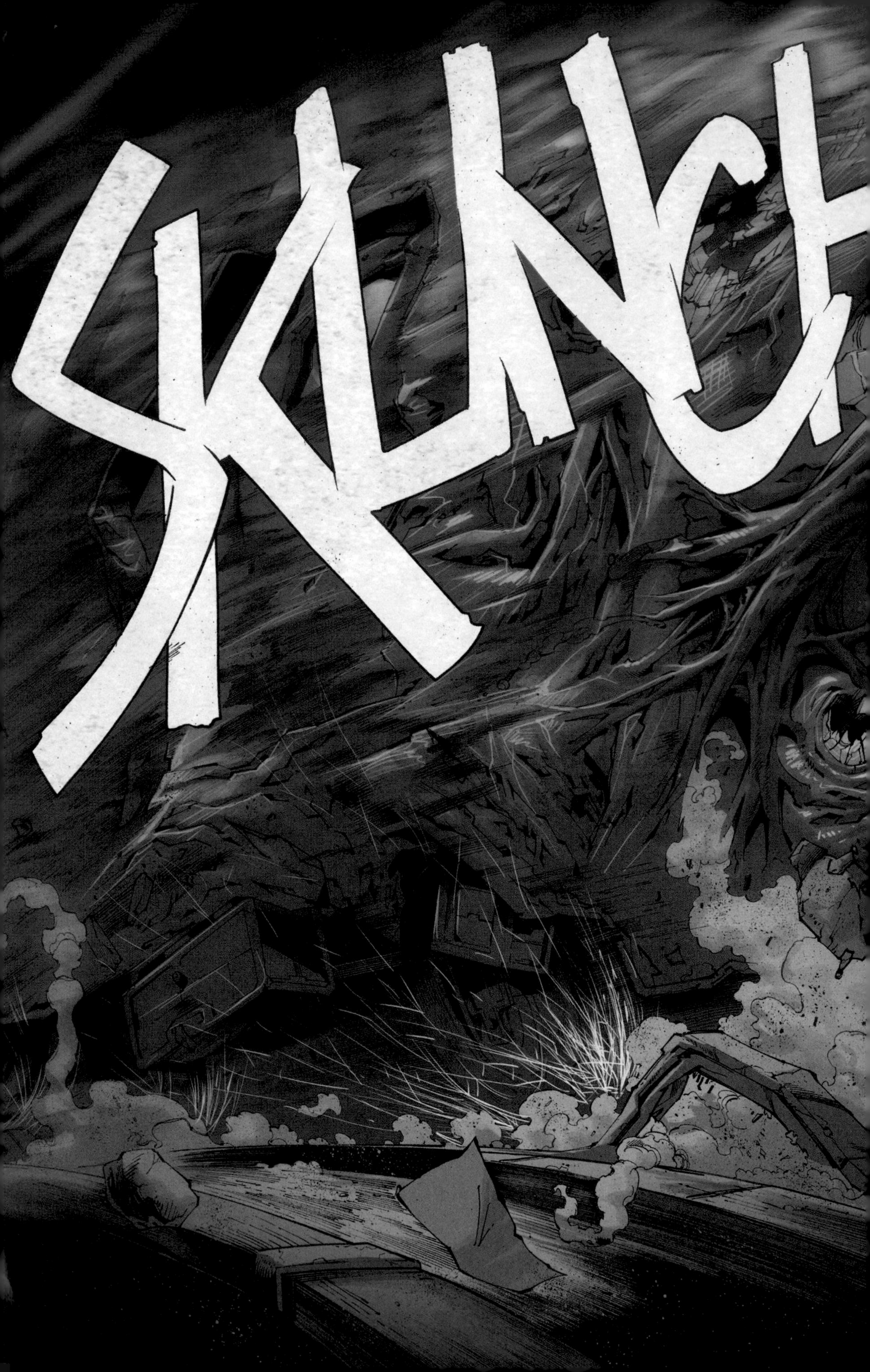
SKLNCH

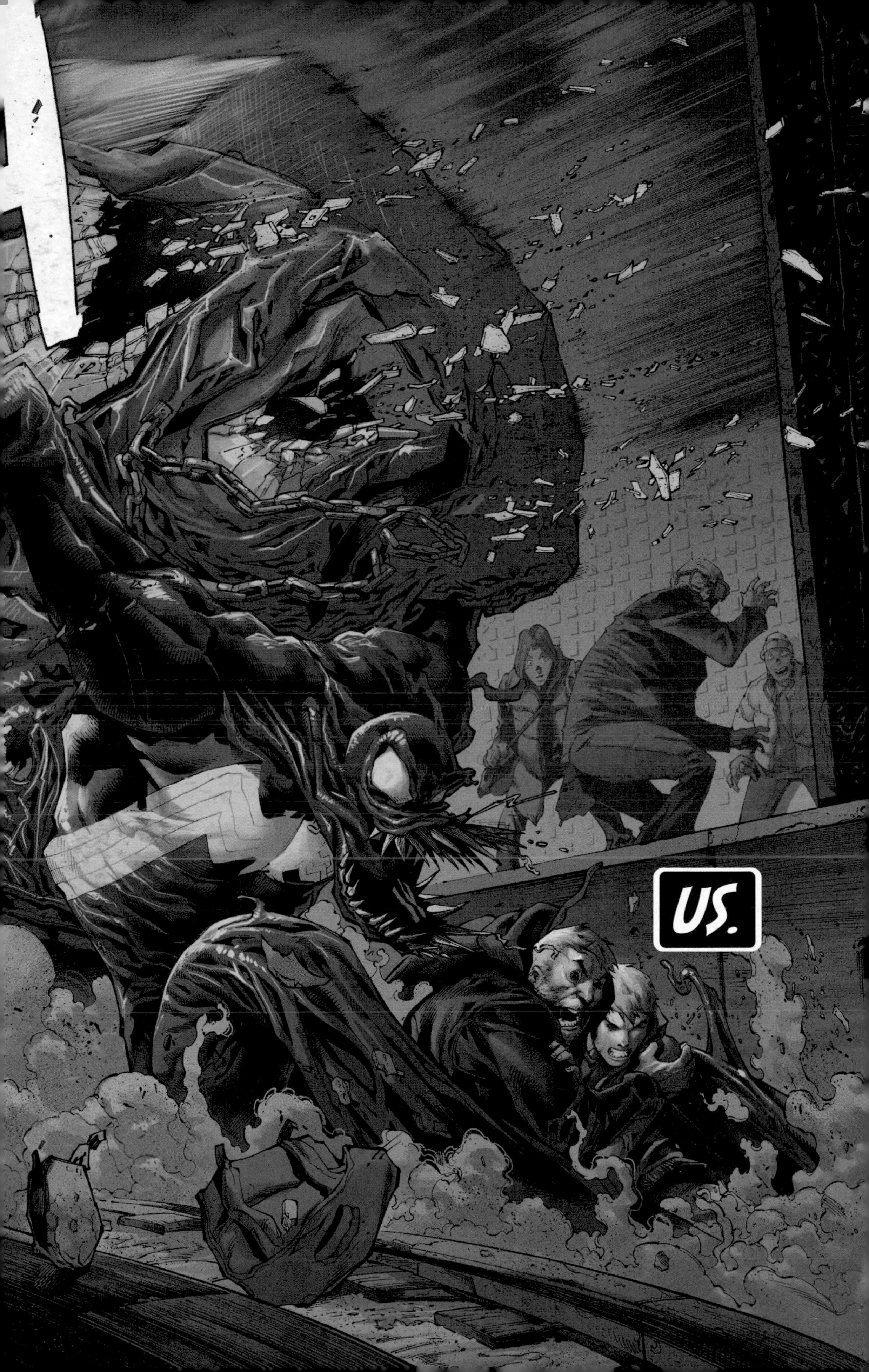
US.

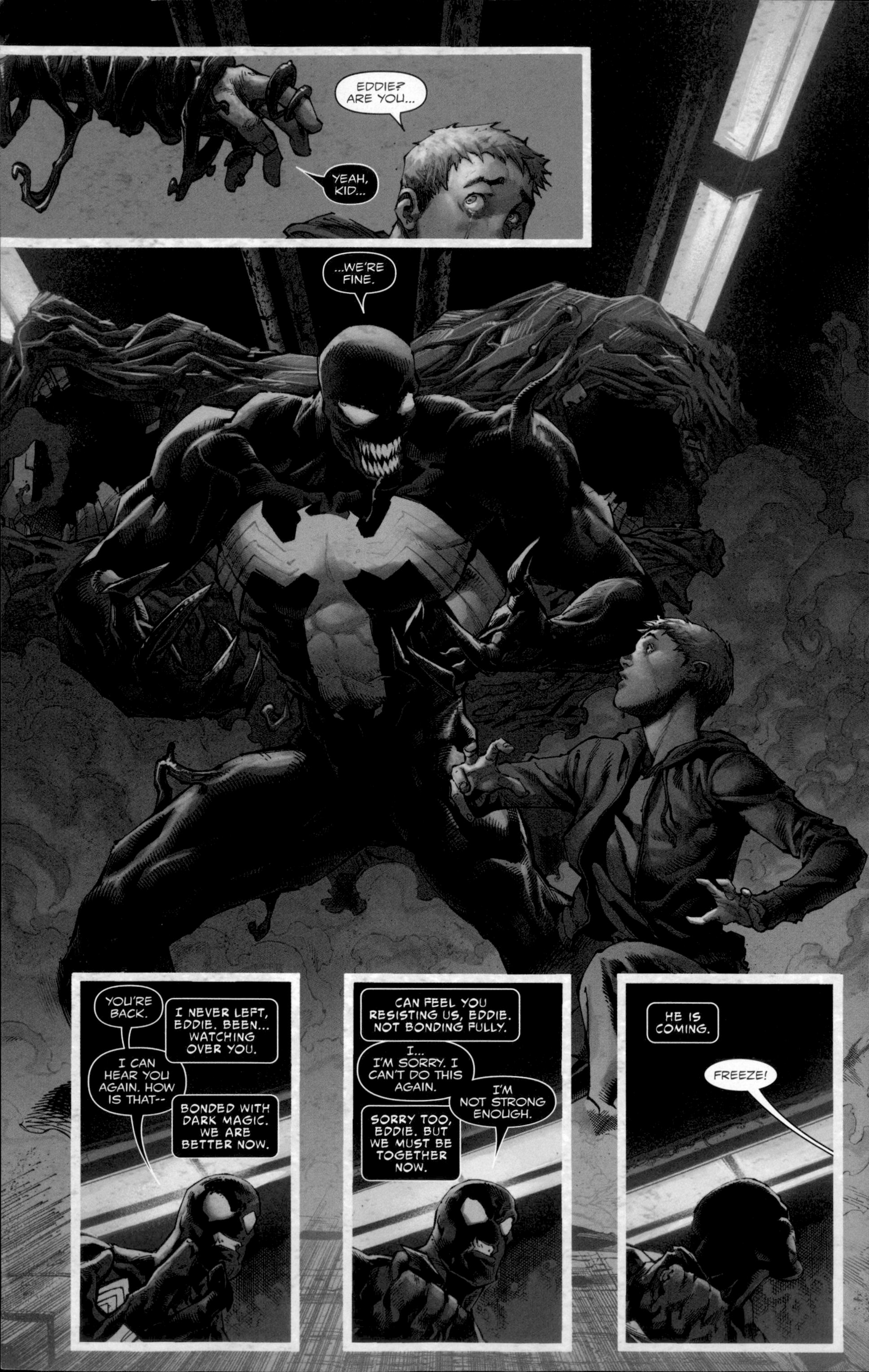
EDDIE? ARE YOU...
YEAH, KID...
...WE'RE FINE.
YOU'RE BACK.
I NEVER LEFT, EDDIE. BEEN... WATCHING OVER YOU.
I CAN HEAR YOU AGAIN. HOW IS THAT--
BONDED WITH DARK MAGIC. WE ARE BETTER NOW.
CAN FEEL YOU RESISTING US, EDDIE. NOT BONDING FULLY.
I... I'M SORRY. I CAN'T DO THIS AGAIN.
I'M NOT STRONG ENOUGH.
SORRY TOO, EDDIE. BUT WE MUST BE TOGETHER NOW.
HE IS COMING.
FREEZE!

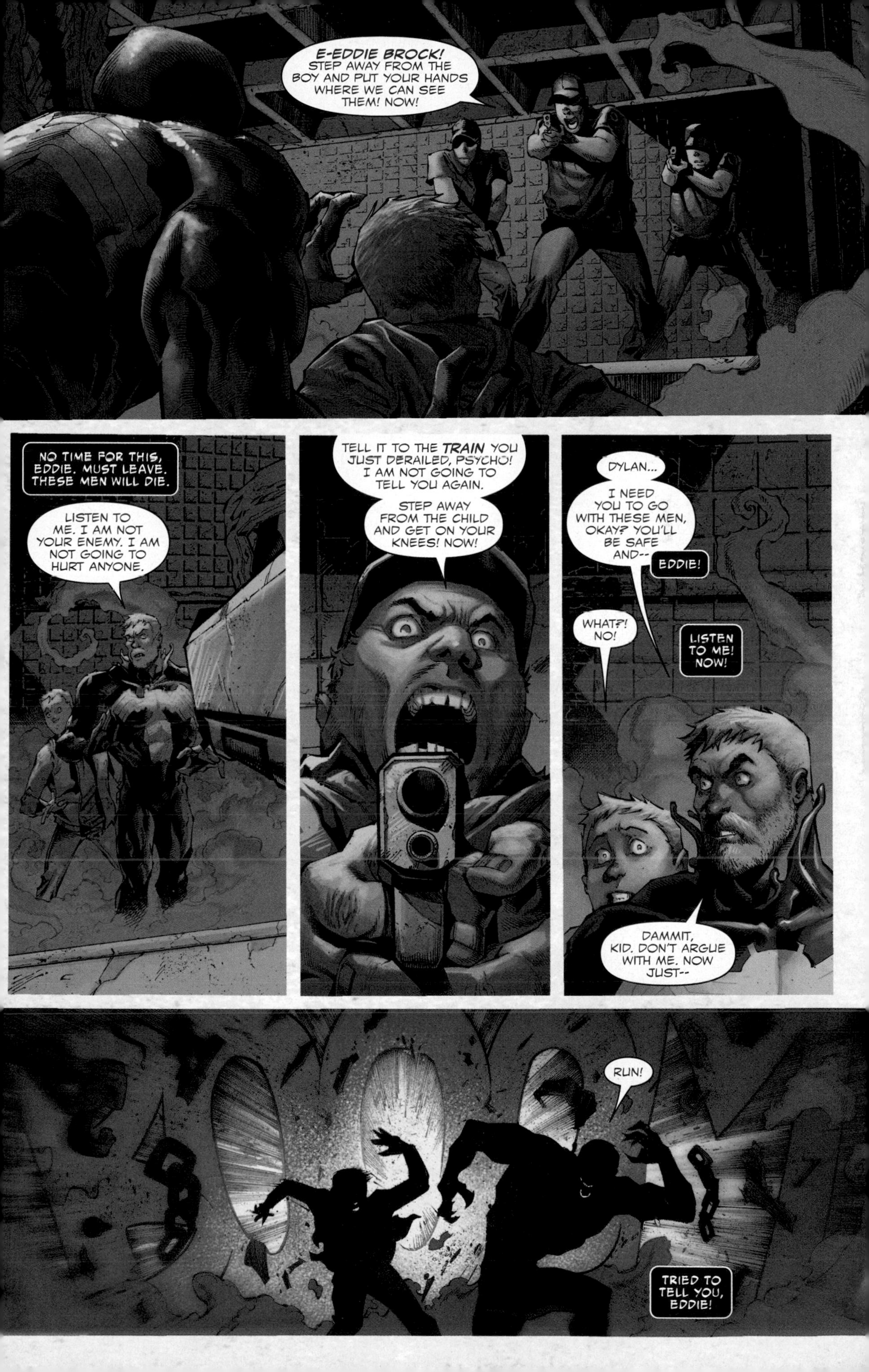
E-EDDIE BROCK! STEP AWAY FROM THE BOY AND PUT YOUR HANDS WHERE WE CAN SEE THEM! NOW!
NO TIME FOR THIS, EDDIE. MUST LEAVE. THESE MEN WILL DIE.
LISTEN TO ME. I AM NOT YOUR ENEMY. I AM NOT GOING TO HURT ANYONE.
TELL IT TO THE TRAIN YOU JUST DERAILED, PSYCHO! I AM NOT GOING TO TELL YOU AGAIN.
STEP AWAY FROM THE CHILD AND GET ON YOUR KNEES! NOW!
DYLAN...
I NEED YOU TO GO WITH THESE MEN, OKAY? YOU'LL BE SAFE AND--
EDDIE!
WHAT?! NO!
LISTEN TO ME! NOW!
DAMMIT, KID. DON'T ARGUE WITH ME. NOW JUST--
RUN!
TRIED TO TELL YOU, EDDIE!

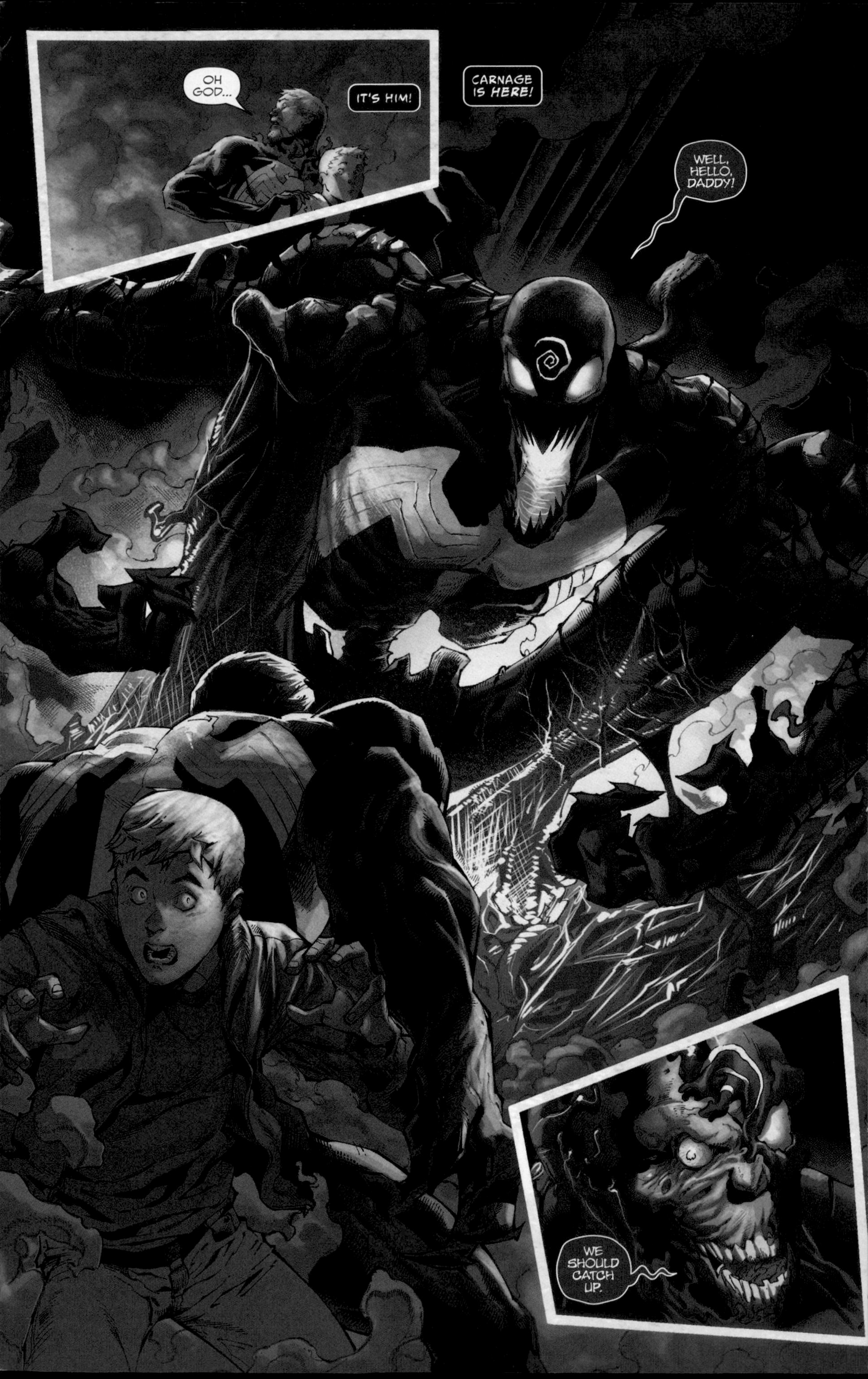
OH GOD...
IT'S HIM!
CARNAGE IS HERE!
WELL, HELLO, DADDY!
WE SHOULD CATCH UP.

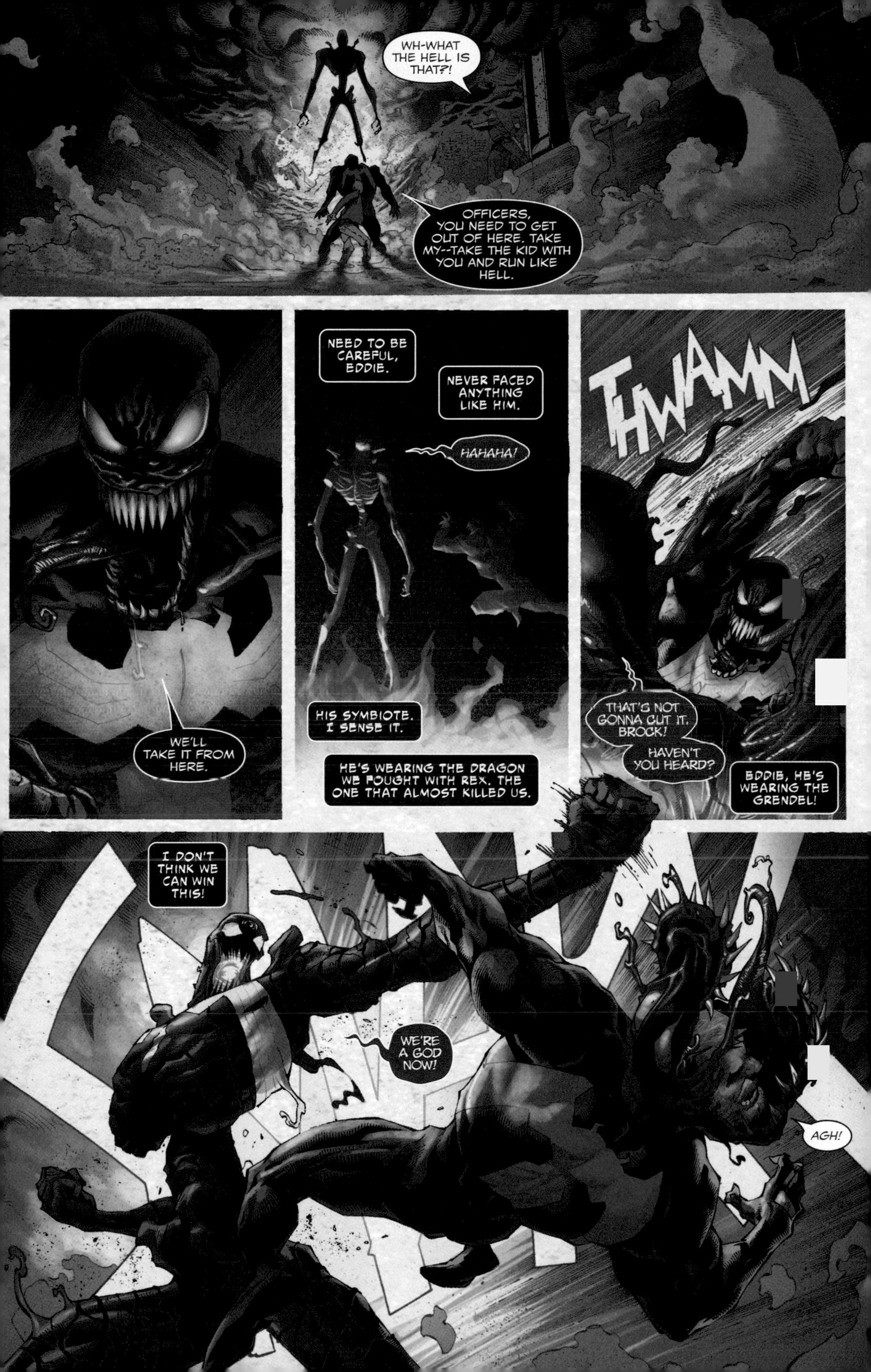
WH-WHAT THE HELL IS THAT?!
OFFICERS, YOU NEED TO GET OUT OF HERE. TAKE MY--TAKE THE KID WITH YOU AND RUN LIKE HELL.
WE'LL TAKE IT FROM HERE.
NEED TO BE CAREFUL, EDDIE.
NEVER FACED ANYTHING LIKE HIM.
HAHAHA!
HIS SYMBIOTE. I SENSE IT.
HE'S WEARING THE DRAGON WE FOUGHT WITH REX. THE ONE THAT ALMOST KILLED US.
THWAMM
THAT'S NOT GONNA CUT IT, BROCK!
HAVEN'T YOU HEARD?
EDDIE, HE'S WEARING THE GRENDEL!
I DON'T THINK WE CAN WIN THIS!
WE'RE A GOD NOW!
AGH!

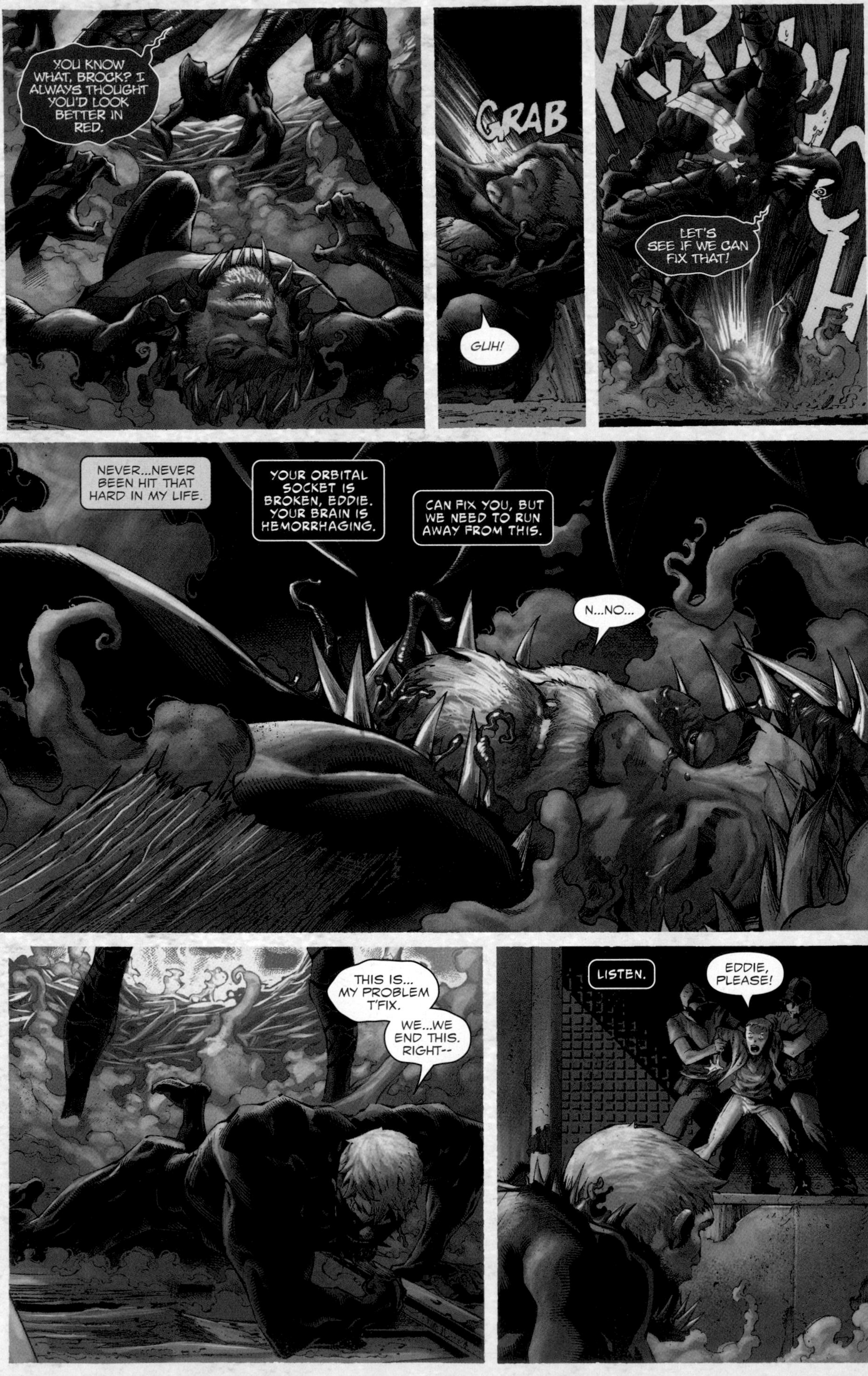
YOU KNOW WHAT, BROCK? I ALWAYS THOUGHT YOU'D LOOK BETTER IN RED.
GRAB
GUH!
LET'S SEE IF WE CAN FIX THAT!
NEVER...NEVER BEEN HIT THAT HARD IN MY LIFE.
YOUR ORBITAL SOCKET IS BROKEN, EDDIE. YOUR BRAIN IS HEMORRHAGING.
CAN FIX YOU, BUT WE NEED TO RUN AWAY FROM THIS.
N...NO...
THIS IS... MY PROBLEM T'FIX.
WE...WE END THIS. RIGHT--
LISTEN.
EDDIE, PLEASE!

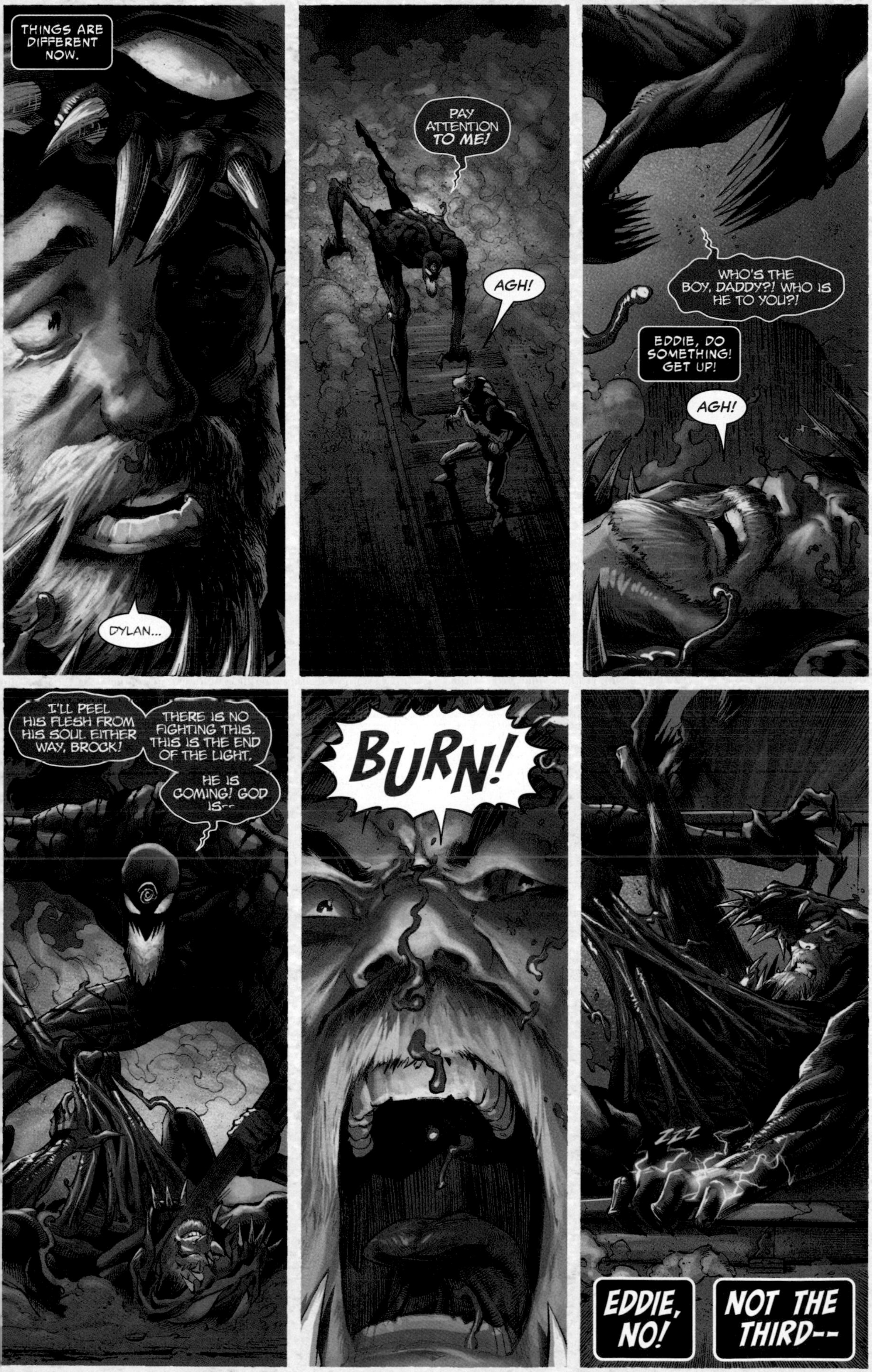
THINGS ARE DIFFERENT NOW.
DYLAN...
PAY ATTENTION TO ME!
AGH!
WHO'S THE BOY, DADDY?! WHO IS HE TO YOU?!
EDDIE, DO SOMETHING! GET UP!
AGH!
I'LL PEEL HIS FLESH FROM HIS SOUL EITHER WAY, BROCK!
THERE IS NO FIGHTING THIS. THIS IS THE END OF THE LIGHT.
HE IS COMING! GOD IS--
BURN!
ZZZ
EDDIE, NO!
NOT THE THIRD--

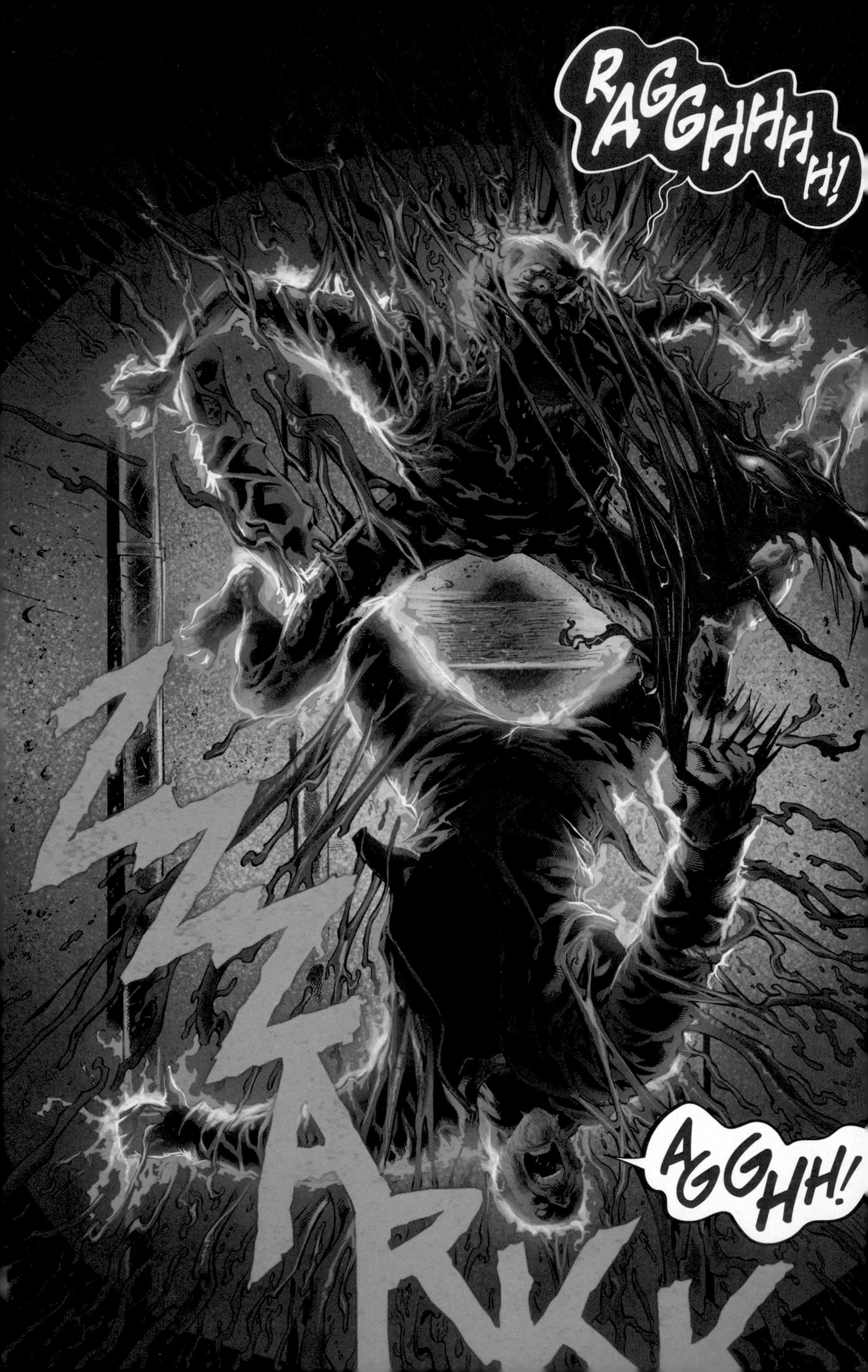
RAGGHHHHH!
AGGHH!
ZZARKK

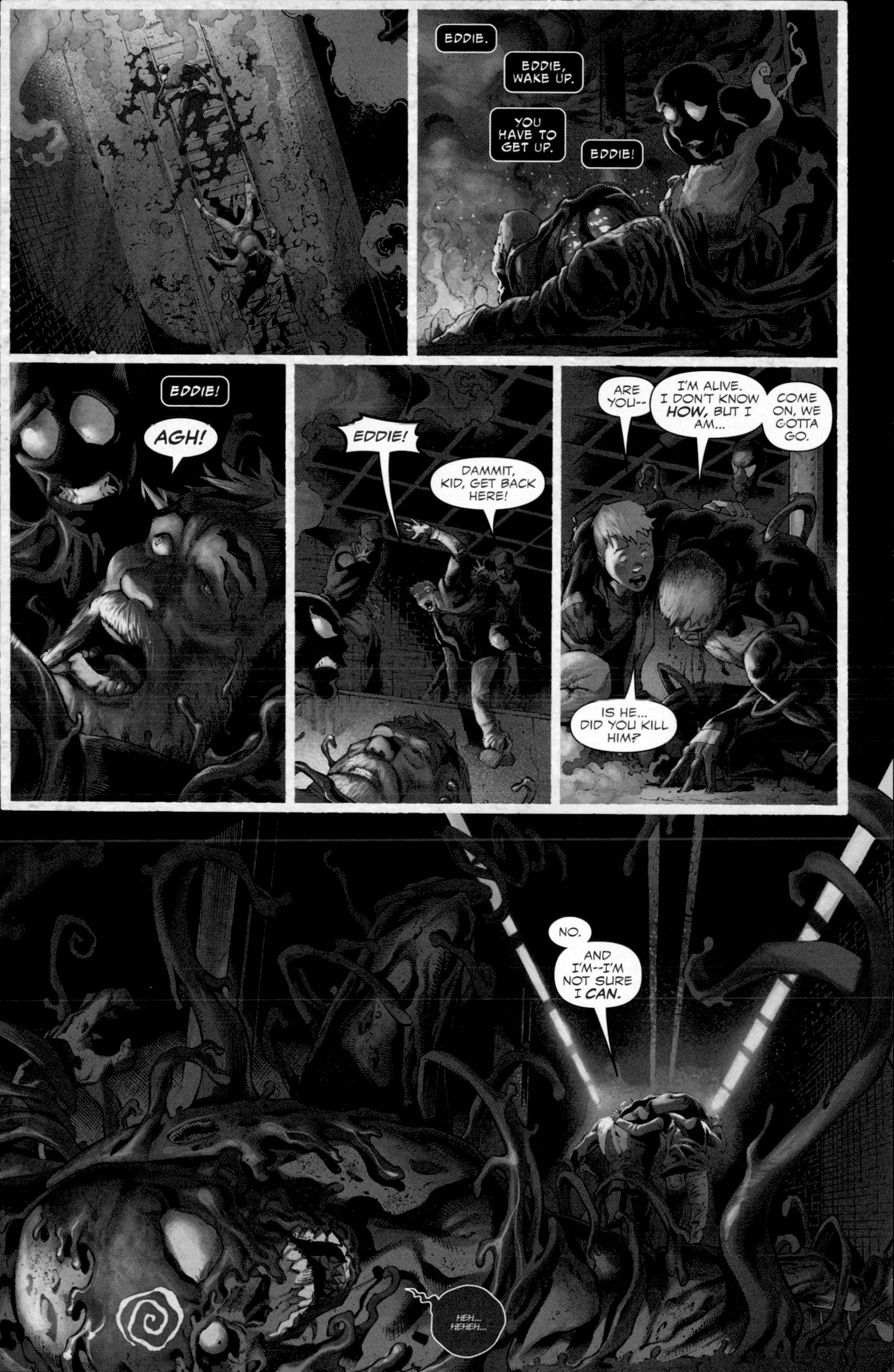
EDDIE.
EDDIE, WAKE UP.
YOU HAVE TO GET UP.
EDDIE!
EDDIE!
AGH!
EDDIE!
DAMMIT, KID, GET BACK HERE!
ARE YOU--
I'M ALIVE. I DON'T KNOW HOW, BUT I AM...
COME ON, WE GOTTA GO.
IS HE... DID YOU KILL HIM?
NO.
AND I'M--I'M NOT SURE I CAN.
HEH... HEHEH...

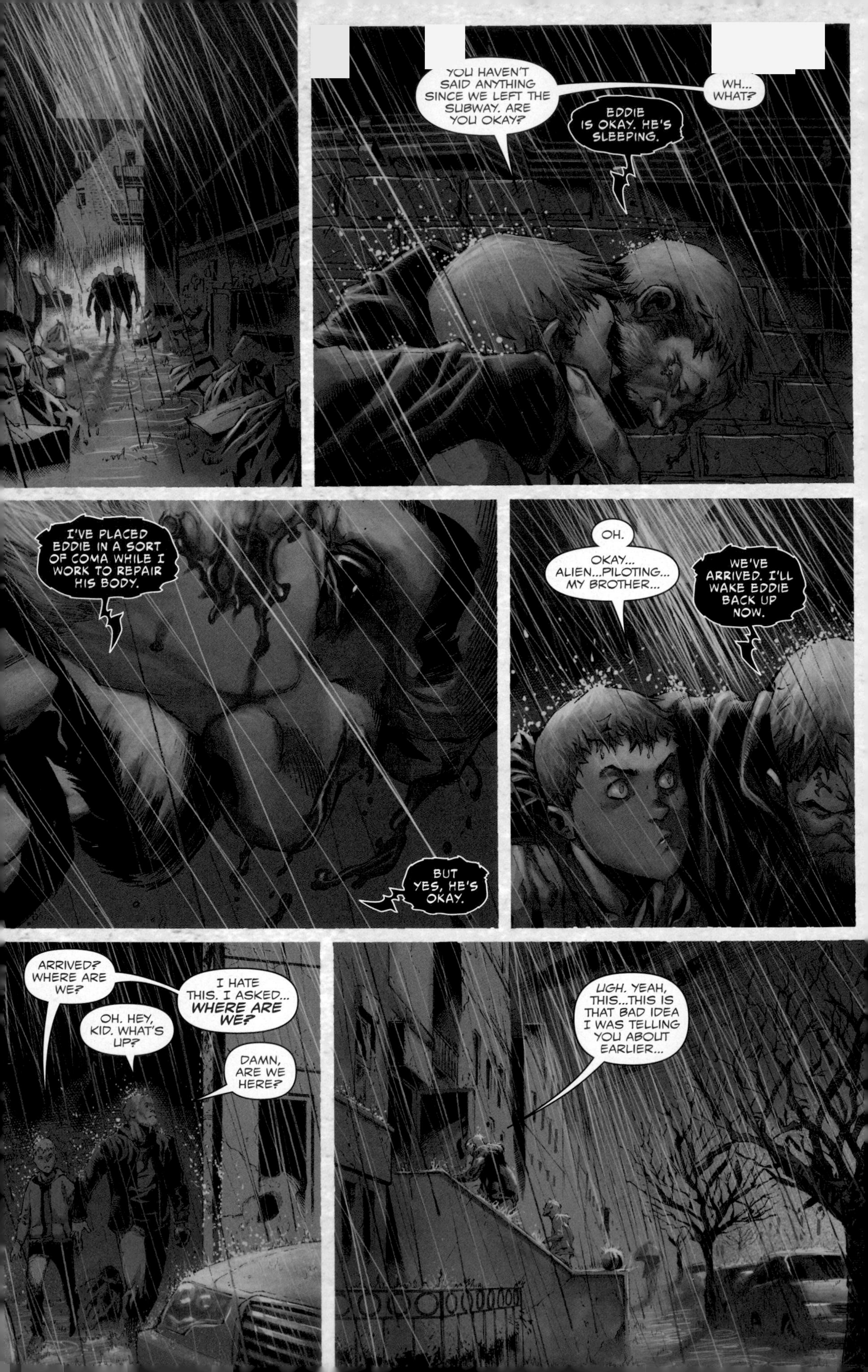
YOU HAVEN'T SAID ANYTHING SINCE WE LEFT THE SUBWAY. ARE YOU OKAY?
WH... WHAT?
EDDIE IS OKAY. HE'S SLEEPING.
I'VE PLACED EDDIE IN A SORT OF COMA WHILE I WORK TO REPAIR HIS BODY.
BUT YES, HE'S OKAY.
OH.
OKAY... ALIEN...PILOTING... MY BROTHER...
WE'VE ARRIVED. I'LL WAKE EDDIE BACK UP NOW.
ARRIVED? WHERE ARE WE?
I HATE THIS. I ASKED... ***WHERE ARE WE?***
OH. HEY, KID. WHAT'S UP?
DAMN, ARE WE HERE?
UGH. YEAH, THIS...THIS IS THAT BAD IDEA I WAS TELLING YOU ABOUT EARLIER...

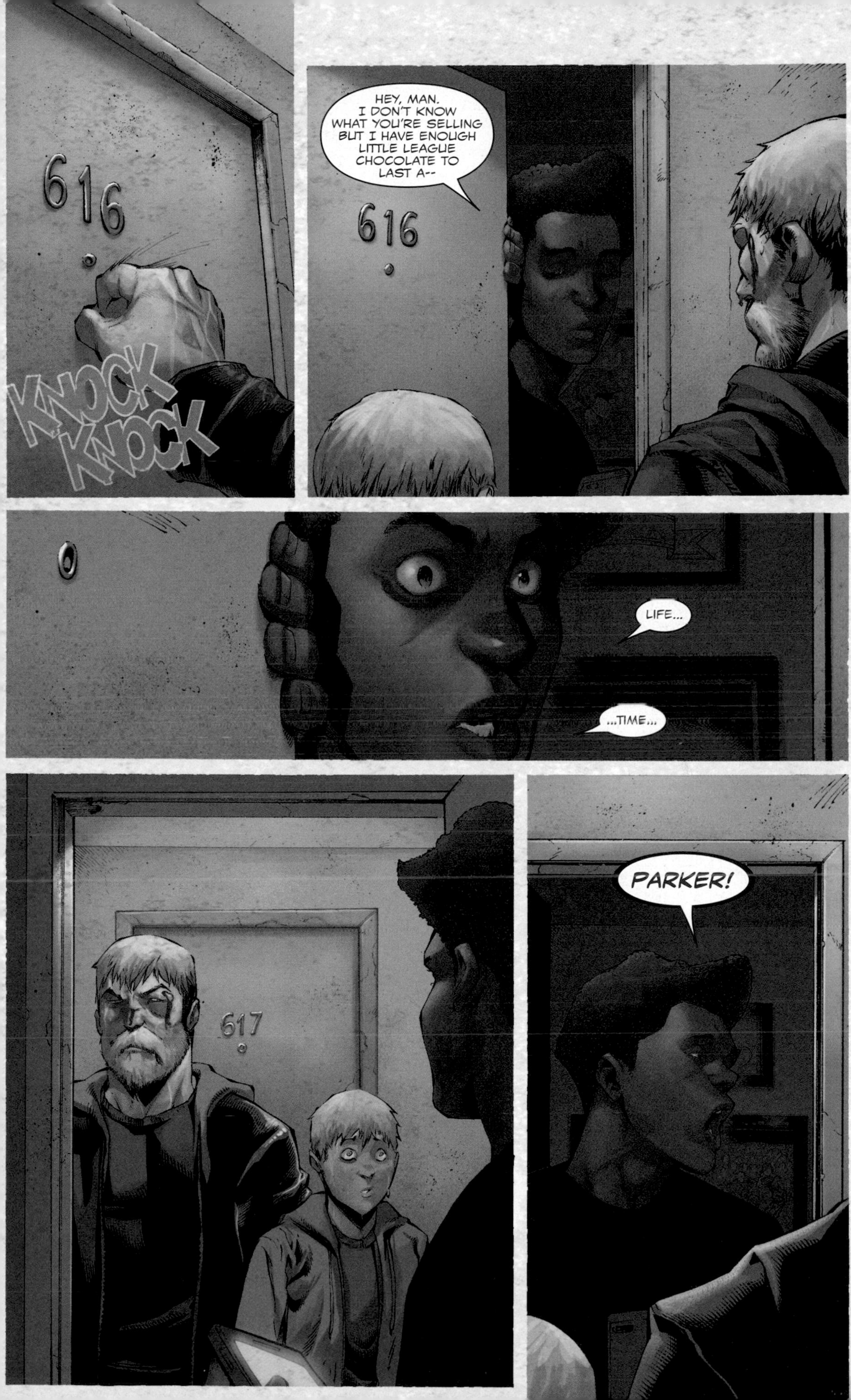
KNOCK KNOCK
HEY, MAN. I DON'T KNOW WHAT YOU'RE SELLING BUT I HAVE ENOUGH LITTLE LEAGUE CHOCOLATE TO LAST A--
616
LIFE...
...TIME...
617
PARKER!

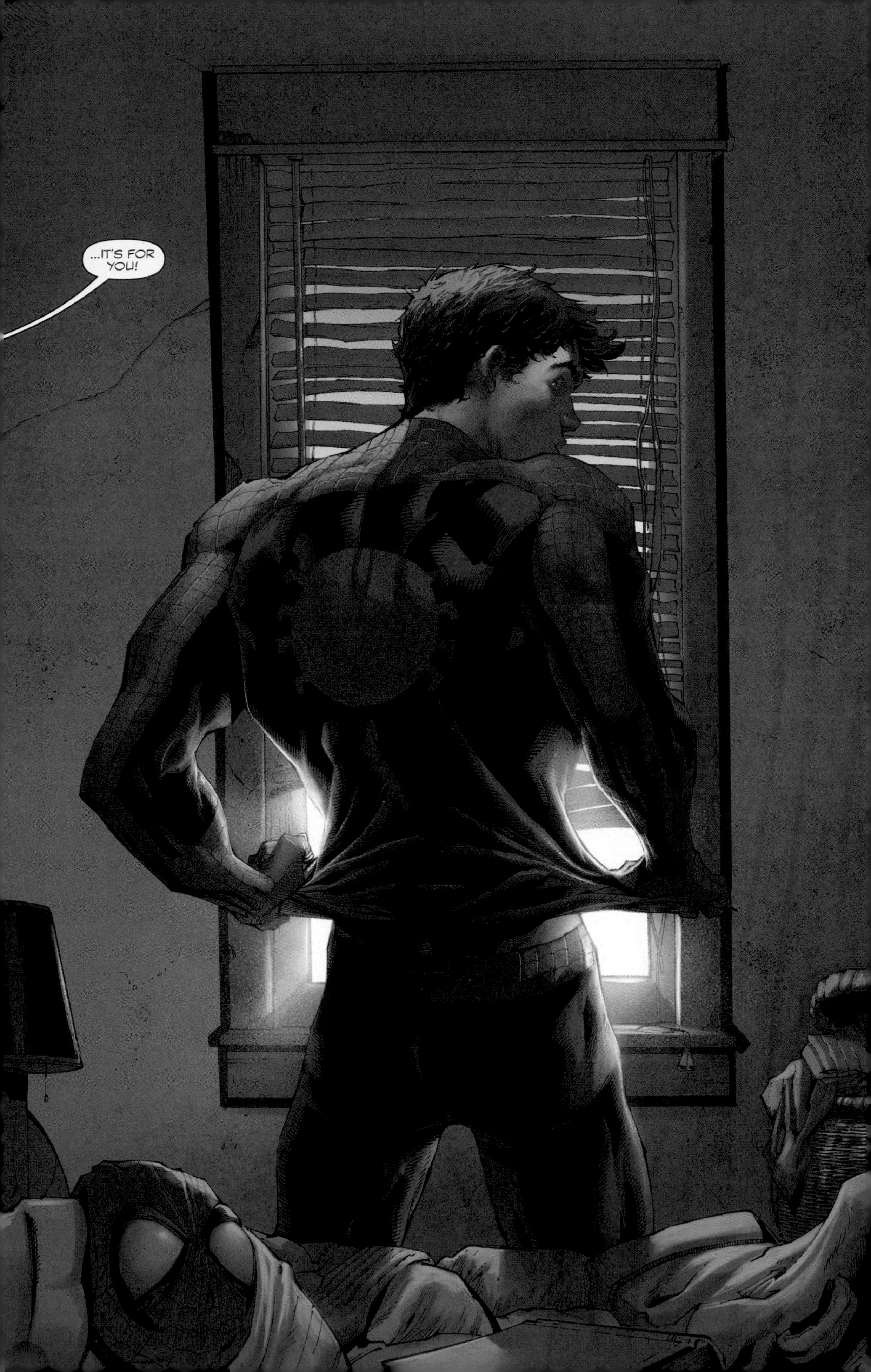
...IT'S FOR YOU!

CHAPTER TWO:

THE GOD SON

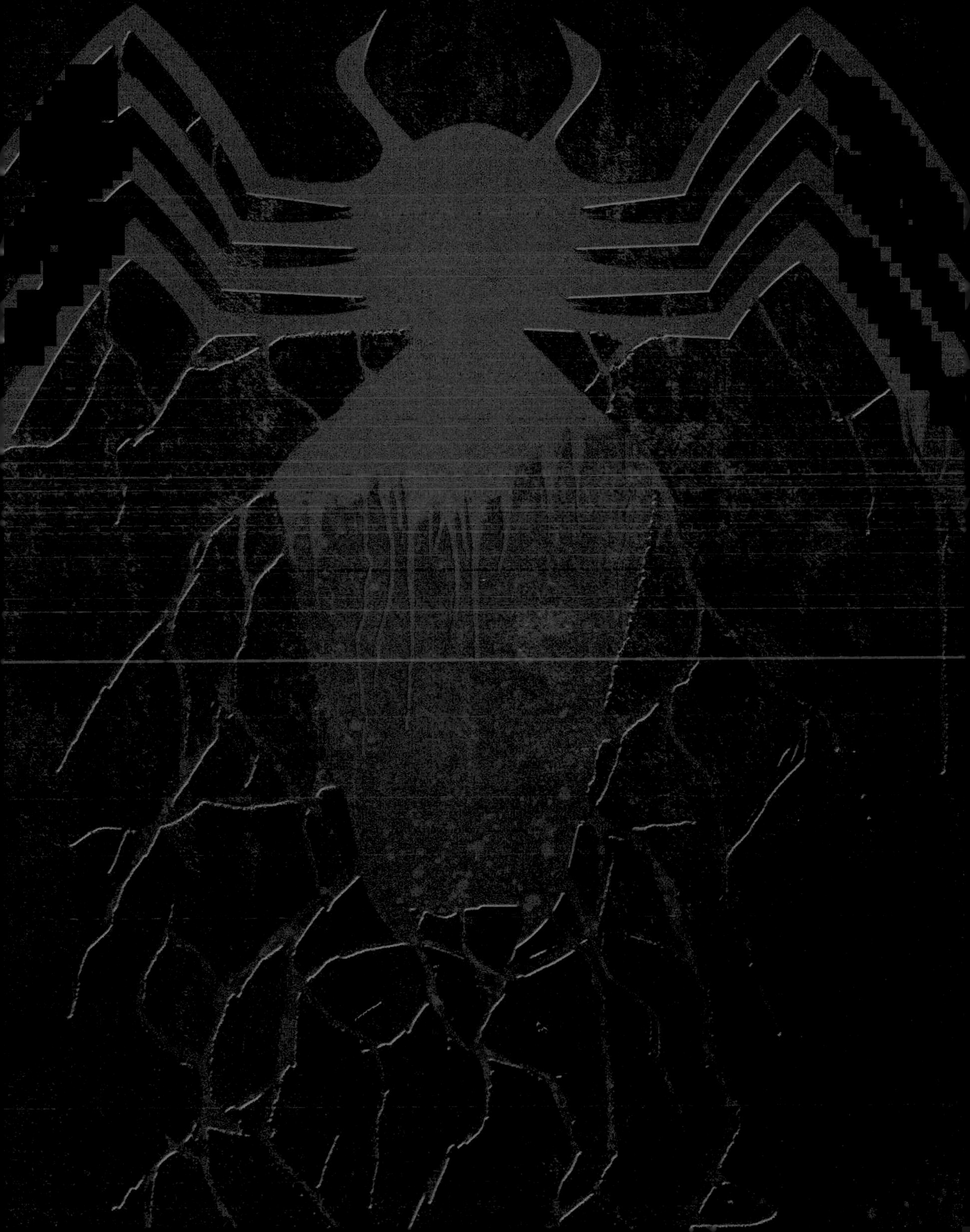

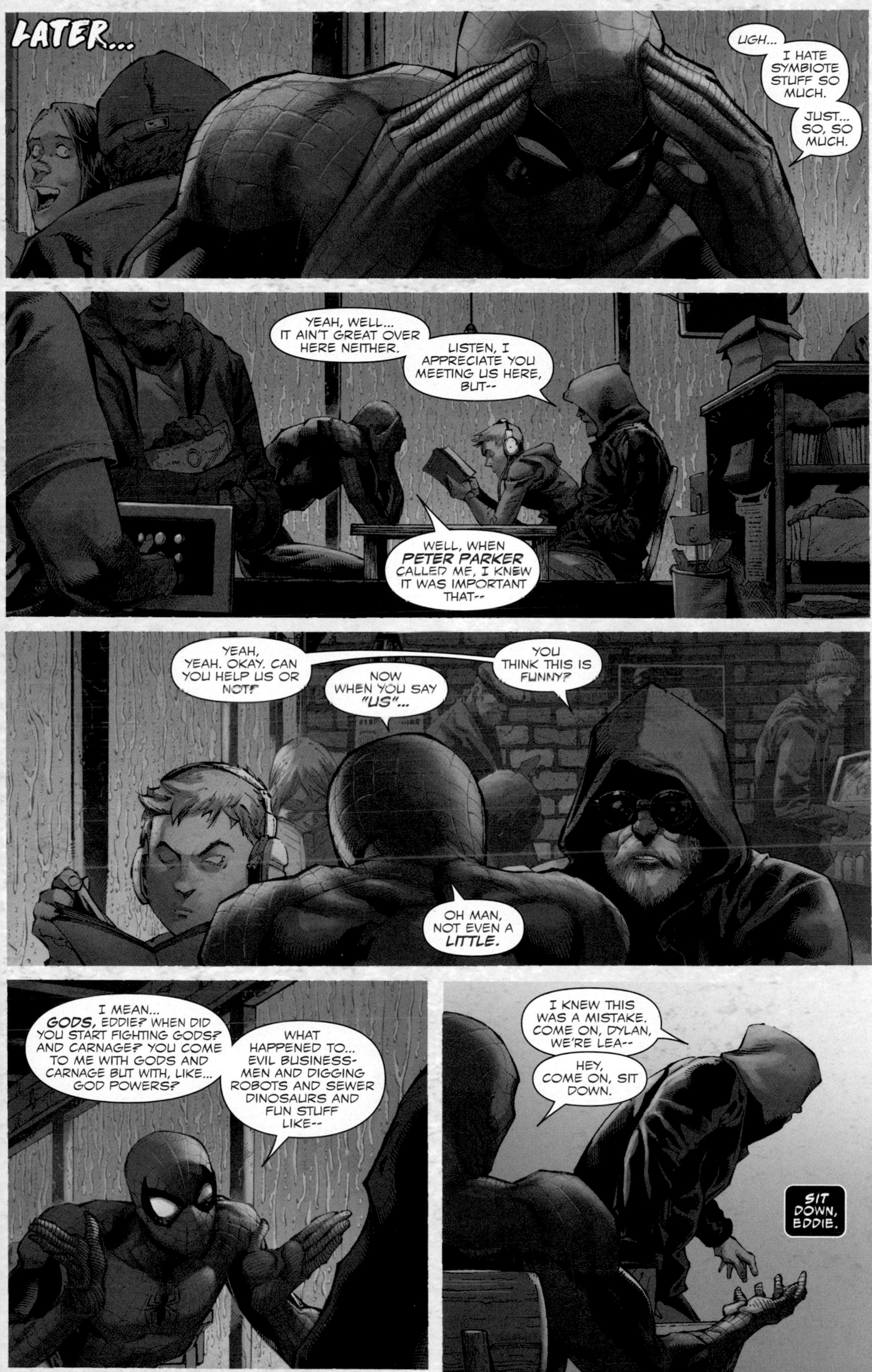
LATER...
UGH... I HATE SYMBIOTE STUFF SO MUCH.
JUST... SO, SO MUCH.
YEAH, WELL... IT AIN'T GREAT OVER HERE NEITHER.
LISTEN, I APPRECIATE YOU MEETING US HERE, BUT--
WELL, WHEN PETER PARKER CALLED ME, I KNEW IT WAS IMPORTANT THAT--
YEAH, YEAH. OKAY. CAN YOU HELP US OR NOT?
NOW WHEN YOU SAY "US"...
YOU THINK THIS IS FUNNY?
OH MAN, NOT EVEN A LITTLE.
I MEAN... GODS, EDDIE? WHEN DID YOU START FIGHTING GODS? AND CARNAGE? YOU COME TO ME WITH GODS AND CARNAGE BUT WITH, LIKE... GOD POWERS?
WHAT HAPPENED TO... EVIL BUSINESS-MEN AND DIGGING ROBOTS AND SEWER DINOSAURS AND FUN STUFF LIKE--
I KNEW THIS WAS A MISTAKE. COME ON, DYLAN, WE'RE LEA--
HEY, COME ON, SIT DOWN.
SIT DOWN, EDDIE.

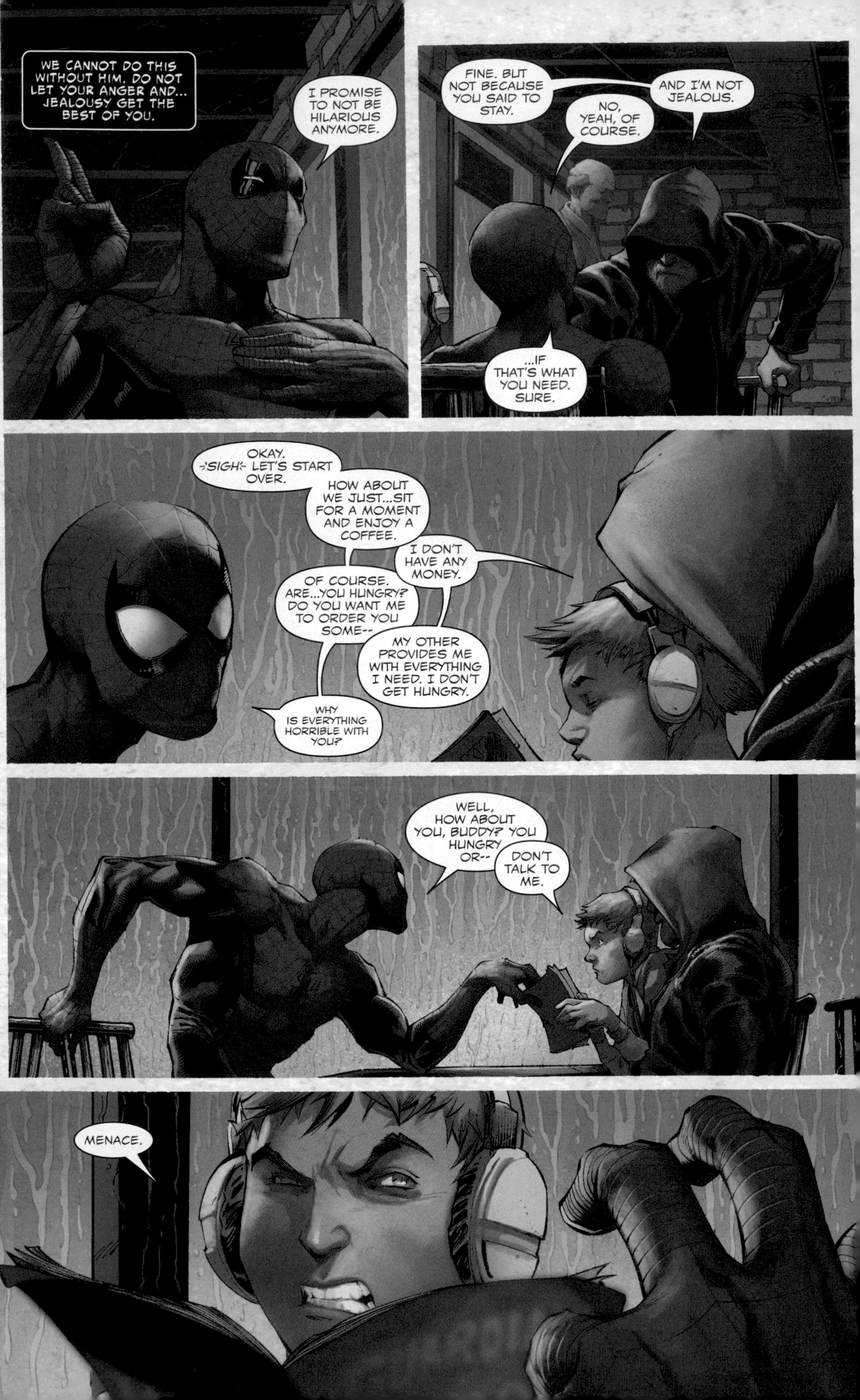
WE CANNOT DO THIS WITHOUT HIM. DO NOT LET YOUR ANGER AND... JEALOUSY GET THE BEST OF YOU.
I PROMISE TO NOT BE HILARIOUS ANYMORE.
FINE. BUT NOT BECAUSE YOU SAID TO STAY.
AND I'M NOT JEALOUS.
NO, YEAH, OF COURSE.
...IF THAT'S WHAT YOU NEED. SURE.
OKAY. -SIGH- LET'S START OVER.
HOW ABOUT WE JUST...SIT FOR A MOMENT AND ENJOY A COFFEE.
I DON'T HAVE ANY MONEY.
OF COURSE. ARE...YOU HUNGRY? DO YOU WANT ME TO ORDER YOU SOME--
MY OTHER PROVIDES ME WITH EVERYTHING I NEED. I DON'T GET HUNGRY.
WHY IS EVERYTHING HORRIBLE WITH YOU?
WELL, HOW ABOUT YOU, BUDDY? YOU HUNGRY OR--
DON'T TALK TO ME.
MENACE.

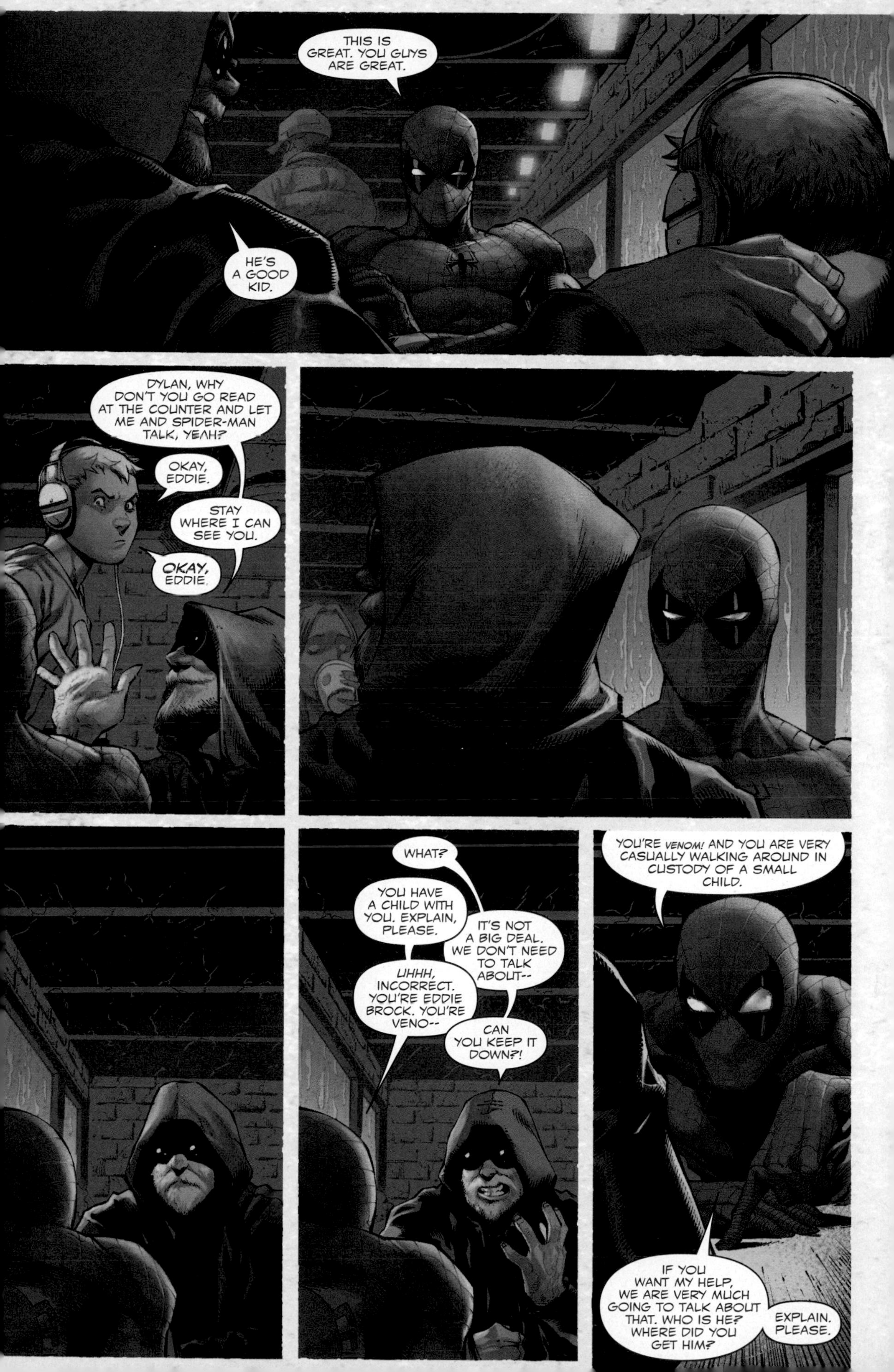
THIS IS GREAT. YOU GUYS ARE GREAT.
HE'S A GOOD KID.
DYLAN, WHY DON'T YOU GO READ AT THE COUNTER AND LET ME AND SPIDER-MAN TALK, YEAH?
OKAY, EDDIE.
STAY WHERE I CAN SEE YOU.
OKAY, EDDIE.
WHAT?
YOU HAVE A CHILD WITH YOU. EXPLAIN, PLEASE.
IT'S NOT A BIG DEAL. WE DON'T NEED TO TALK ABOUT--
UHHH, INCORRECT. YOU'RE EDDIE BROCK. YOU'RE VENO--
CAN YOU KEEP IT DOWN?!
YOU'RE VENOM! AND YOU ARE VERY CASUALLY WALKING AROUND IN CUSTODY OF A SMALL CHILD.
IF YOU WANT MY HELP, WE ARE VERY MUCH GOING TO TALK ABOUT THAT. WHO IS HE? WHERE DID YOU GET HIM?
EXPLAIN. PLEASE.

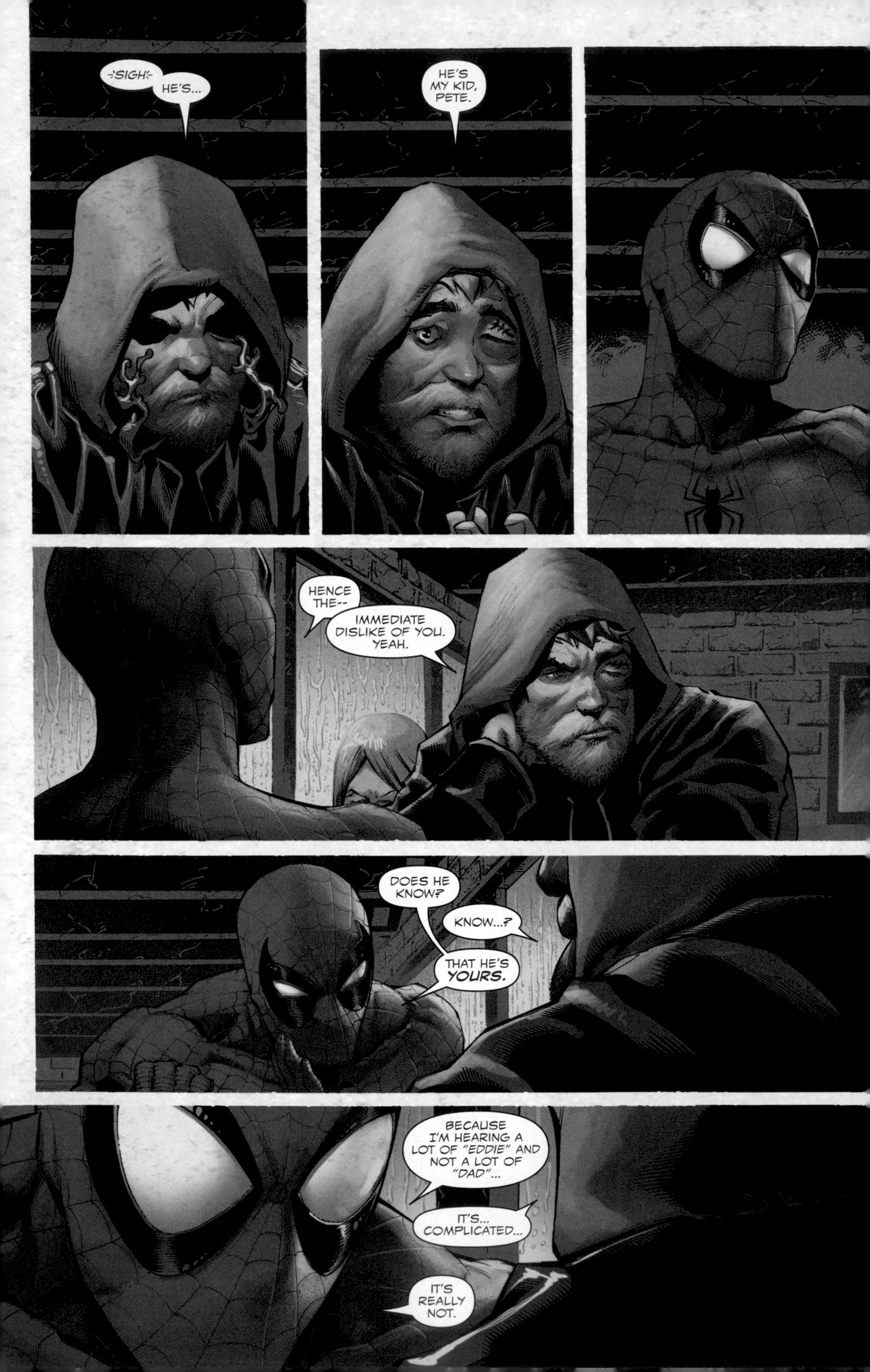

-SIGH-
HE'S...
HE'S MY KID, PETE.
HENCE THE--
IMMEDIATE DISLIKE OF YOU. YEAH.
DOES HE KNOW?
KNOW...?
THAT HE'S YOURS.
BECAUSE I'M HEARING A LOT OF "EDDIE" AND NOT A LOT OF "DAD"...
IT'S... COMPLICATED...
IT'S REALLY NOT.

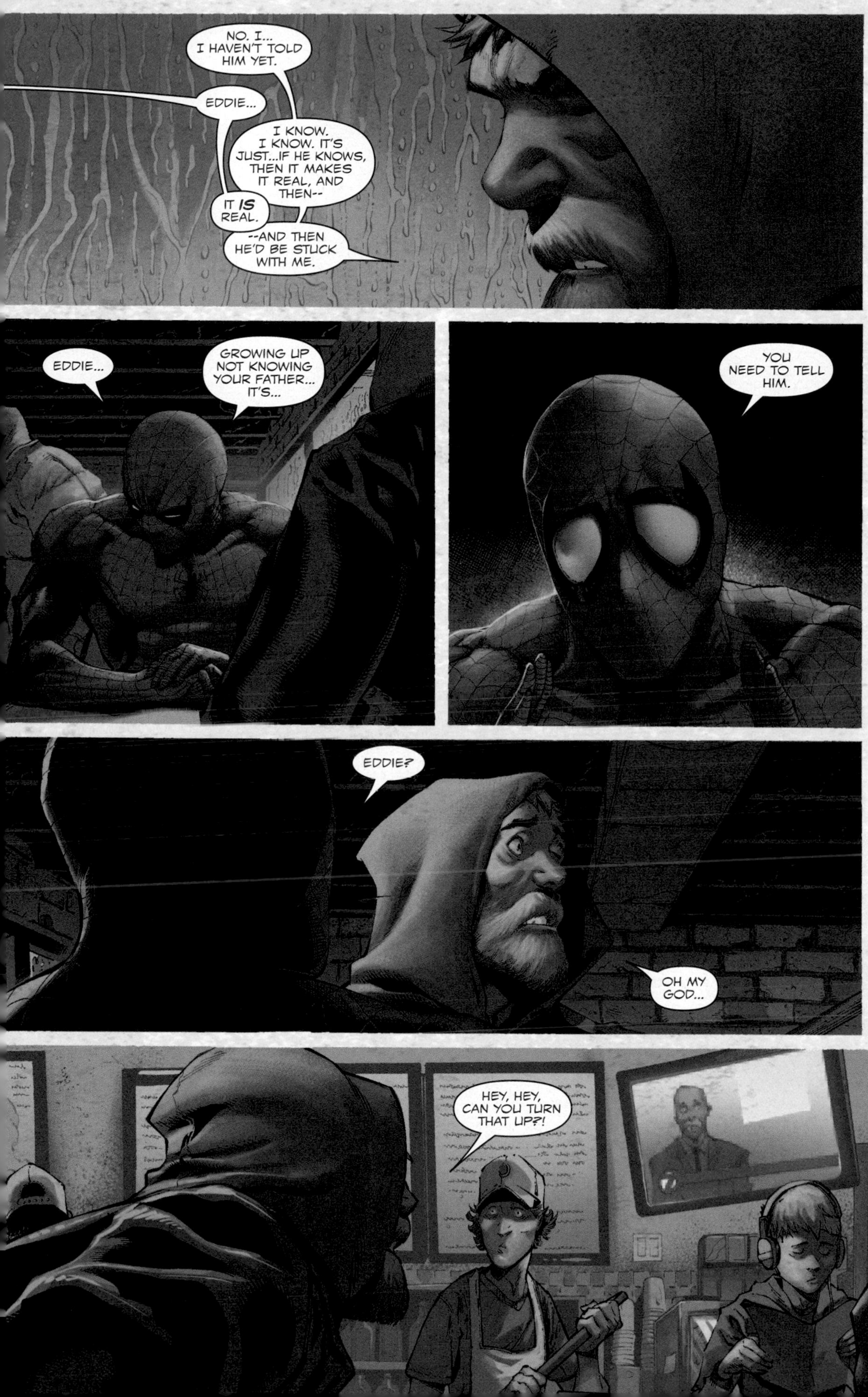
NO. I... I HAVEN'T TOLD HIM YET.
EDDIE...
I KNOW. I KNOW. IT'S JUST...IF HE KNOWS, THEN IT MAKES IT REAL, AND THEN--
IT IS REAL.
--AND THEN HE'D BE STUCK WITH ME.
EDDIE...
GROWING UP NOT KNOWING YOUR FATHER... IT'S...
YOU NEED TO TELL HIM.
EDDIE?
OH MY GOD...
HEY, HEY, CAN YOU TURN THAT UP?!

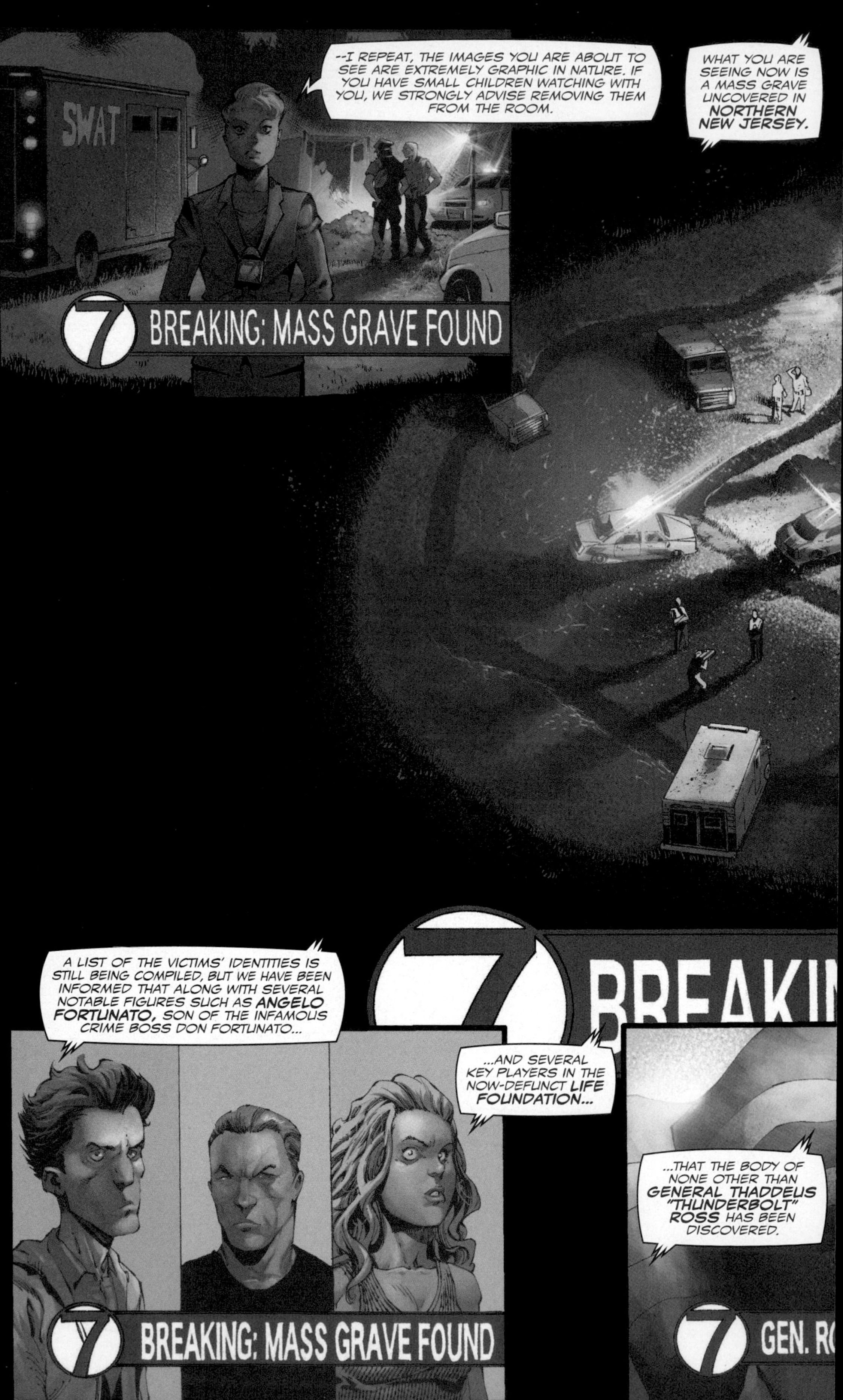

--I REPEAT, THE IMAGES YOU ARE ABOUT TO SEE ARE EXTREMELY GRAPHIC IN NATURE. IF YOU HAVE SMALL CHILDREN WATCHING WITH YOU, WE STRONGLY ADVISE REMOVING THEM FROM THE ROOM.
SWAT
7 BREAKING: MASS GRAVE FOUND
WHAT YOU ARE SEEING NOW IS A MASS GRAVE UNCOVERED IN NORTHERN NEW JERSEY.
A LIST OF THE VICTIMS' IDENTITIES IS STILL BEING COMPILED, BUT WE HAVE BEEN INFORMED THAT ALONG WITH SEVERAL NOTABLE FIGURES SUCH AS ANGELO FORTUNATO, SON OF THE INFAMOUS CRIME BOSS DON FORTUNATO...
...AND SEVERAL KEY PLAYERS IN THE NOW-DEFUNCT LIFE FOUNDATION...
7 BREAKING: MASS GRAVE FOUND
...THAT THE BODY OF NONE OTHER THAN GENERAL THADDEUS "THUNDERBOLT" ROSS HAS BEEN DISCOVERED.

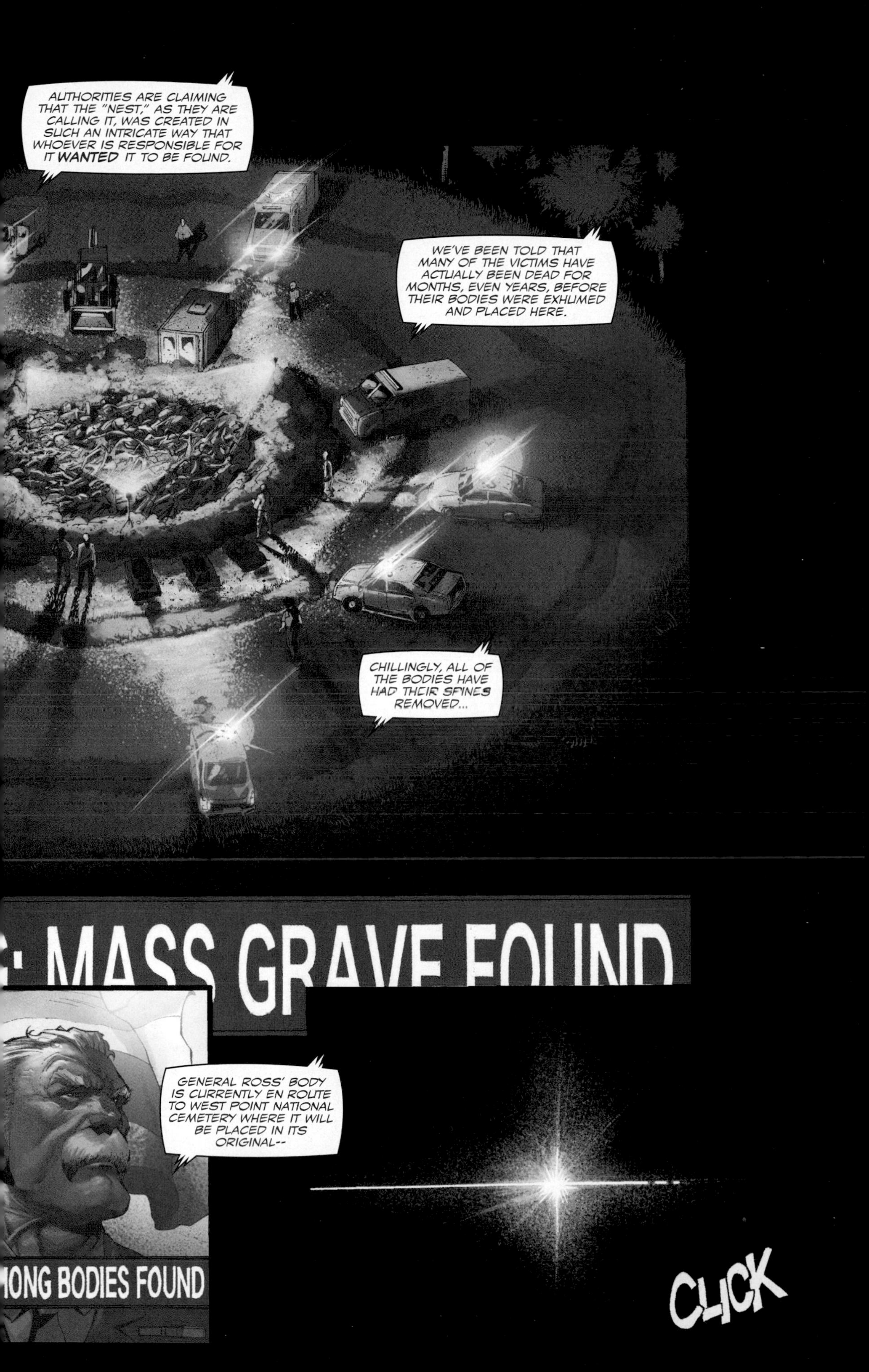

AUTHORITIES ARE CLAIMING THAT THE "NEST," AS THEY ARE CALLING IT, WAS CREATED IN SUCH AN INTRICATE WAY THAT WHOEVER IS RESPONSIBLE FOR IT **WANTED** IT TO BE FOUND.

WE'VE BEEN TOLD THAT MANY OF THE VICTIMS HAVE ACTUALLY BEEN DEAD FOR MONTHS, EVEN YEARS, BEFORE THEIR BODIES WERE EXHUMED AND PLACED HERE.

CHILLINGLY, ALL OF THE BODIES HAVE HAD THEIR SPINES REMOVED...

: MASS GRAVE FOUND

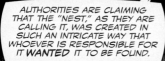

GENERAL ROSS' BODY IS CURRENTLY EN ROUTE TO WEST POINT NATIONAL CEMETERY WHERE IT WILL BE PLACED IN ITS ORIGINAL--

ONG BODIES FOUND

CLICK

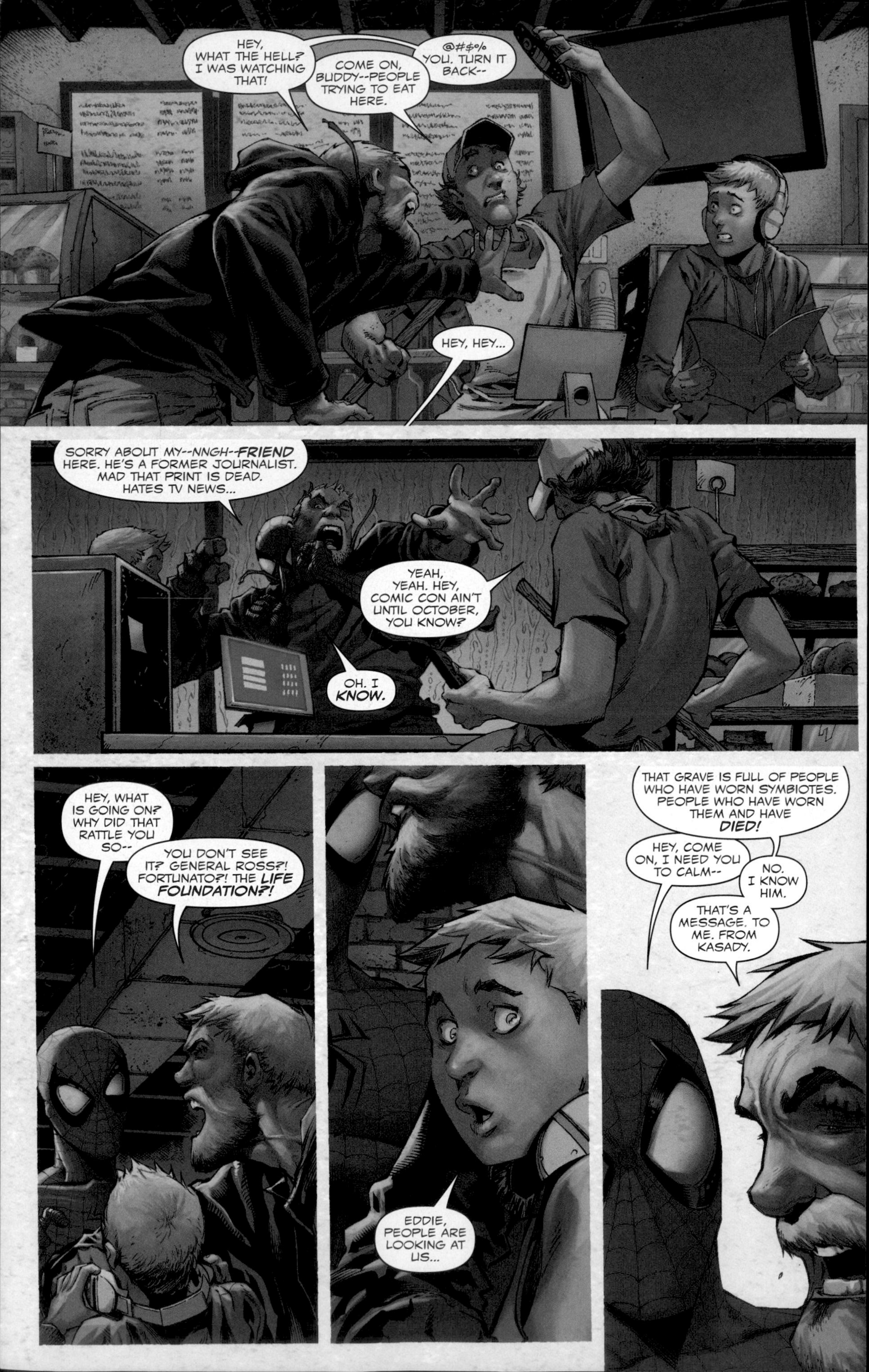
HEY, WHAT THE HELL? I WAS WATCHING THAT!
COME ON, BUDDY--PEOPLE TRYING TO EAT HERE.
@#$% YOU. TURN IT BACK--
HEY, HEY...
SORRY ABOUT MY--NNGH--FRIEND HERE. HE'S A FORMER JOURNALIST. MAD THAT PRINT IS DEAD. HATES TV NEWS...
YEAH, YEAH. HEY, COMIC CON AIN'T UNTIL OCTOBER, YOU KNOW?
OH. I KNOW.
HEY, WHAT IS GOING ON? WHY DID THAT RATTLE YOU SO--
YOU DON'T SEE IT? GENERAL ROSS?! FORTUNATO?! THE LIFE FOUNDATION?!
EDDIE, PEOPLE ARE LOOKING AT US...
THAT GRAVE IS FULL OF PEOPLE WHO HAVE WORN SYMBIOTES. PEOPLE WHO HAVE WORN THEM AND HAVE DIED!
HEY, COME ON, I NEED YOU TO CALM--
NO. I KNOW HIM.
THAT'S A MESSAGE. TO ME. FROM KASADY.

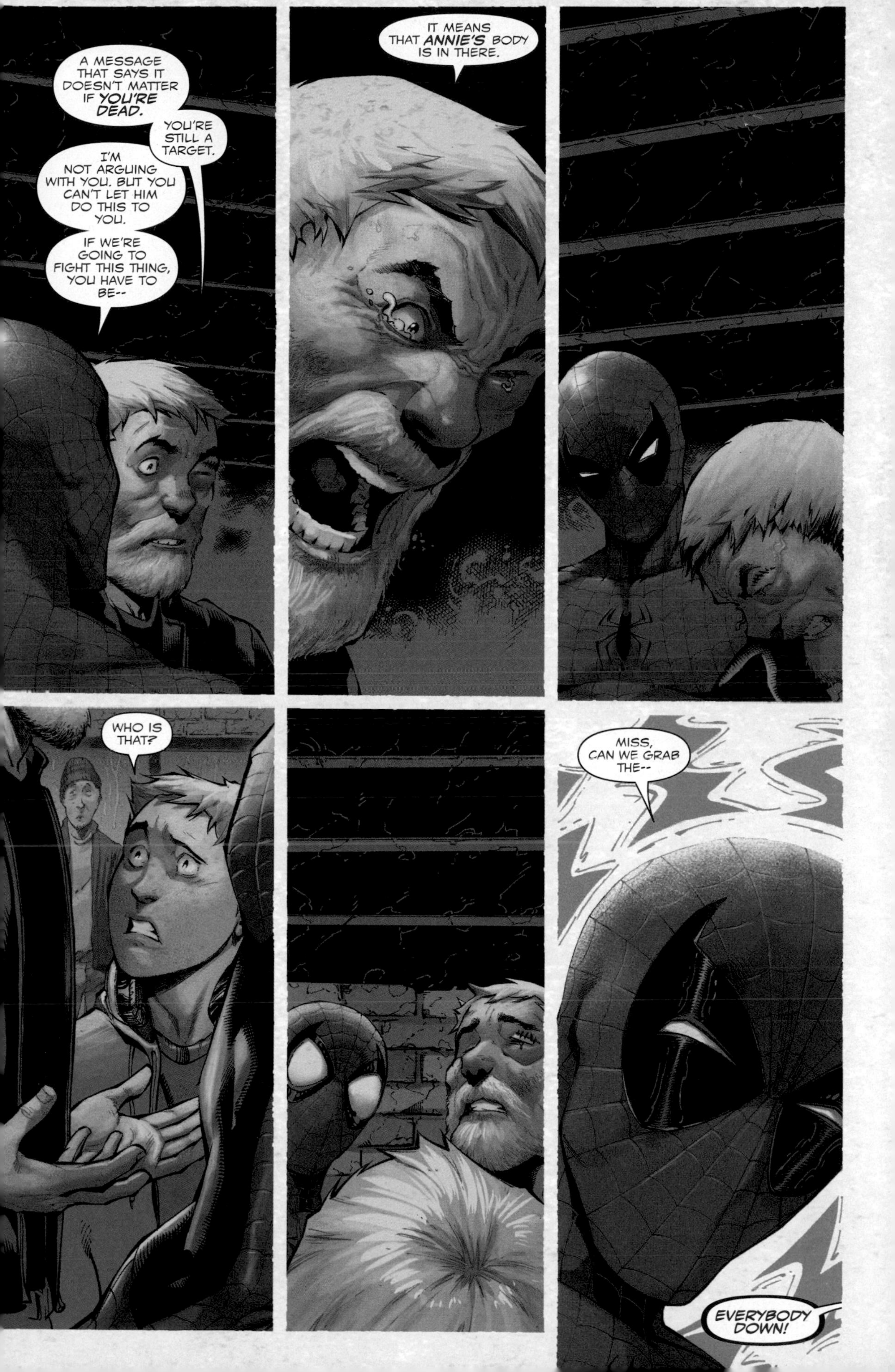
A MESSAGE THAT SAYS IT DOESN'T MATTER IF YOU'RE DEAD.
YOU'RE STILL A TARGET.
I'M NOT ARGUING WITH YOU. BUT YOU CAN'T LET HIM DO THIS TO YOU.
IF WE'RE GOING TO FIGHT THIS THING, YOU HAVE TO BE--
IT MEANS THAT ANNIE'S BODY IS IN THERE.
WHO IS THAT?
MISS, CAN WE GRAB THE--
EVERYBODY DOWN!

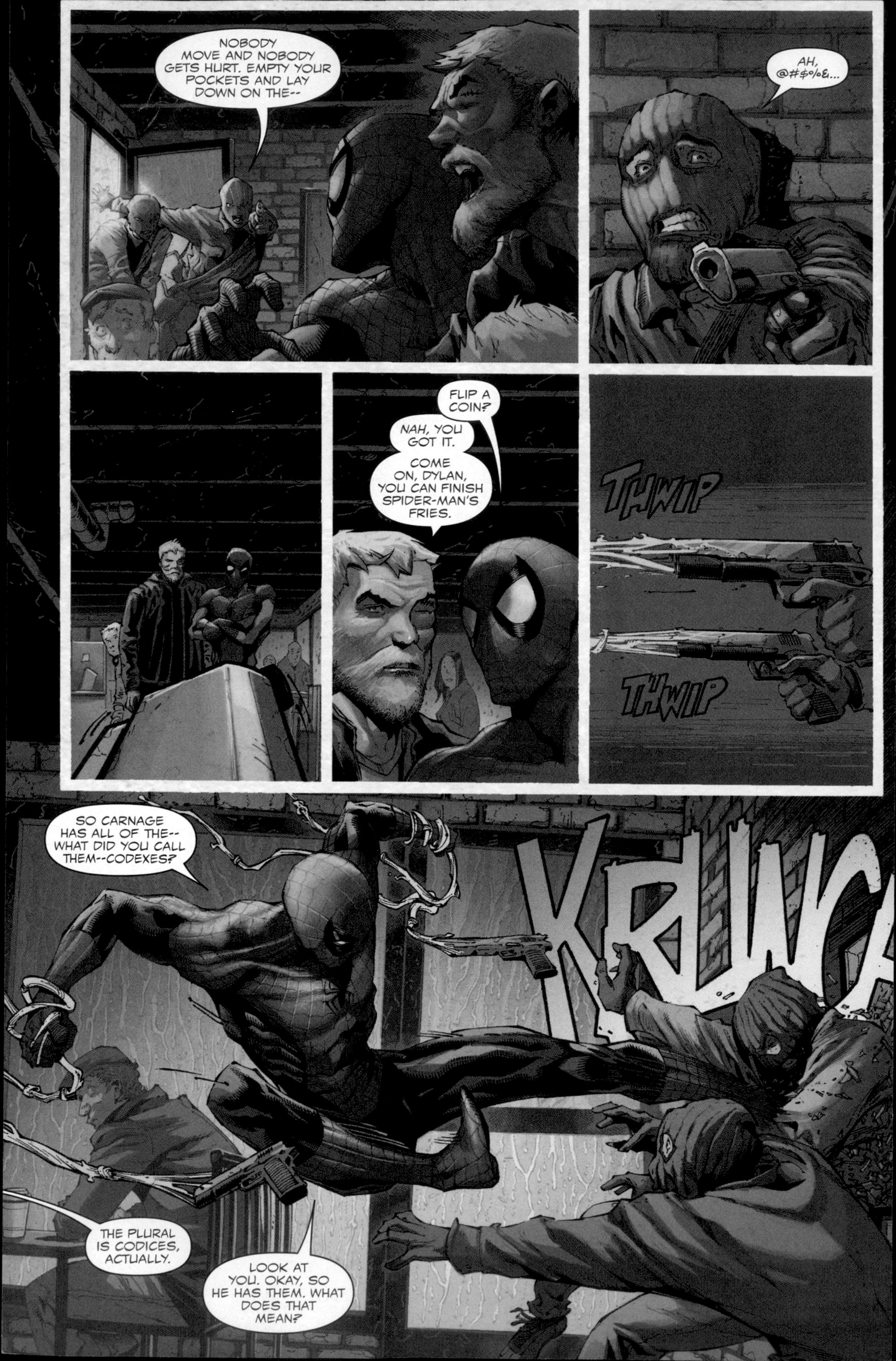
NOBODY MOVE AND NOBODY GETS HURT. EMPTY YOUR POCKETS AND LAY DOWN ON THE--
AH, @#$%&...
FLIP A COIN?
NAH, YOU GOT IT.
COME ON, DYLAN, YOU CAN FINISH SPIDER-MAN'S FRIES.
THWIP
THWIP
SO CARNAGE HAS ALL OF THE--WHAT DID YOU CALL THEM--CODEXES?
KRUNC
THE PLURAL IS CODICES, ACTUALLY.
LOOK AT YOU. OKAY, SO HE HAS THEM. WHAT DOES THAT MEAN?

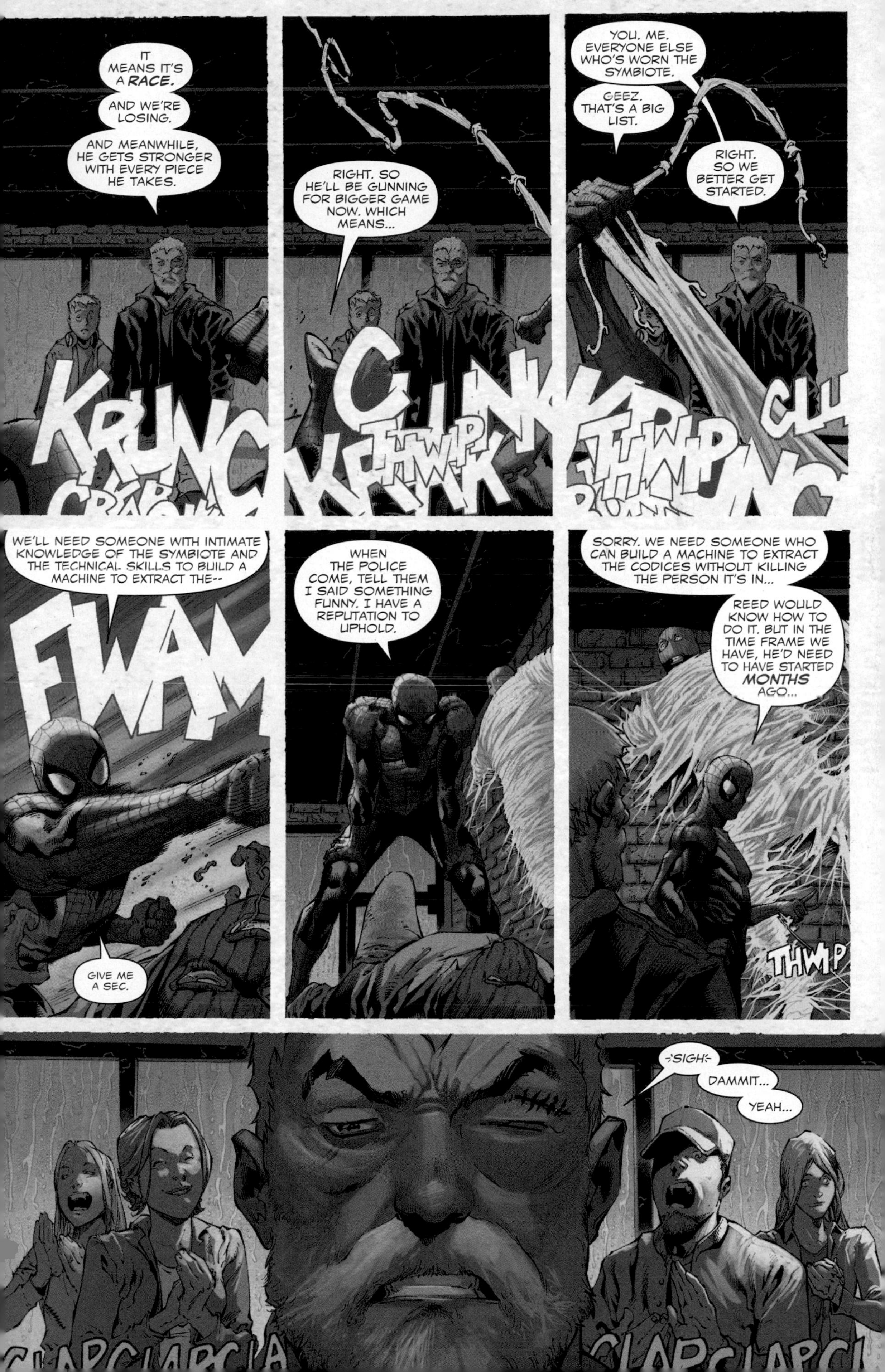
IT MEANS IT'S A RACE.
AND WE'RE LOSING.
AND MEANWHILE, HE GETS STRONGER WITH EVERY PIECE HE TAKES.
RIGHT. SO HE'LL BE GUNNING FOR BIGGER GAME NOW. WHICH MEANS...
YOU. ME. EVERYONE ELSE WHO'S WORN THE SYMBIOTE.
GEEZ. THAT'S A BIG LIST.
RIGHT. SO WE BETTER GET STARTED.
KRUNC
CLUNK
THWIP
THWIP
WE'LL NEED SOMEONE WITH INTIMATE KNOWLEDGE OF THE SYMBIOTE AND THE TECHNICAL SKILLS TO BUILD A MACHINE TO EXTRACT THE--
FWA
GIVE ME A SEC.
WHEN THE POLICE COME, TELL THEM I SAID SOMETHING FUNNY. I HAVE A REPUTATION TO UPHOLD.
SORRY. WE NEED SOMEONE WHO CAN BUILD A MACHINE TO EXTRACT THE CODICES WITHOUT KILLING THE PERSON IT'S IN...
REED WOULD KNOW HOW TO DO IT. BUT IN THE TIME FRAME WE HAVE, HE'D NEED TO HAVE STARTED MONTHS AGO...
THWIP
-SIGH-
DAMMIT...
YEAH...

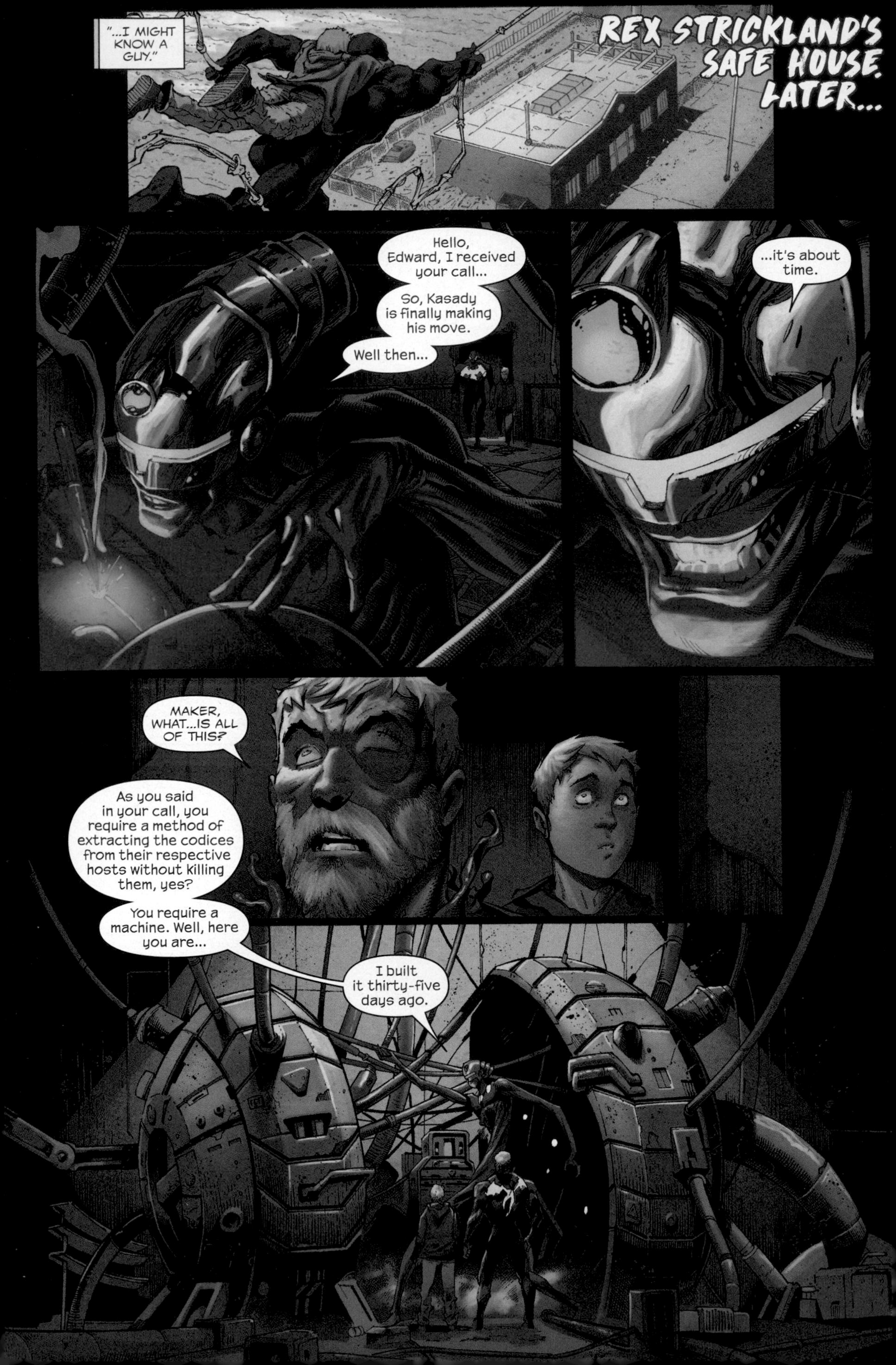
"...I MIGHT KNOW A GUY."
REX STRICKLAND'S SAFE HOUSE. LATER...
Hello, Edward, I received your call...
So, Kasady is finally making his move.
Well then...
...it's about time.
MAKER, WHAT...IS ALL OF THIS?
As you said in your call, you require a method of extracting the codices from their respective hosts without killing them, yes?
You require a machine. Well, here you are...
I built it thirty-five days ago.

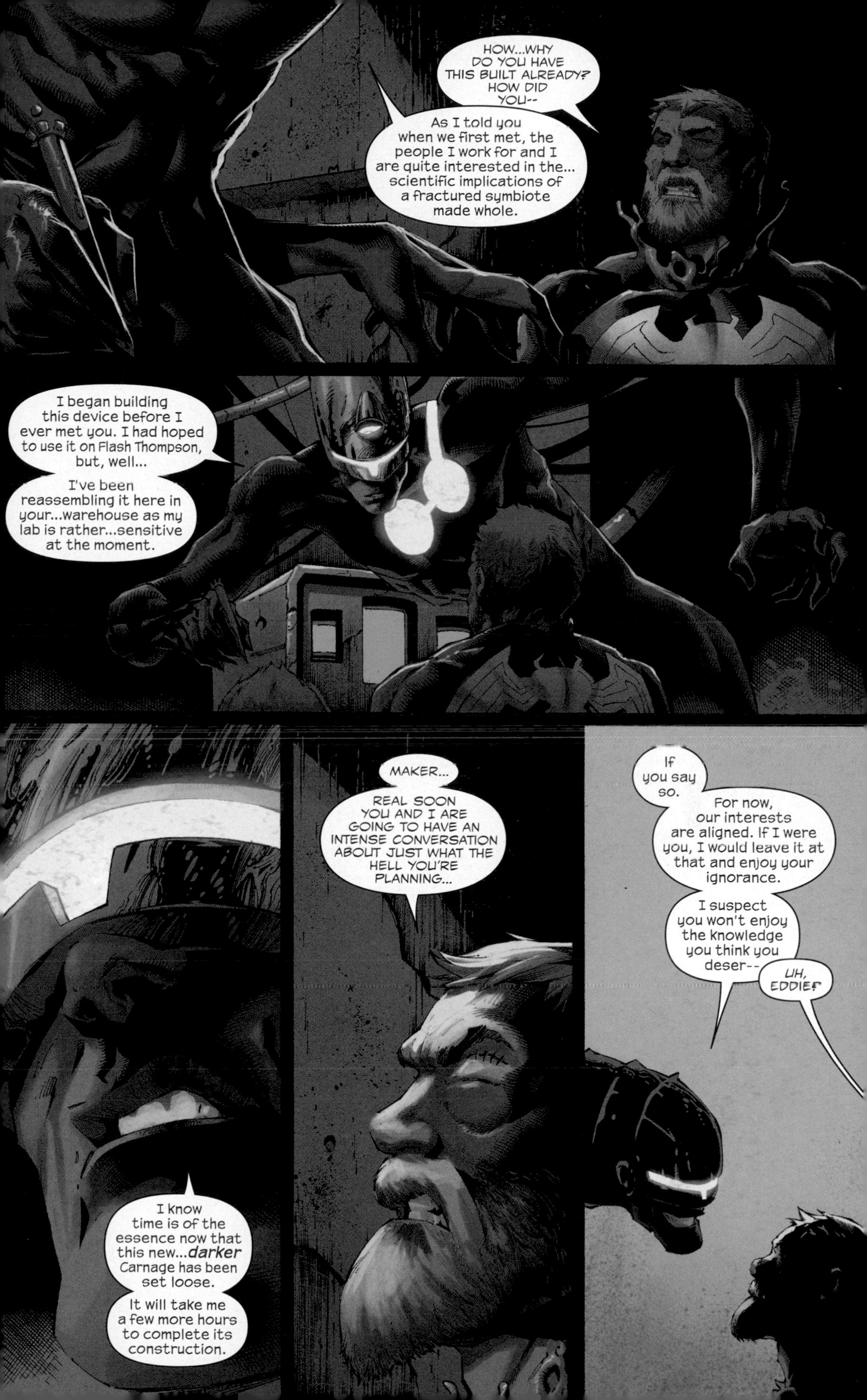
HOW...WHY DO YOU HAVE THIS BUILT ALREADY? HOW DID YOU--
As I told you when we first met, the people I work for and I are quite interested in the... scientific implications of a fractured symbiote made whole.
I began building this device before I ever met you. I had hoped to use it on Flash Thompson, but, well...
I've been reassembling it here in your...warehouse as my lab is rather...sensitive at the moment.
I know time is of the essence now that this new...*darker* Carnage has been set loose.
It will take me a few more hours to complete its construction.
MAKER...
REAL SOON YOU AND I ARE GOING TO HAVE AN INTENSE CONVERSATION ABOUT JUST WHAT THE HELL YOU'RE PLANNING...
If you say so.
For now, our interests are aligned. If I were you, I would leave it at that and enjoy your ignorance.
I suspect you won't enjoy the knowledge you think you deser--
UH, EDDIE?

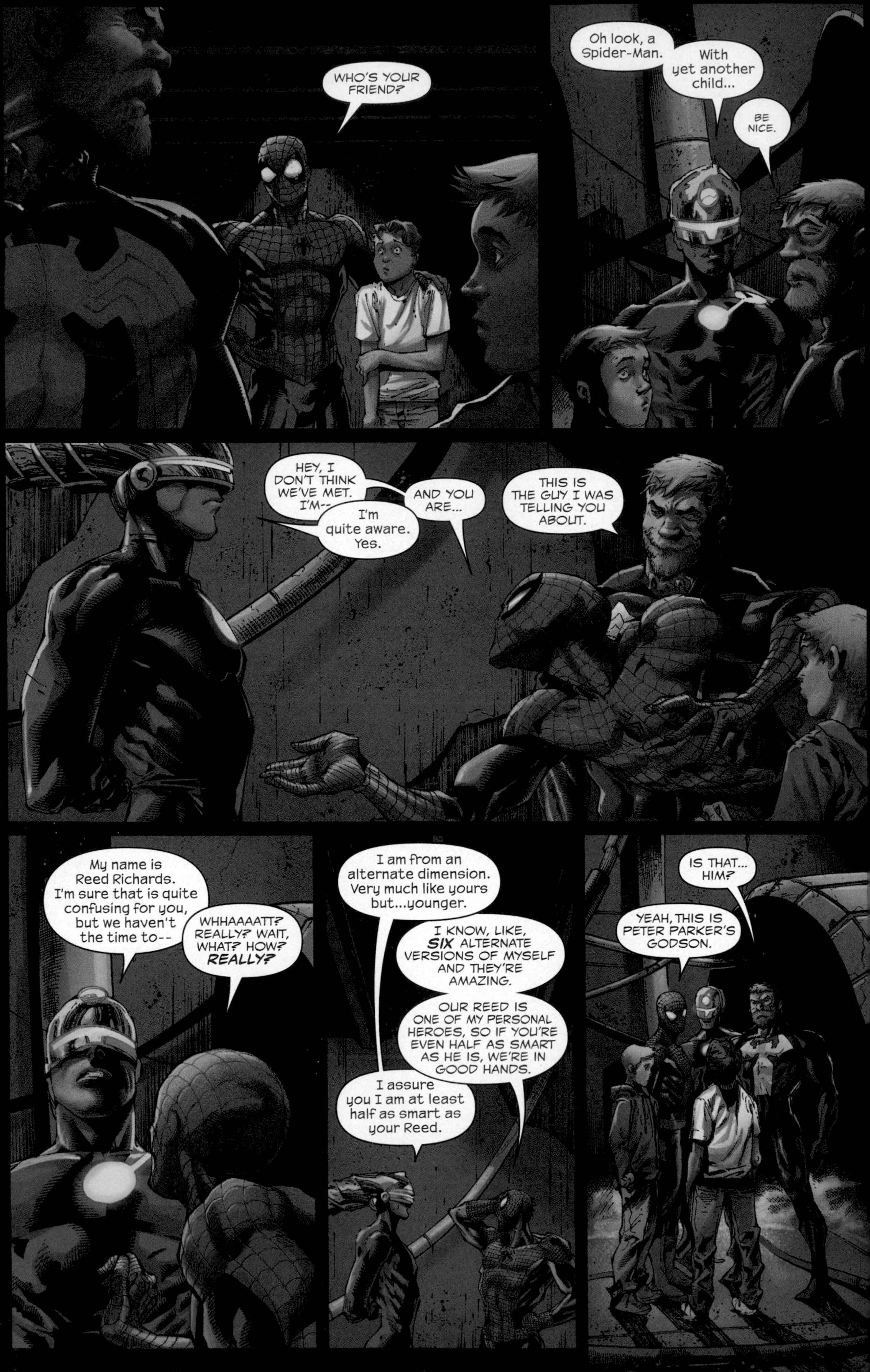
WHO'S YOUR FRIEND?
Oh look, a Spider-Man.
With yet another child...
BE NICE.
HEY, I DON'T THINK WE'VE MET. I'M--
I'm quite aware. Yes.
AND YOU ARE...
THIS IS THE GUY I WAS TELLING YOU ABOUT.
My name is Reed Richards. I'm sure that is quite confusing for you, but we haven't the time to--
WHHAAAATT? REALLY? WAIT, WHAT? HOW? REALLY?
I am from an alternate dimension. Very much like yours but...younger.
I KNOW, LIKE, SIX ALTERNATE VERSIONS OF MYSELF AND THEY'RE AMAZING.
OUR REED IS ONE OF MY PERSONAL HEROES, SO IF YOU'RE EVEN HALF AS SMART AS HE IS, WE'RE IN GOOD HANDS.
I assure you I am at least half as smart as your Reed.
IS THAT... HIM?
YEAH, THIS IS PETER PARKER'S GODSON.

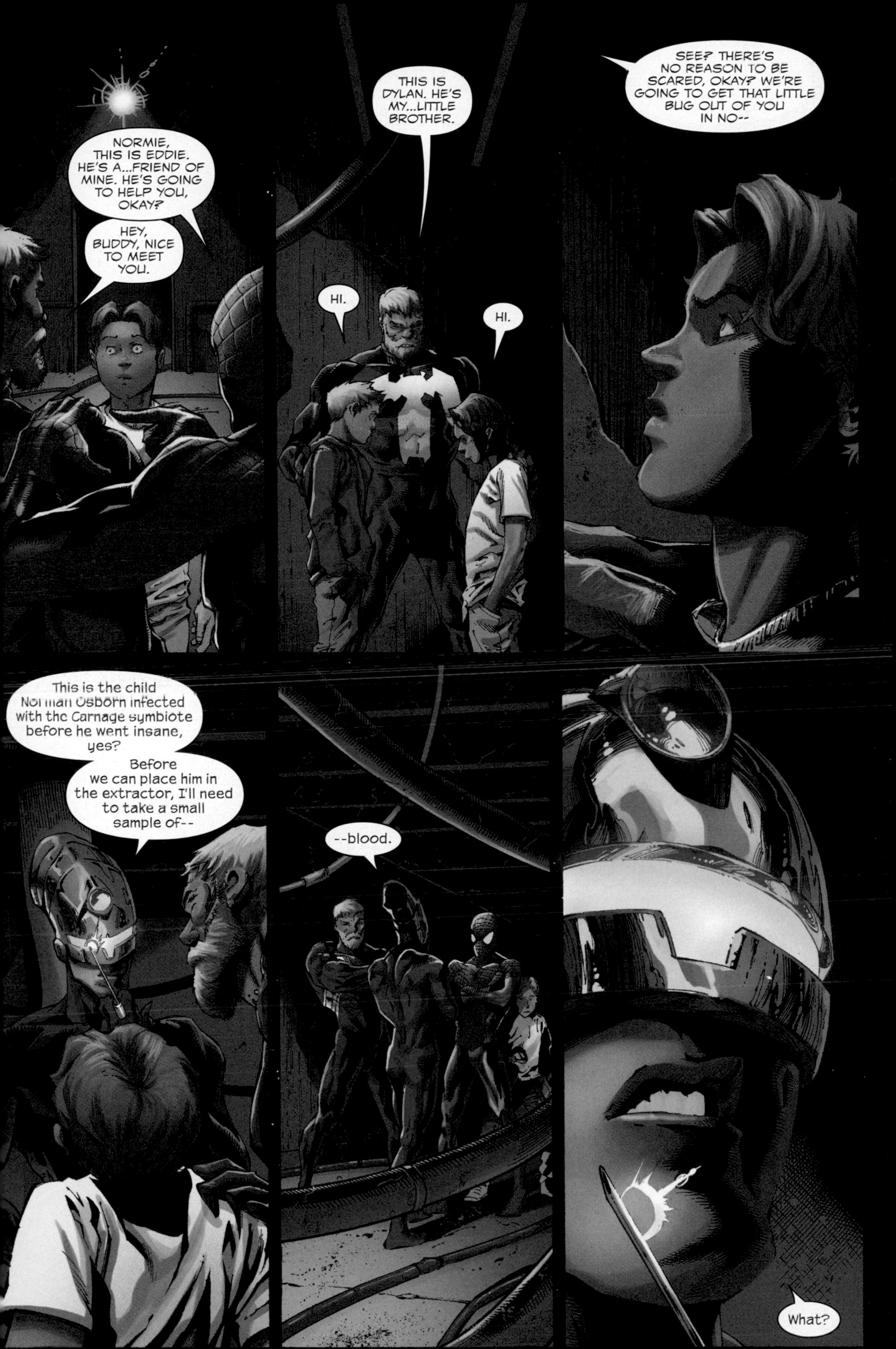

NORMIE, THIS IS EDDIE. HE'S A...FRIEND OF MINE. HE'S GOING TO HELP YOU, OKAY?
HEY, BUDDY, NICE TO MEET YOU.
THIS IS DYLAN. HE'S MY...LITTLE BROTHER.
HI.
HI.
SEE? THERE'S NO REASON TO BE SCARED, OKAY? WE'RE GOING TO GET THAT LITTLE BUG OUT OF YOU IN NO--
This is the child Norman Osborn infected with the Carnage symbiote before he went insane, yes?
Before we can place him in the extractor, I'll need to take a small sample of--
--blood.
What?

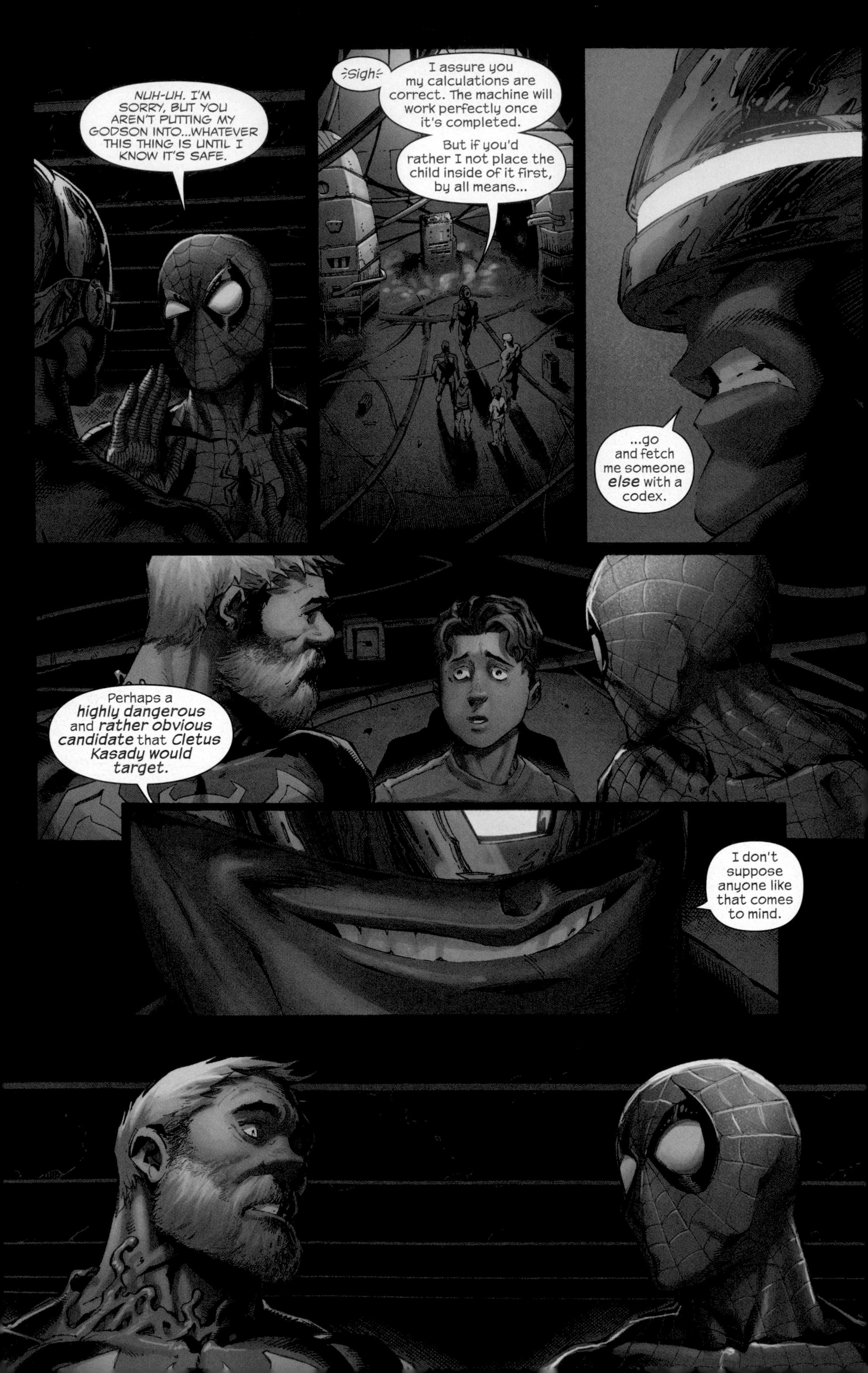
NUH-UH. I'M SORRY, BUT YOU AREN'T PUTTING MY GODSON INTO...WHATEVER THIS THING IS UNTIL I KNOW IT'S SAFE.
Sigh
I assure you my calculations are correct. The machine will work perfectly once it's completed.
But if you'd rather I not place the child inside of it first, by all means...
...go and fetch me someone else with a codex.
Perhaps a highly dangerous and rather obvious candidate that Cletus Kasady would target.
I don't suppose anyone like that comes to mind.

CHAPTER THREE:

THE LONG RED DARK

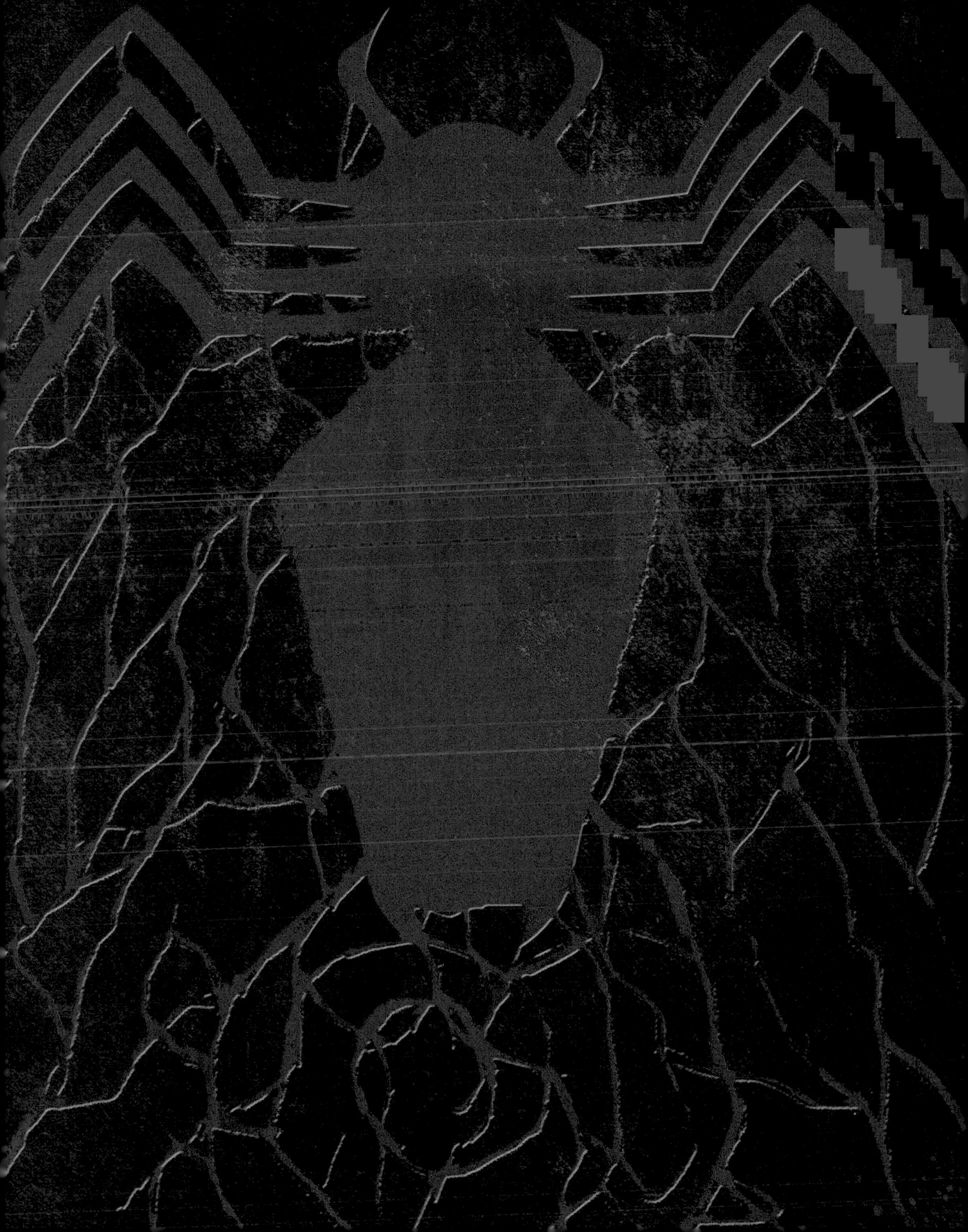

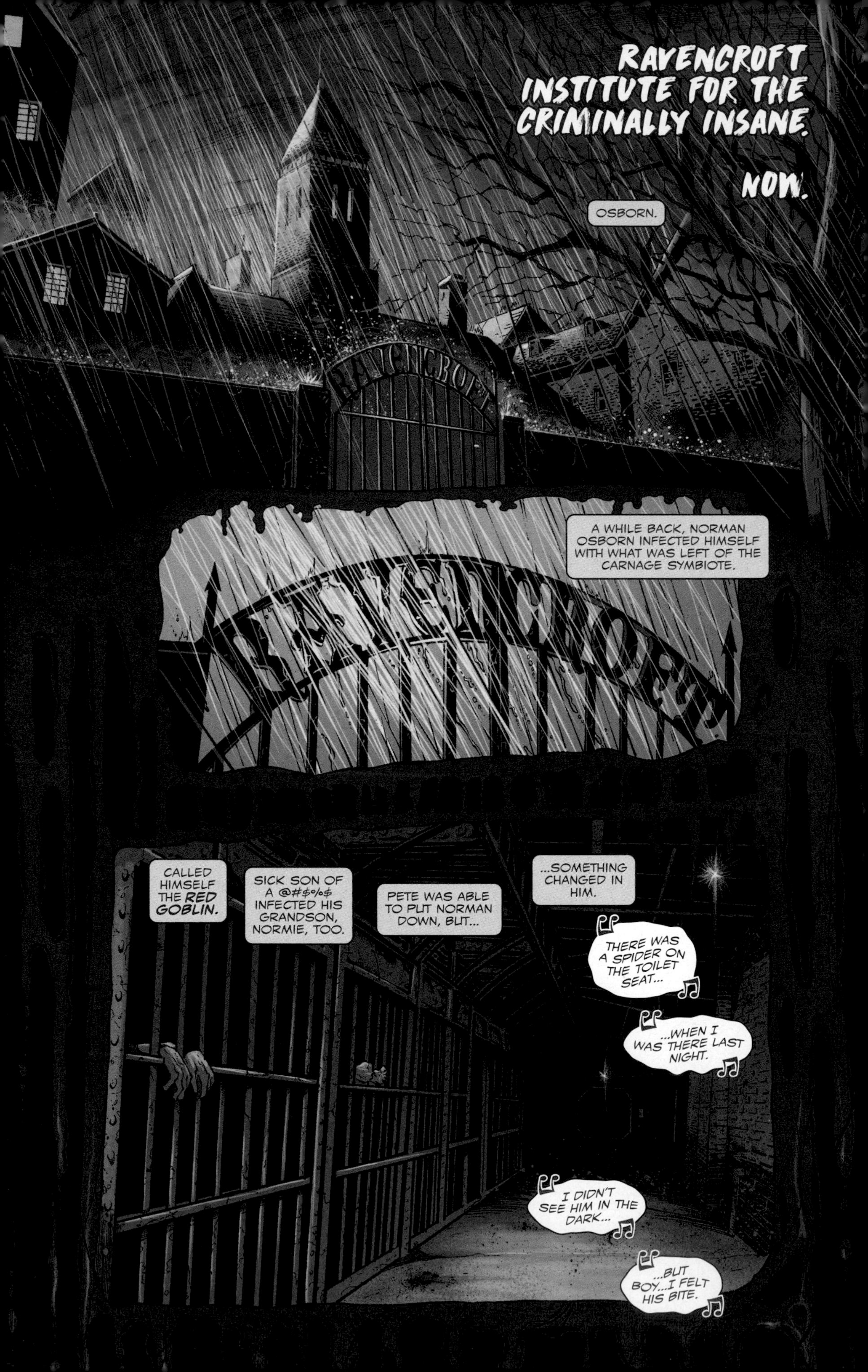
RAVENCROFT INSTITUTE FOR THE CRIMINALLY INSANE.
NOW.
OSBORN.
A WHILE BACK, NORMAN OSBORN INFECTED HIMSELF WITH WHAT WAS LEFT OF THE CARNAGE SYMBIOTE.
CALLED HIMSELF THE RED GOBLIN.
SICK SON OF A @#$%$ INFECTED HIS GRANDSON, NORMIE, TOO.
PETE WAS ABLE TO PUT NORMAN DOWN, BUT...
...SOMETHING CHANGED IN HIM.
THERE WAS A SPIDER ON THE TOILET SEAT...
...WHEN I WAS THERE LAST NIGHT.
I DIDN'T SEE HIM IN THE DARK...
...BUT BOY...I FELT HIS BITE.

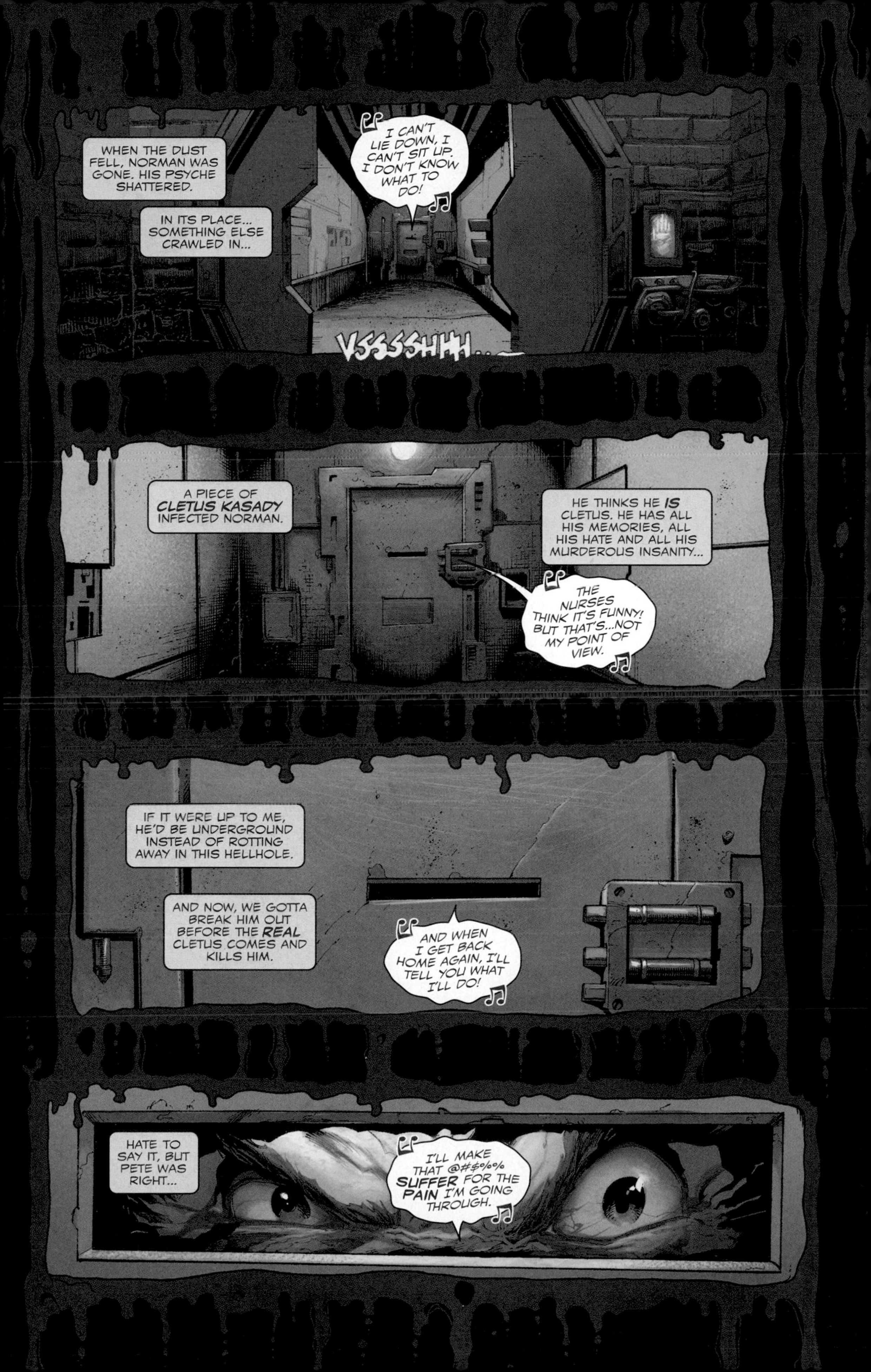
WHEN THE DUST FELL, NORMAN WAS GONE. HIS PSYCHE SHATTERED.
IN ITS PLACE... SOMETHING ELSE CRAWLED IN...
I CAN'T LIE DOWN, I CAN'T SIT UP. I DON'T KNOW WHAT TO DO!
VSSSSHHH...
A PIECE OF CLETUS KASADY INFECTED NORMAN.
HE THINKS HE IS CLETUS. HE HAS ALL HIS MEMORIES, ALL HIS HATE AND ALL HIS MURDEROUS INSANITY...
THE NURSES THINK IT'S FUNNY! BUT THAT'S...NOT MY POINT OF VIEW.
IF IT WERE UP TO ME, HE'D BE UNDERGROUND INSTEAD OF ROTTING AWAY IN THIS HELLHOLE.
AND NOW, WE GOTTA BREAK HIM OUT BEFORE THE REAL CLETUS COMES AND KILLS HIM.
AND WHEN I GET BACK HOME AGAIN, I'LL TELL YOU WHAT I'LL DO!
HATE TO SAY IT, BUT PETE WAS RIGHT...
I'LL MAKE THAT @#$%% SUFFER FOR THE PAIN I'M GOING THROUGH.

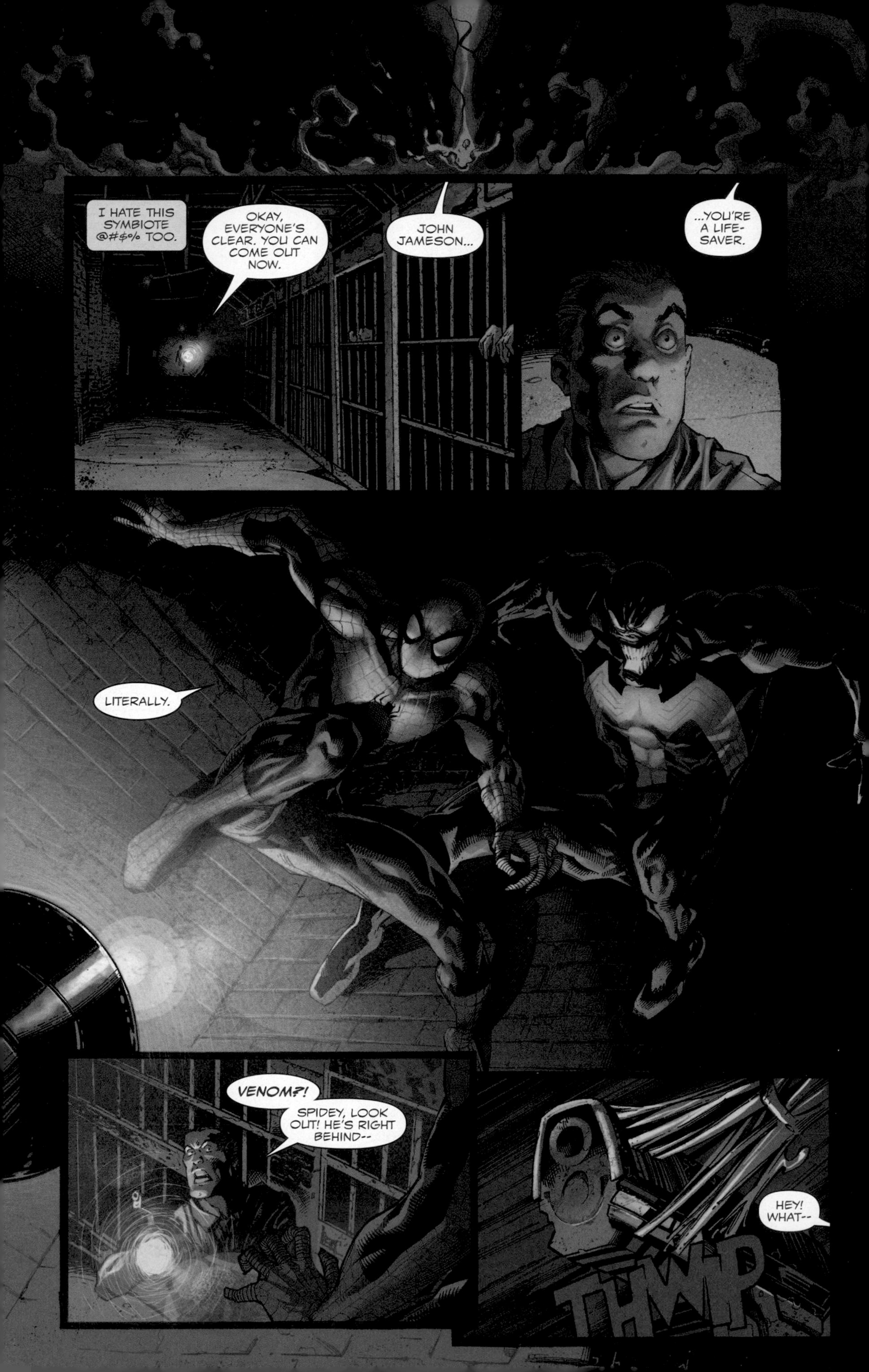
I HATE THIS SYMBIOTE @#$% TOO.
OKAY, EVERYONE'S CLEAR. YOU CAN COME OUT NOW.
JOHN JAMESON...
...YOU'RE A LIFE-SAVER.
LITERALLY.
VENOM?!
SPIDEY, LOOK OUT! HE'S RIGHT BEHIND--
HEY! WHAT--
THWP

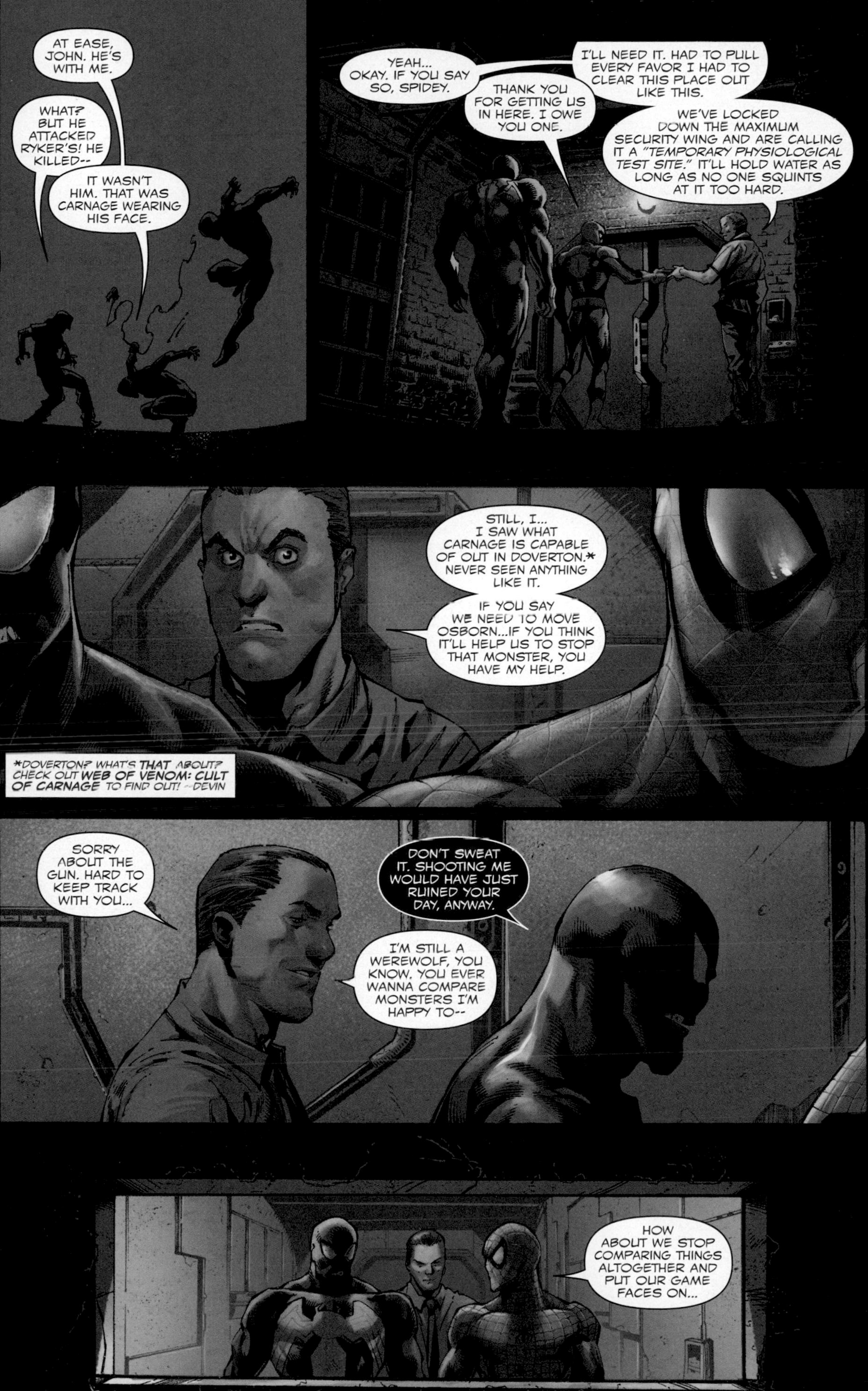
AT EASE, JOHN. HE'S WITH ME.
WHAT? BUT HE ATTACKED RYKER'S! HE KILLED--
IT WASN'T HIM. THAT WAS CARNAGE WEARING HIS FACE.
YEAH... OKAY. IF YOU SAY SO, SPIDEY.
THANK YOU FOR GETTING US IN HERE. I OWE YOU ONE.
I'LL NEED IT. HAD TO PULL EVERY FAVOR I HAD TO CLEAR THIS PLACE OUT LIKE THIS.
WE'VE LOCKED DOWN THE MAXIMUM SECURITY WING AND ARE CALLING IT A "TEMPORARY PHYSIOLOGICAL TEST SITE." IT'LL HOLD WATER AS LONG AS NO ONE SQUINTS AT IT TOO HARD.
STILL, I... I SAW WHAT CARNAGE IS CAPABLE OF OUT IN DOVERTON.* NEVER SEEN ANYTHING LIKE IT.
IF YOU SAY WE NEED TO MOVE OSBORN...IF YOU THINK IT'LL HELP US TO STOP THAT MONSTER, YOU HAVE MY HELP.
*DOVERTON? WHAT'S THAT ABOUT? CHECK OUT WEB OF VENOM: CULT OF CARNAGE TO FIND OUT! --DEVIN
SORRY ABOUT THE GUN. HARD TO KEEP TRACK WITH YOU...
DON'T SWEAT IT. SHOOTING ME WOULD HAVE JUST RUINED YOUR DAY, ANYWAY.
I'M STILL A WEREWOLF, YOU KNOW. YOU EVER WANNA COMPARE MONSTERS I'M HAPPY TO--
HOW ABOUT WE STOP COMPARING THINGS ALTOGETHER AND PUT OUR GAME FACES ON...

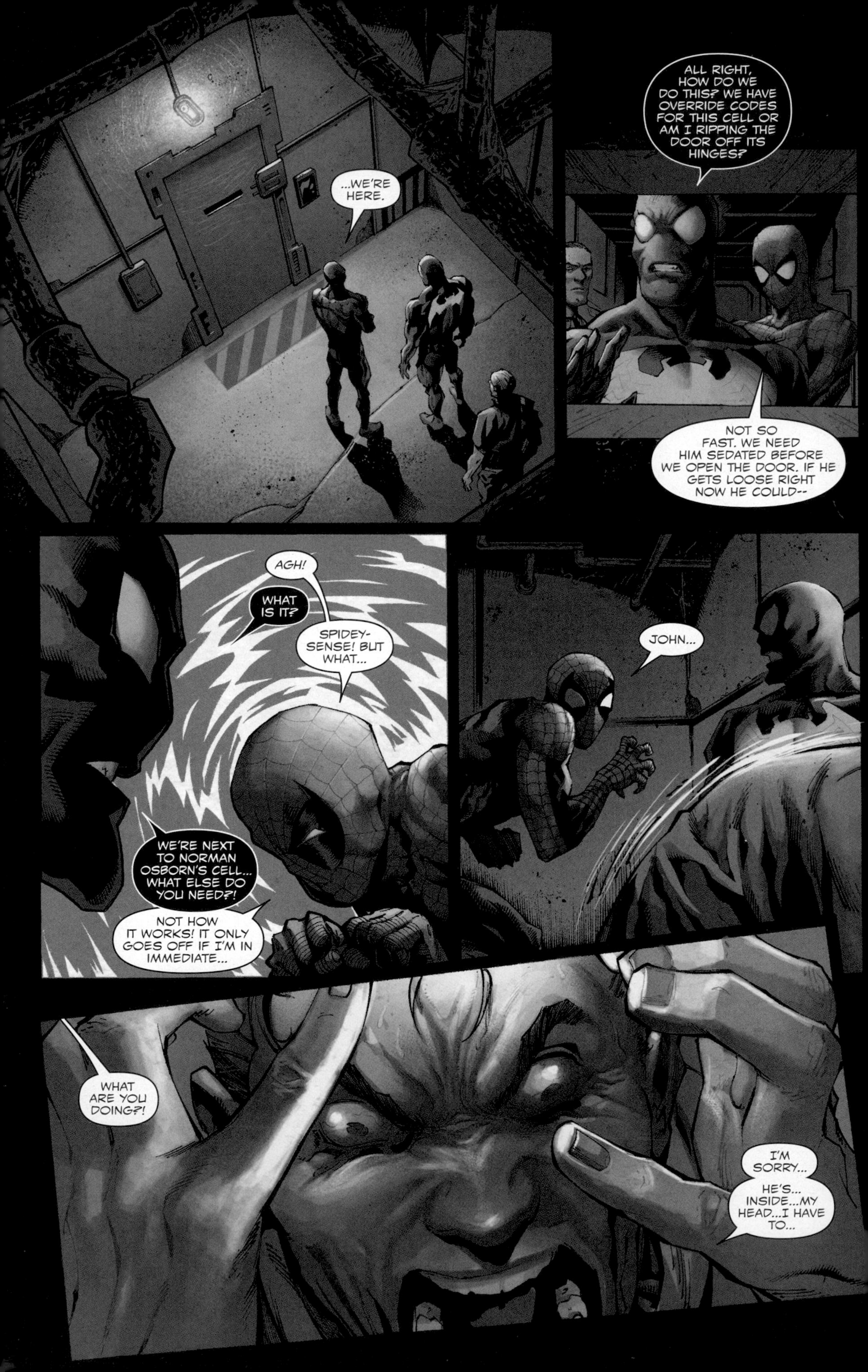
...WE'RE HERE.
ALL RIGHT, HOW DO WE DO THIS? WE HAVE OVERRIDE CODES FOR THIS CELL OR AM I RIPPING THE DOOR OFF ITS HINGES?
NOT SO FAST. WE NEED HIM SEDATED BEFORE WE OPEN THE DOOR. IF HE GETS LOOSE RIGHT NOW HE COULD--
AGH!
WHAT IS IT?
SPIDEY-SENSE! BUT WHAT...
WE'RE NEXT TO NORMAN OSBORN'S CELL... WHAT ELSE DO YOU NEED?!
NOT HOW IT WORKS! IT ONLY GOES OFF IF I'M IN IMMEDIATE...
JOHN...
WHAT ARE YOU DOING?!
I'M SORRY...
HE'S... INSIDE...MY HEAD...I HAVE TO...

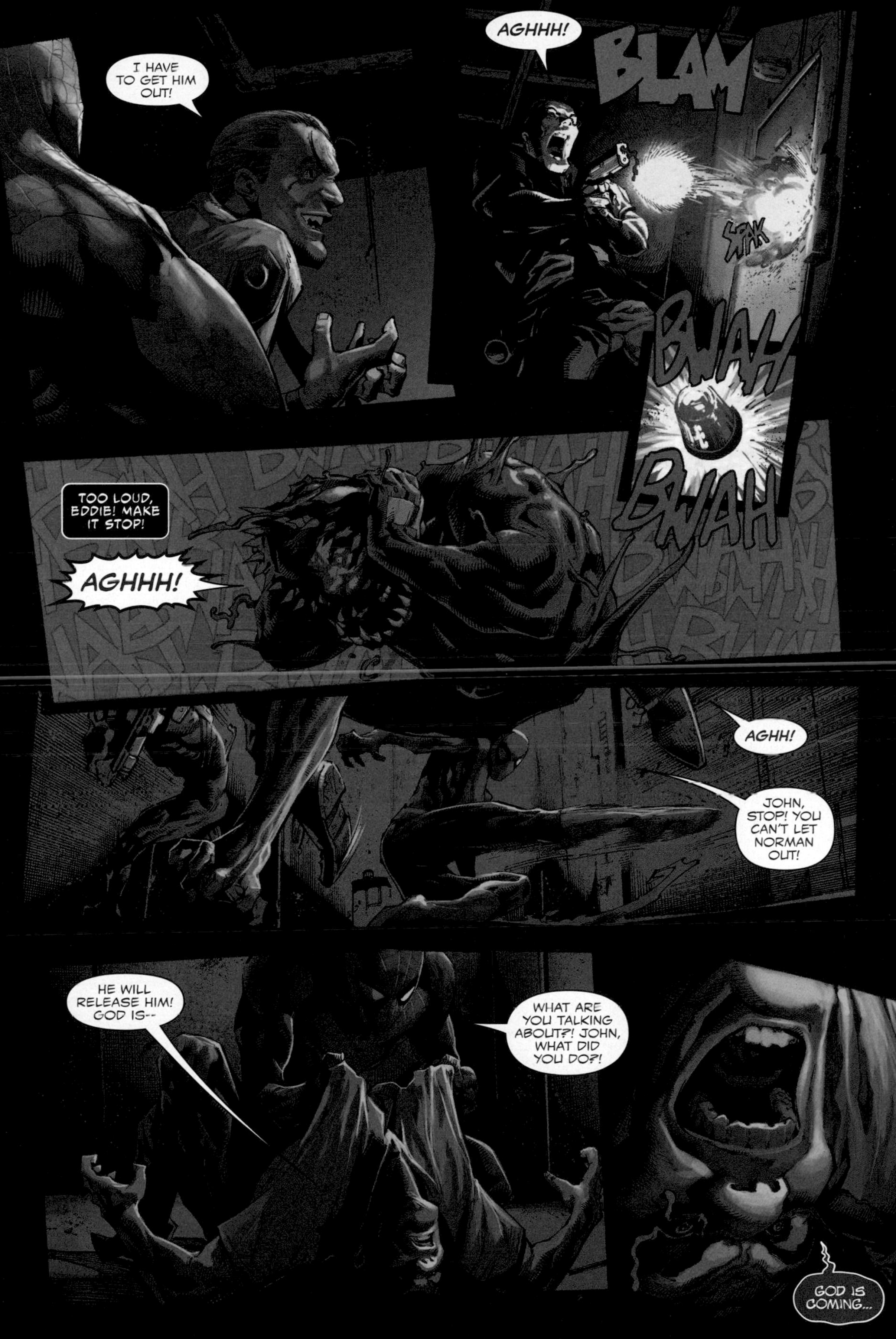
I HAVE TO GET HIM OUT!
AGHHH!
BLAM
SPAK
BWAH
BWAH
TOO LOUD, EDDIE! MAKE IT STOP!
AGHHH!
AGHH!
JOHN, STOP! YOU CAN'T LET NORMAN OUT!
HE WILL RELEASE HIM! GOD IS--
WHAT ARE YOU TALKING ABOUT?! JOHN, WHAT DID YOU DO?!
GOD IS COMING...

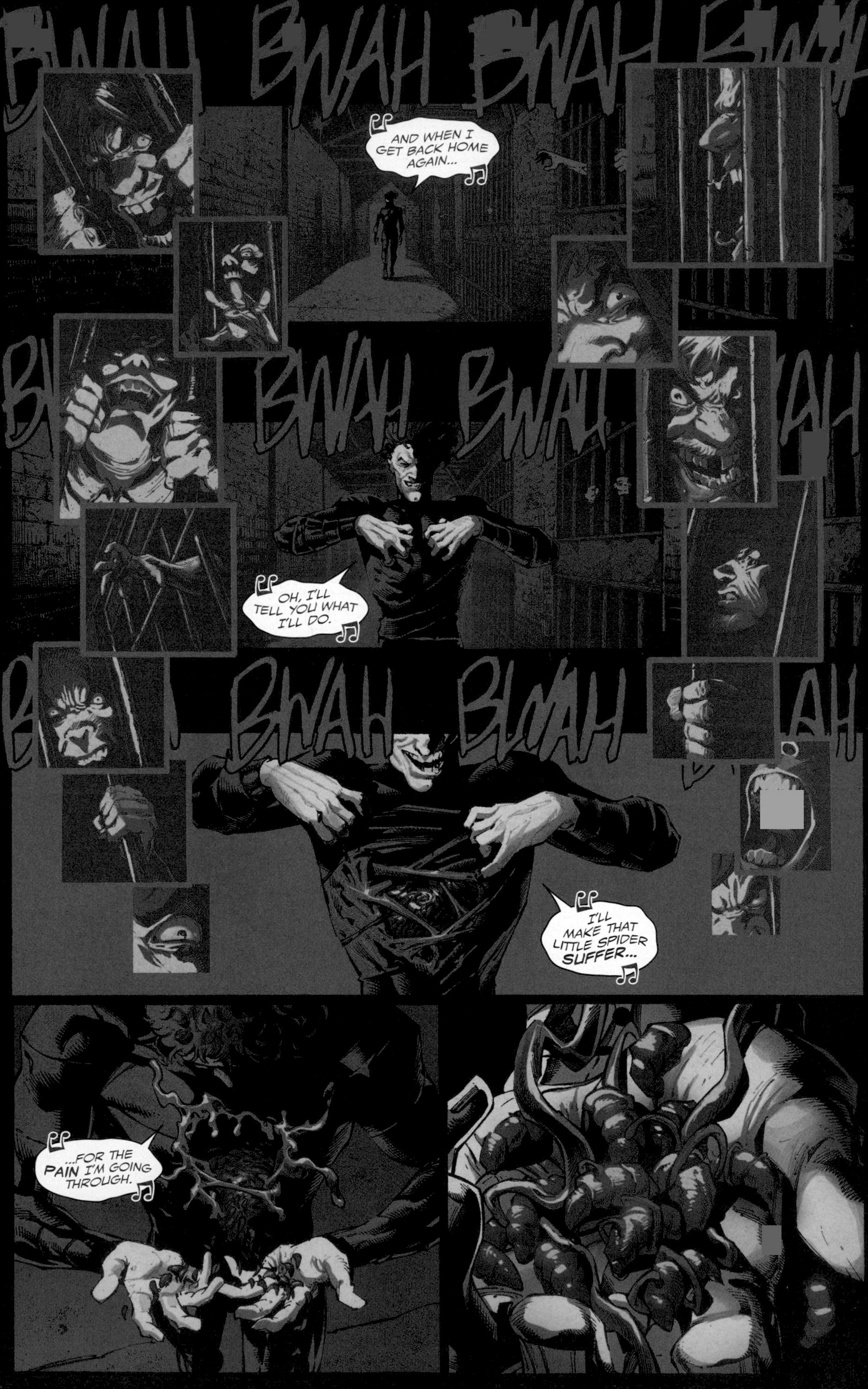
BWAH BWAH BWAH BWAH
AND WHEN I GET BACK HOME AGAIN...
BWAH BWAH BWAH
OH, I'LL TELL YOU WHAT I'LL DO.
BWAH BWAH
I'LL MAKE THAT LITTLE SPIDER SUFFER...
...FOR THE PAIN I'M GOING THROUGH.

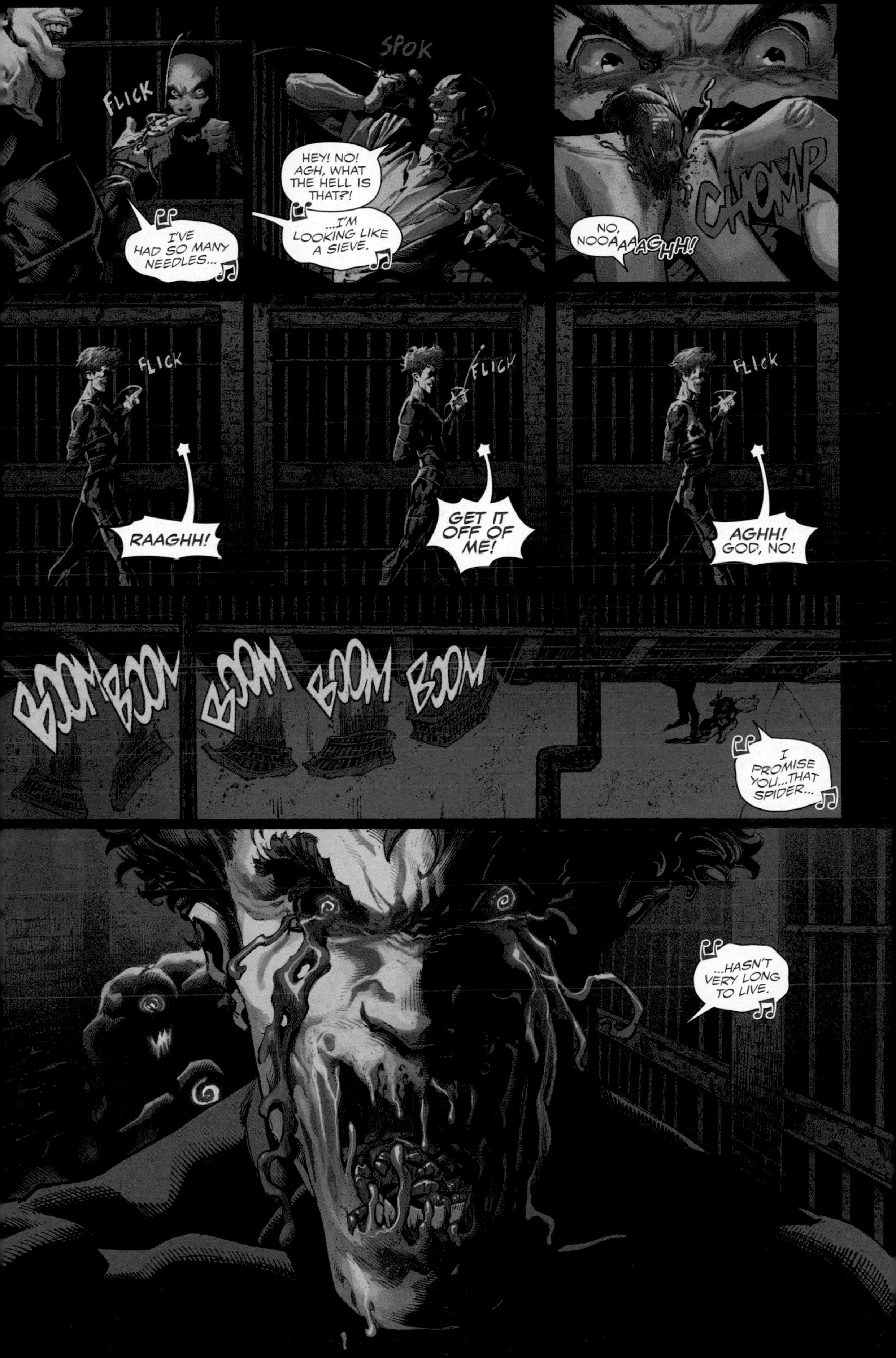

FLICK
I'VE HAD SO MANY NEEDLES...
SPOK
HEY! NO! AGH, WHAT THE HELL IS THAT?!
...I'M LOOKING LIKE A SIEVE.
CHOMP
NO, NOOAAAAGHH!
FLICK
RAAGHH!
FLICK
GET IT OFF OF ME!
FLICK
AGHH! GOD, NO!
BOOM BOOM BOOM BOOM BOOM
I PROMISE YOU...THAT SPIDER...
...HASN'T VERY LONG TO LIVE.

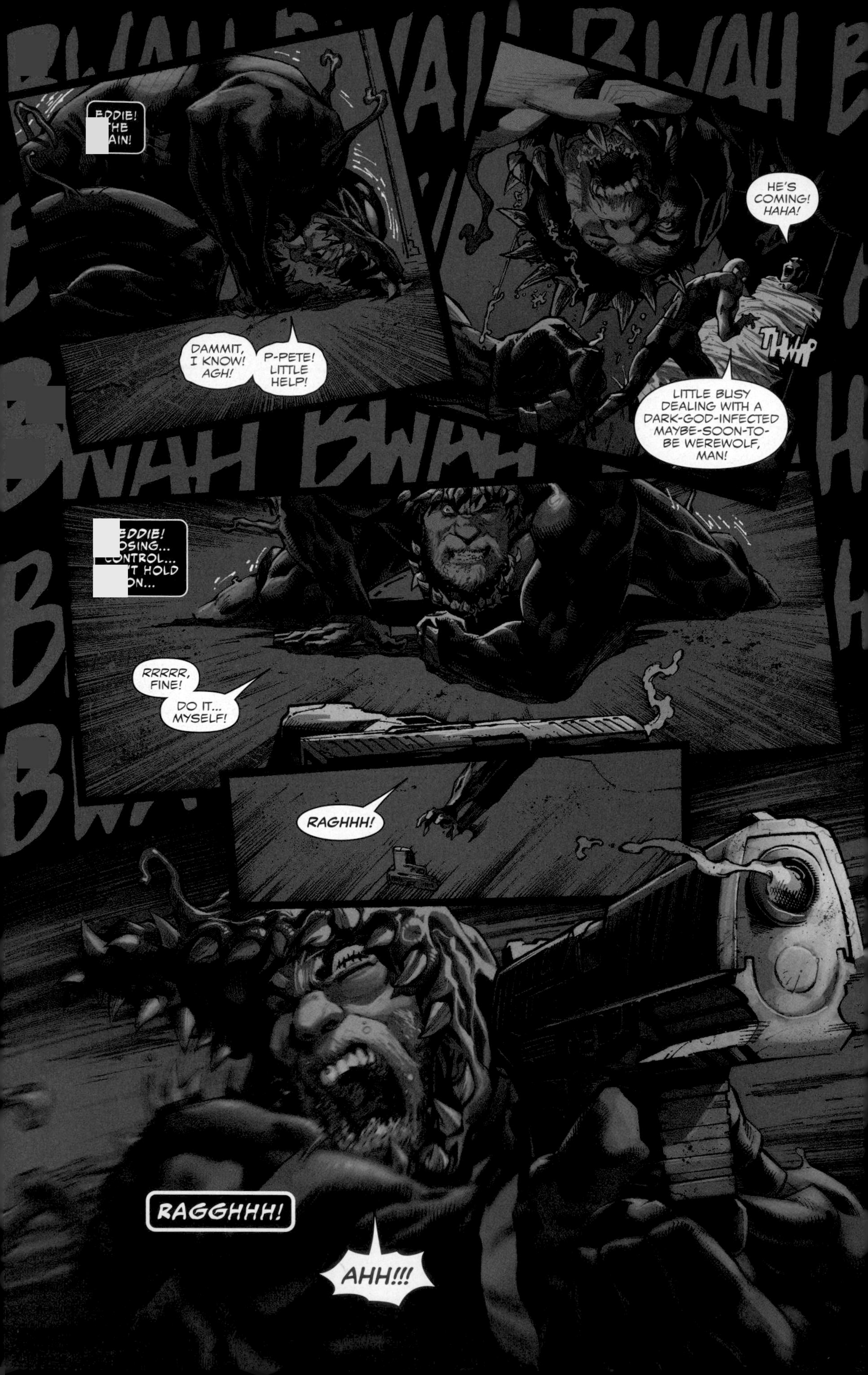

BWAH BWAH BWAH
EDDIE! [redacted]THE [redacted]AIN!
DAMMIT, I KNOW! AGH!
P-PETE! LITTLE HELP!
HE'S COMING! HAHA!
THWIP
LITTLE BUSY DEALING WITH A DARK-GOD-INFECTED MAYBE-SOON-TO-BE WEREWOLF, MAN!
BWAH BWAH
[redacted]EDDIE! [redacted]OSING... [redacted]ONTROL... [redacted]T HOLD [redacted]ON...
RRRRR, FINE!
DO IT... MYSELF!
RAGHHH!
RAGGHHH!
AHH!!!

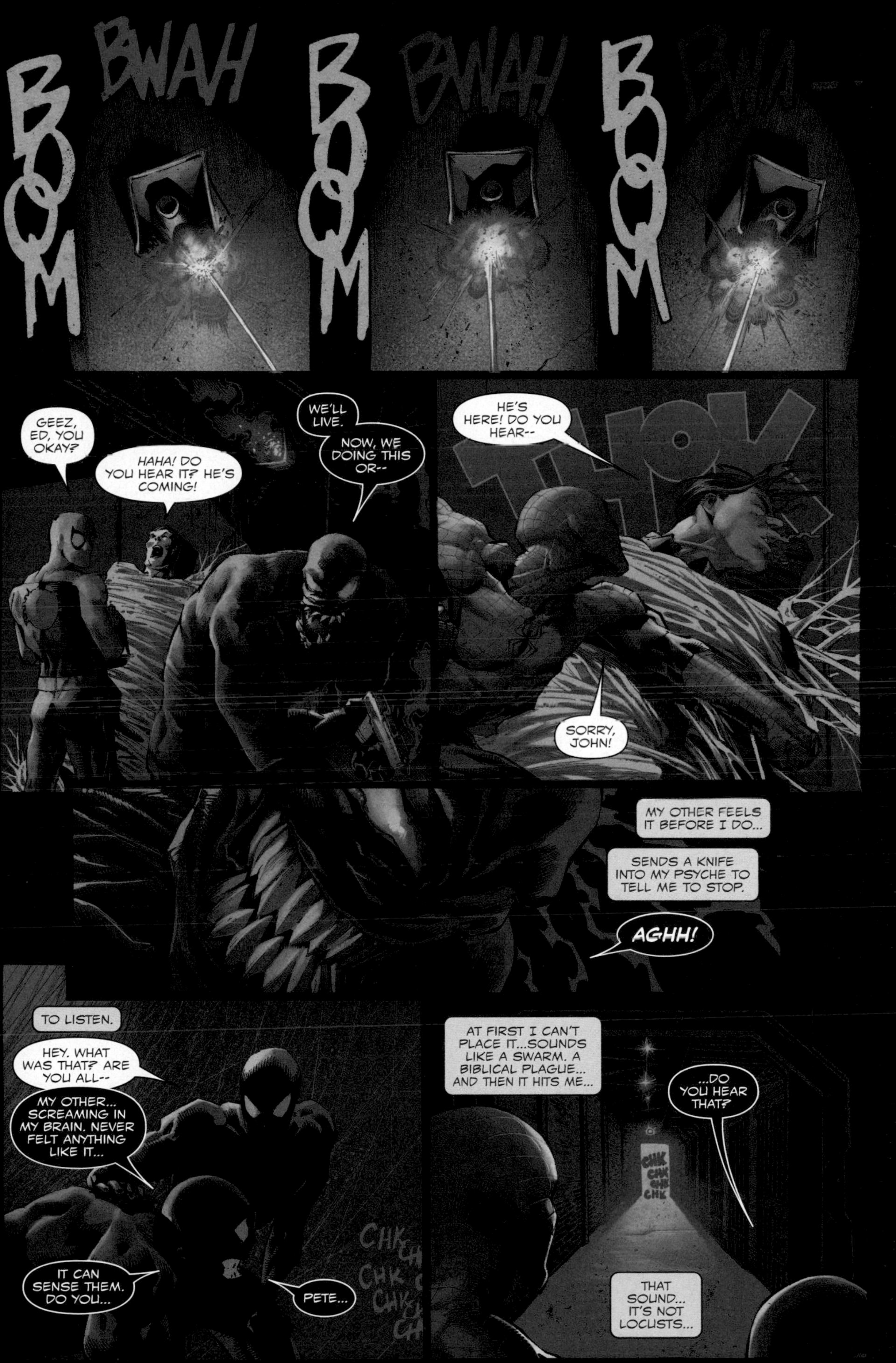
BOOM
BWAH
BOOM
BWAH
BOOM
GEEZ, ED, YOU OKAY?
HAHA! DO YOU HEAR IT? HE'S COMING!
WE'LL LIVE.
NOW, WE DOING THIS OR--
HE'S HERE! DO YOU HEAR--
THOK
SORRY, JOHN!
MY OTHER FEELS IT BEFORE I DO...
SENDS A KNIFE INTO MY PSYCHE TO TELL ME TO STOP.
AGHH!
TO LISTEN.
HEY. WHAT WAS THAT? ARE YOU ALL--
MY OTHER... SCREAMING IN MY BRAIN. NEVER FELT ANYTHING LIKE IT...
IT CAN SENSE THEM. DO YOU...
PETE...
AT FIRST I CAN'T PLACE IT...SOUNDS LIKE A SWARM. A BIBLICAL PLAGUE... AND THEN IT HITS ME...
...DO YOU HEAR THAT?
CHK CHK CHK CHK
THAT SOUND... IT'S NOT LOCUSTS...

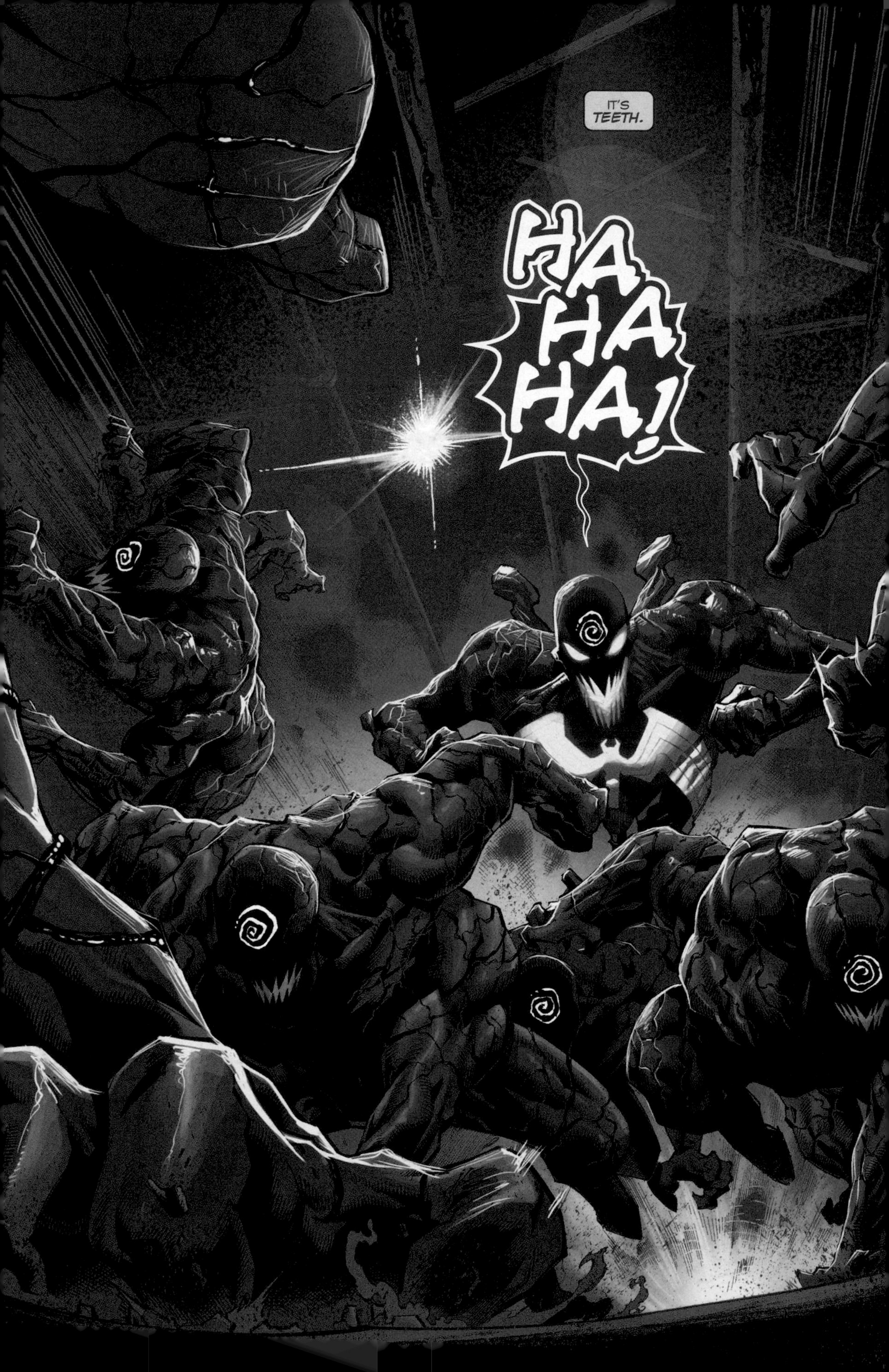
IT'S TEETH.
HA HA HA HA!

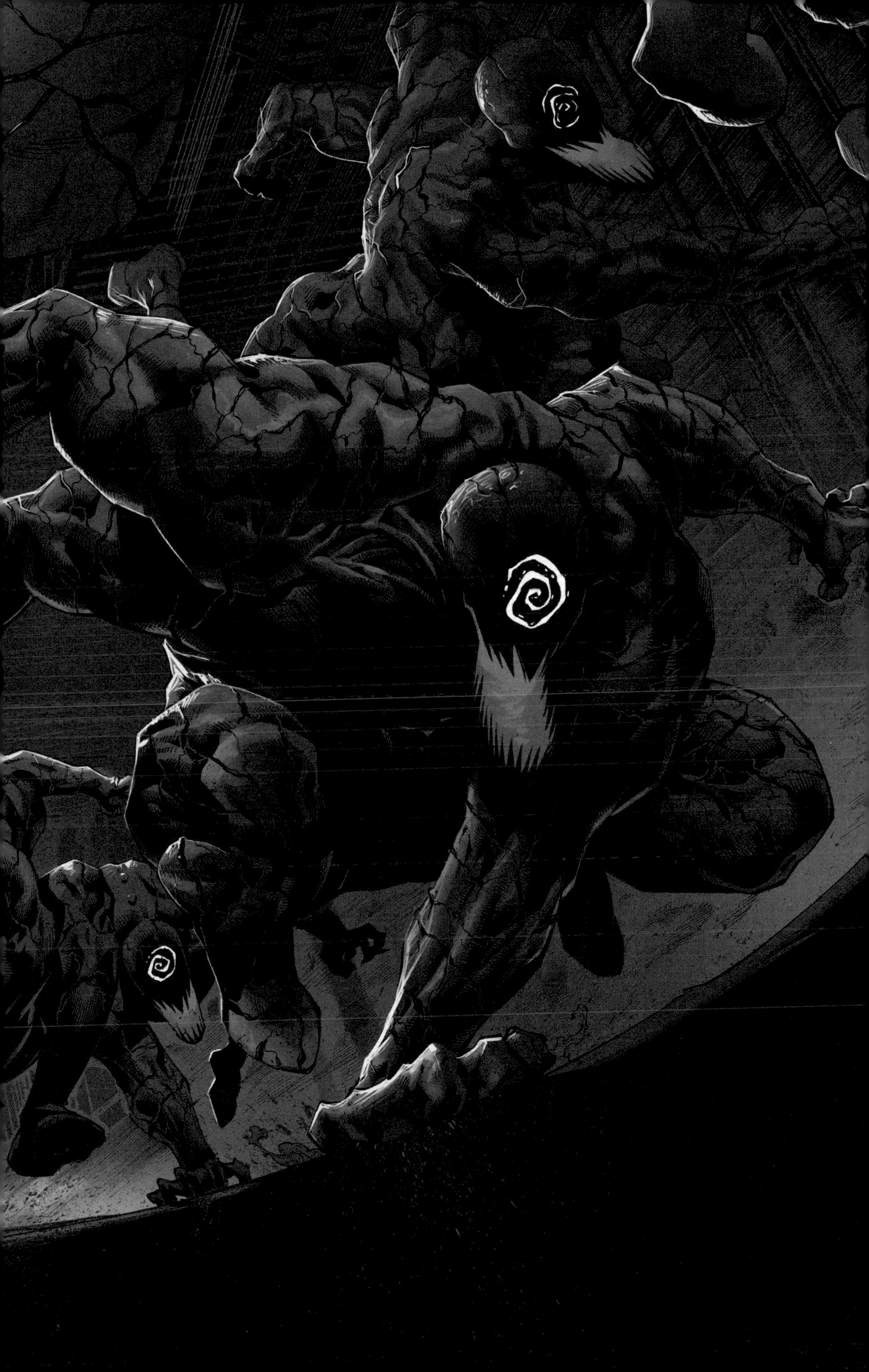

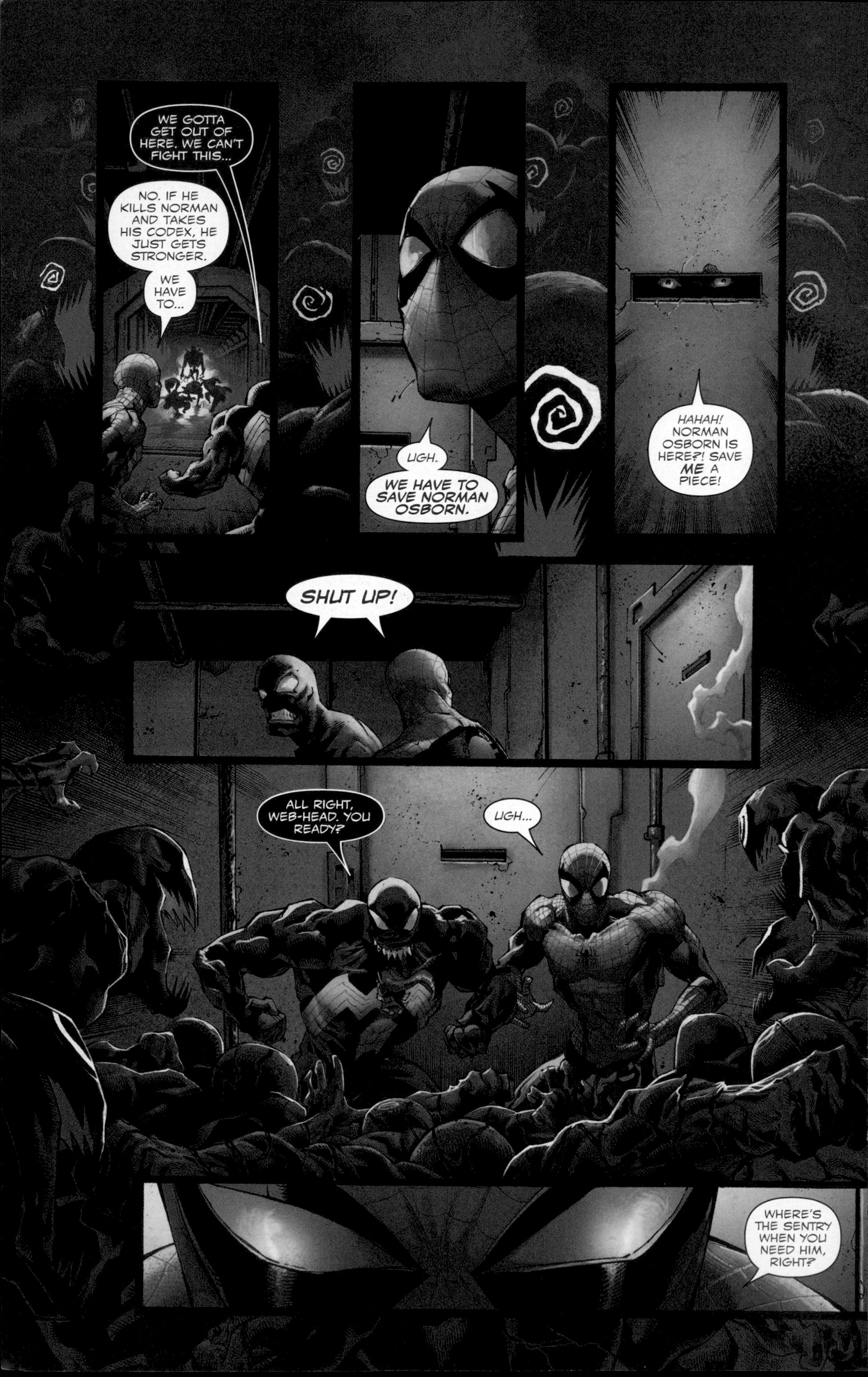
WE GOTTA GET OUT OF HERE. WE CAN'T FIGHT THIS...
NO. IF HE KILLS NORMAN AND TAKES HIS CODEX, HE JUST GETS STRONGER.
WE HAVE TO...
UGH.
WE HAVE TO SAVE NORMAN OSBORN.
HAHAH! NORMAN OSBORN IS HERE?! SAVE ME A PIECE!
SHUT UP!
ALL RIGHT, WEB-HEAD. YOU READY?
UGH...
WHERE'S THE SENTRY WHEN YOU NEED HIM, RIGHT?

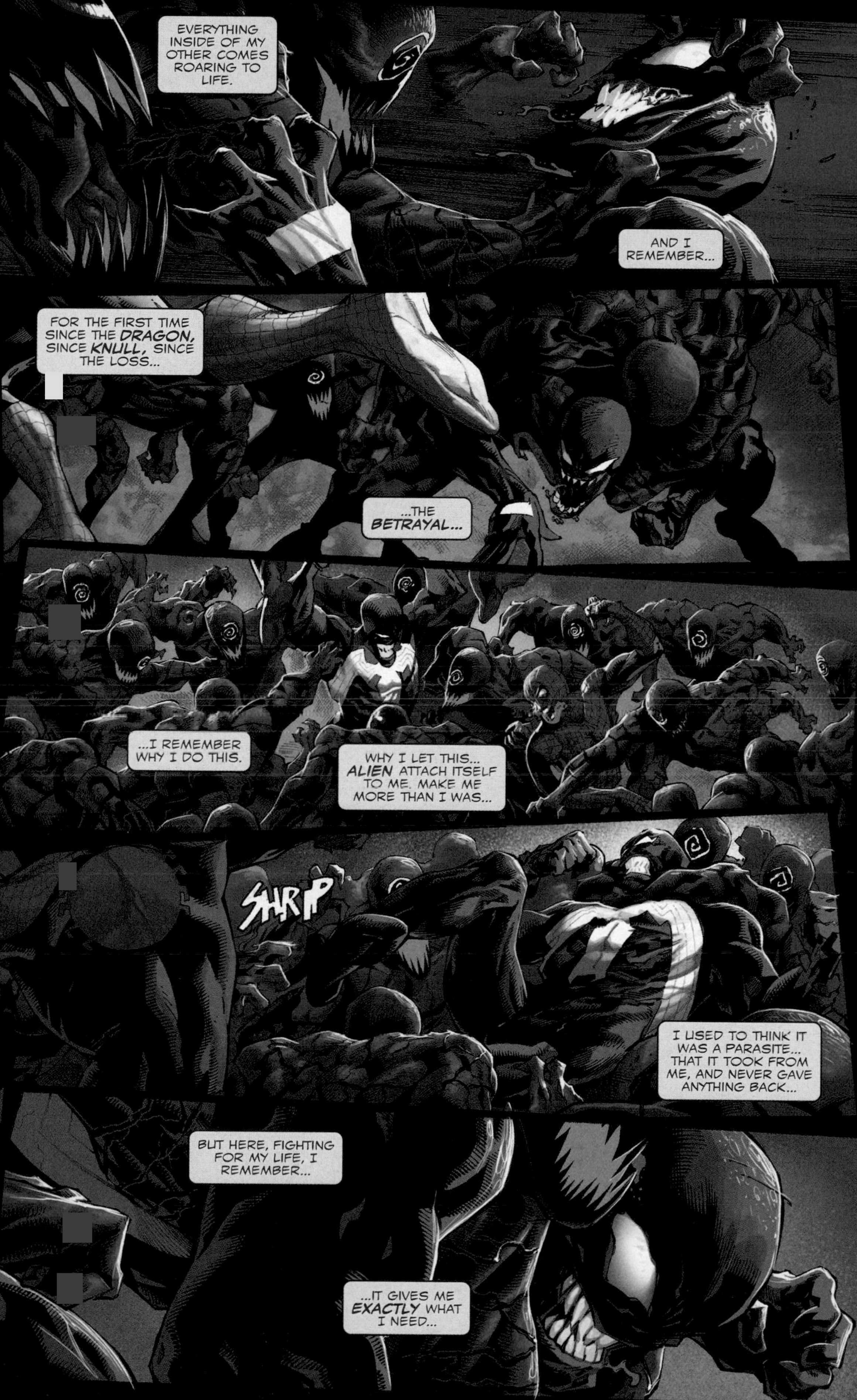
EVERYTHING INSIDE OF MY OTHER COMES ROARING TO LIFE.
AND I REMEMBER...
FOR THE FIRST TIME SINCE THE DRAGON, SINCE KNULL, SINCE THE LOSS...
...THE BETRAYAL...
...I REMEMBER WHY I DO THIS.
WHY I LET THIS... ALIEN ATTACH ITSELF TO ME. MAKE ME MORE THAN I WAS...
SHRIP
I USED TO THINK IT WAS A PARASITE... THAT IT TOOK FROM ME, AND NEVER GAVE ANYTHING BACK...
BUT HERE, FIGHTING FOR MY LIFE, I REMEMBER...
...IT GIVES ME EXACTLY WHAT I NEED...

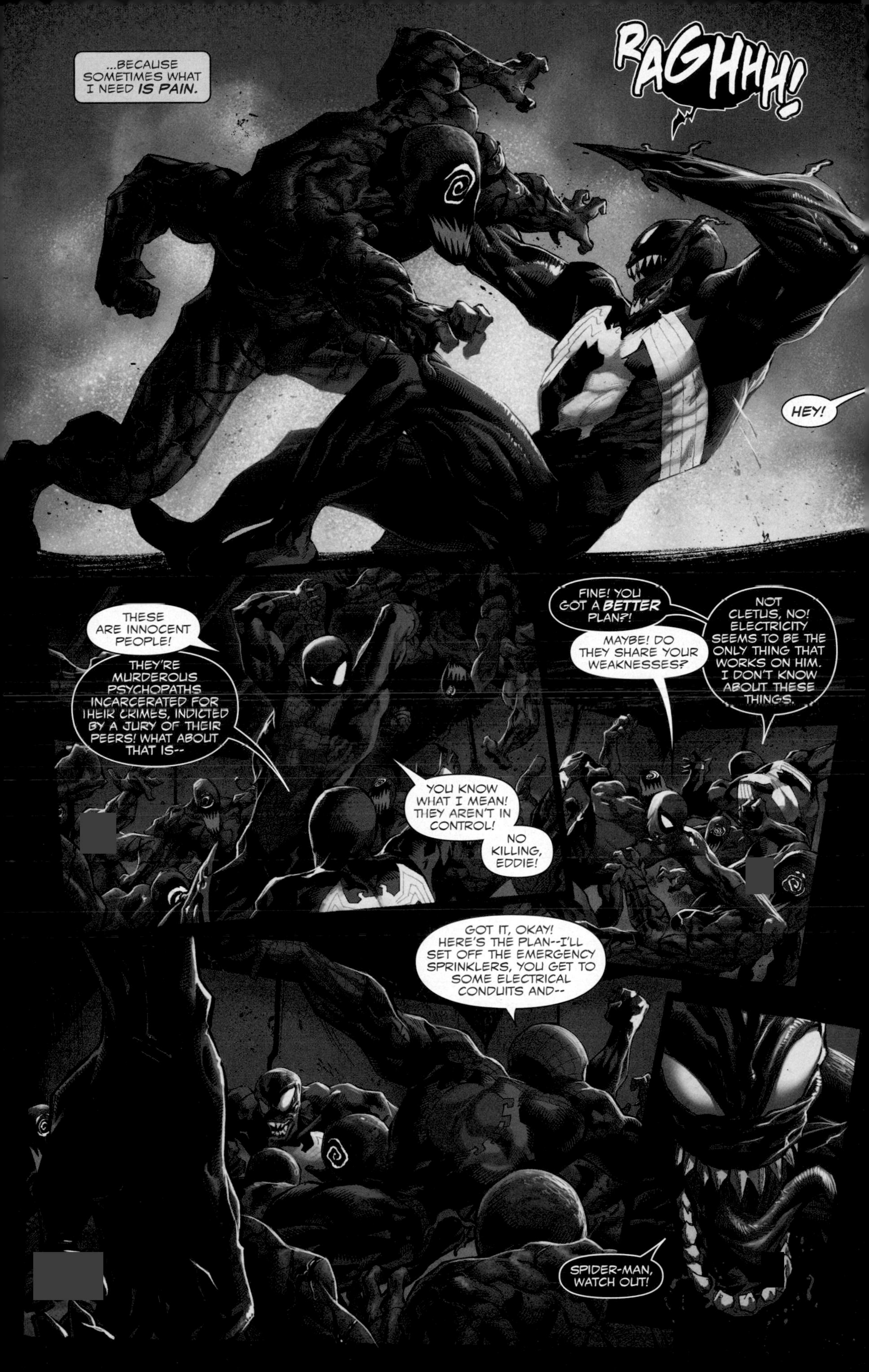

...BECAUSE SOMETIMES WHAT I NEED IS PAIN.
RAGHHH!
HEY!
THESE ARE INNOCENT PEOPLE!
THEY'RE MURDEROUS PSYCHOPATHS INCARCERATED FOR THEIR CRIMES, INDICTED BY A JURY OF THEIR PEERS! WHAT ABOUT THAT IS--
YOU KNOW WHAT I MEAN! THEY AREN'T IN CONTROL!
NO KILLING, EDDIE!
FINE! YOU GOT A BETTER PLAN?!
MAYBE! DO THEY SHARE YOUR WEAKNESSES?
NOT CLETUS, NO! ELECTRICITY SEEMS TO BE THE ONLY THING THAT WORKS ON HIM. I DON'T KNOW ABOUT THESE THINGS.
GOT IT, OKAY! HERE'S THE PLAN--I'LL SET OFF THE EMERGENCY SPRINKLERS, YOU GET TO SOME ELECTRICAL CONDUITS AND--
SPIDER-MAN, WATCH OUT!

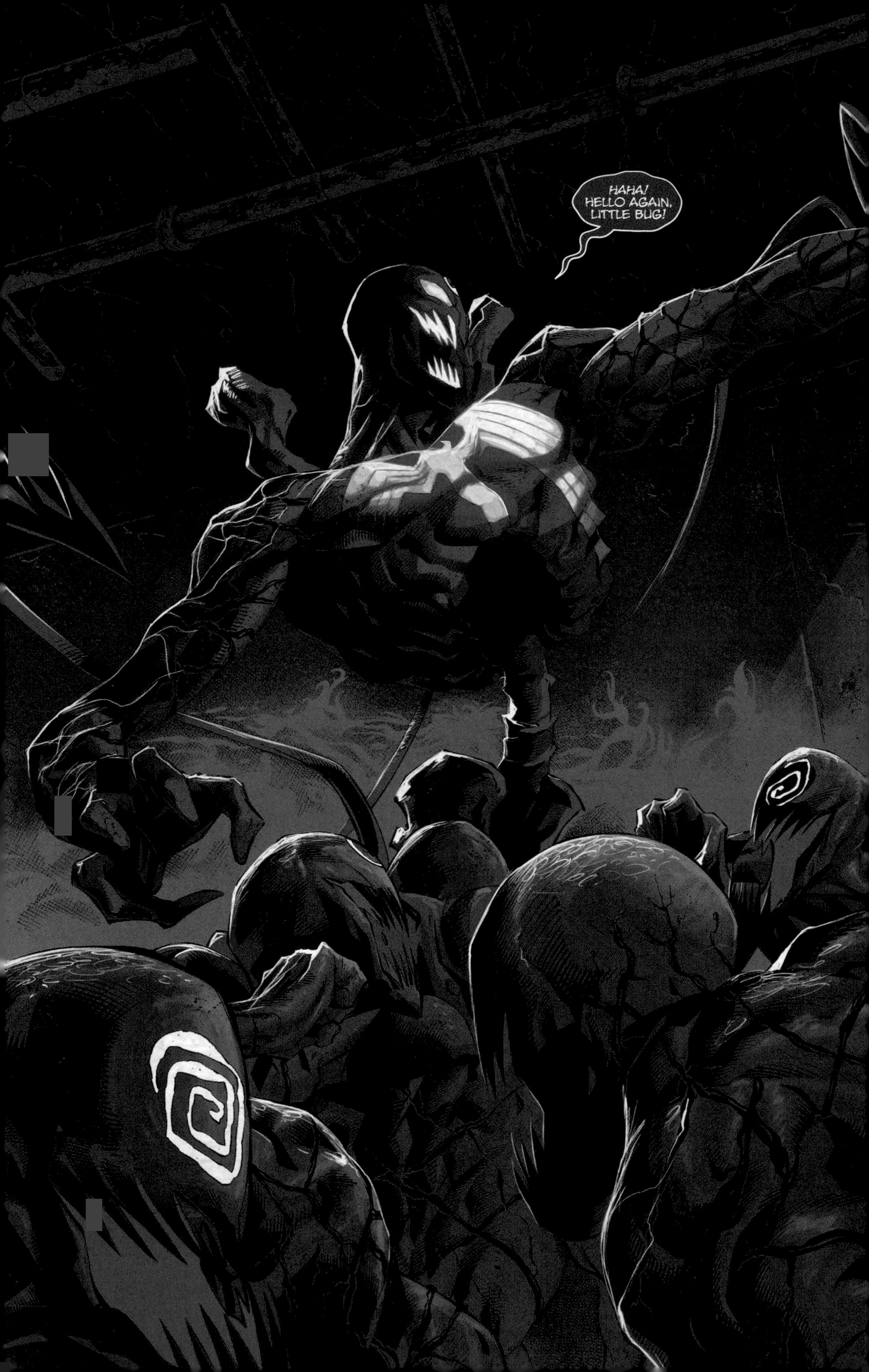
HAHA! HELLO AGAIN, LITTLE BUG!

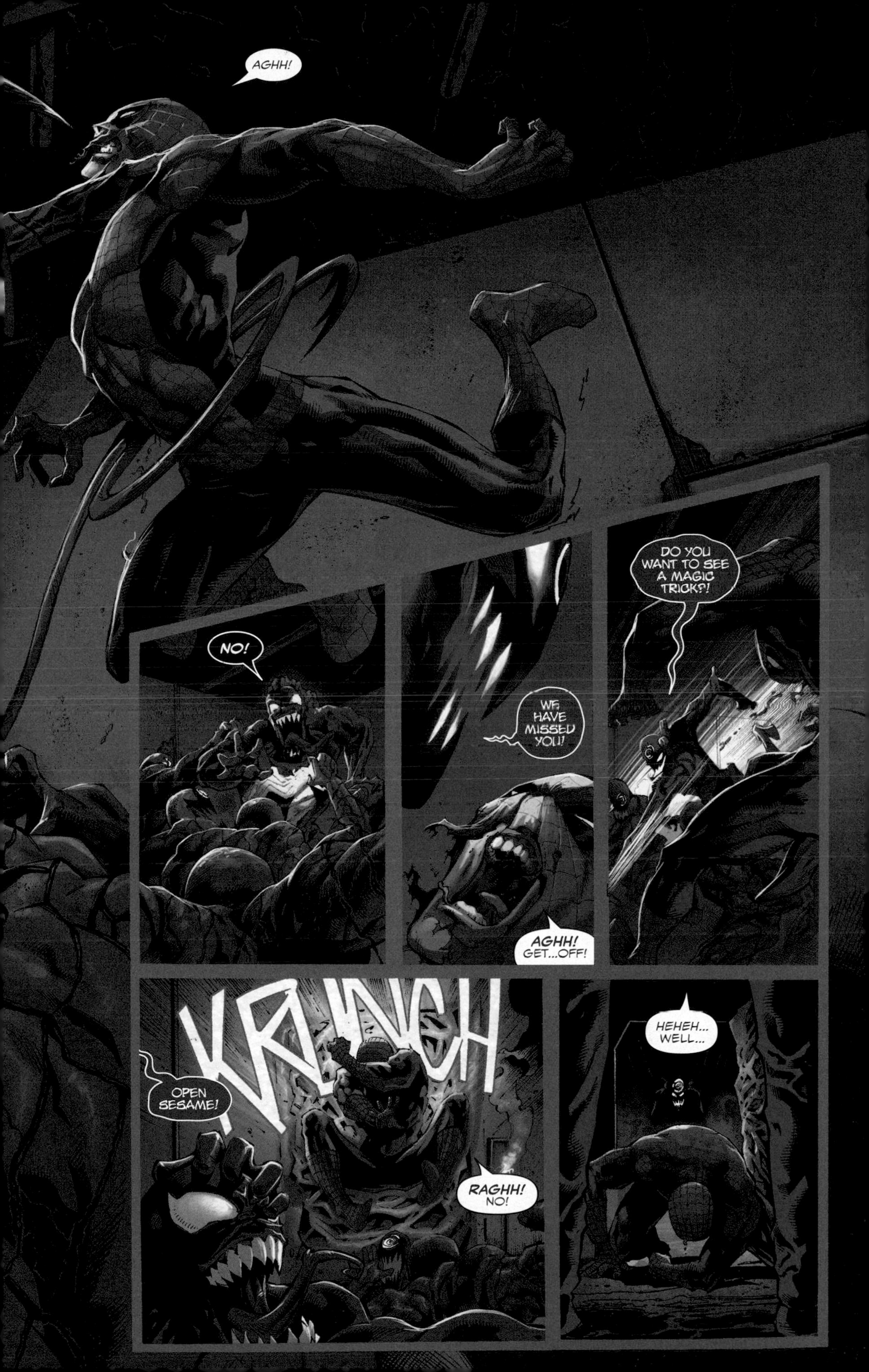
AGHH!
NO!
WE HAVE MISSED YOU!
AGHH! GET...OFF!
DO YOU WANT TO SEE A MAGIC TRICK?!
OPEN SESAME!
KRUNCH
RAGHH! NO!
HEHEH... WELL...

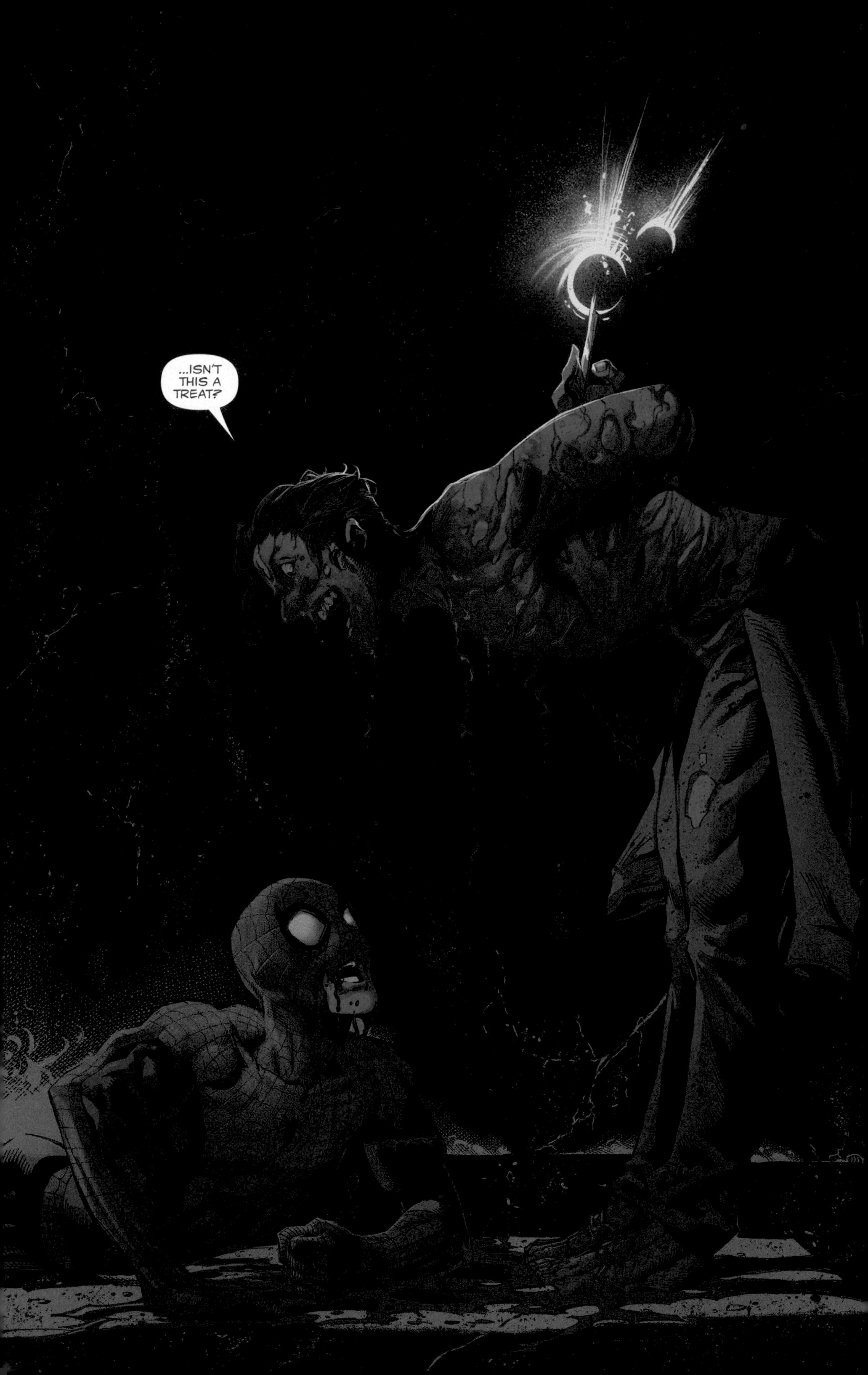
...ISN'T THIS A TREAT?

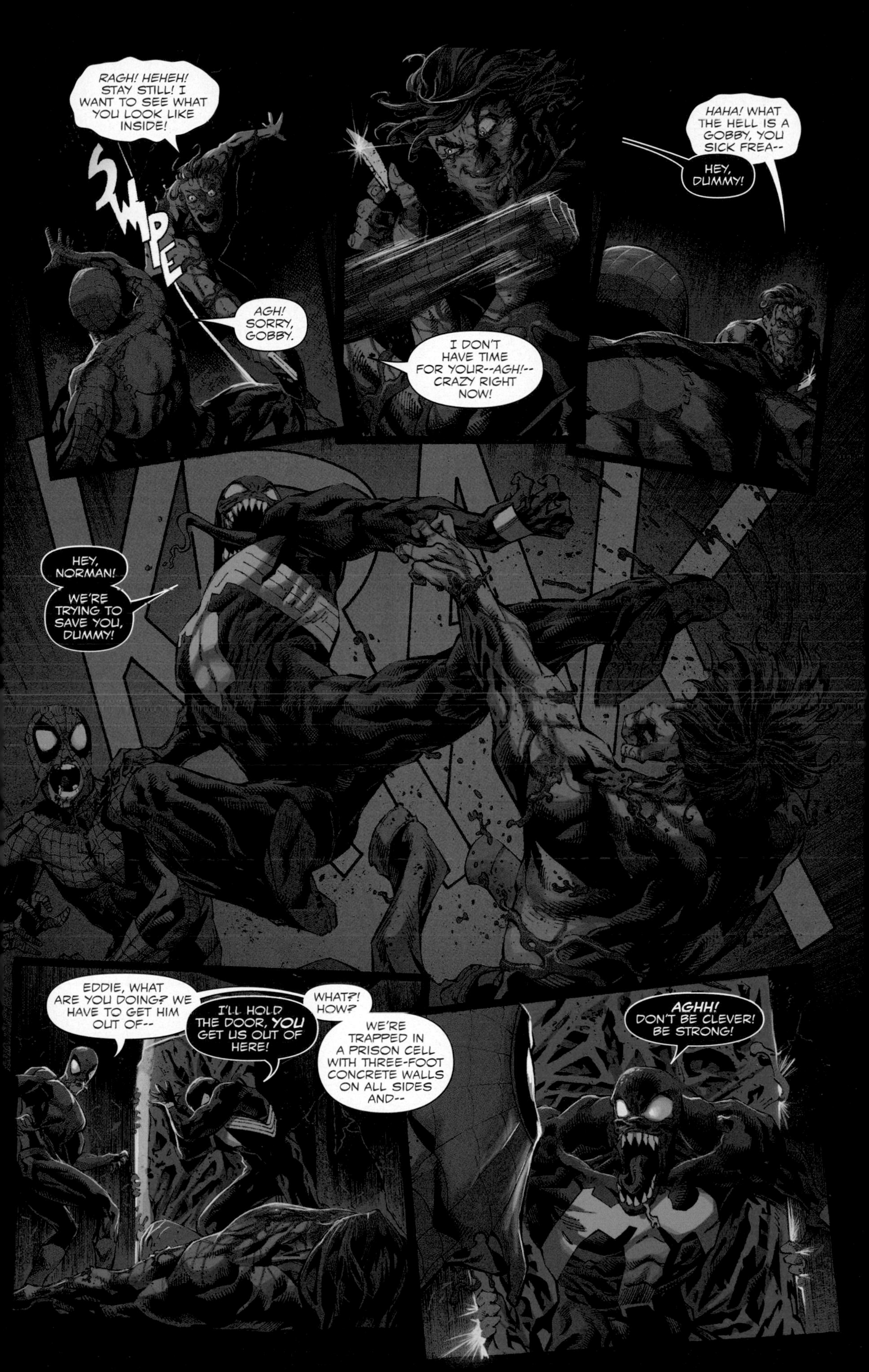
RAGH! HEHEH! STAY STILL! I WANT TO SEE WHAT YOU LOOK LIKE INSIDE!
SWIPE
AGH! SORRY, GOBBY.
I DON'T HAVE TIME FOR YOUR--AGH!-- CRAZY RIGHT NOW!
HAHA! WHAT THE HELL IS A GOBBY, YOU SICK FREA--
HEY, DUMMY!
HEY, NORMAN!
WE'RE TRYING TO SAVE YOU, DUMMY!
EDDIE, WHAT ARE YOU DOING? WE HAVE TO GET HIM OUT OF--
I'LL HOLD THE DOOR, YOU GET US OUT OF HERE!
WHAT?! HOW?
WE'RE TRAPPED IN A PRISON CELL WITH THREE-FOOT CONCRETE WALLS ON ALL SIDES AND--
AGHH! DON'T BE CLEVER! BE STRONG!

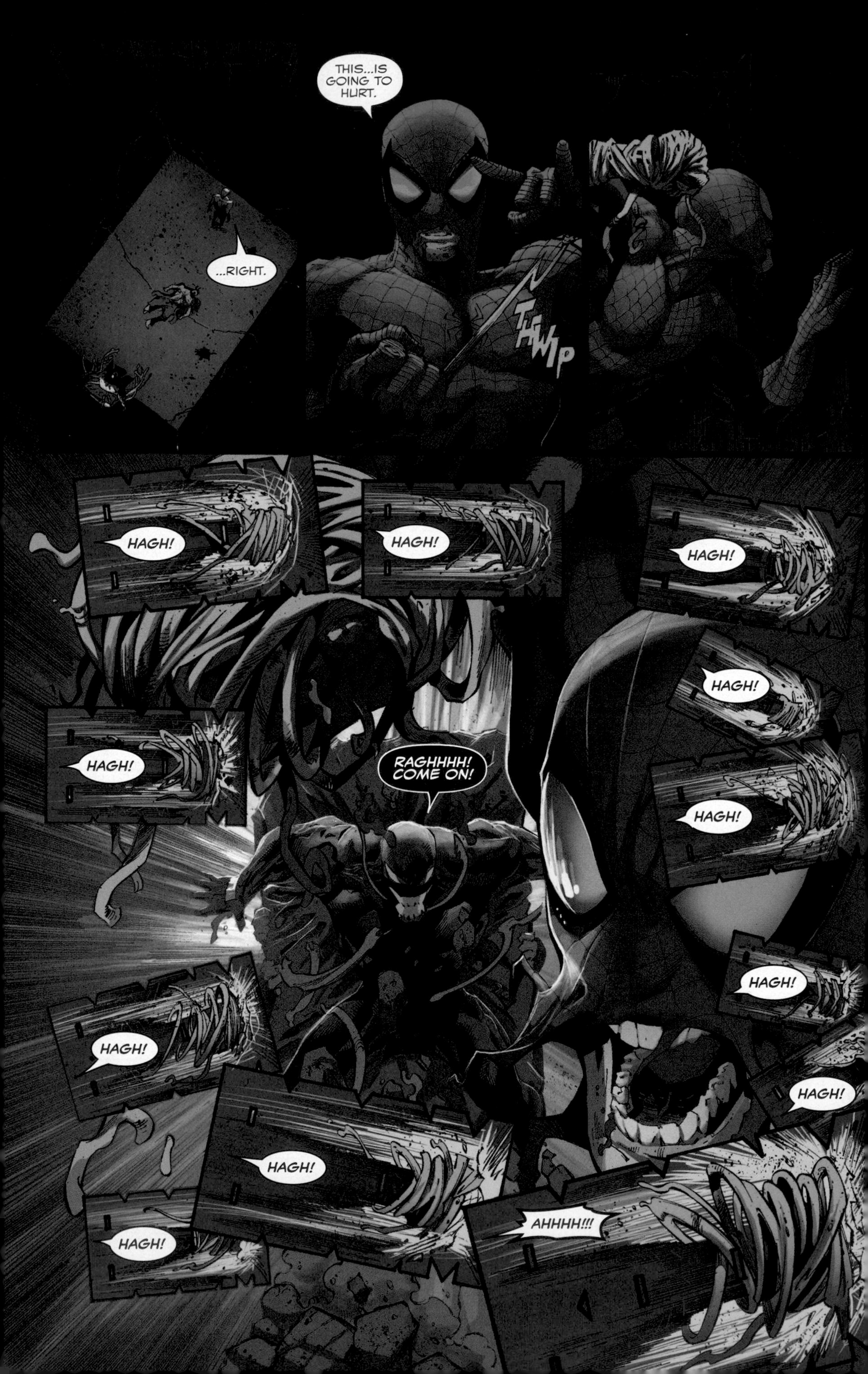
THIS...IS GOING TO HURT.
...RIGHT.
THWIP
HAGH!
HAGH!
HAGH!
HAGH!
HAGH!
RAGHHHH! COME ON!
HAGH!
HAGH!
HAGH!
HAGH!
HAGH!
HAGH!
AHHHH!!!

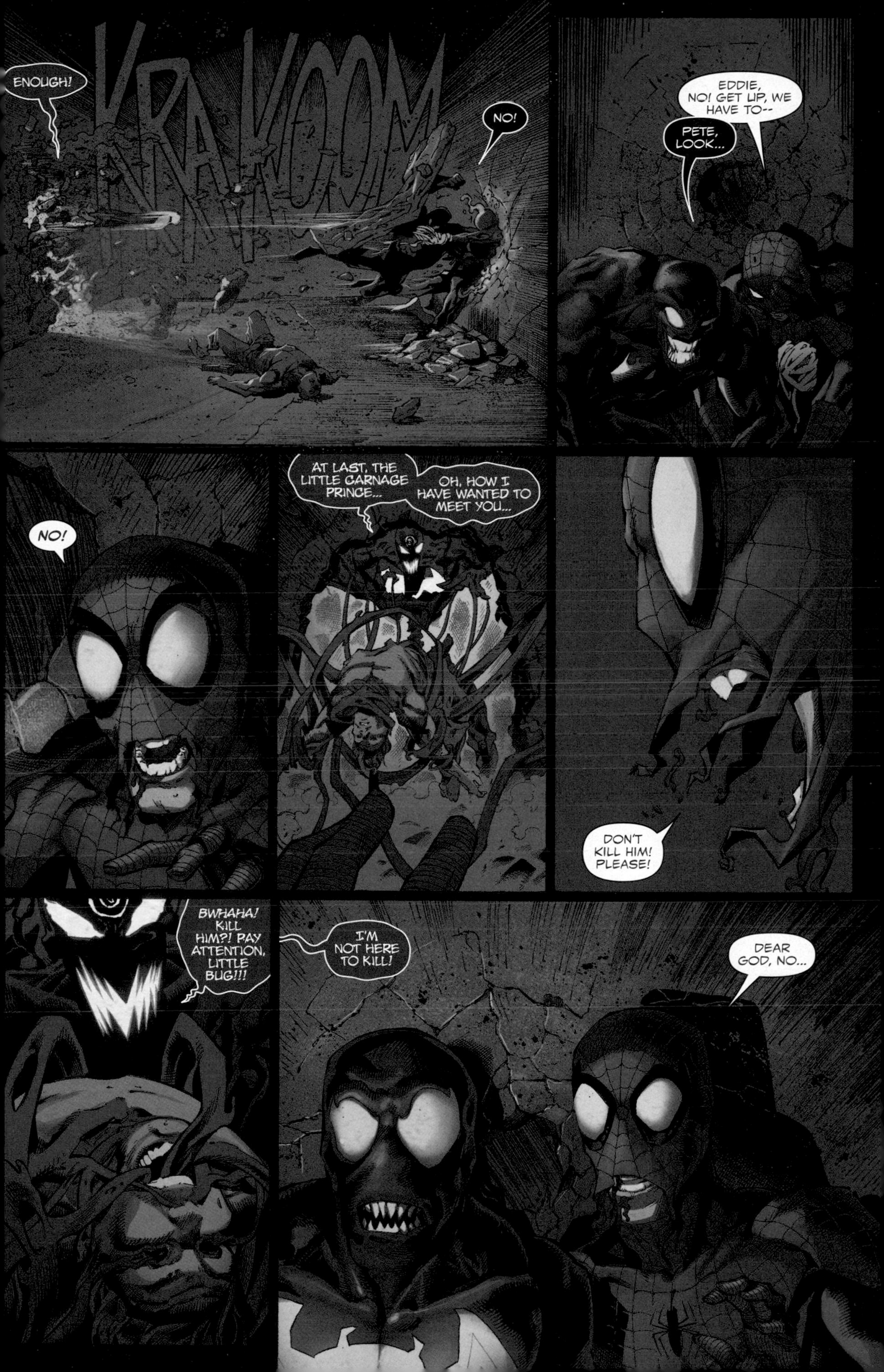
ENOUGH!
KRAKOOM
NO!
EDDIE, NO! GET UP, WE HAVE TO--
PETE, LOOK...
NO!
AT LAST, THE LITTLE CARNAGE PRINCE...
OH, HOW I HAVE WANTED TO MEET YOU...
DON'T KILL HIM! PLEASE!
BWHAHA! KILL HIM?! PAY ATTENTION, LITTLE BUG!!!
I'M NOT HERE TO KILL!
DEAR GOD, NO...

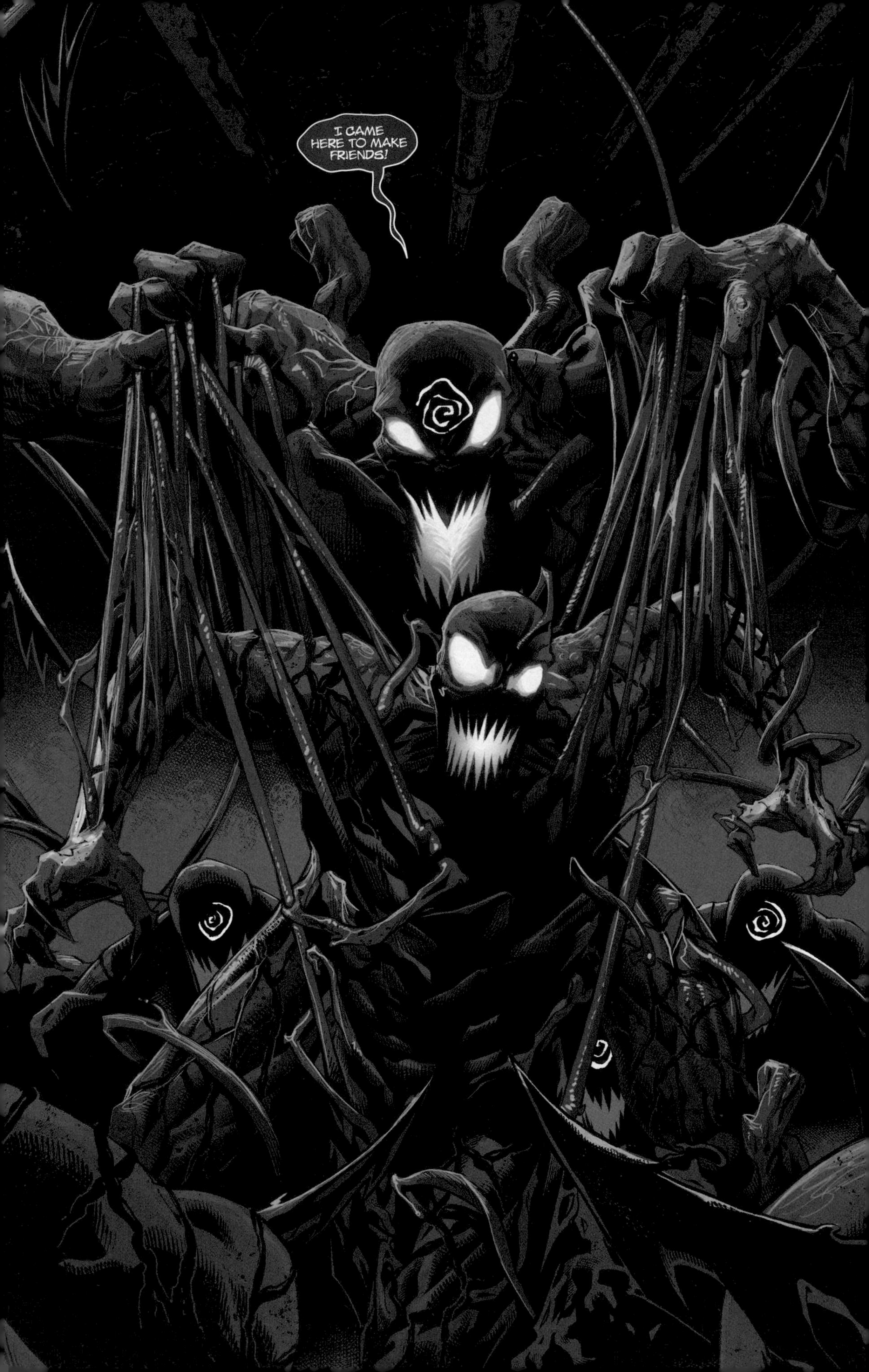
I CAME HERE TO MAKE FRIENDS!

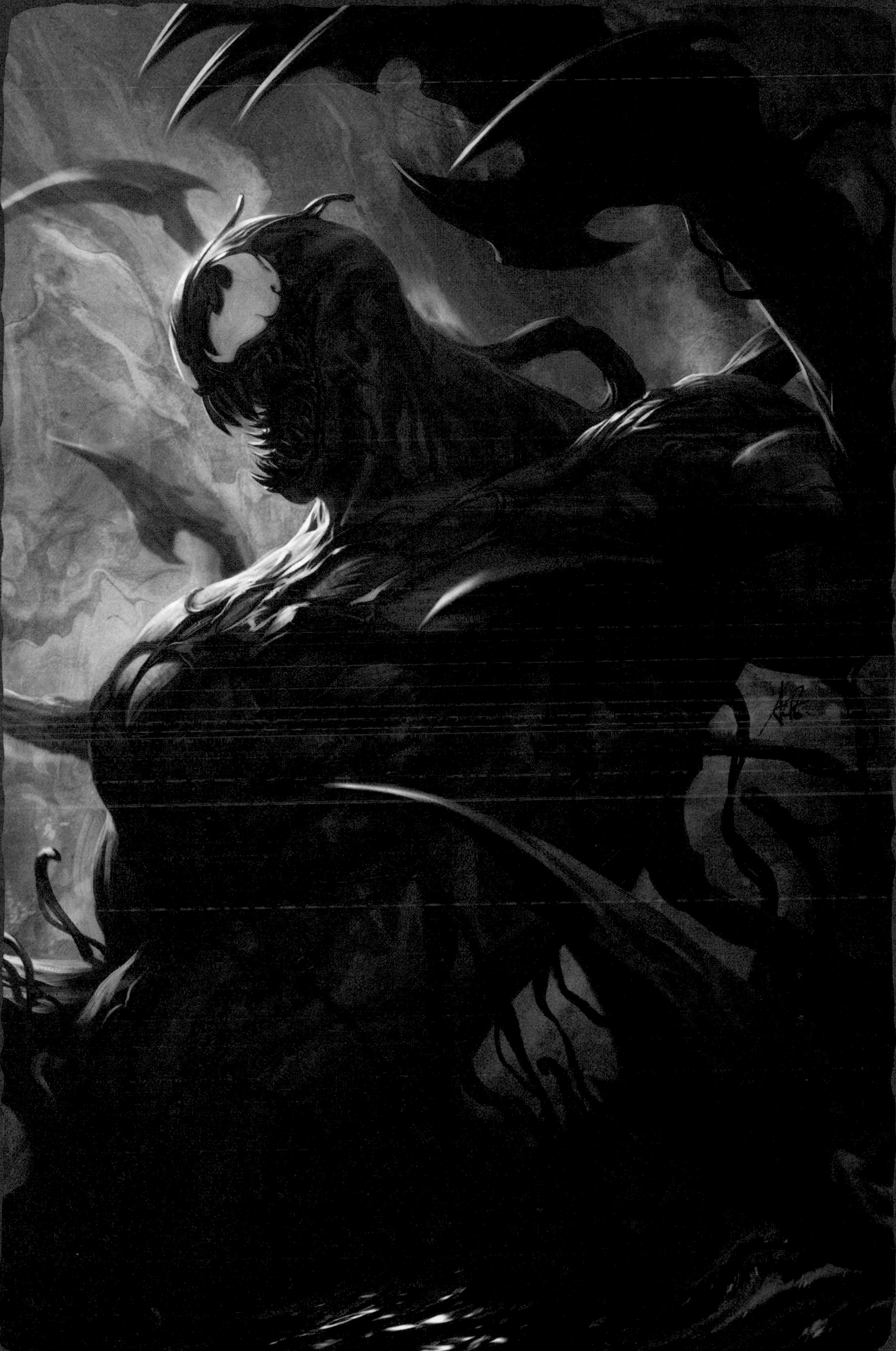

STANLEY "ARTGERM" LAU

#1 Variant

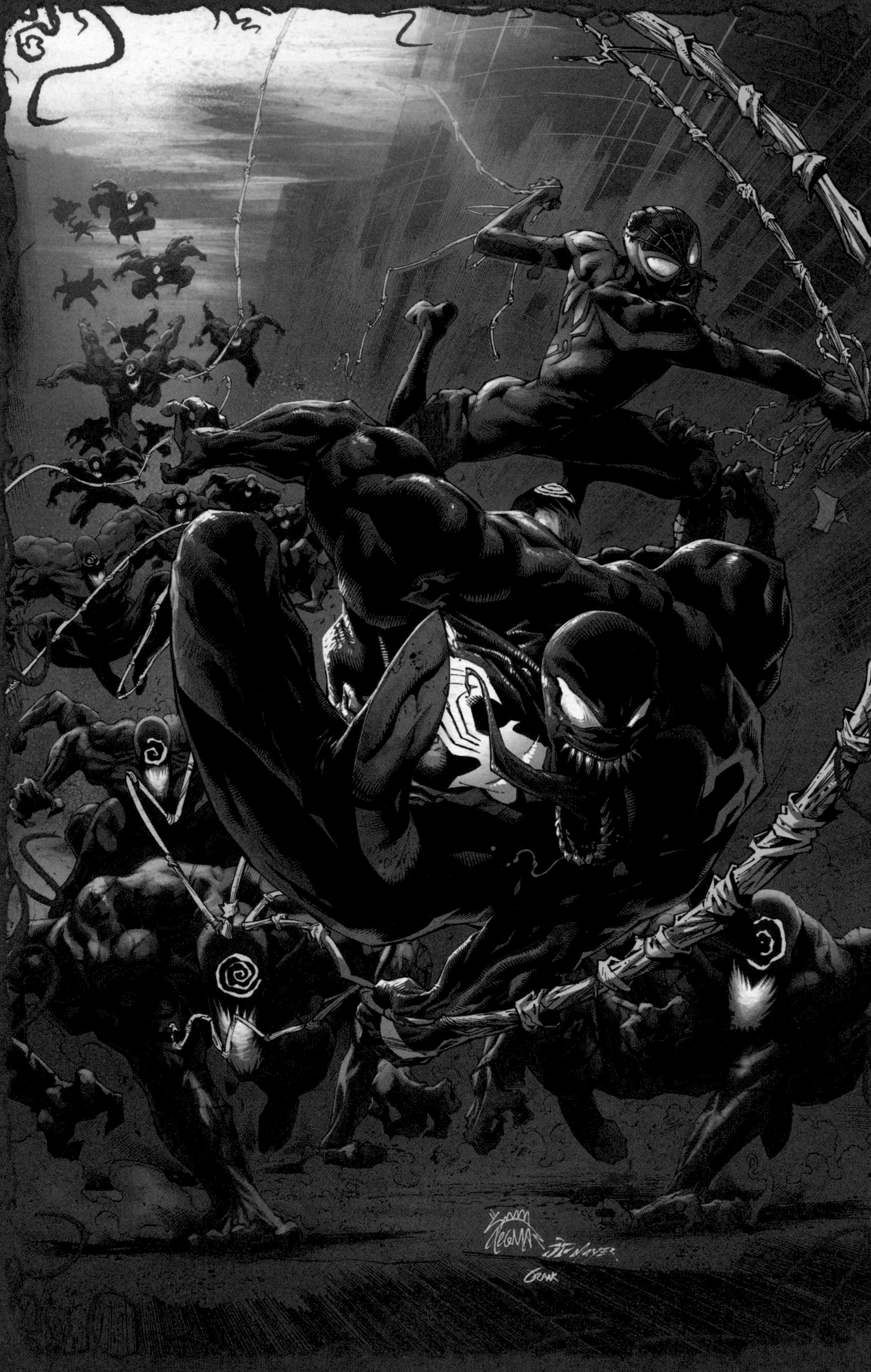

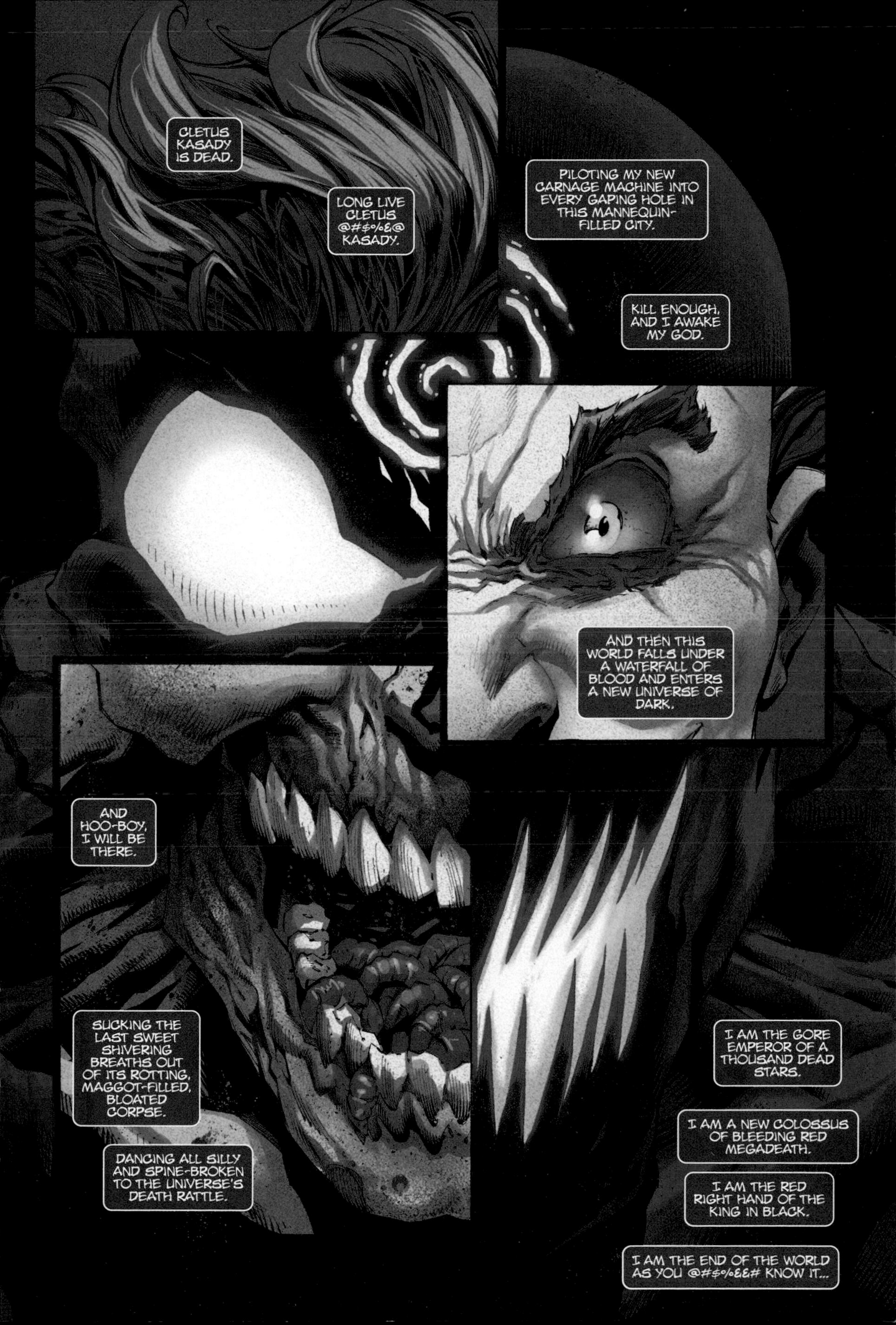
CLETUS KASADY IS DEAD.
LONG LIVE CLETUS @#$%&@ KASADY.
PILOTING MY NEW CARNAGE MACHINE INTO EVERY GAPING HOLE IN THIS MANNEQUIN-FILLED CITY.
KILL ENOUGH, AND I AWAKE MY GOD.
AND THEN THIS WORLD FALLS UNDER A WATERFALL OF BLOOD AND ENTERS A NEW UNIVERSE OF DARK.
AND HOO-BOY, I WILL BE THERE.
SUCKING THE LAST SWEET SHIVERING BREATHS OUT OF ITS ROTTING, MAGGOT-FILLED, BLOATED CORPSE.
DANCING ALL SILLY AND SPINE-BROKEN TO THE UNIVERSE'S DEATH RATTLE.
I AM THE GORE EMPEROR OF A THOUSAND DEAD STARS.
I AM A NEW COLOSSUS OF BLEEDING RED MEGADEATH.
I AM THE RED RIGHT HAND OF THE KING IN BLACK.
I AM THE END OF THE WORLD AS YOU @#$%&&# KNOW IT...

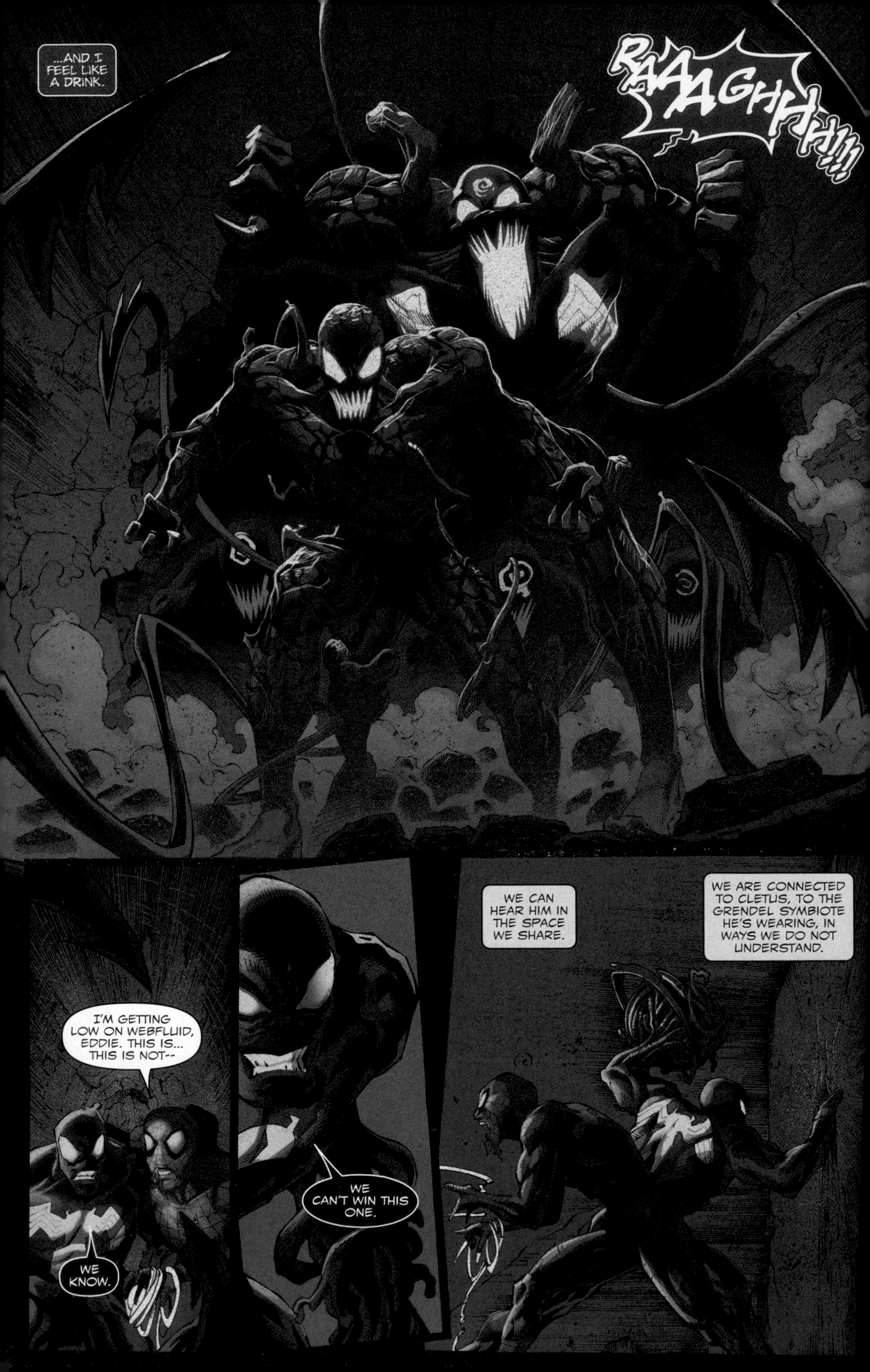...AND I FEEL LIKE A DRINK.
RAAAGHHH!!!
I'M GETTING LOW ON WEBFLUID, EDDIE. THIS IS... THIS IS NOT--
WE KNOW.
WE CAN'T WIN THIS ONE.
WE CAN HEAR HIM IN THE SPACE WE SHARE.
WE ARE CONNECTED TO CLETUS, TO THE GRENDEL SYMBIOTE HE'S WEARING, IN WAYS WE DO NOT UNDERSTAND.

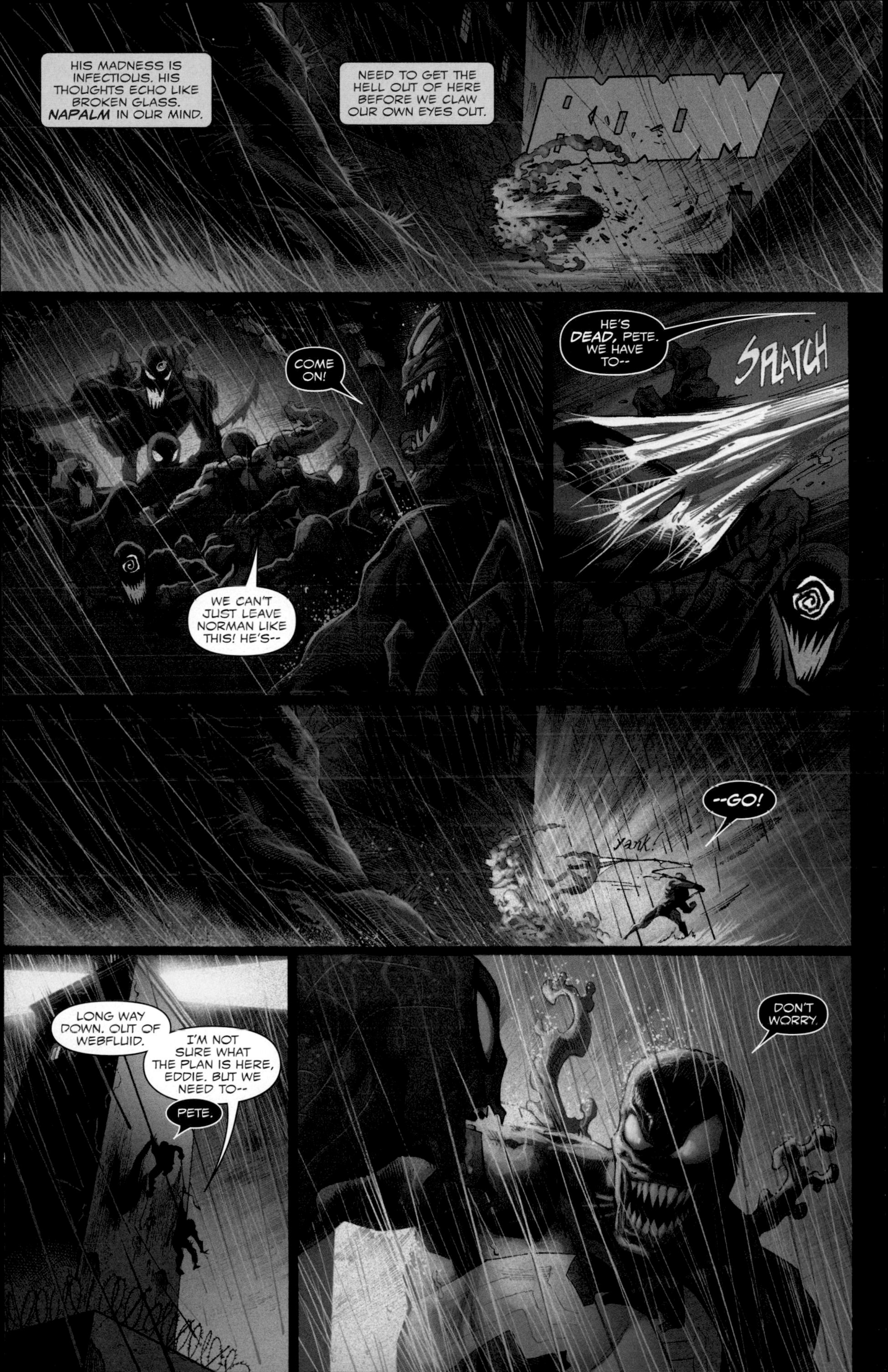
HIS MADNESS IS INFECTIOUS. HIS THOUGHTS ECHO LIKE BROKEN GLASS. NAPALM IN OUR MIND.
NEED TO GET THE HELL OUT OF HERE BEFORE WE CLAW OUR OWN EYES OUT.
COME ON!
WE CAN'T JUST LEAVE NORMAN LIKE THIS! HE'S--
HE'S DEAD, PETE. WE HAVE TO--
SPLATCH
--GO!
YANK!
LONG WAY DOWN. OUT OF WEBFLUID.
I'M NOT SURE WHAT THE PLAN IS HERE, EDDIE. BUT WE NEED TO--
PETE.
DON'T WORRY.

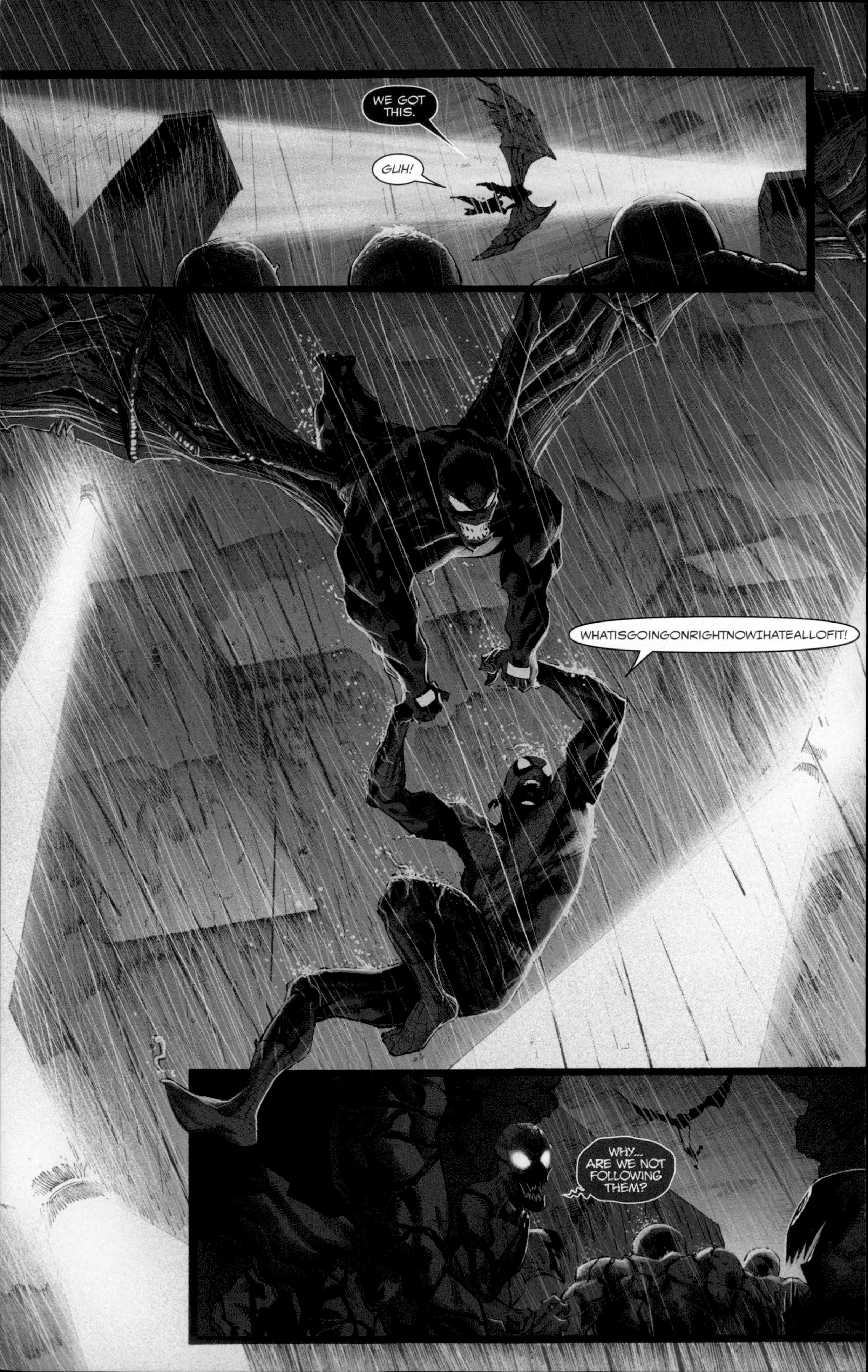
WE GOT THIS.
GUH!
WHATISGOINGONRIGHTNOWIHATEALLOFIT!
WHY... ARE WE NOT FOLLOWING THEM?

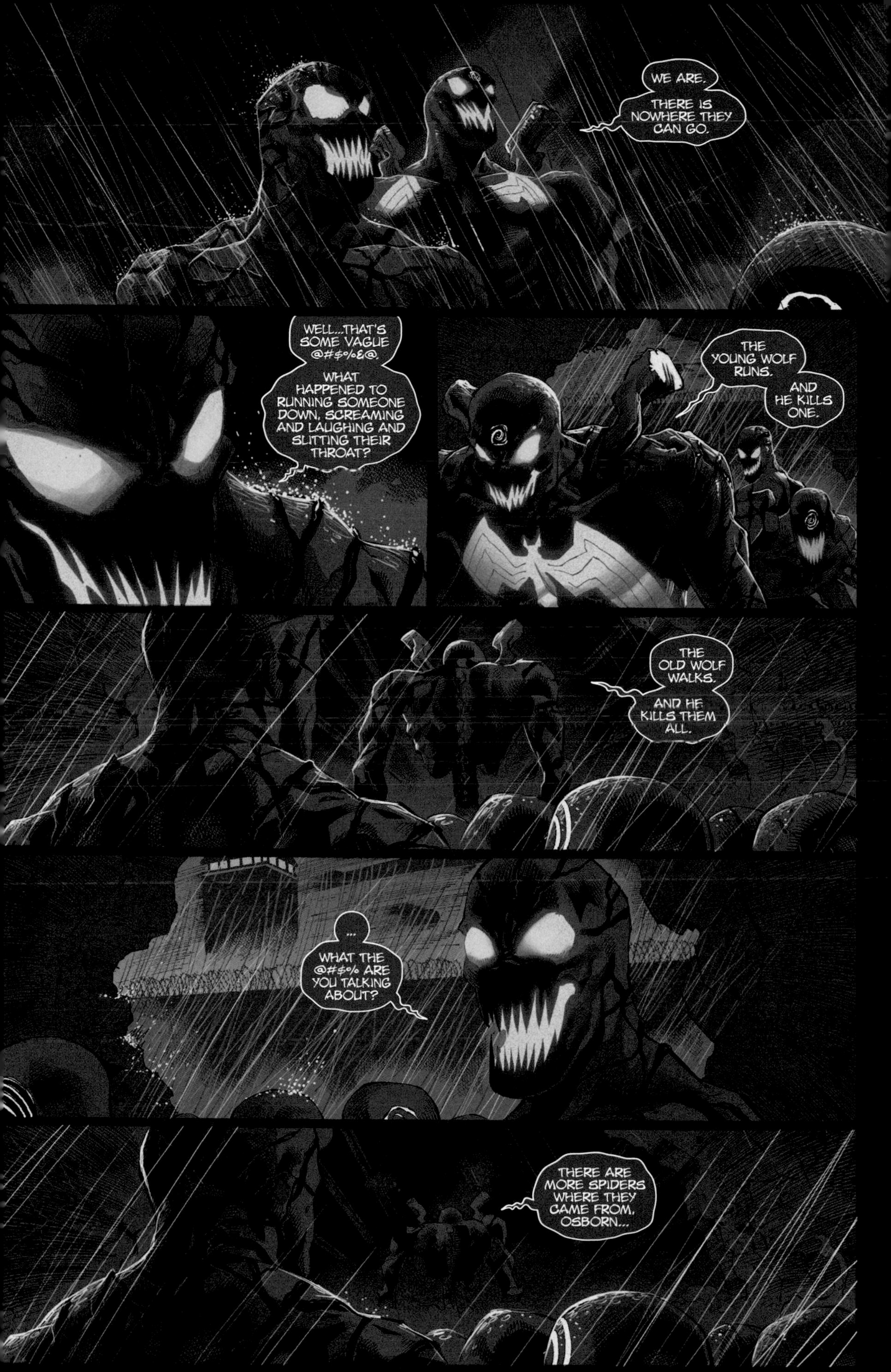
WE ARE.
THERE IS NOWHERE THEY CAN GO.
WELL...THAT'S SOME VAGUE @#$%&@.
WHAT HAPPENED TO RUNNING SOMEONE DOWN, SCREAMING AND LAUGHING AND SLITTING THEIR THROAT?
THE YOUNG WOLF RUNS.
AND HE KILLS ONE.
THE OLD WOLF WALKS.
AND HE KILLS THEM ALL.
...
WHAT THE @#$% ARE YOU TALKING ABOUT?
THERE ARE MORE SPIDERS WHERE THEY CAME FROM, OSBORN...

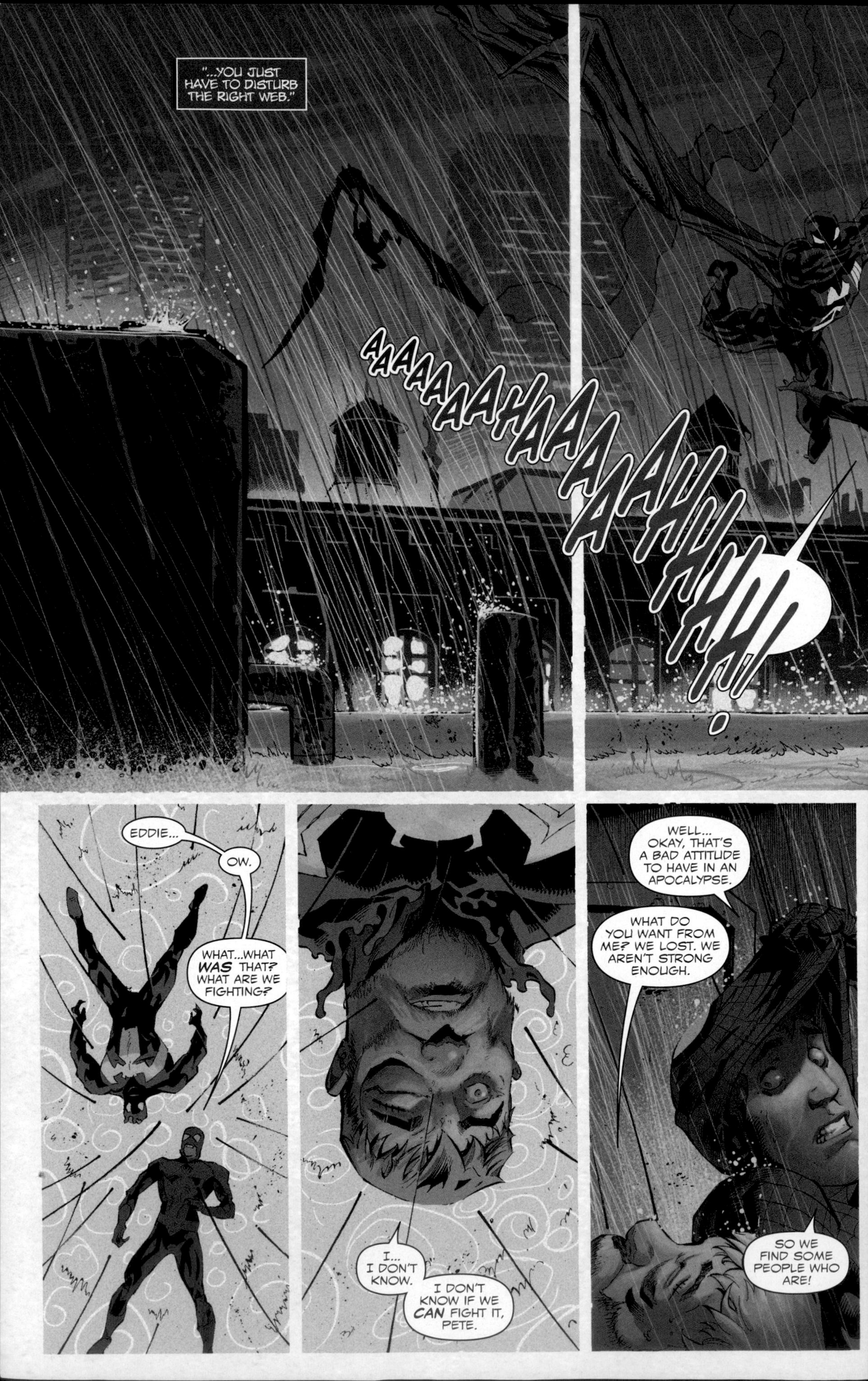
"...YOU JUST HAVE TO DISTURB THE RIGHT WEB."
AAAAAAAHAAAAAAHHHHHH!
EDDIE...
OW.
WHAT...WHAT WAS THAT? WHAT ARE WE FIGHTING?
I... I DON'T KNOW.
I DON'T KNOW IF WE CAN FIGHT IT, PETE.
WELL... OKAY, THAT'S A BAD ATTITUDE TO HAVE IN AN APOCALYPSE.
WHAT DO YOU WANT FROM ME? WE LOST. WE AREN'T STRONG ENOUGH.
SO WE FIND SOME PEOPLE WHO ARE!

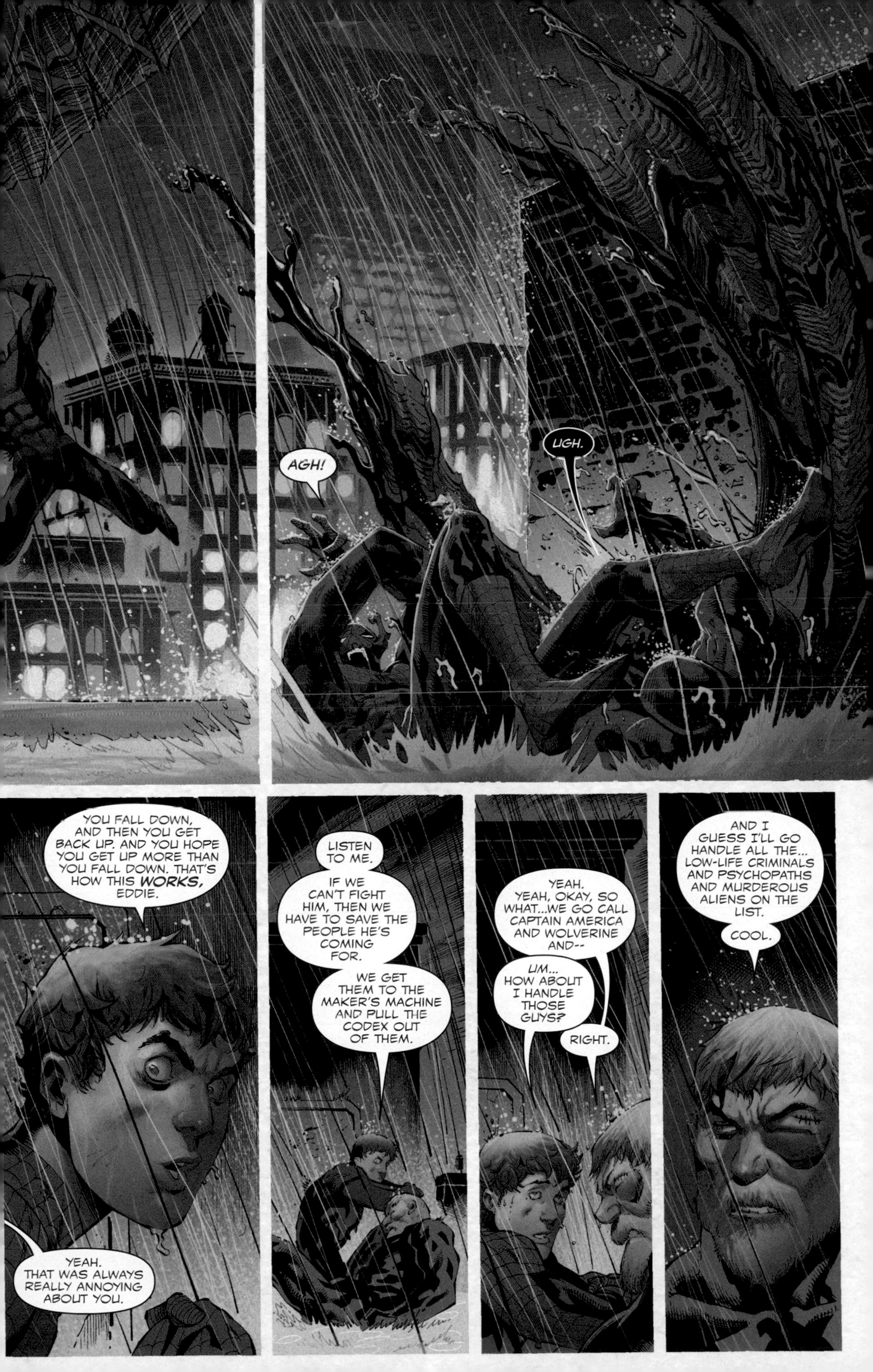
AGH!
UGH.
YOU FALL DOWN, AND THEN YOU GET BACK UP. AND YOU HOPE YOU GET UP MORE THAN YOU FALL DOWN. THAT'S HOW THIS WORKS, EDDIE.
YEAH. THAT WAS ALWAYS REALLY ANNOYING ABOUT YOU.
LISTEN TO ME.
IF WE CAN'T FIGHT HIM, THEN WE HAVE TO SAVE THE PEOPLE HE'S COMING FOR.
WE GET THEM TO THE MAKER'S MACHINE AND PULL THE CODEX OUT OF THEM.
YEAH. YEAH, OKAY, SO WHAT...WE GO CALL CAPTAIN AMERICA AND WOLVERINE AND--
UM... HOW ABOUT I HANDLE THOSE GUYS?
RIGHT.
AND I GUESS I'LL GO HANDLE ALL THE... LOW-LIFE CRIMINALS AND PSYCHOPATHS AND MURDEROUS ALIENS ON THE LIST.
COOL.

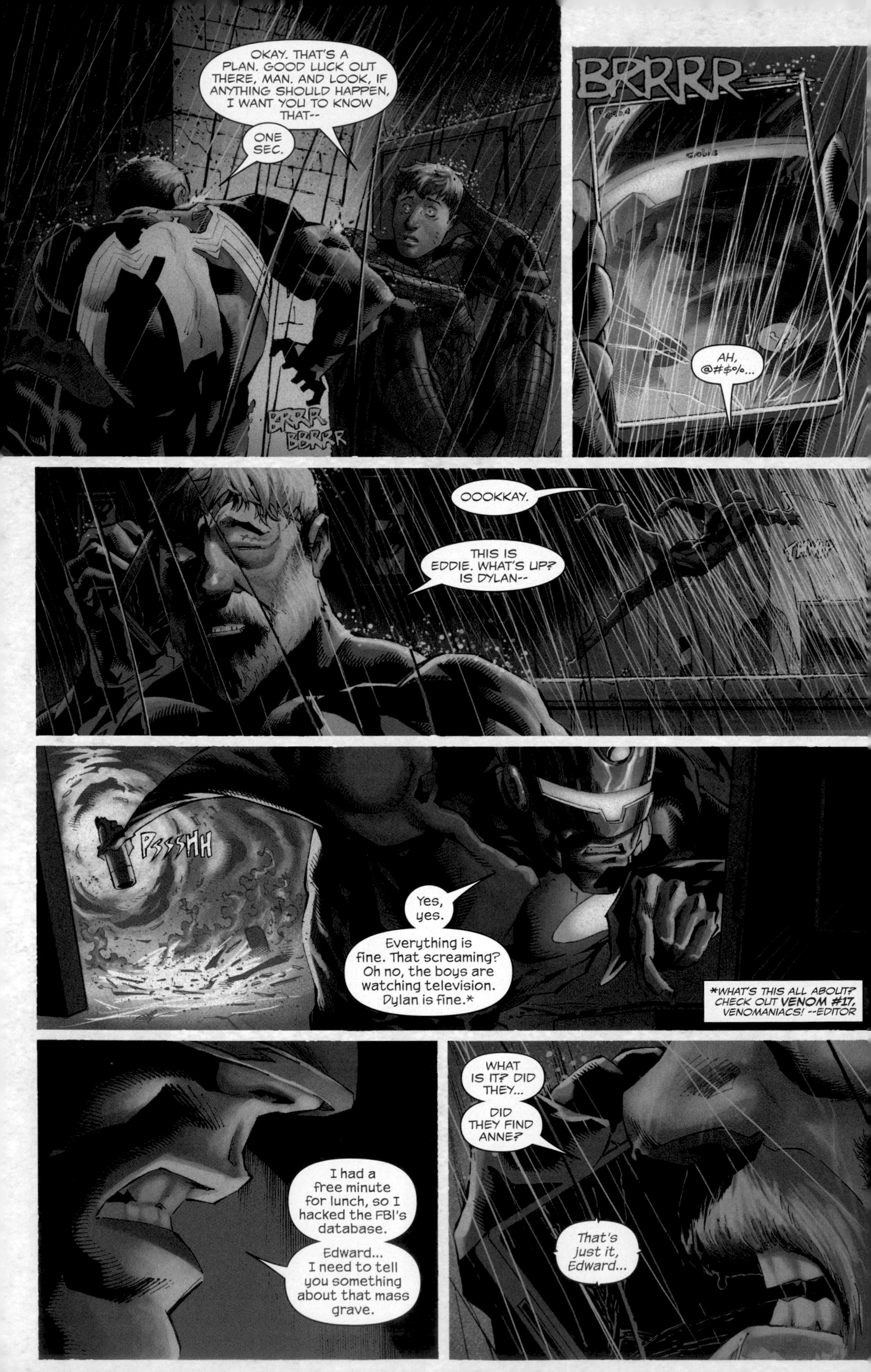

OKAY. THAT'S A PLAN. GOOD LUCK OUT THERE, MAN. AND LOOK, IF ANYTHING SHOULD HAPPEN, I WANT YOU TO KNOW THAT--
ONE SEC.
BRRR BBRRR
BRRRR
AH, @#$%...
OOOKKAY.
THIS IS EDDIE. WHAT'S UP? IS DYLAN--
PSSSHH
Yes, yes.
Everything is fine. That screaming? Oh no, the boys are watching television. Dylan is fine.*
*WHAT'S THIS ALL ABOUT? CHECK OUT VENOM #17, VENOMANIACS! --EDITOR
I had a free minute for lunch, so I hacked the FBI's database.
Edward... I need to tell you something about that mass grave.
WHAT IS IT? DID THEY...
DID THEY FIND ANNE?
That's just it, Edward...

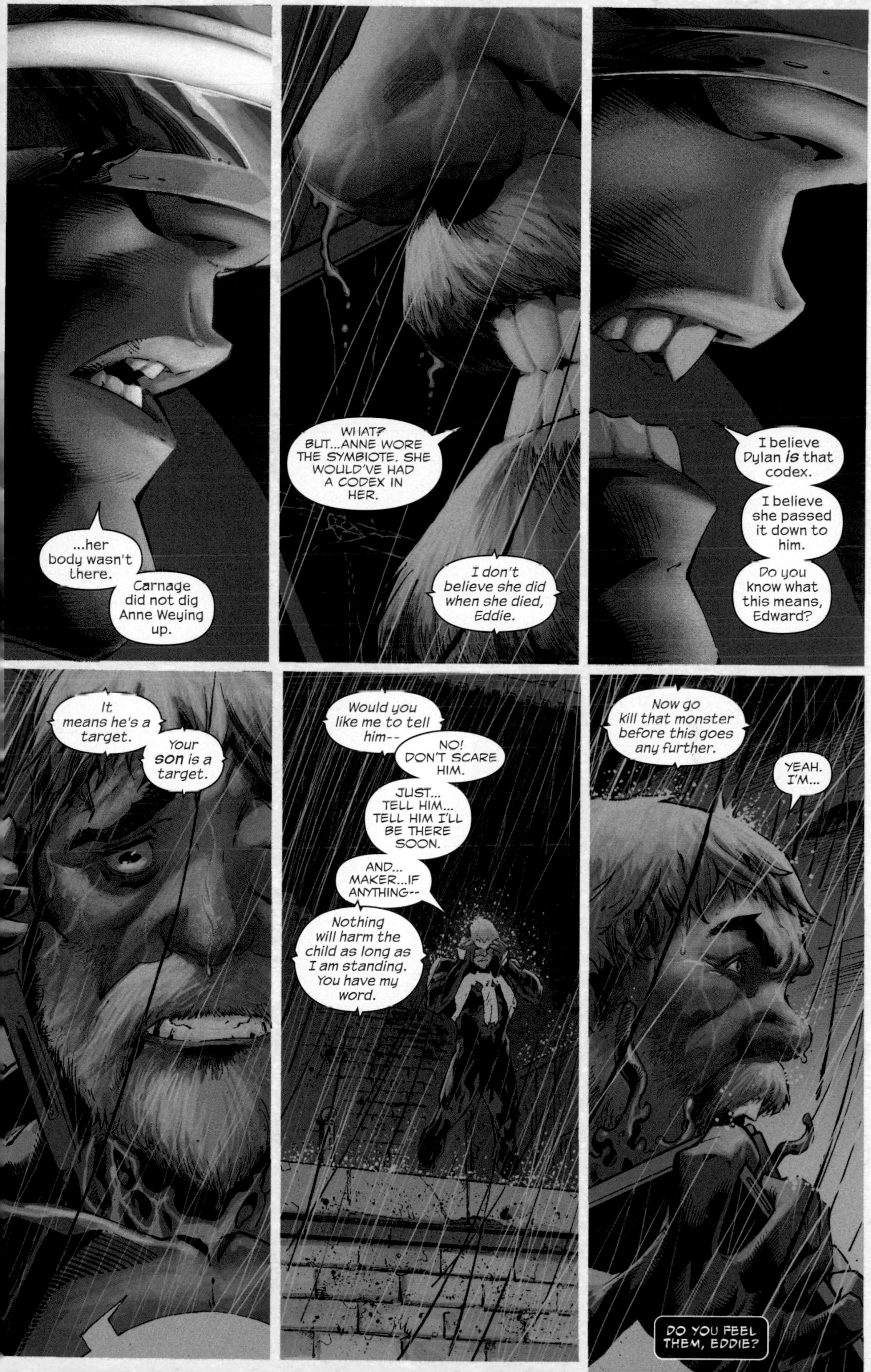
...her body wasn't there.
Carnage did not dig Anne Weying up.
WHAT? BUT...ANNE WORE THE SYMBIOTE. SHE WOULD'VE HAD A CODEX IN HER.
I don't believe she did when she died, Eddie.
I believe Dylan *is* that codex.
I believe she passed it down to him.
Do you know what this means, Edward?
It means he's a target.
Your **son** is a target.
Would you like me to tell him--
NO! DON'T SCARE HIM.
JUST... TELL HIM... TELL HIM I'LL BE THERE SOON.
AND... MAKER...IF ANYTHING--
Nothing will harm the child as long as I am standing. You have my word.
Now go kill that monster before this goes any further.
YEAH. I'M...
DO YOU FEEL THEM, EDDIE?

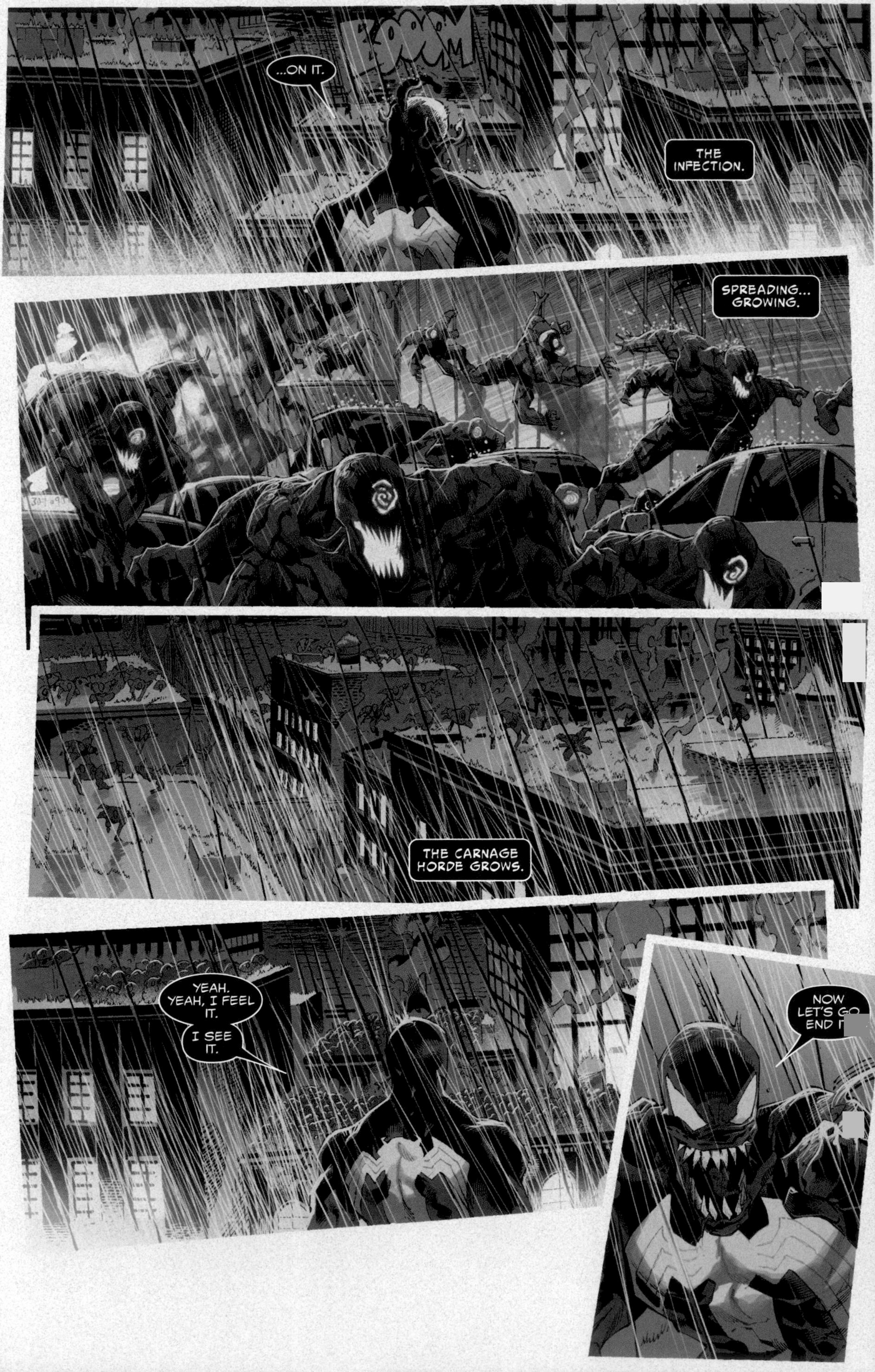
BOOM
...ON IT.
THE INFECTION.
SPREADING... GROWING.
THE CARNAGE HORDE GROWS.
YEAH. YEAH, I FEEL IT.
I SEE IT.
NOW LET'S GO END I

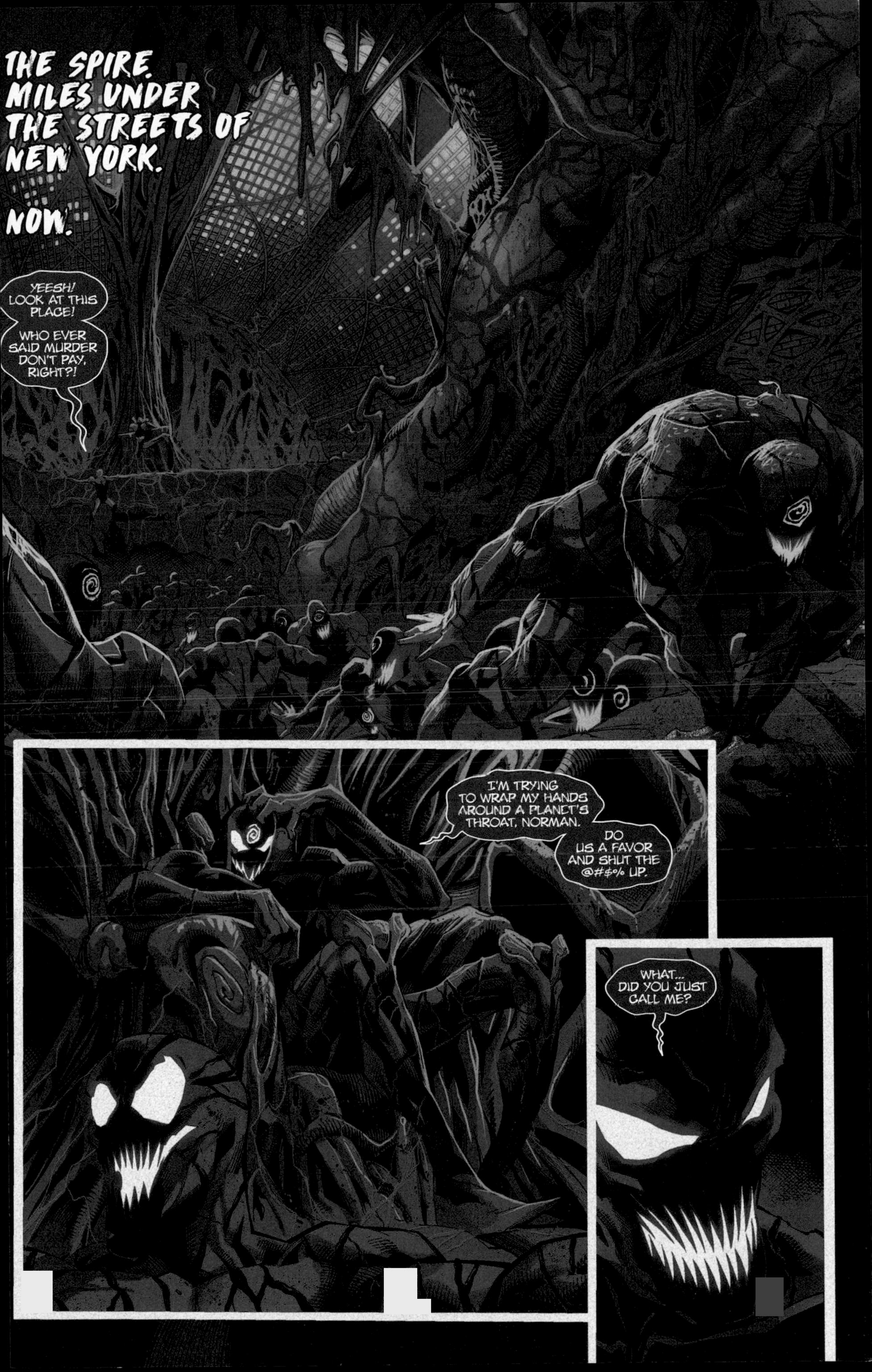
THE SPIRE. MILES UNDER THE STREETS OF NEW YORK.
NOW.
YEESH! LOOK AT THIS PLACE!
WHO EVER SAID MURDER DON'T PAY, RIGHT?!
I'M TRYING TO WRAP MY HANDS AROUND A PLANET'S THROAT, NORMAN.
DO US A FAVOR AND SHUT THE @#$% UP.
WHAT... DID YOU JUST CALL ME?

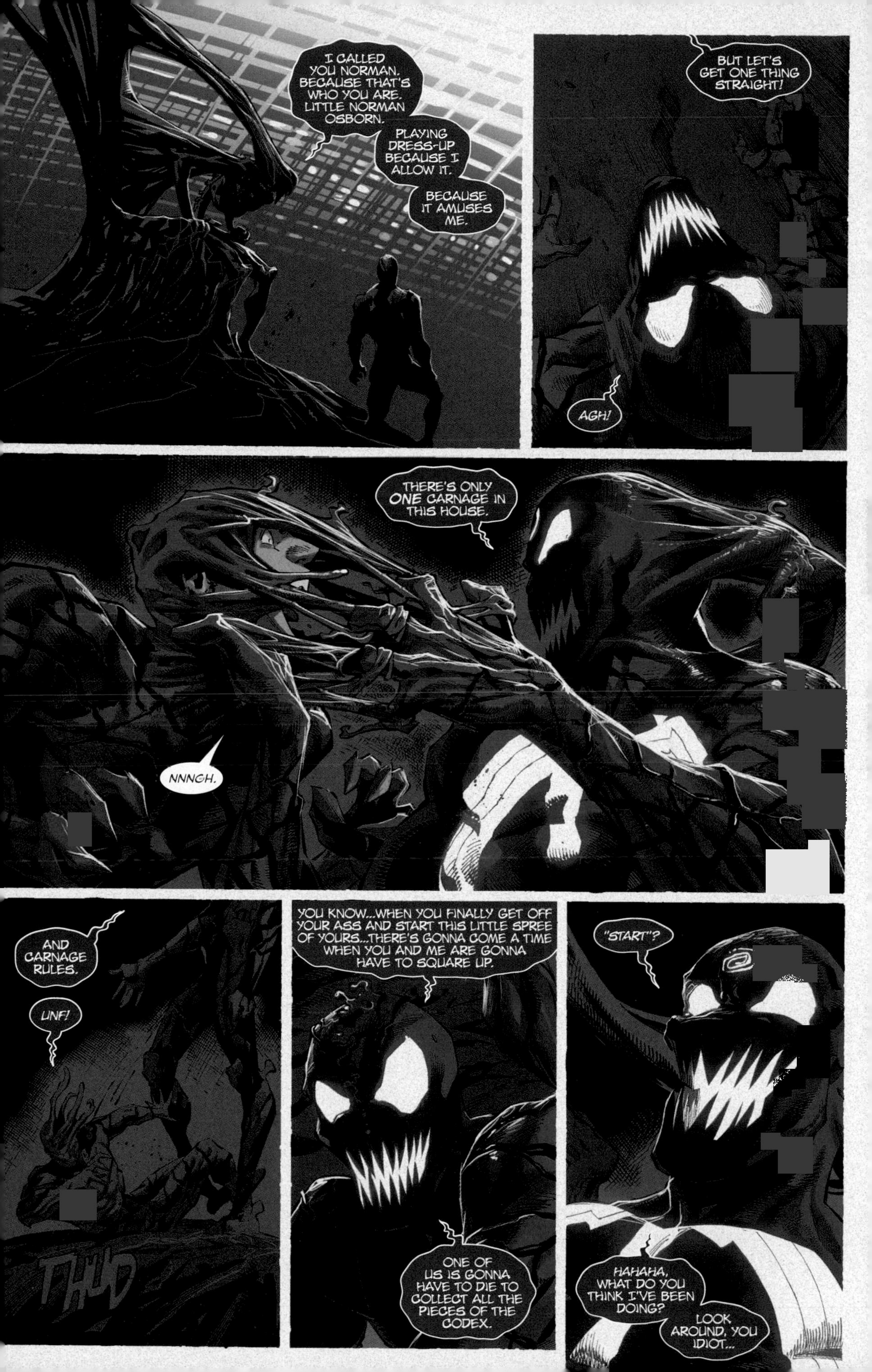
I CALLED YOU NORMAN. BECAUSE THAT'S WHO YOU ARE. LITTLE NORMAN OSBORN.
PLAYING DRESS-UP BECAUSE I ALLOW IT.
BECAUSE IT AMUSES ME.
BUT LET'S GET ONE THING STRAIGHT!
AGH!
THERE'S ONLY ONE CARNAGE IN THIS HOUSE.
NNNGH.
AND CARNAGE RULES.
UNF!
THUD
YOU KNOW...WHEN YOU FINALLY GET OFF YOUR ASS AND START THIS LITTLE SPREE OF YOURS...THERE'S GONNA COME A TIME WHEN YOU AND ME ARE GONNA HAVE TO SQUARE UP.
ONE OF US IS GONNA HAVE TO DIE TO COLLECT ALL THE PIECES OF THE CODEX.
"START"?
HAHAHA, WHAT DO YOU THINK I'VE BEEN DOING?
LOOK AROUND, YOU IDIOT...

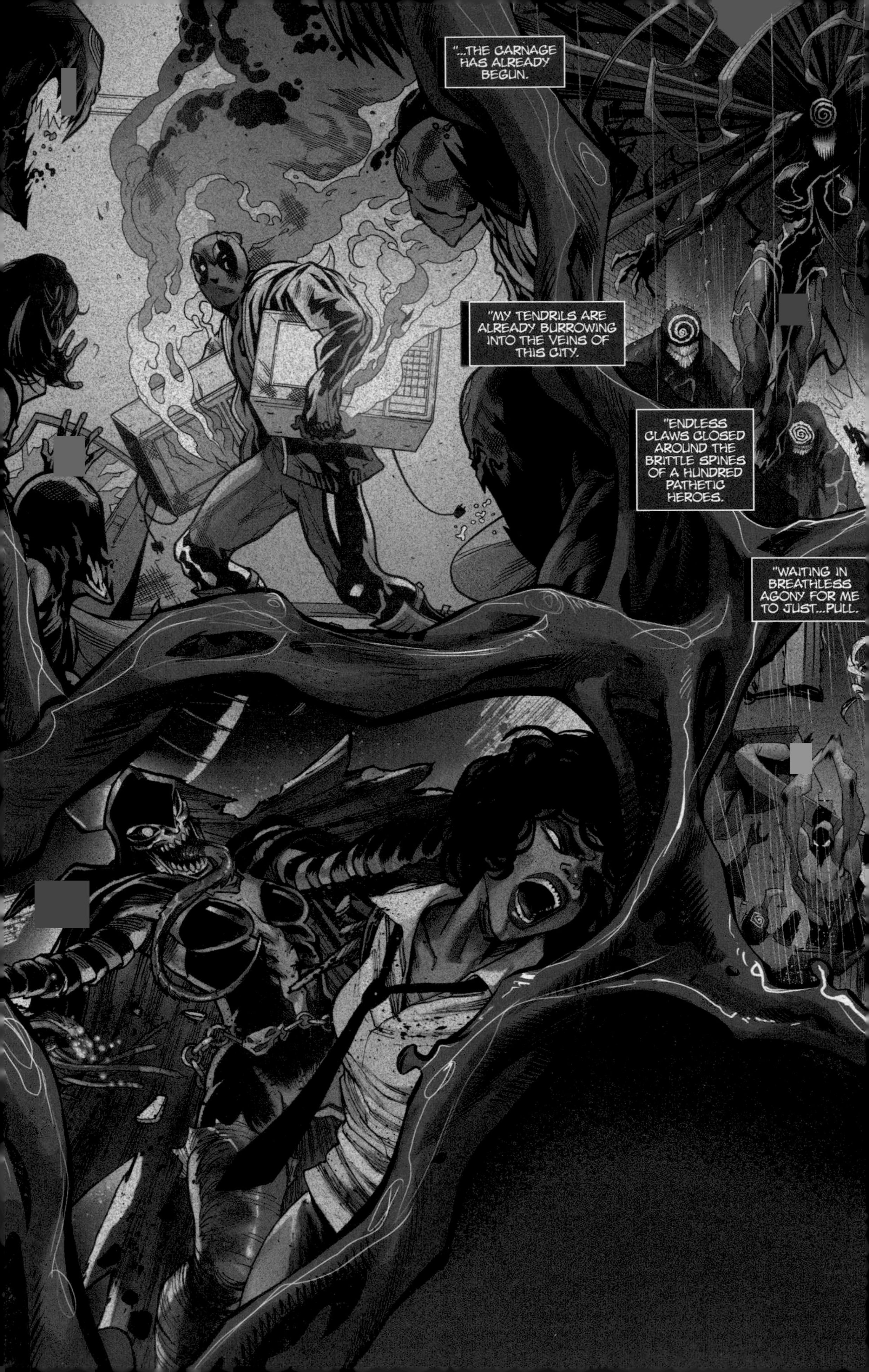
"...THE CARNAGE HAS ALREADY BEGUN.
"MY TENDRILS ARE ALREADY BURROWING INTO THE VEINS OF THIS CITY.
"ENDLESS CLAWS CLOSED AROUND THE BRITTLE SPINES OF A HUNDRED PATHETIC HEROES.
"WAITING IN BREATHLESS AGONY FOR ME TO JUST...PULL.

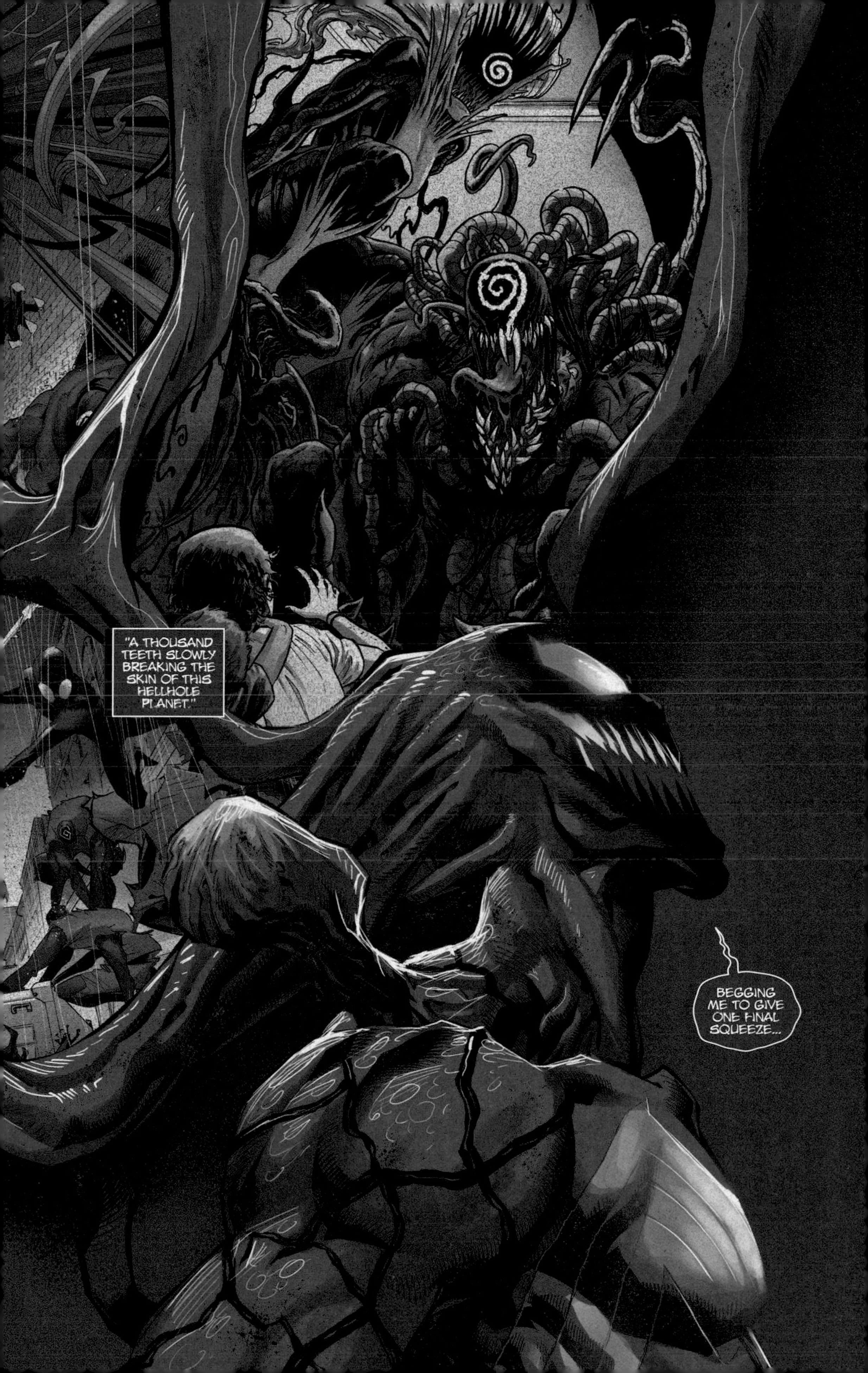
"A THOUSAND TEETH SLOWLY BREAKING THE SKIN OF THIS HELLHOLE PLANET."
BEGGING ME TO GIVE ONE FINAL SQUEEZE...

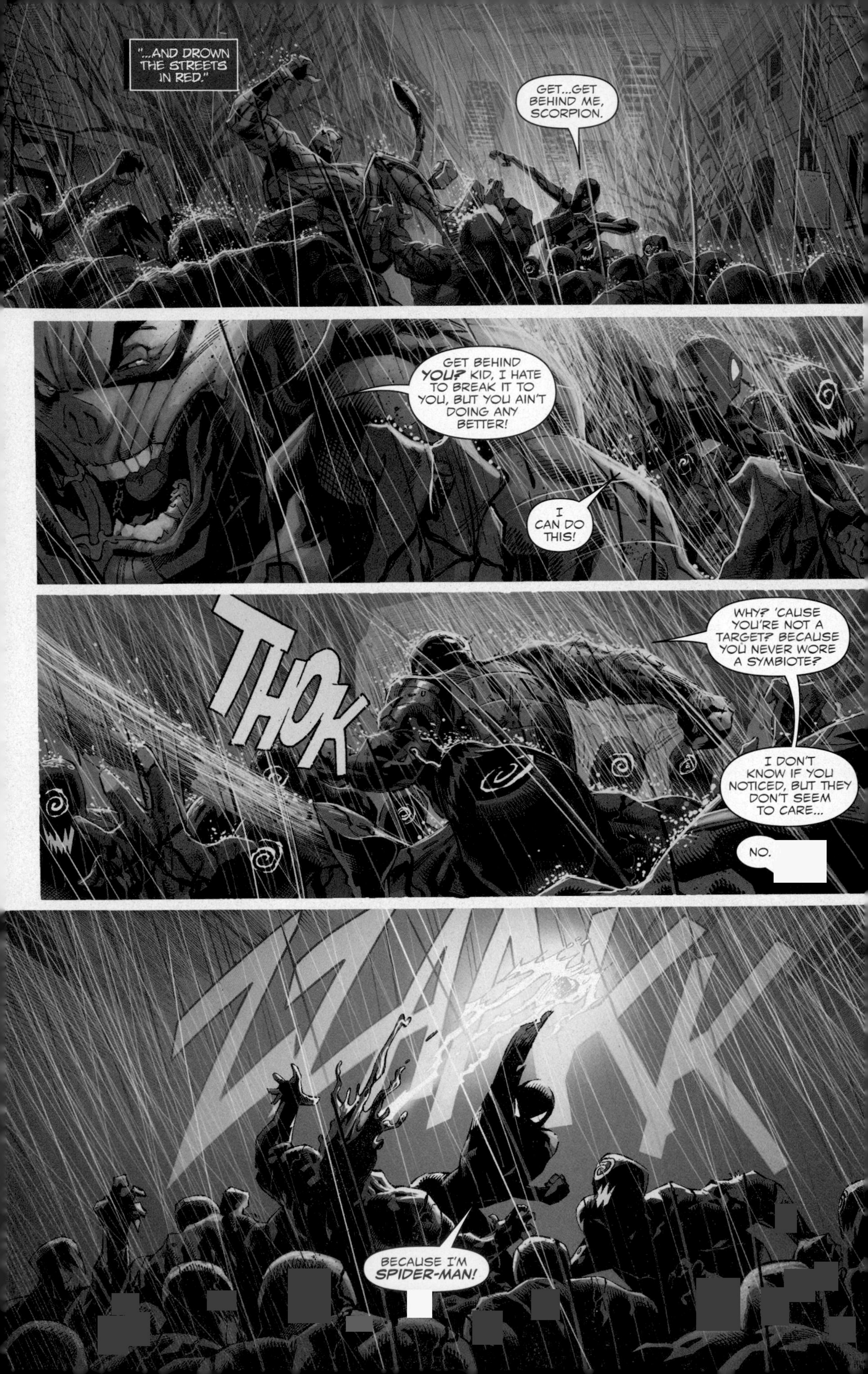
"...AND DROWN THE STREETS IN RED."
GET...GET BEHIND ME, SCORPION.
GET BEHIND YOU? KID, I HATE TO BREAK IT TO YOU, BUT YOU AIN'T DOING ANY BETTER!
I CAN DO THIS!
THOK
WHY? 'CAUSE YOU'RE NOT A TARGET? BECAUSE YOU NEVER WORE A SYMBIOTE?
I DON'T KNOW IF YOU NOTICED, BUT THEY DON'T SEEM TO CARE...
NO.
ZZAAKK
BECAUSE I'M SPIDER-MAN!

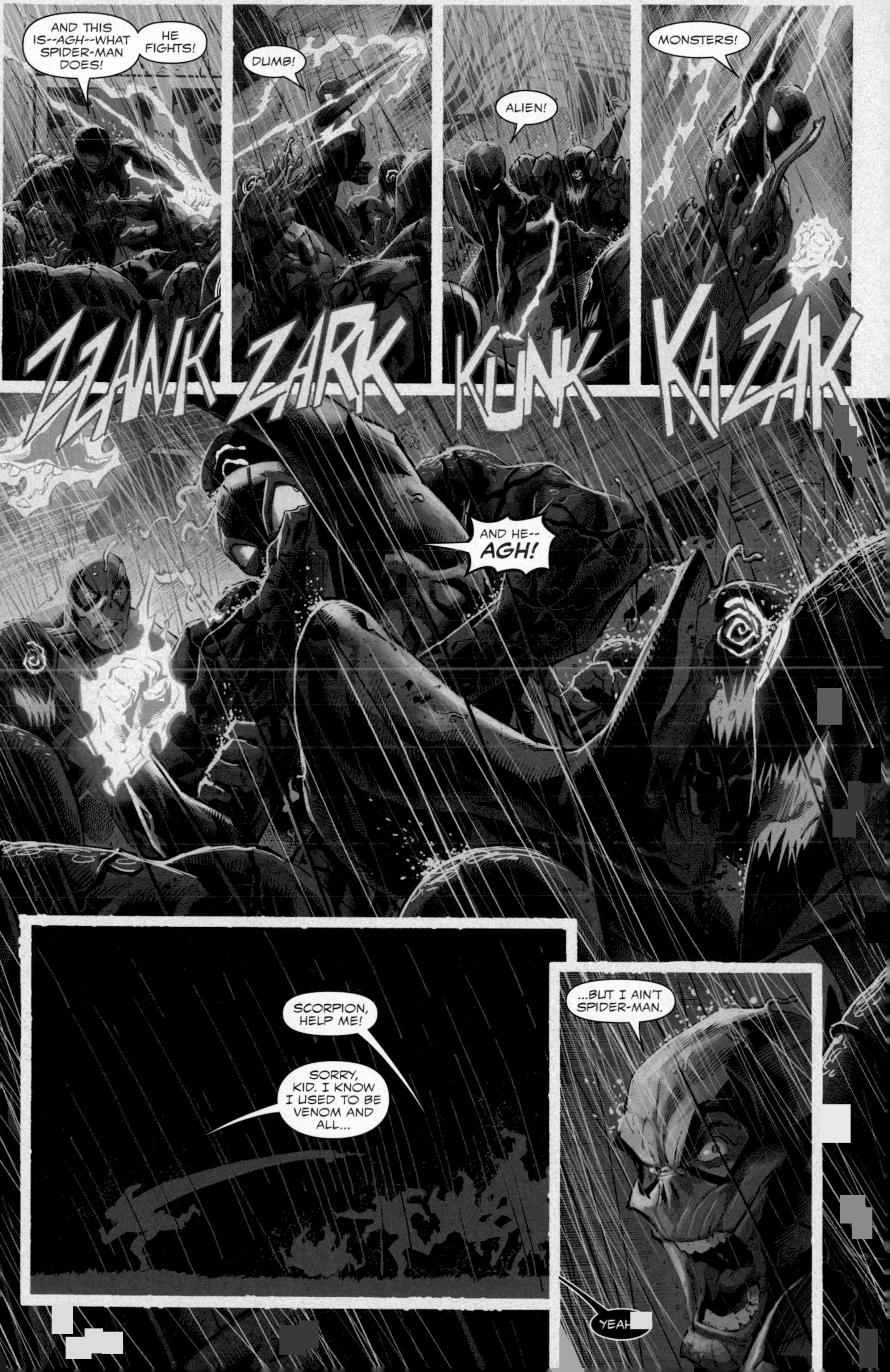
AND THIS IS--AGH--WHAT SPIDER-MAN DOES!
HE FIGHTS!
DUMB!
ALIEN!
MONSTERS!
ZZANK
ZARK
KUNK
KA ZAK
AND HE-- AGH!
SCORPION, HELP ME!
SORRY, KID. I KNOW I USED TO BE VENOM AND ALL...
...BUT I AIN'T SPIDER-MAN.
YEAH

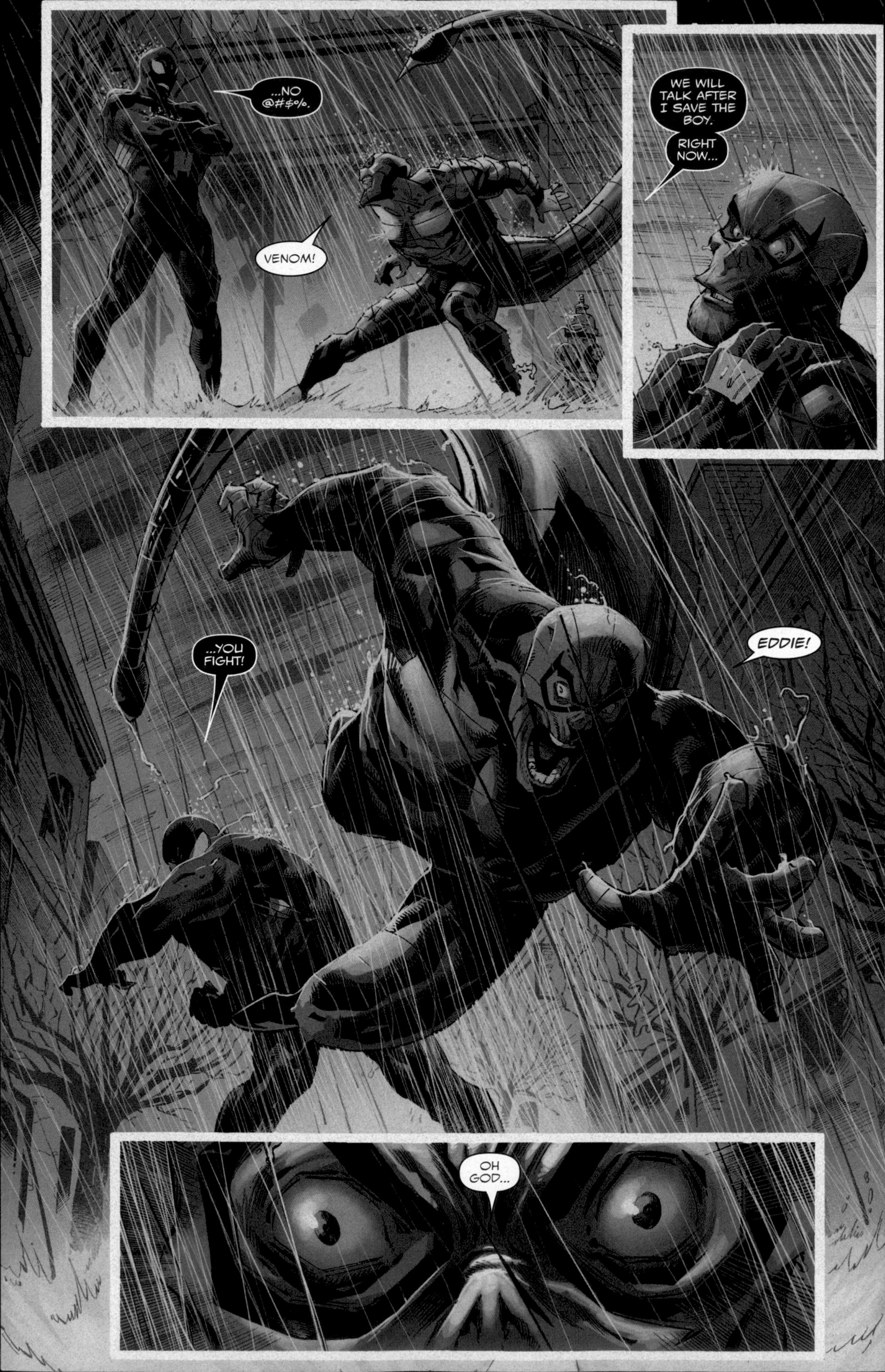
...NO @#$%.
VENOM!
WE WILL TALK AFTER I SAVE THE BOY.
RIGHT NOW...
...YOU FIGHT!
EDDIE!
OH GOD...

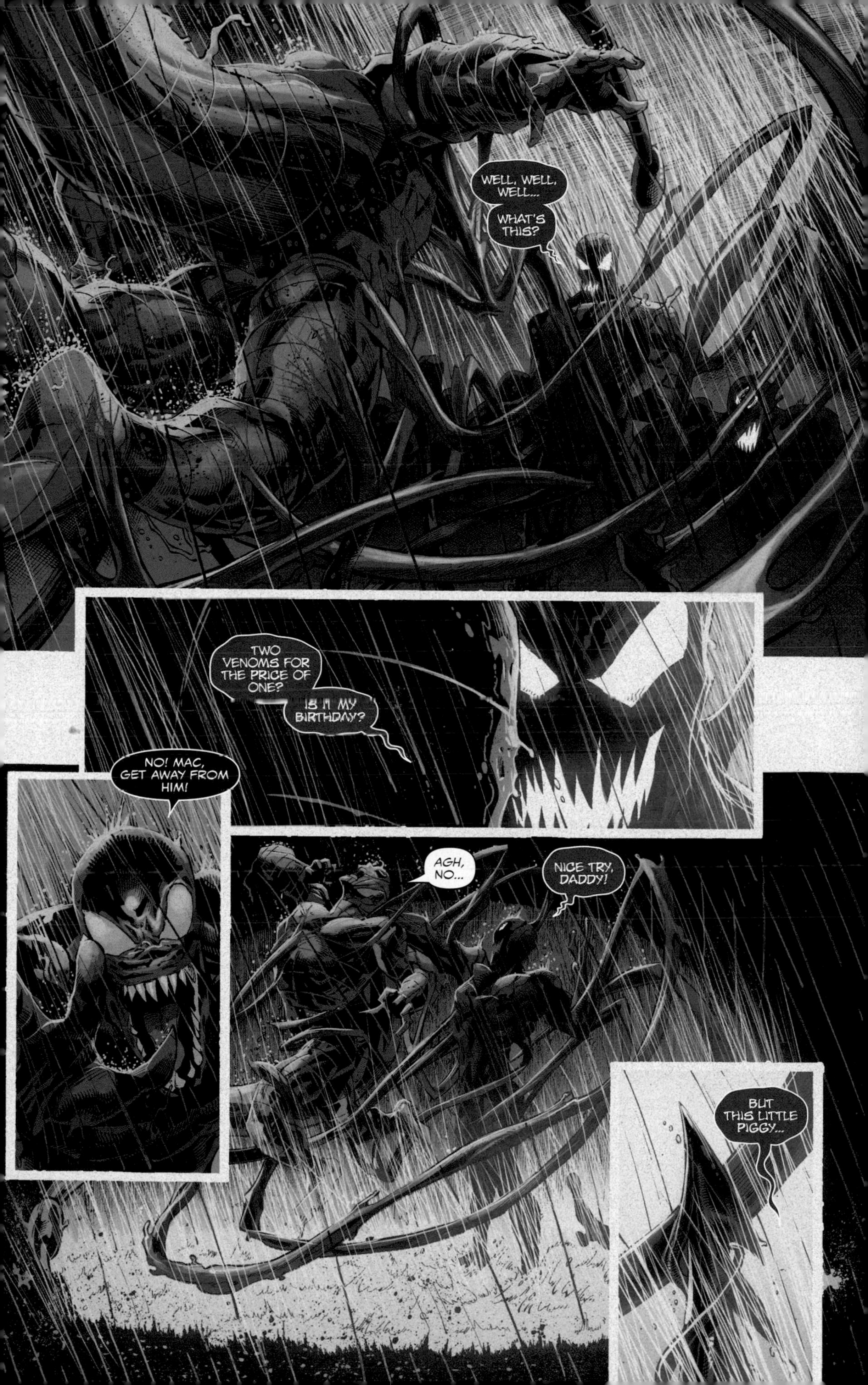
WELL, WELL, WELL...
WHAT'S THIS?
TWO VENOMS FOR THE PRICE OF ONE?
IS IT MY BIRTHDAY?
NO! MAC, GET AWAY FROM HIM!
AGH, NO...
NICE TRY, DADDY!
BUT THIS LITTLE PIGGY...

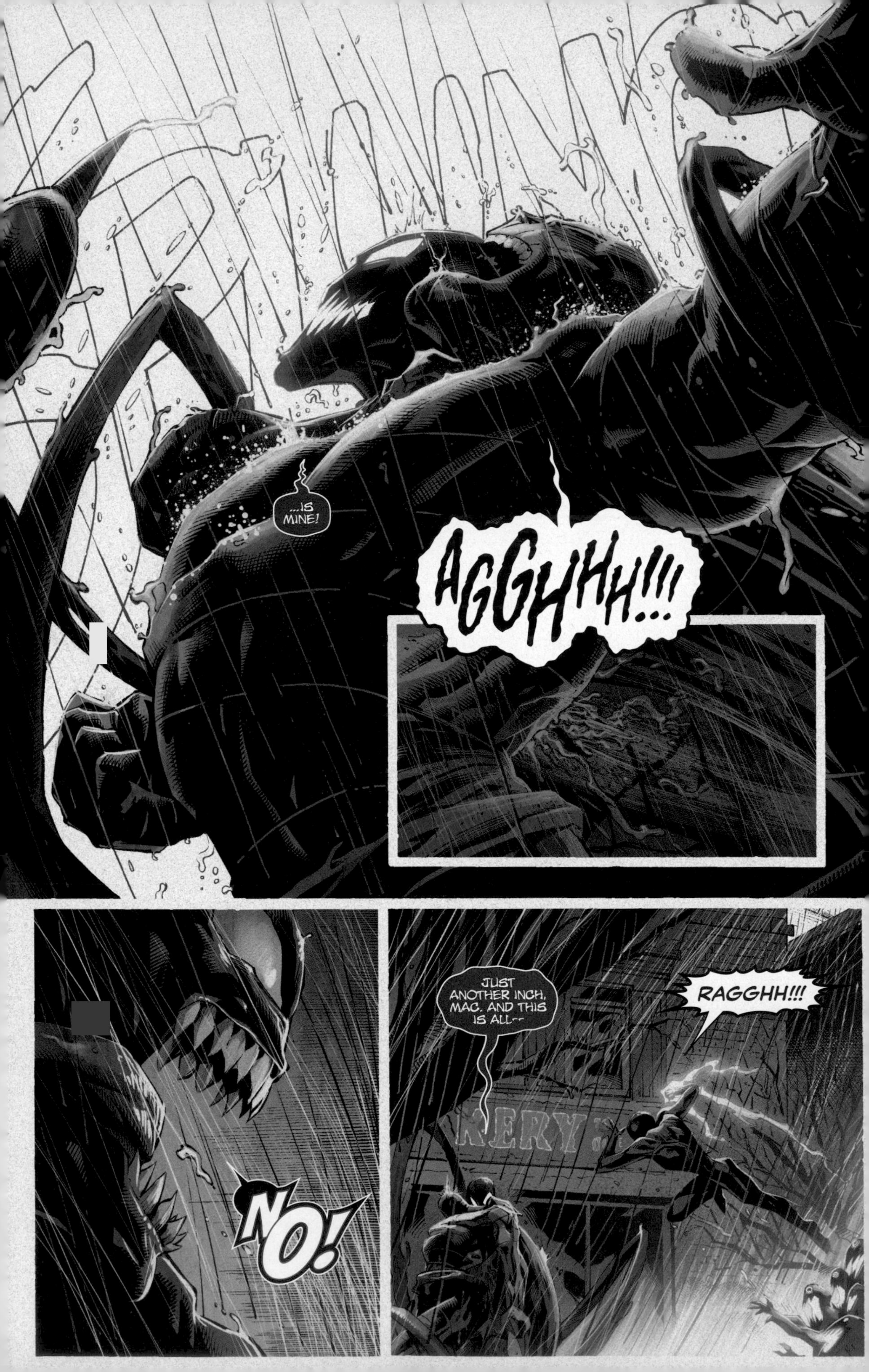
...IS MINE!
AGGHHH!!!
NO!
JUST ANOTHER INCH, MAC. AND THIS IS ALL--
RAGGHH!!!
KERY

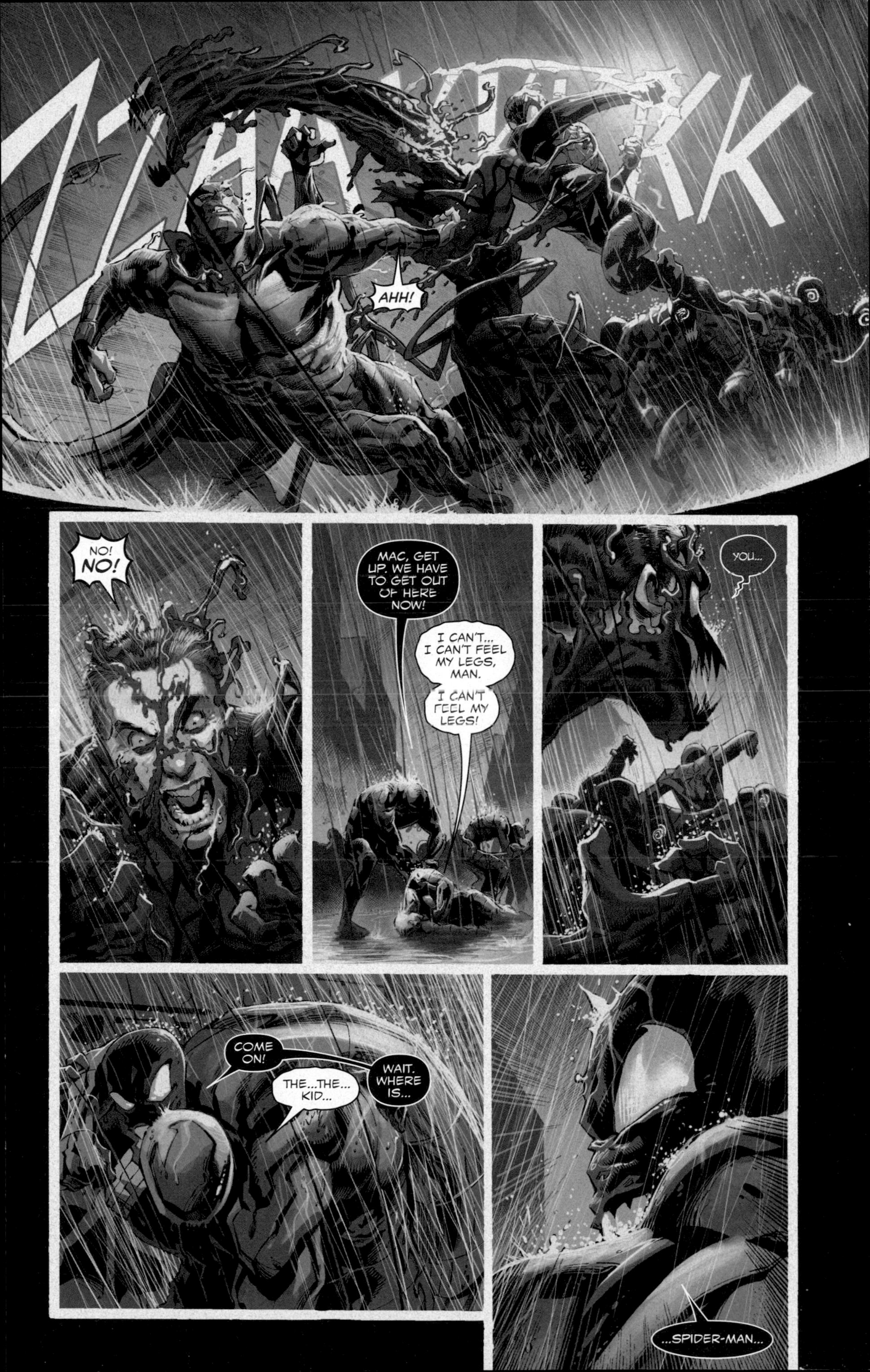
AHH!
NO! NO!
MAC, GET UP. WE HAVE TO GET OUT OF HERE NOW!
I CAN'T... I CAN'T FEEL MY LEGS, MAN.
I CAN'T FEEL MY LEGS!
YOU...
COME ON!
WAIT. WHERE IS...
THE...THE... KID...
...SPIDER-MAN...

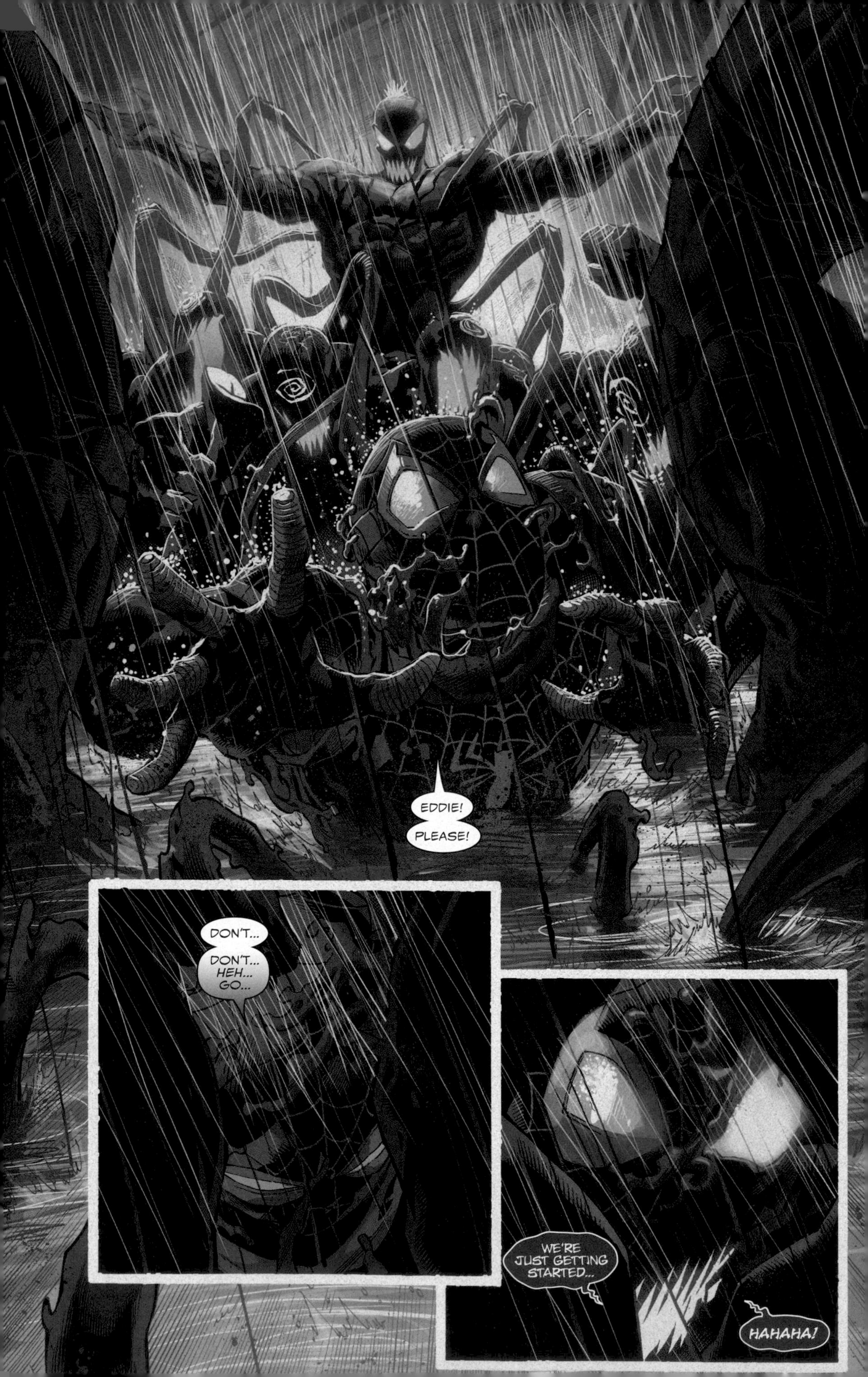
EDDIE!
PLEASE!
DON'T...
DON'T... HEH... GO...
WE'RE JUST GETTING STARTED...
HAHAHA!

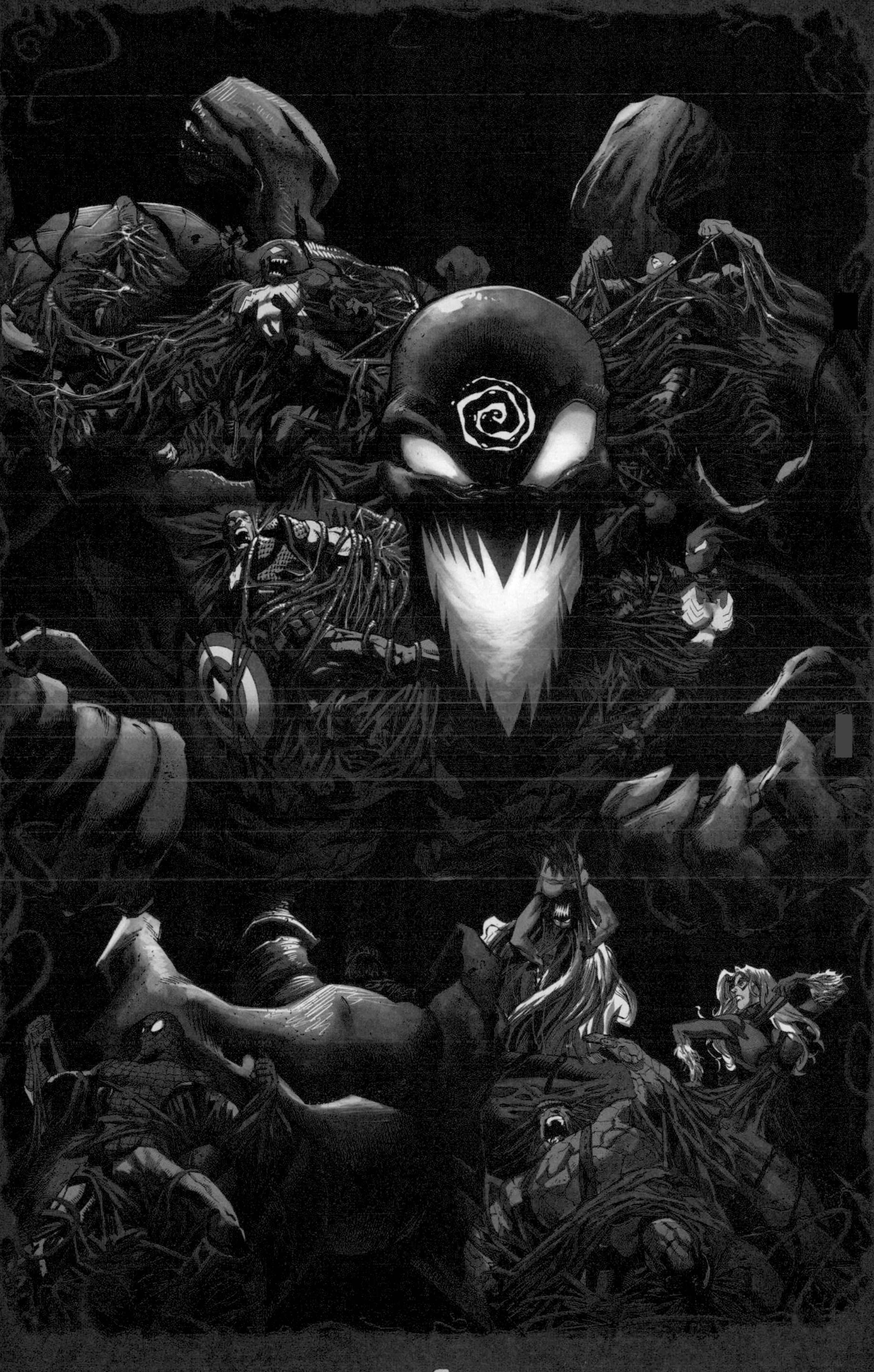

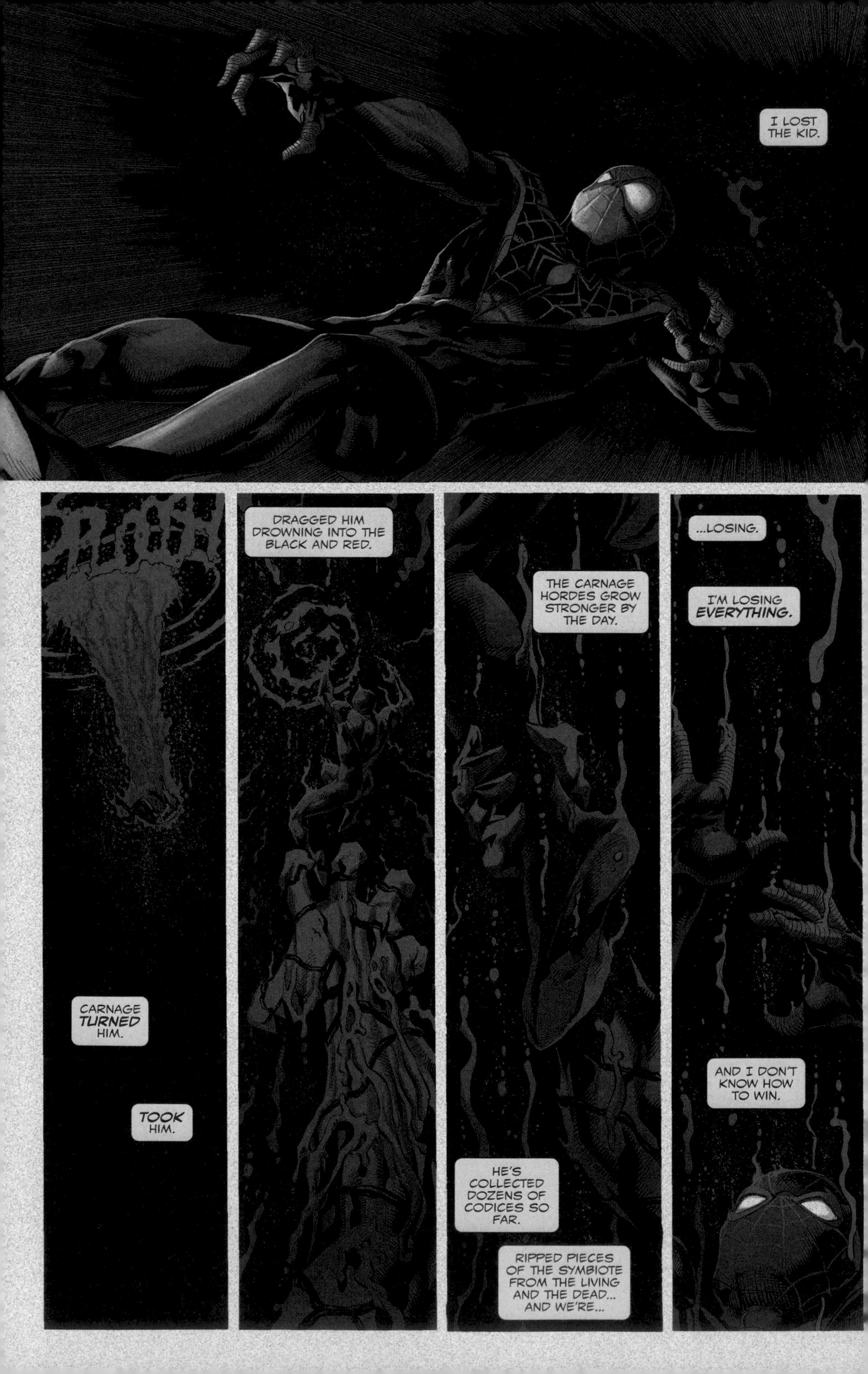
I LOST THE KID.
CARNAGE *TURNED* HIM.
TOOK HIM.
DRAGGED HIM DROWNING INTO THE BLACK AND RED.
THE CARNAGE HORDES GROW STRONGER BY THE DAY.
HE'S COLLECTED DOZENS OF CODICES SO FAR.
RIPPED PIECES OF THE SYMBIOTE FROM THE LIVING AND THE DEAD... AND WE'RE...
...LOSING.
I'M LOSING ***EVERYTHING.***
AND I DON'T KNOW HOW TO WIN.

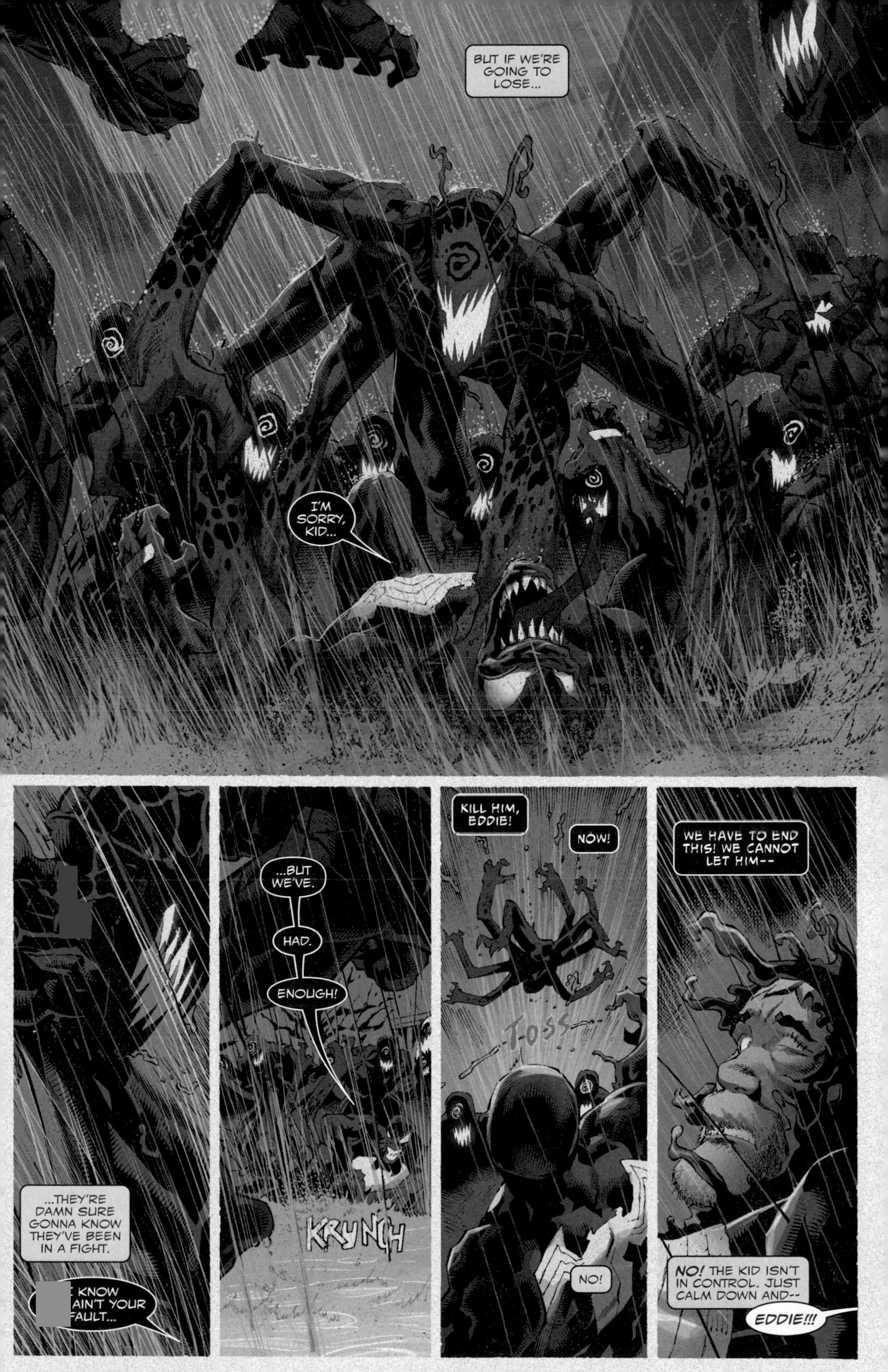
BUT IF WE'RE GOING TO LOSE...
I'M SORRY, KID...
...THEY'RE DAMN SURE GONNA KNOW THEY'VE BEEN IN A FIGHT.
[redacted] KNOW [redacted] AIN'T YOUR FAULT...
...BUT WE'VE.
HAD.
ENOUGH!
KRUNCH
KILL HIM, EDDIE!
NOW!
TOSS
NO!
WE HAVE TO END THIS! WE CANNOT LET HIM--
NO! THE KID ISN'T IN CONTROL. JUST CALM DOWN AND--
EDDIE!!!

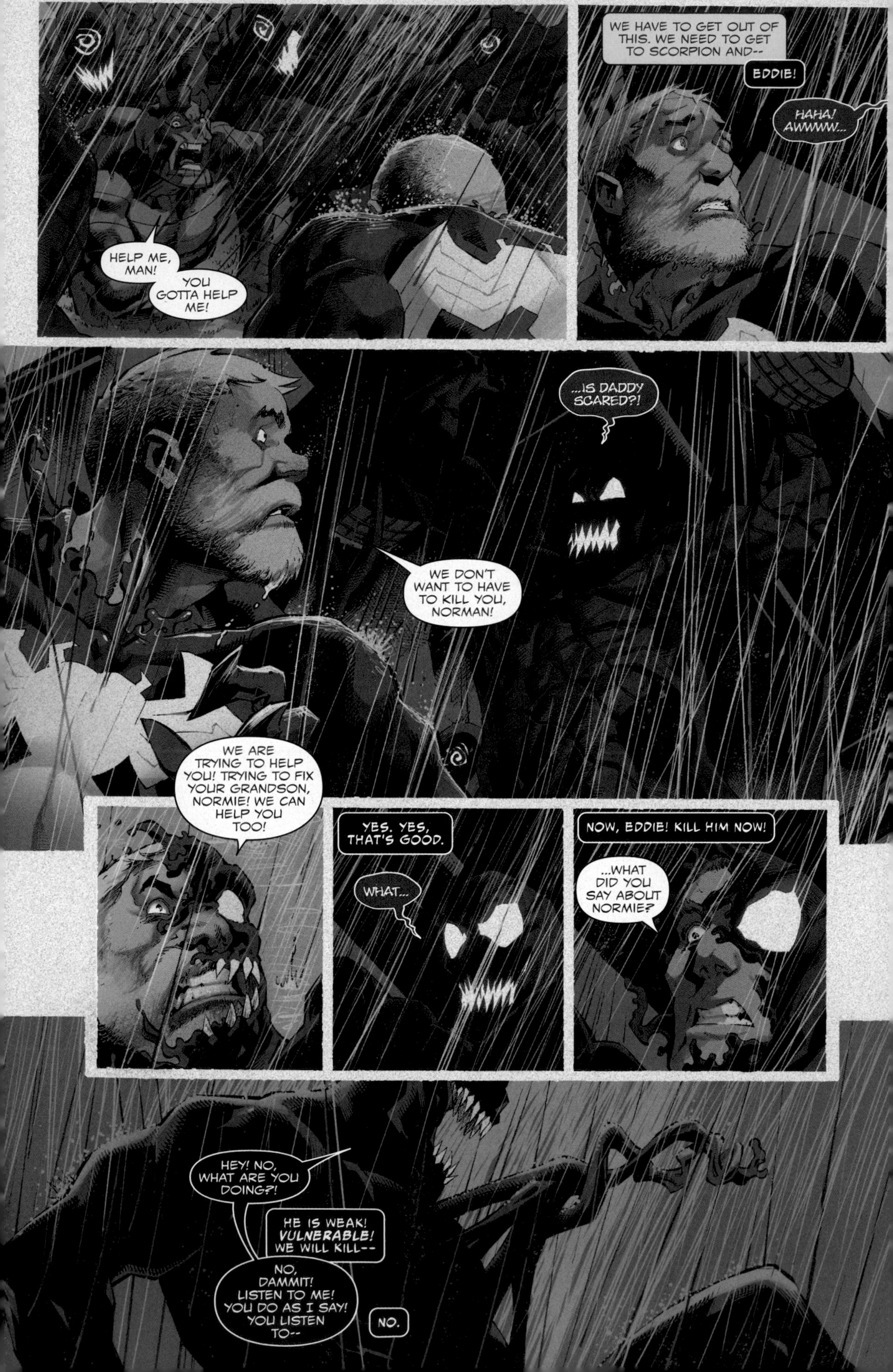
HELP ME, MAN!
YOU GOTTA HELP ME!
WE HAVE TO GET OUT OF THIS. WE NEED TO GET TO SCORPION AND--
EDDIE!
HAHA! AWWWW...
...IS DADDY SCARED?!
WE DON'T WANT TO HAVE TO KILL YOU, NORMAN!
WE ARE TRYING TO HELP YOU! TRYING TO FIX YOUR GRANDSON, NORMIE! WE CAN HELP YOU TOO!
YES. YES, THAT'S GOOD.
WHAT...
NOW, EDDIE! KILL HIM NOW!
...WHAT DID YOU SAY ABOUT NORMIE?
HEY! NO, WHAT ARE YOU DOING?!
HE IS WEAK! VULNERABLE! WE WILL KILL--
NO, DAMMIT! LISTEN TO ME! YOU DO AS I SAY! YOU LISTEN TO--
NO.

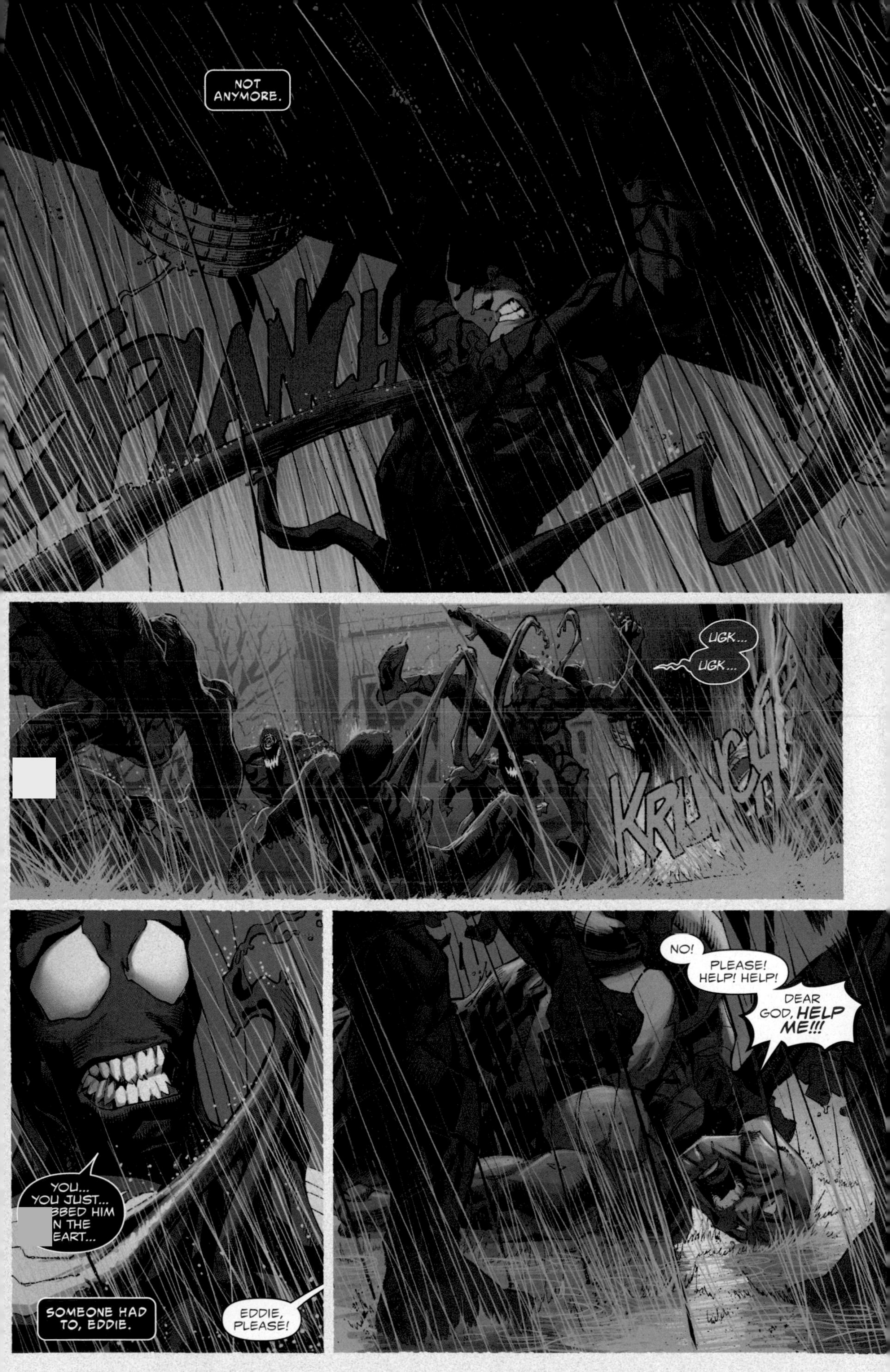
NOT ANYMORE.
UGK...
UGK...
KRUNCH
YOU... YOU JUST... BBED HIM N THE EART...
SOMEONE HAD TO, EDDIE.
EDDIE, PLEASE!
NO!
PLEASE! HELP! HELP!
DEAR GOD, HELP ME!!!

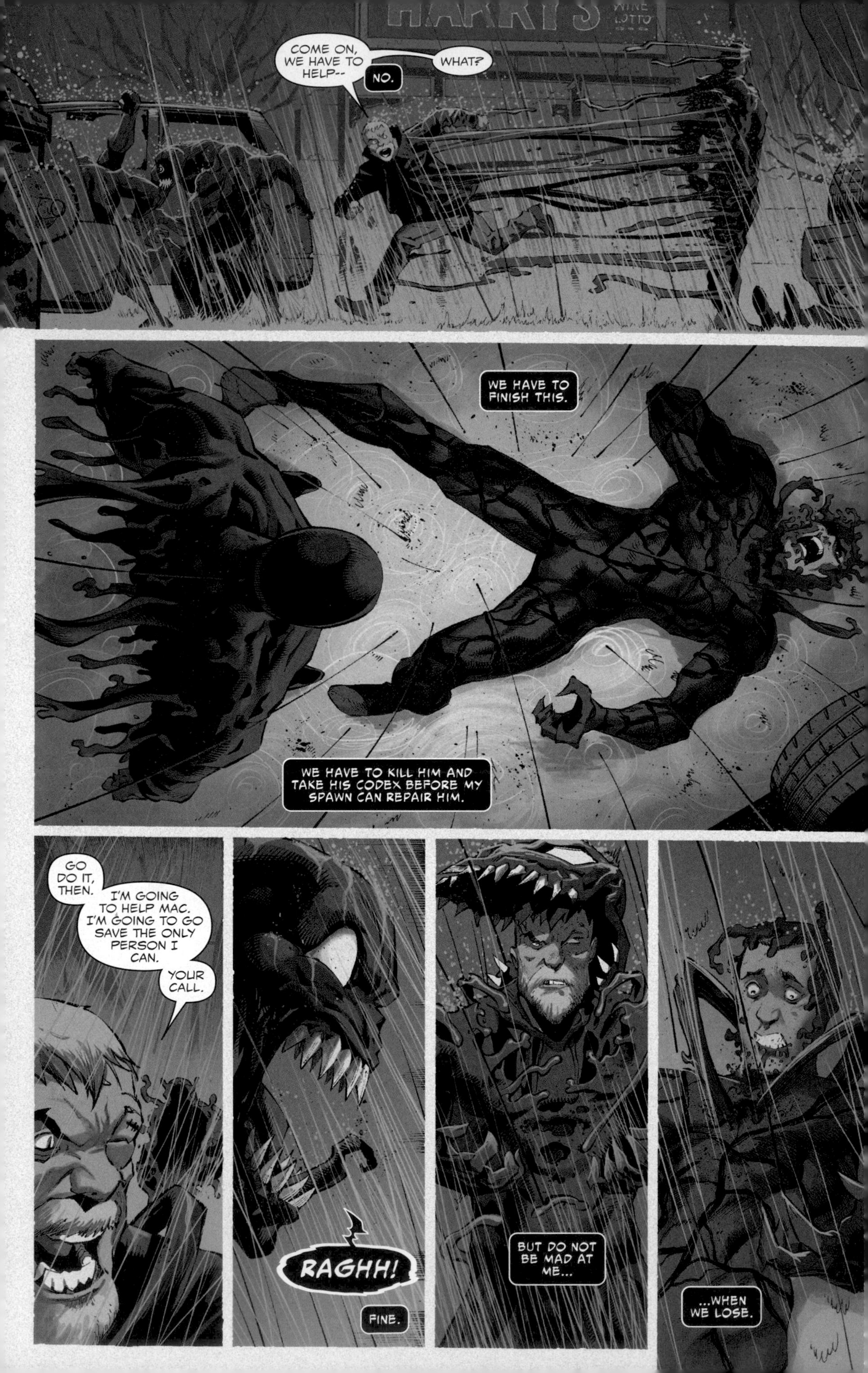

COME ON, WE HAVE TO HELP--
WHAT?
NO.
WE HAVE TO FINISH THIS.
WE HAVE TO KILL HIM AND TAKE HIS CODEX BEFORE MY SPAWN CAN REPAIR HIM.
GO DO IT, THEN.
I'M GOING TO HELP MAC. I'M GOING TO GO SAVE THE ONLY PERSON I CAN.
YOUR CALL.
RAGHH!
FINE.
BUT DO NOT BE MAD AT ME...
...WHEN WE LOSE.

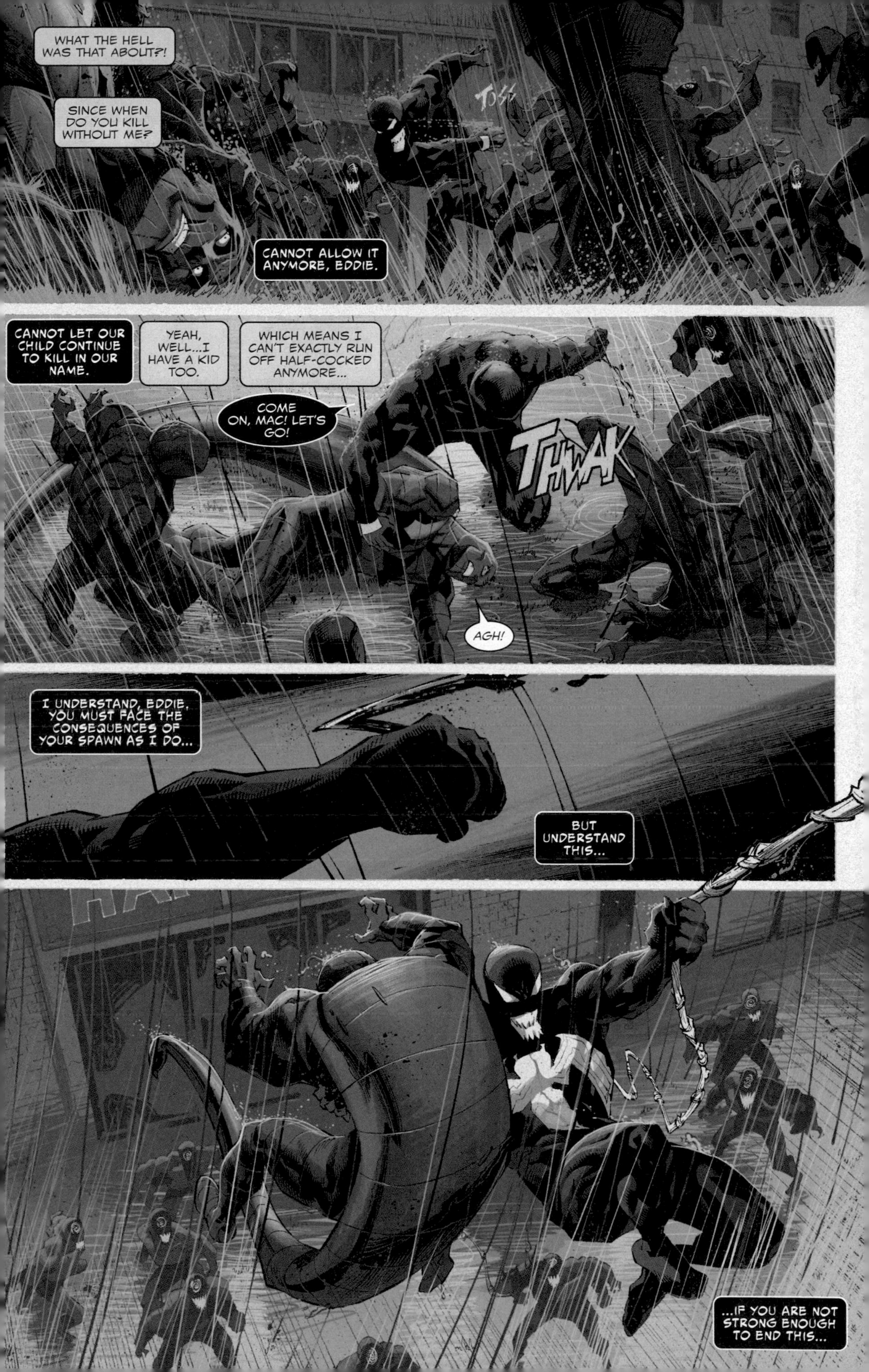
WHAT THE HELL WAS THAT ABOUT?!
SINCE WHEN DO YOU KILL WITHOUT ME?
TOSS
CANNOT ALLOW IT ANYMORE, EDDIE.
CANNOT LET OUR CHILD CONTINUE TO KILL IN OUR NAME.
YEAH, WELL...I HAVE A KID TOO.
WHICH MEANS I CAN'T EXACTLY RUN OFF HALF-COCKED ANYMORE...
COME ON, MAC! LET'S GO!
THWAK
AGH!
I UNDERSTAND, EDDIE. YOU MUST FACE THE CONSEQUENCES OF YOUR SPAWN AS I DO...
BUT UNDERSTAND THIS...
...IF YOU ARE NOT STRONG ENOUGH TO END THIS...

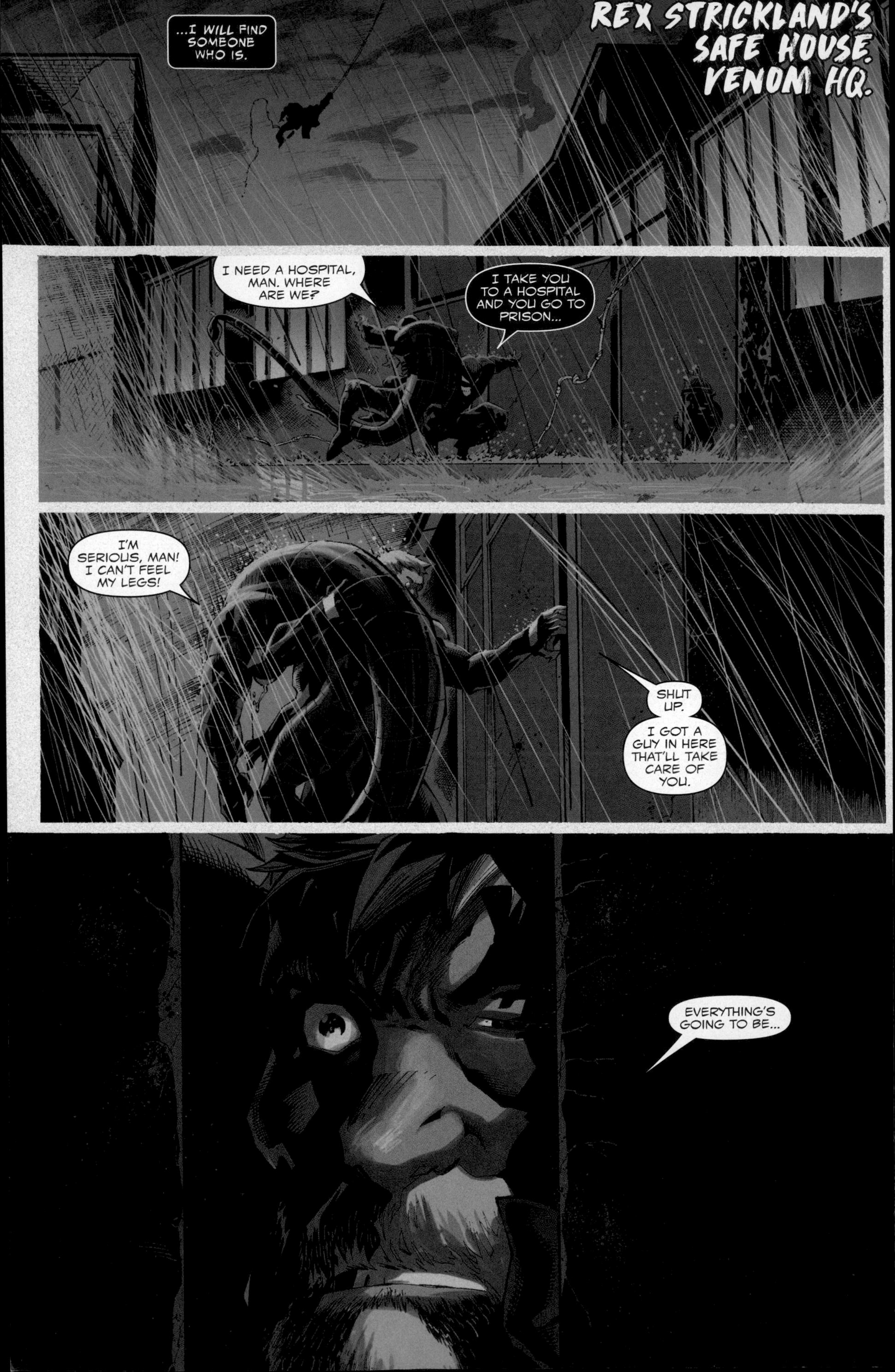

...I WILL FIND SOMEONE WHO IS.
REX STRICKLAND'S SAFE HOUSE. VENOM HQ.
I NEED A HOSPITAL, MAN. WHERE ARE WE?
I TAKE YOU TO A HOSPITAL AND YOU GO TO PRISON...
I'M SERIOUS, MAN! I CAN'T FEEL MY LEGS!
SHUT UP.
I GOT A GUY IN HERE THAT'LL TAKE CARE OF YOU.
EVERYTHING'S GOING TO BE...

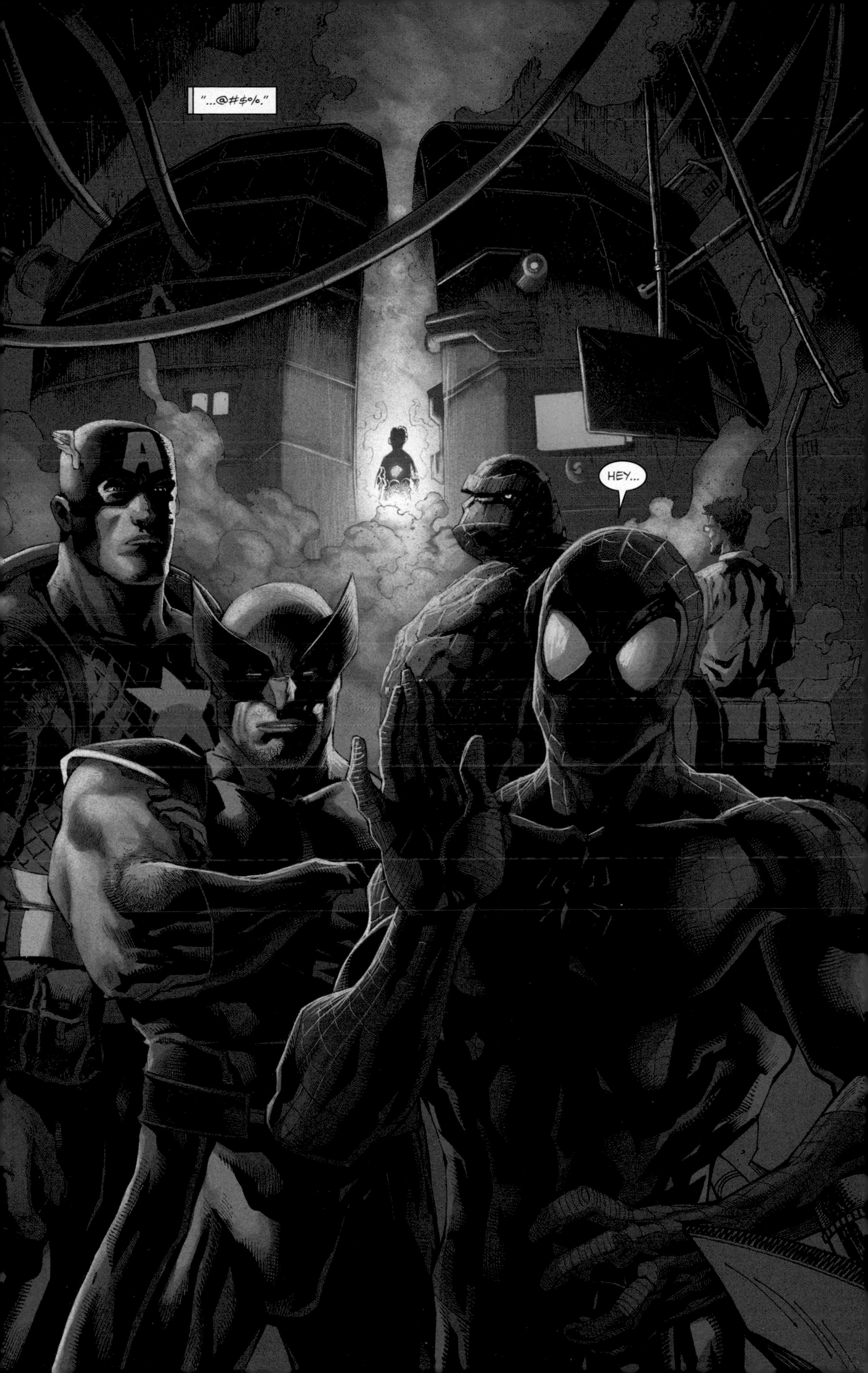
"...@#$%."
HEY...

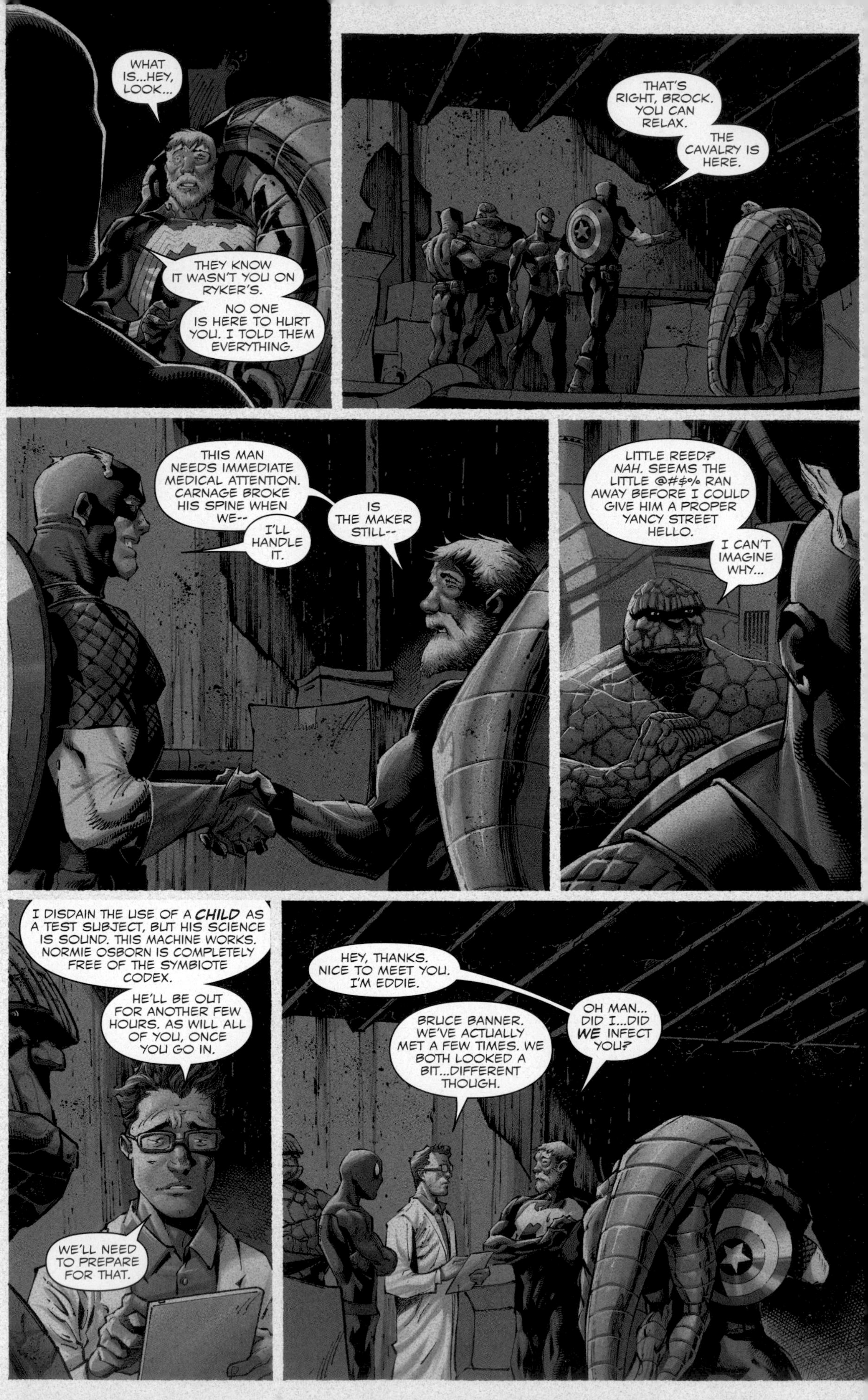
WHAT IS...HEY, LOOK...
THEY KNOW IT WASN'T YOU ON RYKER'S.
NO ONE IS HERE TO HURT YOU. I TOLD THEM EVERYTHING.
THAT'S RIGHT, BROCK. YOU CAN RELAX.
THE CAVALRY IS HERE.
THIS MAN NEEDS IMMEDIATE MEDICAL ATTENTION. CARNAGE BROKE HIS SPINE WHEN WE--
I'LL HANDLE IT.
IS THE MAKER STILL--
LITTLE REED? NAH. SEEMS THE LITTLE @#$% RAN AWAY BEFORE I COULD GIVE HIM A PROPER YANCY STREET HELLO.
I CAN'T IMAGINE WHY...
I DISDAIN THE USE OF A CHILD AS A TEST SUBJECT, BUT HIS SCIENCE IS SOUND. THIS MACHINE WORKS. NORMIE OSBORN IS COMPLETELY FREE OF THE SYMBIOTE CODEX.
HE'LL BE OUT FOR ANOTHER FEW HOURS. AS WILL ALL OF YOU, ONCE YOU GO IN.
WE'LL NEED TO PREPARE FOR THAT.
HEY, THANKS. NICE TO MEET YOU. I'M EDDIE.
BRUCE BANNER. WE'VE ACTUALLY MET A FEW TIMES. WE BOTH LOOKED A BIT...DIFFERENT THOUGH.
OH MAN... DID I...DID WE INFECT YOU?

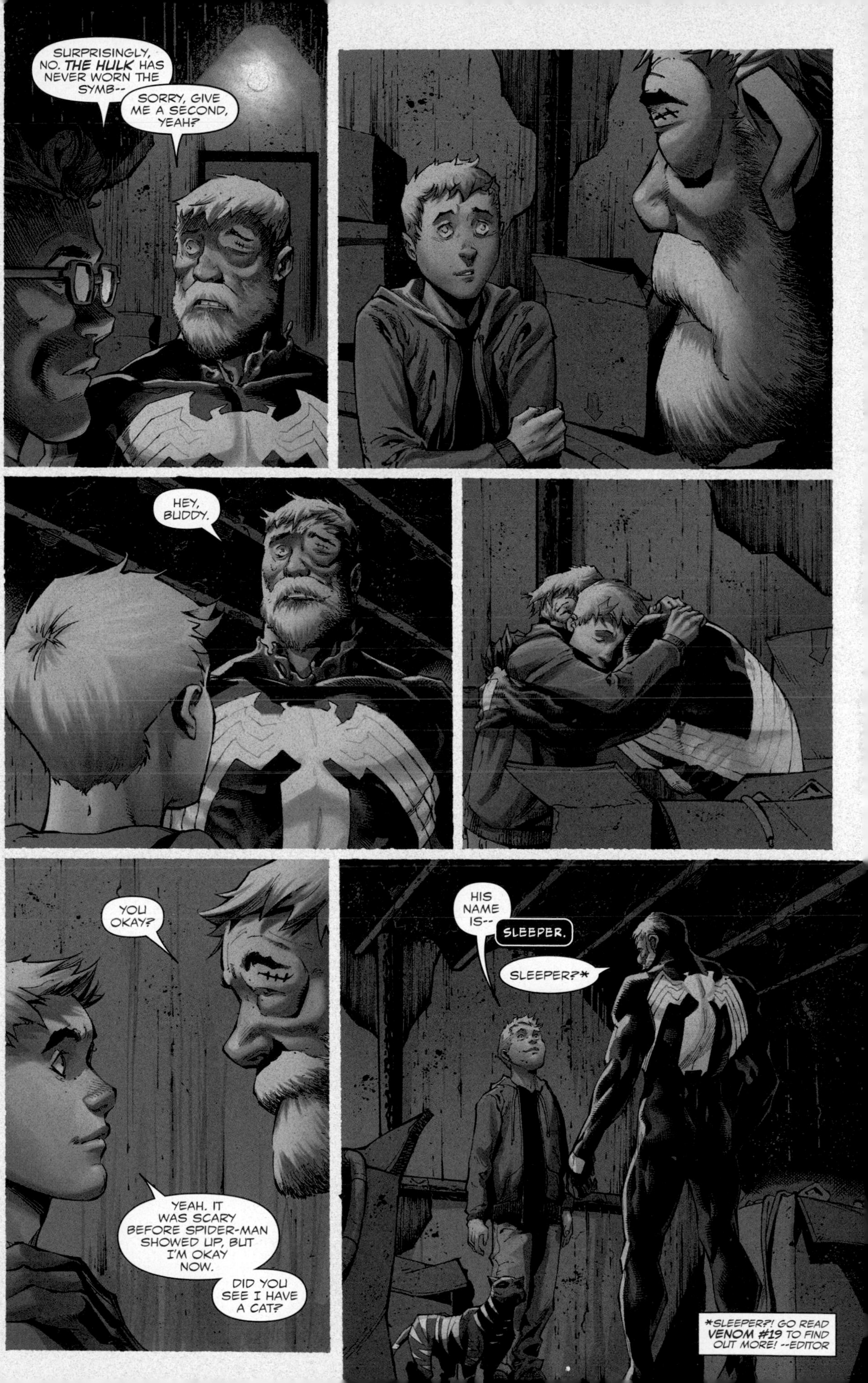
SURPRISINGLY, NO. THE HULK HAS NEVER WORN THE SYMB--
SORRY, GIVE ME A SECOND, YEAH?
HEY, BUDDY.
YOU OKAY?
YEAH. IT WAS SCARY BEFORE SPIDER-MAN SHOWED UP, BUT I'M OKAY NOW.
DID YOU SEE I HAVE A CAT?
HIS NAME IS--
SLEEPER.
SLEEPER?*
*SLEEPER?! GO READ VENOM #19 TO FIND OUT MORE! --EDITOR

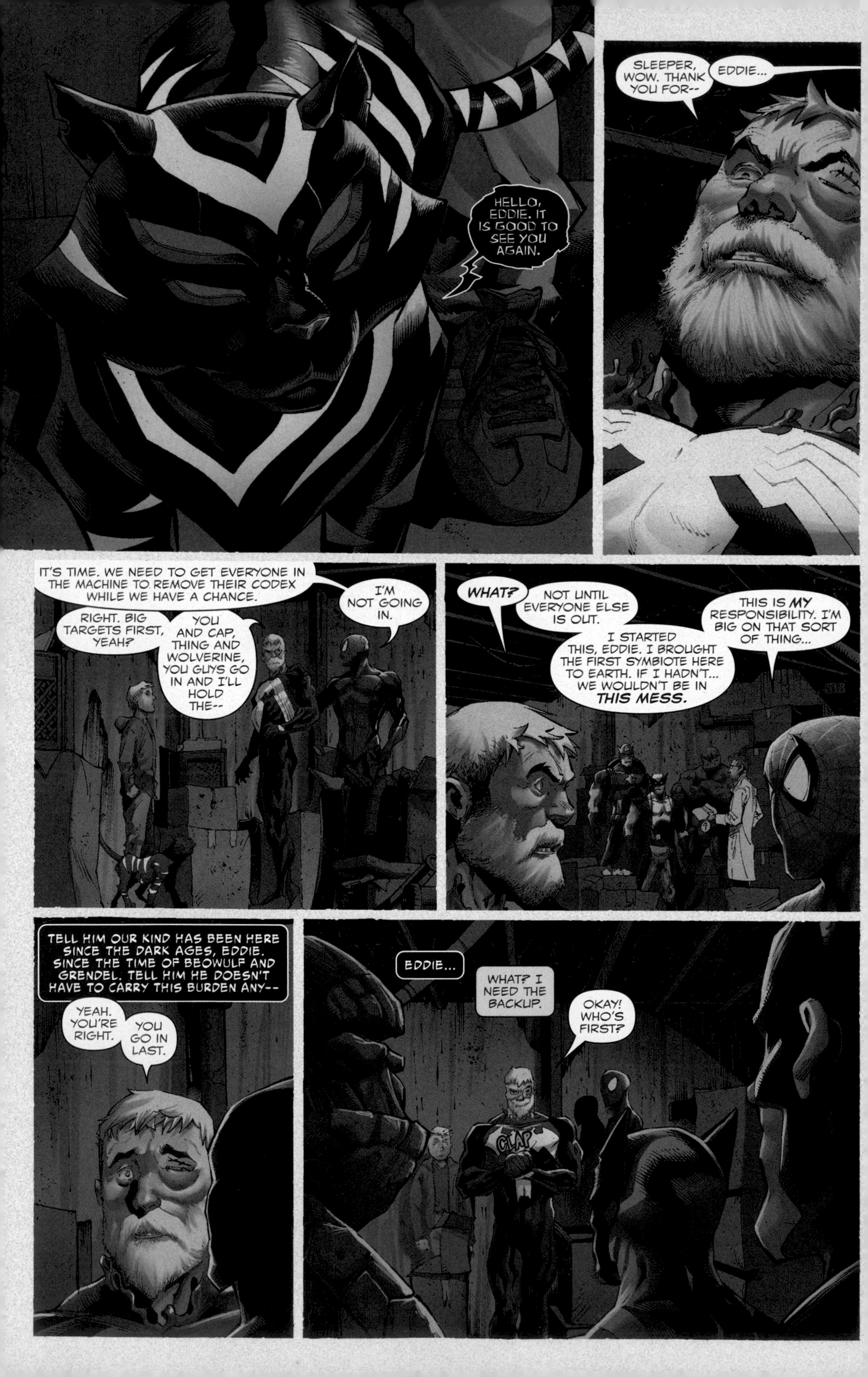
HELLO, EDDIE. IT IS GOOD TO SEE YOU AGAIN.
SLEEPER, WOW. THANK YOU FOR--
EDDIE...
IT'S TIME. WE NEED TO GET EVERYONE IN THE MACHINE TO REMOVE THEIR CODEX WHILE WE HAVE A CHANCE.
I'M NOT GOING IN.
RIGHT. BIG TARGETS FIRST, YEAH?
YOU AND CAP, THING AND WOLVERINE, YOU GUYS GO IN AND I'LL HOLD THE--
WHAT?
NOT UNTIL EVERYONE ELSE IS OUT.
I STARTED THIS, EDDIE. I BROUGHT THE FIRST SYMBIOTE HERE TO EARTH. IF I HADN'T... WE WOULDN'T BE IN THIS MESS.
THIS IS MY RESPONSIBILITY. I'M BIG ON THAT SORT OF THING...
TELL HIM OUR KIND HAS BEEN HERE SINCE THE DARK AGES, EDDIE. SINCE THE TIME OF BEOWULF AND GRENDEL. TELL HIM HE DOESN'T HAVE TO CARRY THIS BURDEN ANY--
YEAH. YOU'RE RIGHT.
YOU GO IN LAST.
EDDIE...
WHAT? I NEED THE BACKUP.
OKAY! WHO'S FIRST?
CLAP

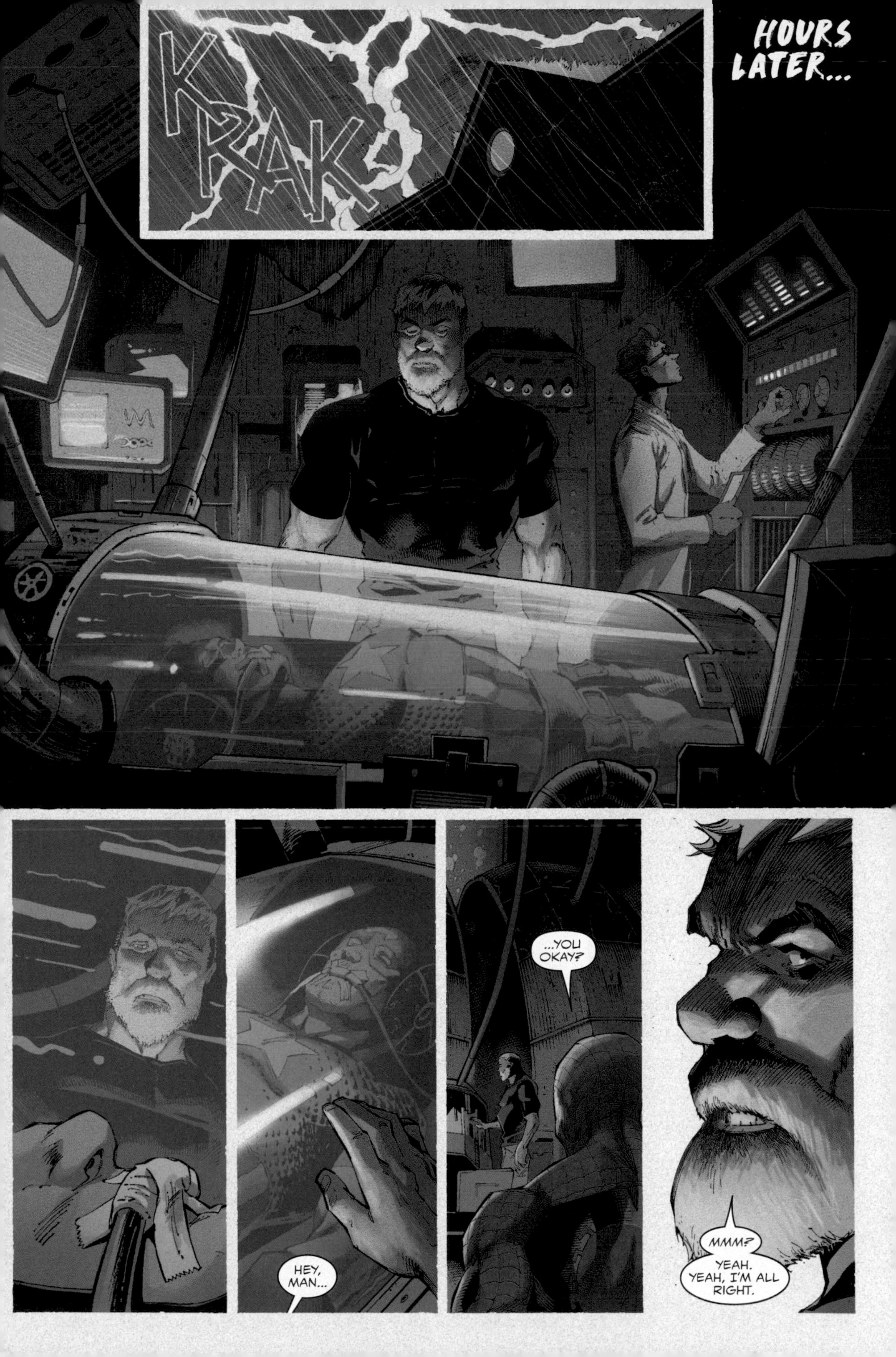
KRAK
HOURS LATER...
HEY, MAN...
...YOU OKAY?
MMM?
YEAH. YEAH, I'M ALL RIGHT.

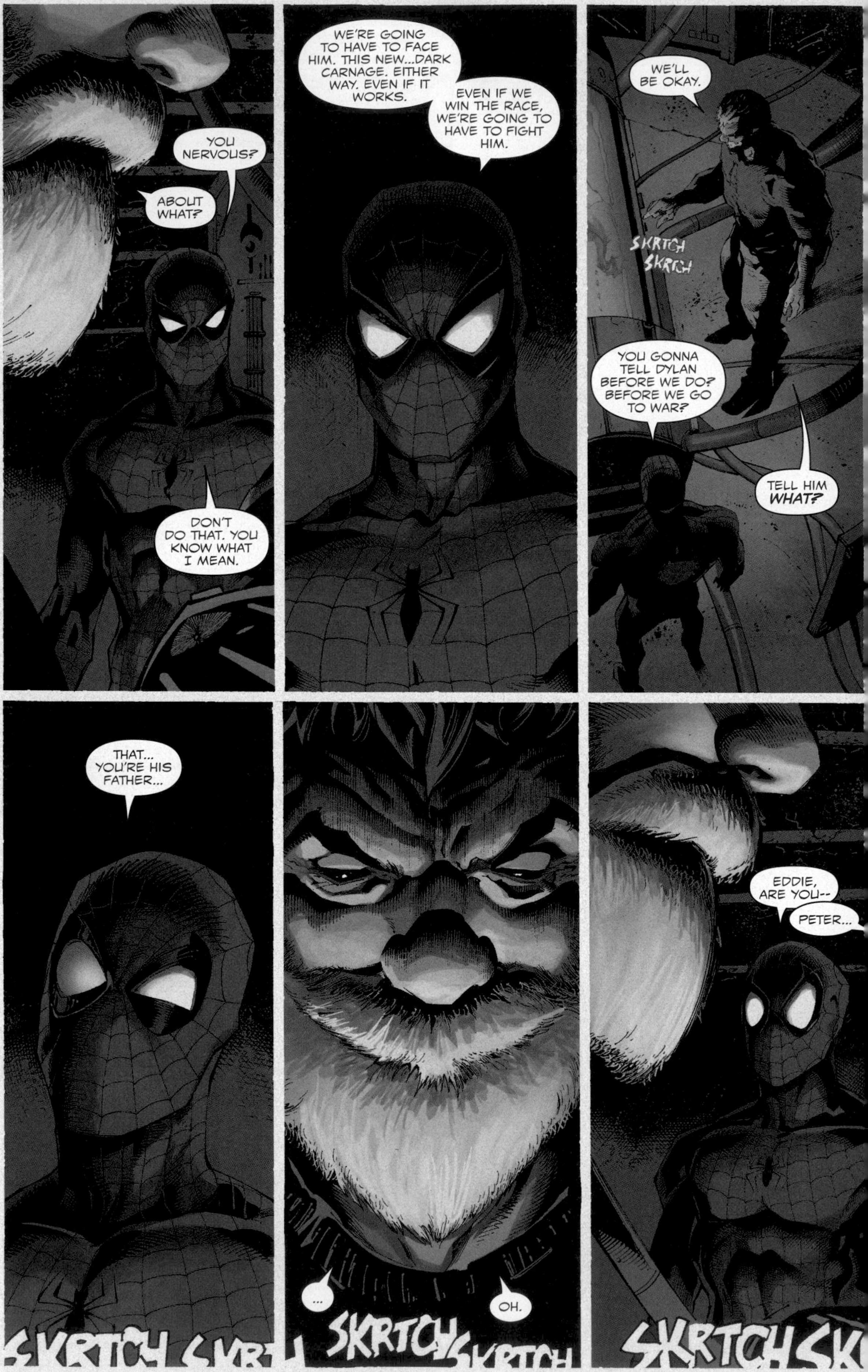

YOU NERVOUS?
ABOUT WHAT?
DON'T DO THAT. YOU KNOW WHAT I MEAN.
WE'RE GOING TO HAVE TO FACE HIM. THIS NEW...DARK CARNAGE. EITHER WAY. EVEN IF IT WORKS.
EVEN IF WE WIN THE RACE, WE'RE GOING TO HAVE TO FIGHT HIM.
WE'LL BE OKAY.
SKRTCH
SKRTCH
YOU GONNA TELL DYLAN BEFORE WE DO? BEFORE WE GO TO WAR?
TELL HIM WHAT?
THAT... YOU'RE HIS FATHER...
...
OH.
SKRTCH
SKRTCH
EDDIE, ARE YOU--
PETER...
SKRTCH

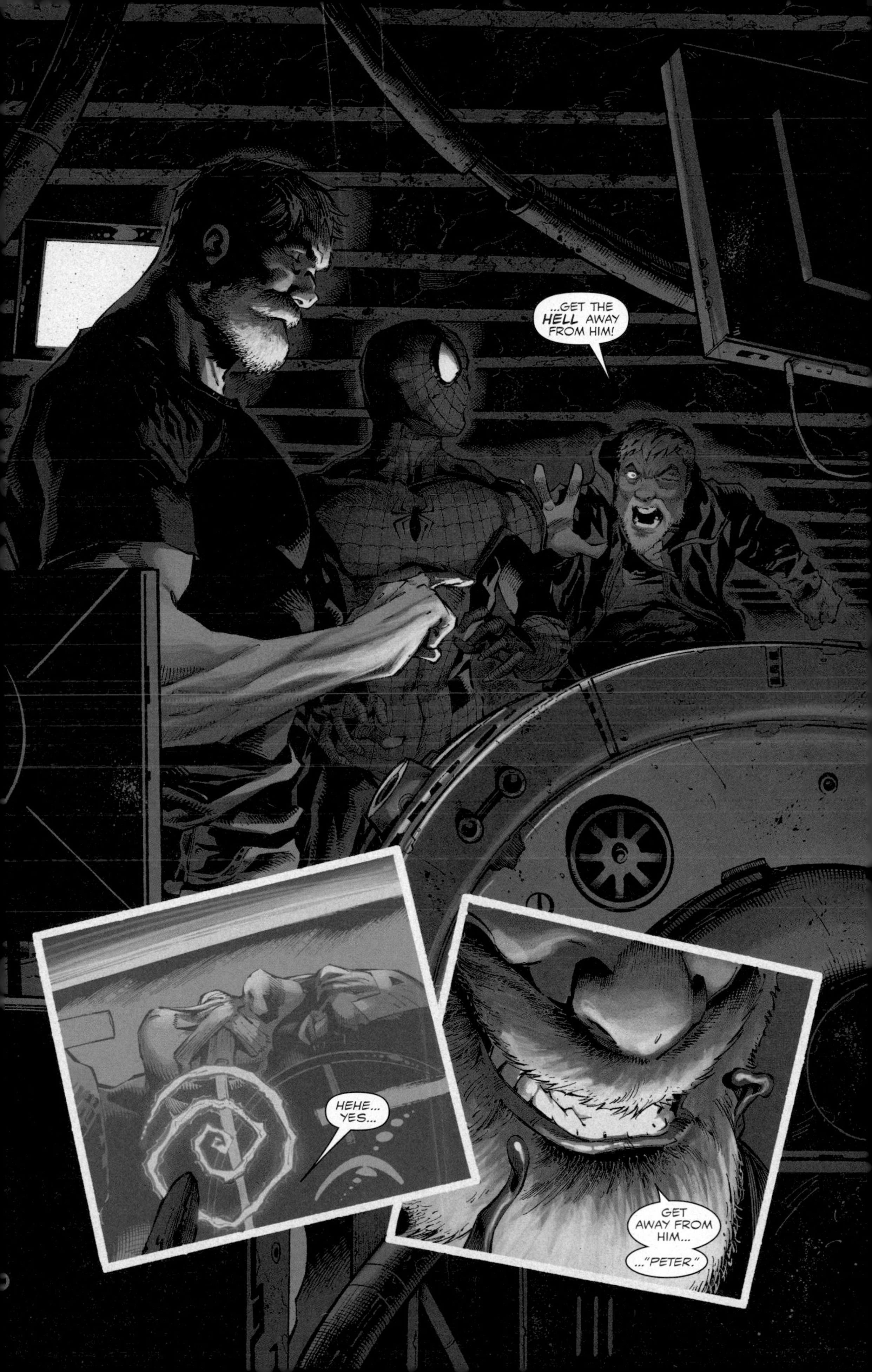
...GET THE HELL AWAY FROM HIM!
HEHE... YES...
GET AWAY FROM HIM...
..."PETER."

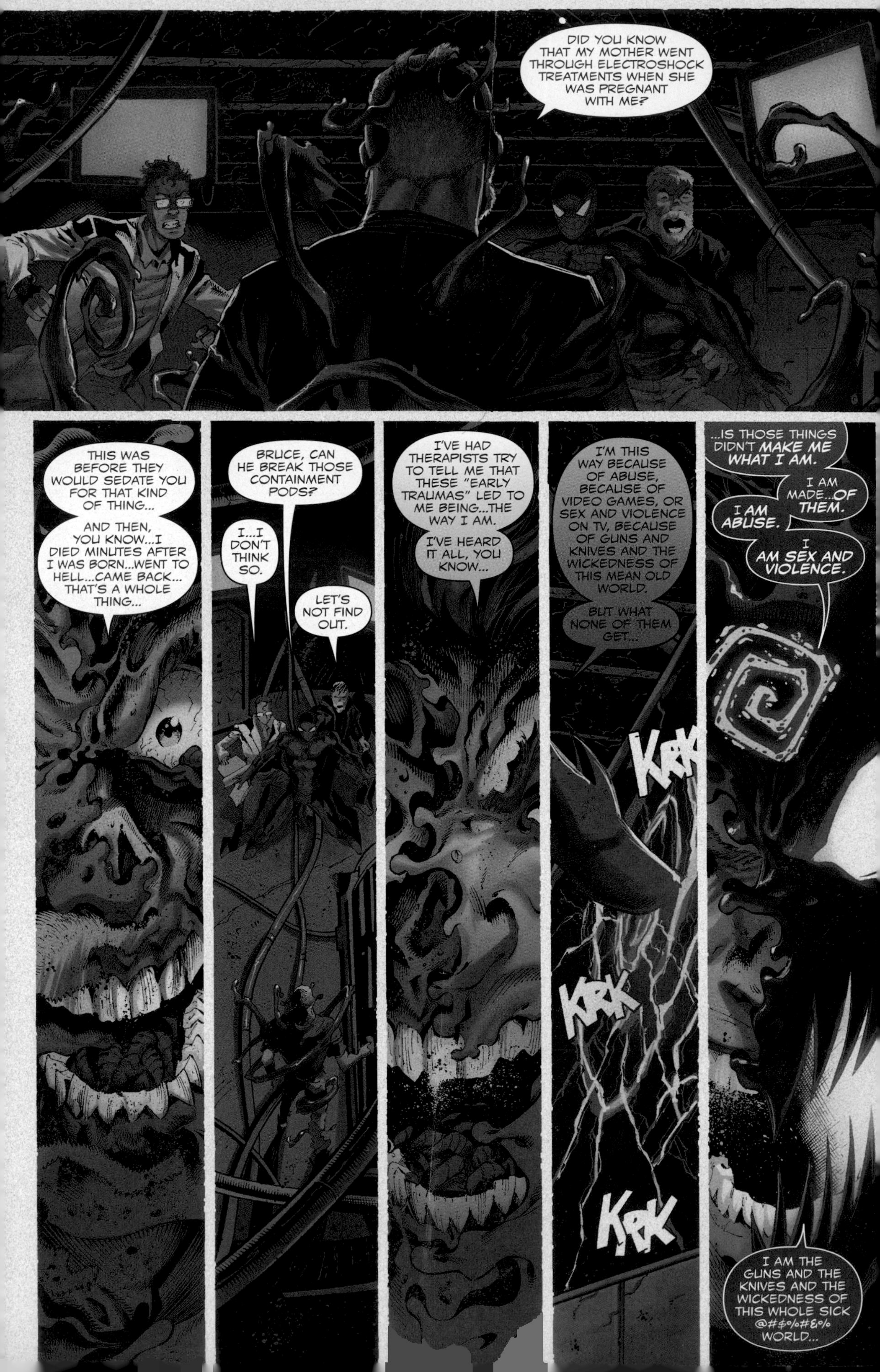
DID YOU KNOW THAT MY MOTHER WENT THROUGH ELECTROSHOCK TREATMENTS WHEN SHE WAS PREGNANT WITH ME?
THIS WAS BEFORE THEY WOULD SEDATE YOU FOR THAT KIND OF THING...
AND THEN, YOU KNOW...I DIED MINUTES AFTER I WAS BORN...WENT TO HELL...CAME BACK... THAT'S A WHOLE THING...
BRUCE, CAN HE BREAK THOSE CONTAINMENT PODS?
I...I DON'T THINK SO.
LET'S NOT FIND OUT.
I'VE HAD THERAPISTS TRY TO TELL ME THAT THESE "EARLY TRAUMAS" LED TO ME BEING...THE WAY I AM.
I'VE HEARD IT ALL, YOU KNOW...
I'M THIS WAY BECAUSE OF ABUSE, BECAUSE OF VIDEO GAMES, OR SEX AND VIOLENCE ON TV, BECAUSE OF GUNS AND KNIVES AND THE WICKEDNESS OF THIS MEAN OLD WORLD.
BUT WHAT NONE OF THEM GET...
KRK
KRK
KRK
...IS THOSE THINGS DIDN'T MAKE ME WHAT I AM.
I AM MADE...OF THEM.
I AM ABUSE.
I AM SEX AND VIOLENCE.
I AM THE GUNS AND THE KNIVES AND THE WICKEDNESS OF THIS WHOLE SICK @#$%#&% WORLD...

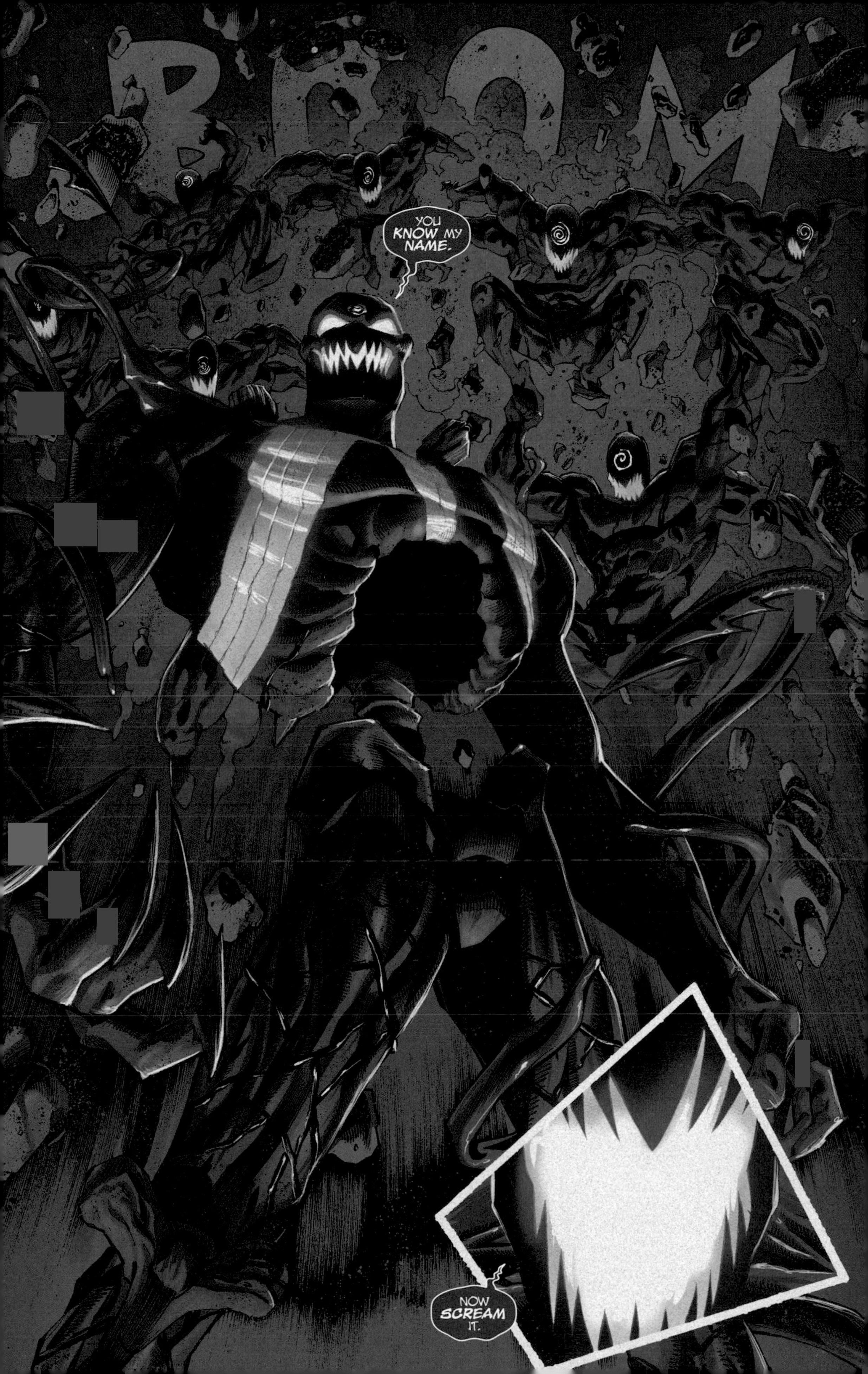
YOU KNOW MY NAME.
NOW SCREAM IT.

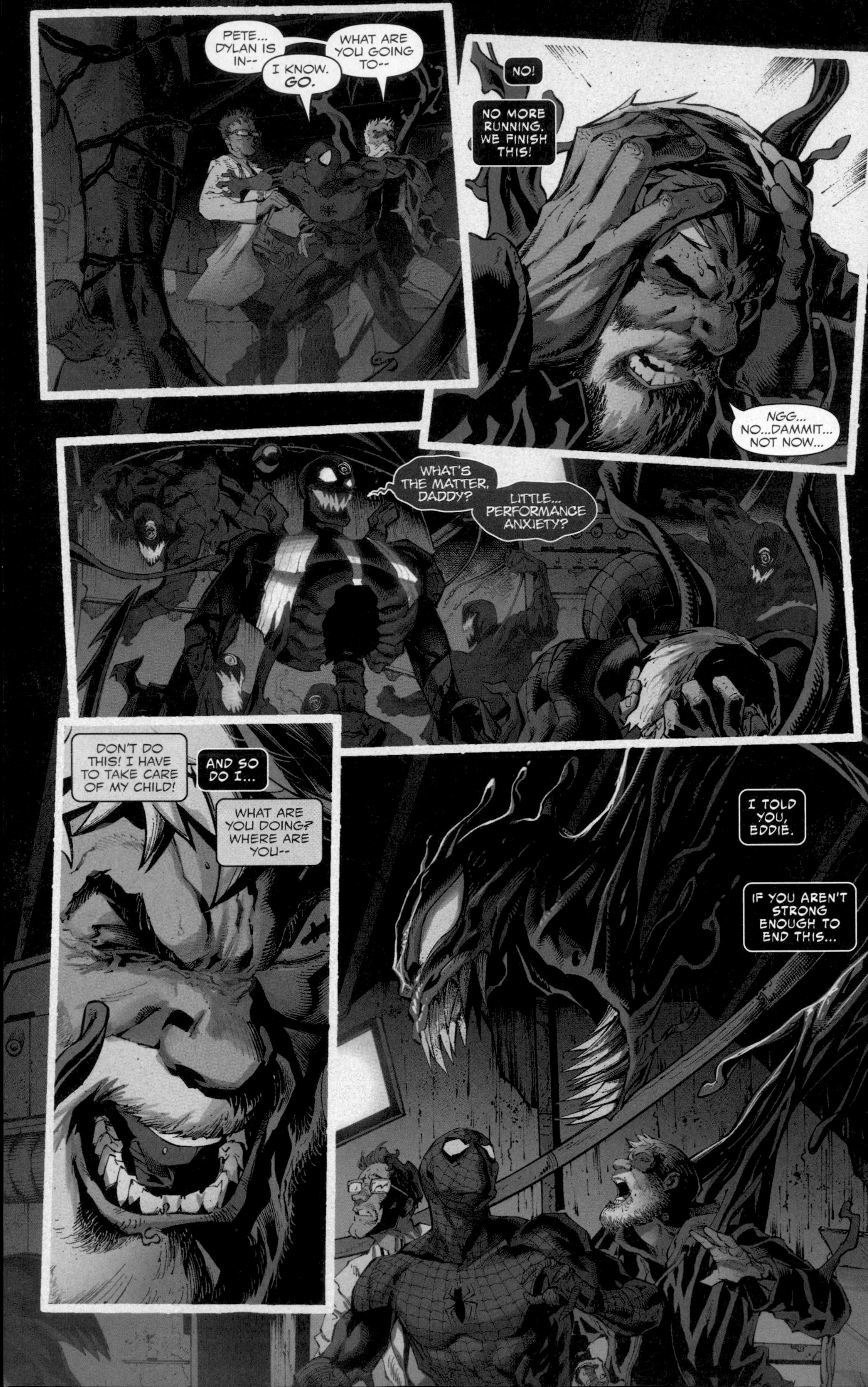
PETE... DYLAN IS IN--
I KNOW. GO.
WHAT ARE YOU GOING TO--
NO!
NO MORE RUNNING. WE FINISH THIS!
NGG... NO...DAMMIT... NOT NOW...
WHAT'S THE MATTER, DADDY?
LITTLE... PERFORMANCE ANXIETY?
DON'T DO THIS! I HAVE TO TAKE CARE OF MY CHILD!
AND SO DO I...
WHAT ARE YOU DOING? WHERE ARE YOU--
I TOLD YOU, EDDIE.
IF YOU AREN'T STRONG ENOUGH TO END THIS...

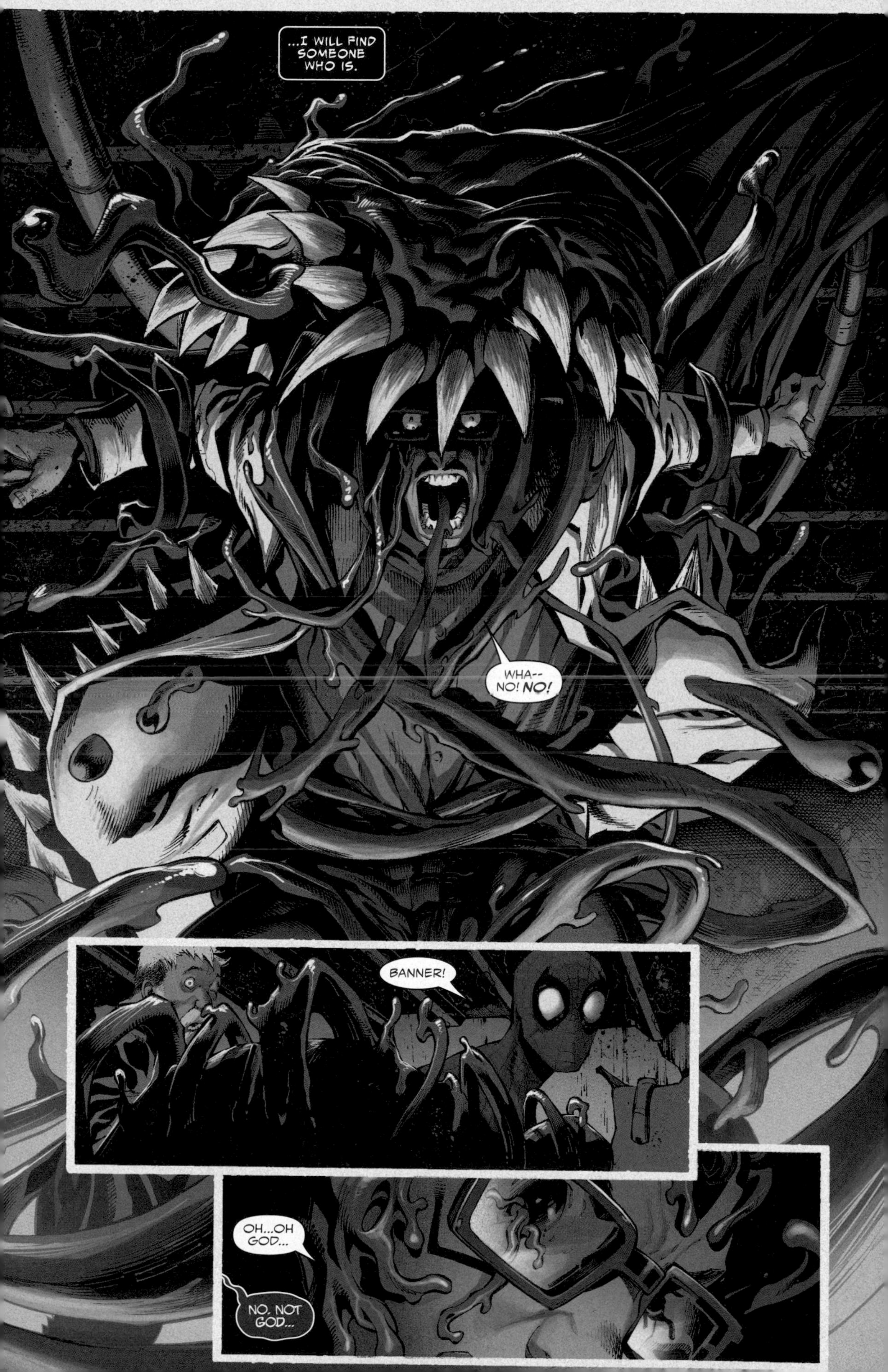
...I WILL FIND SOMEONE WHO IS.
WHA-- NO! NO!
BANNER!
OH...OH GOD...
NO. NOT GOD...

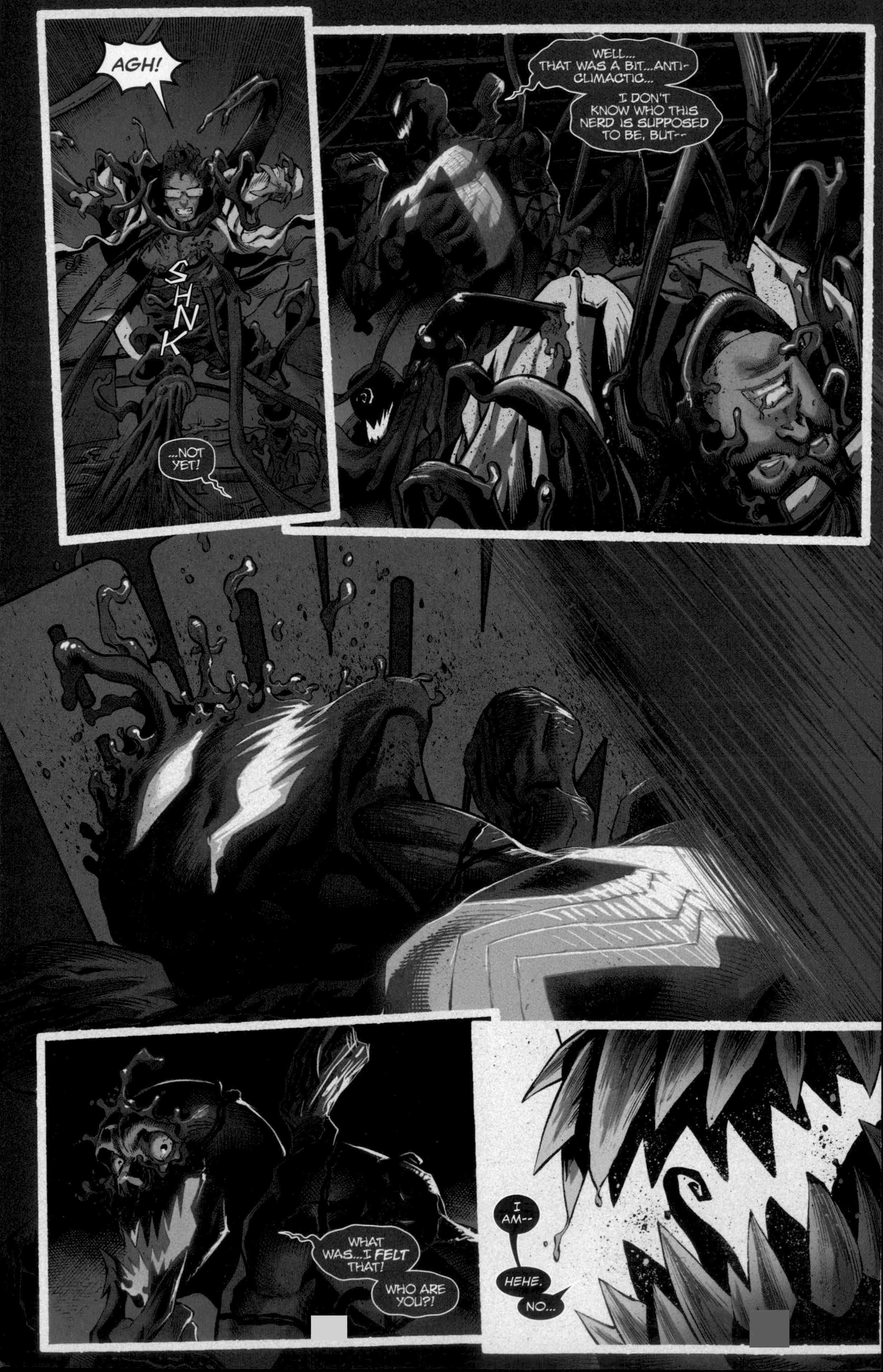
AGH!
SHNK
...NOT YET!
WELL... THAT WAS A BIT...ANTI-CLIMACTIC...
I DON'T KNOW WHO THIS NERD IS SUPPOSED TO BE, BUT--
WHAT WAS...I FELT THAT!
WHO ARE YOU?!
I AM--
HEHE. NO...

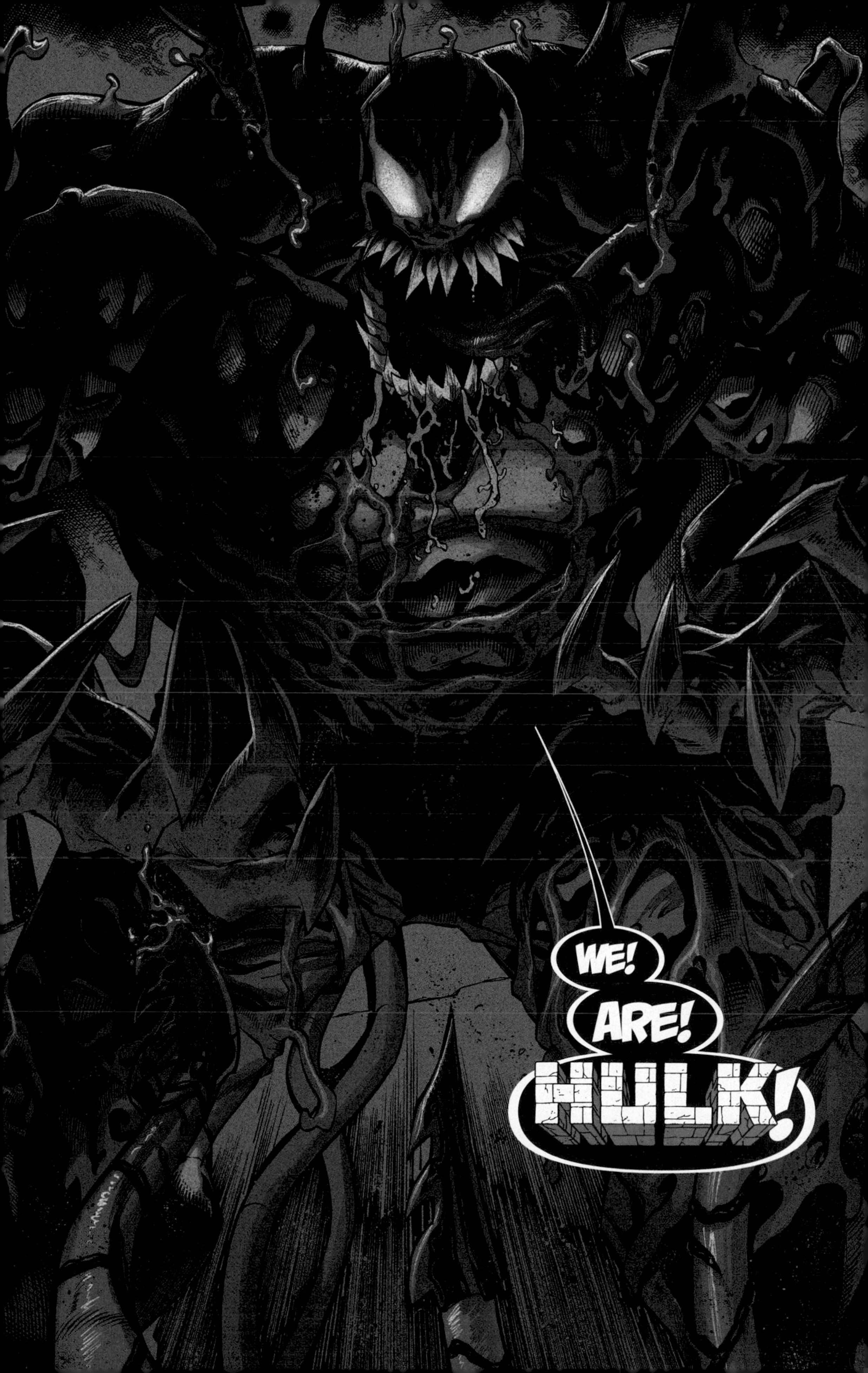
WE!
ARE!
HULK!

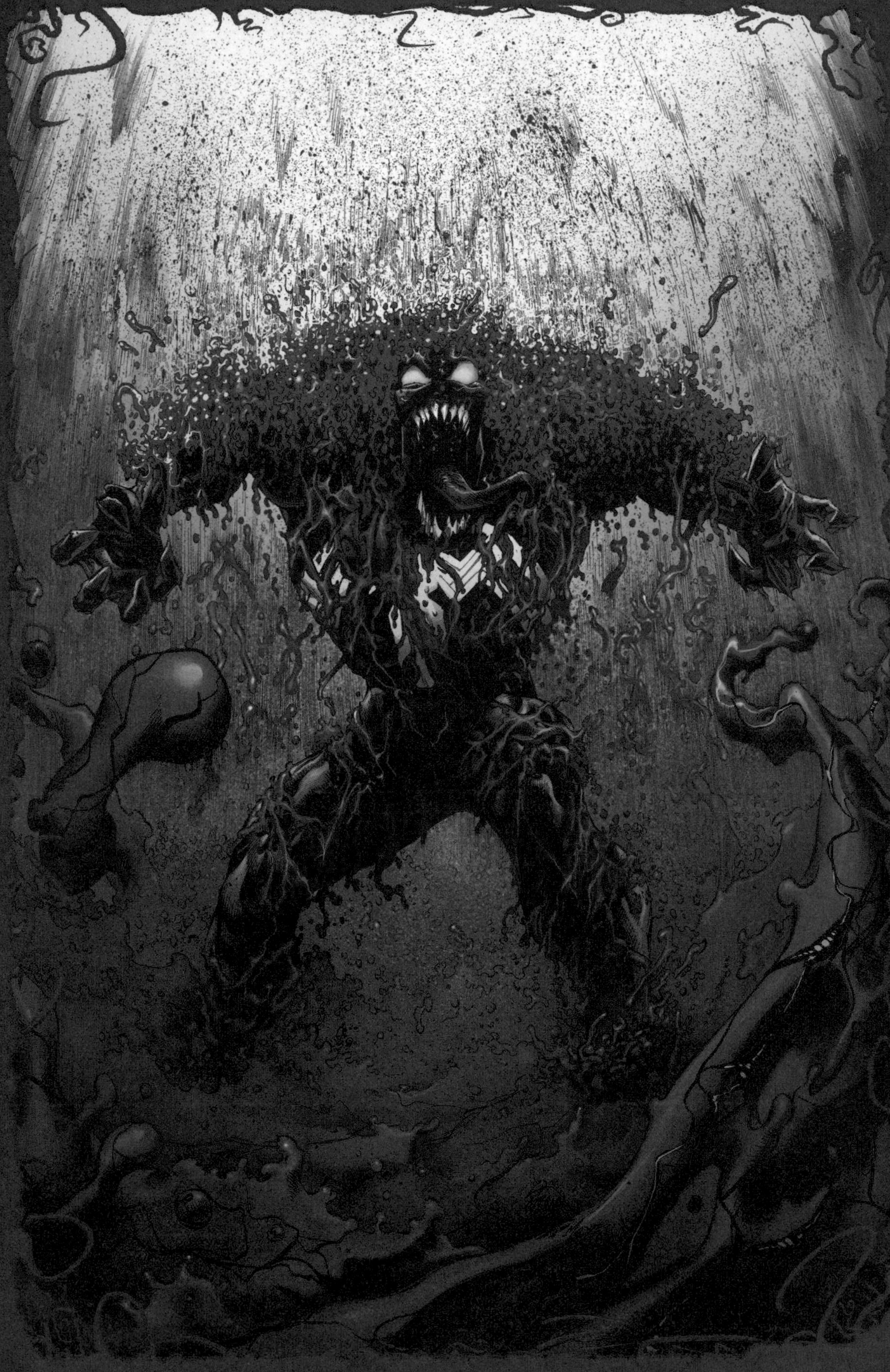

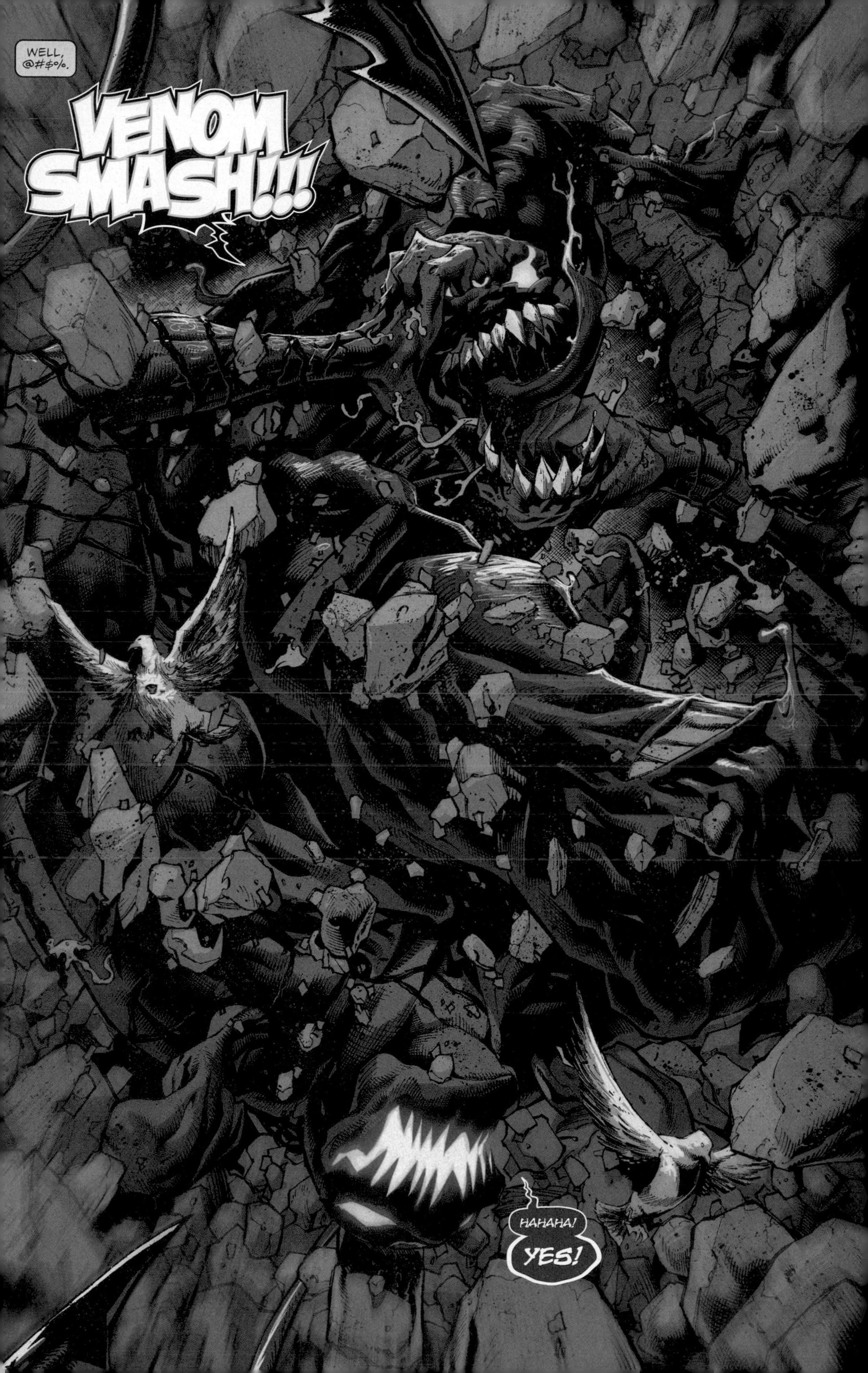
WELL, @#$%.
VENOM SMASH!!!
HAHAHA!
YES!

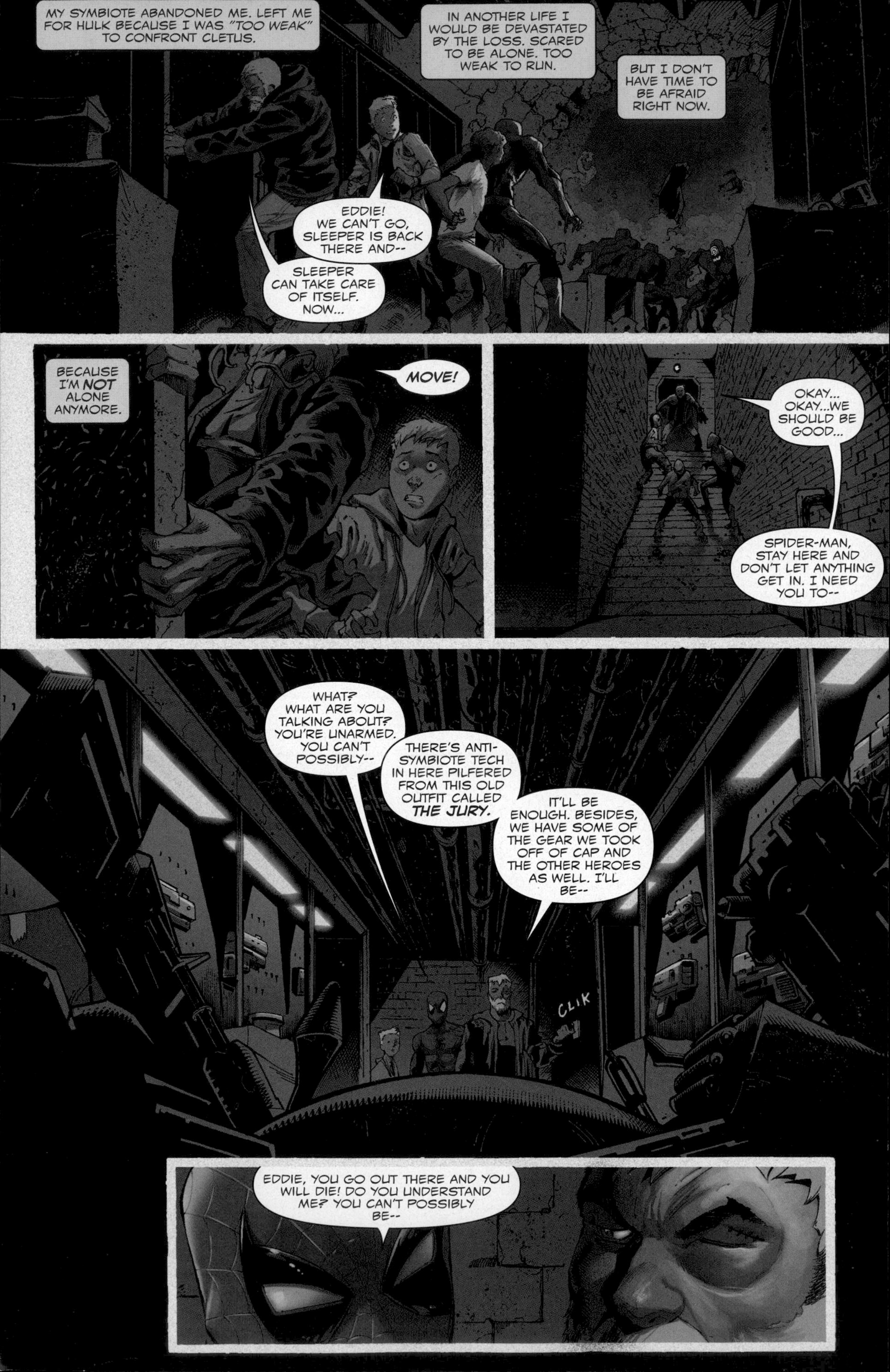
MY SYMBIOTE ABANDONED ME. LEFT ME FOR HULK BECAUSE I WAS "TOO WEAK" TO CONFRONT CLETUS.
IN ANOTHER LIFE I WOULD BE DEVASTATED BY THE LOSS. SCARED TO BE ALONE. TOO WEAK TO RUN.
BUT I DON'T HAVE TIME TO BE AFRAID RIGHT NOW.
EDDIE! WE CAN'T GO, SLEEPER IS BACK THERE AND--
SLEEPER CAN TAKE CARE OF ITSELF. NOW...
BECAUSE I'M NOT ALONE ANYMORE.
MOVE!
OKAY... OKAY...WE SHOULD BE GOOD...
SPIDER-MAN, STAY HERE AND DON'T LET ANYTHING GET IN. I NEED YOU TO--
WHAT? WHAT ARE YOU TALKING ABOUT? YOU'RE UNARMED. YOU CAN'T POSSIBLY--
THERE'S ANTI-SYMBIOTE TECH IN HERE PILFERED FROM THIS OLD OUTFIT CALLED THE JURY.
IT'LL BE ENOUGH. BESIDES, WE HAVE SOME OF THE GEAR WE TOOK OFF OF CAP AND THE OTHER HEROES AS WELL. I'LL BE--
CLIK
EDDIE, YOU GO OUT THERE AND YOU WILL DIE! DO YOU UNDERSTAND ME? YOU CAN'T POSSIBLY BE--

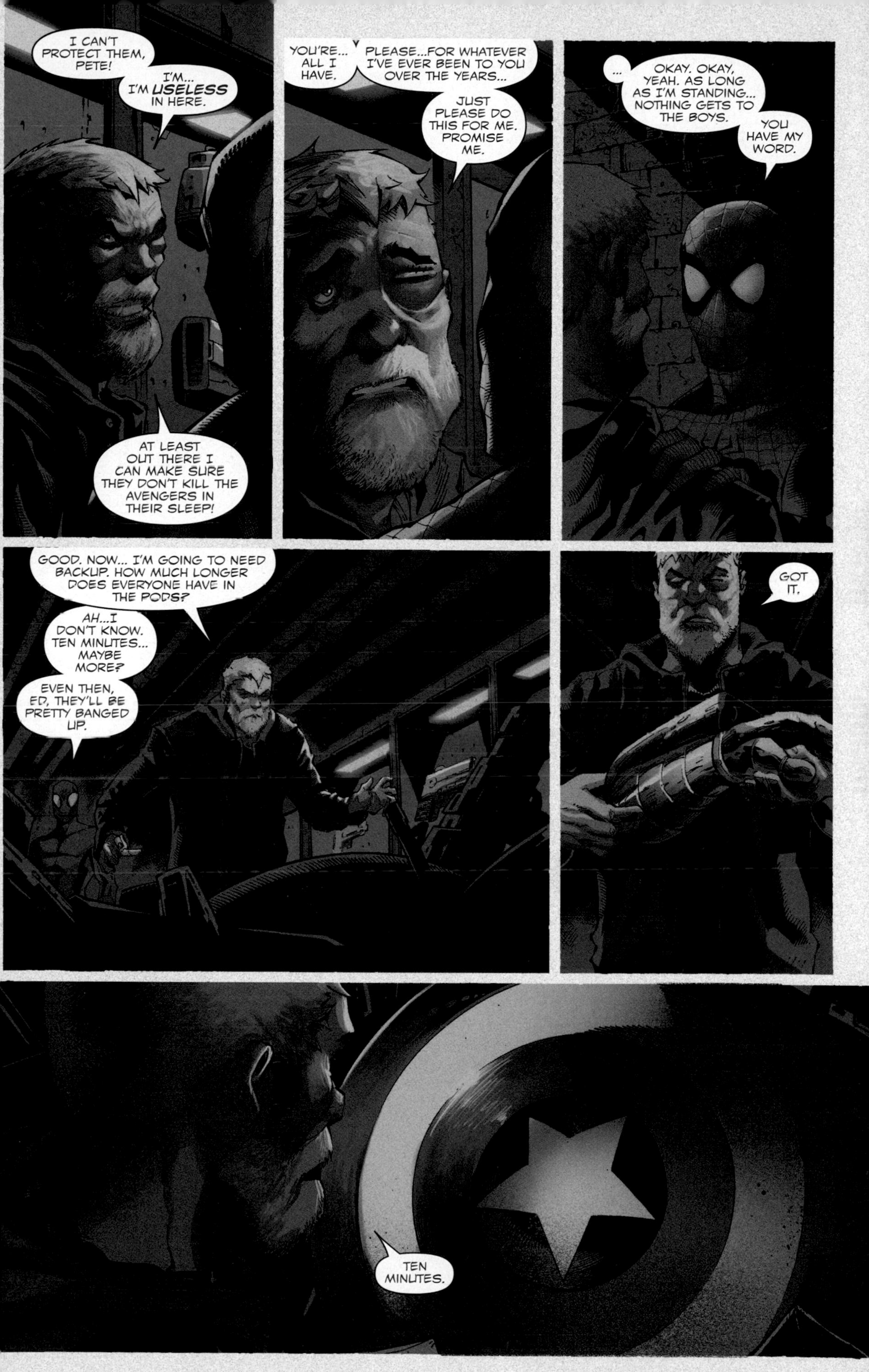
I CAN'T PROTECT THEM, PETE!
I'M... I'M USELESS IN HERE.
AT LEAST OUT THERE I CAN MAKE SURE THEY DON'T KILL THE AVENGERS IN THEIR SLEEP!
YOU'RE... ALL I HAVE.
PLEASE...FOR WHATEVER I'VE EVER BEEN TO YOU OVER THE YEARS...
JUST PLEASE DO THIS FOR ME. PROMISE ME.
...
OKAY. OKAY, YEAH. AS LONG AS I'M STANDING... NOTHING GETS TO THE BOYS.
YOU HAVE MY WORD.
GOOD. NOW... I'M GOING TO NEED BACKUP. HOW MUCH LONGER DOES EVERYONE HAVE IN THE PODS?
AH...I DON'T KNOW. TEN MINUTES... MAYBE MORE?
EVEN THEN, ED, THEY'LL BE PRETTY BANGED UP.
GOT IT.
TEN MINUTES.

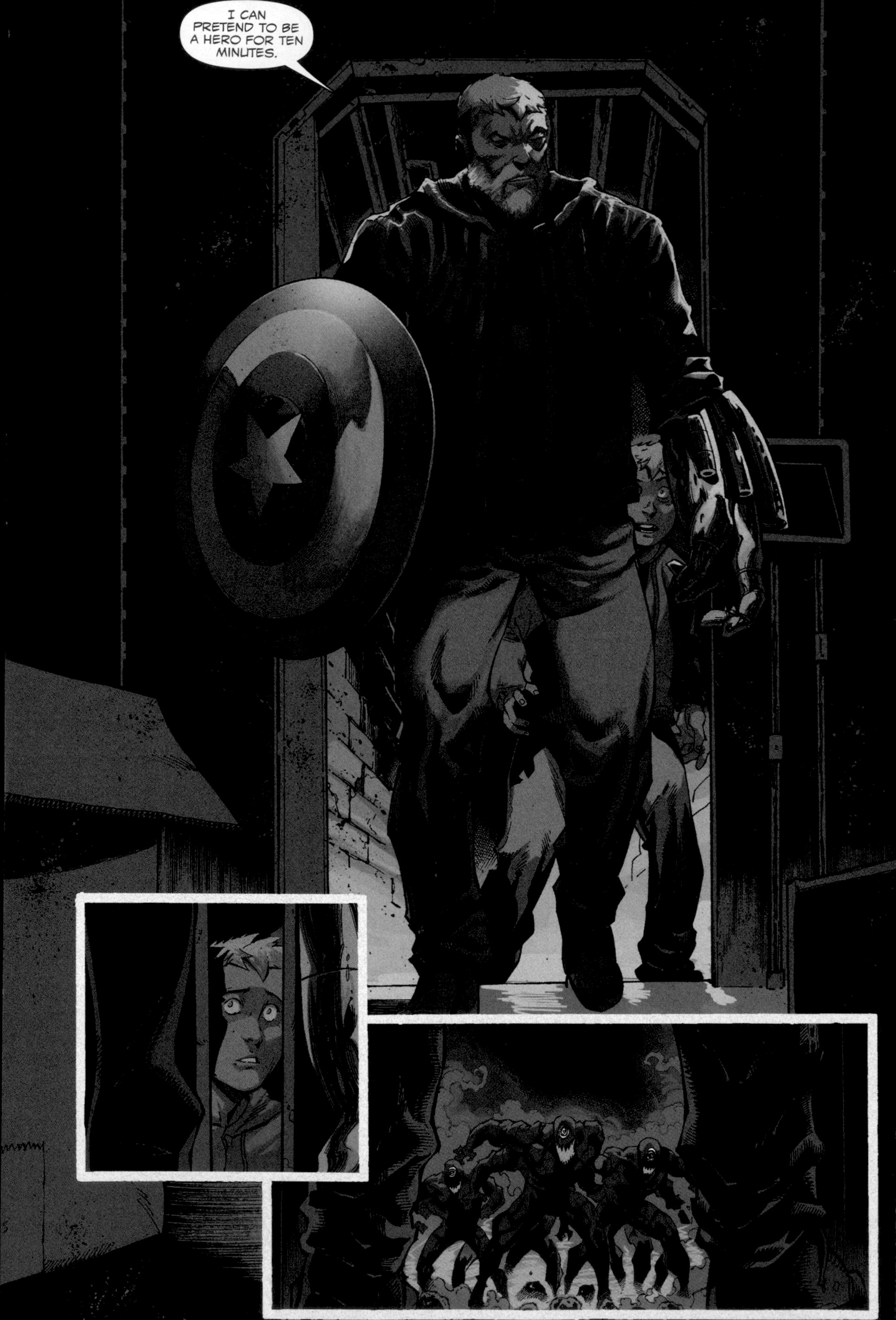
I CAN PRETEND TO BE A HERO FOR TEN MINUTES.

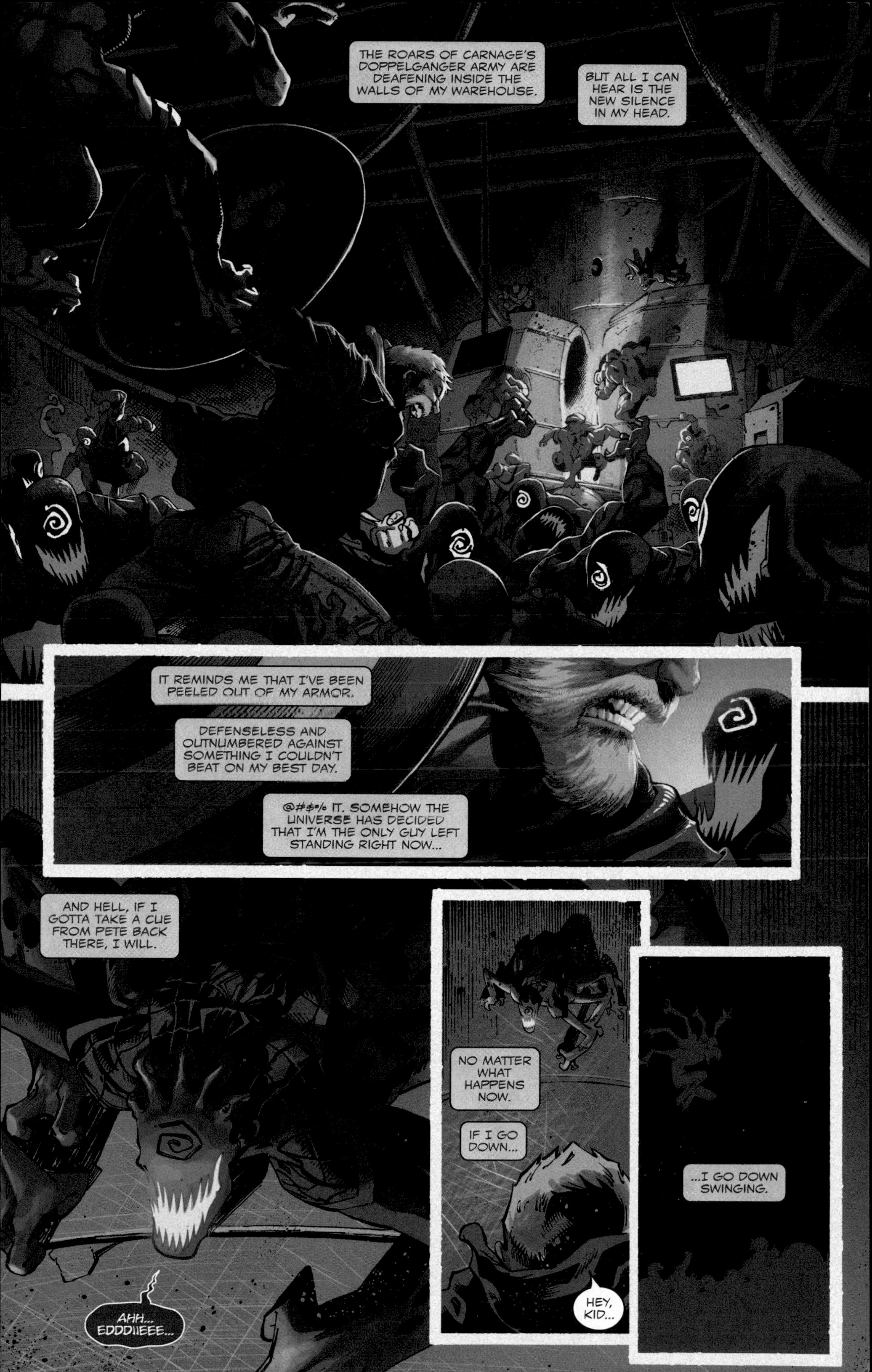
THE ROARS OF CARNAGE'S DOPPELGANGER ARMY ARE DEAFENING INSIDE THE WALLS OF MY WAREHOUSE.
BUT ALL I CAN HEAR IS THE NEW SILENCE IN MY HEAD.
IT REMINDS ME THAT I'VE BEEN PEELED OUT OF MY ARMOR.
DEFENSELESS AND OUTNUMBERED AGAINST SOMETHING I COULDN'T BEAT ON MY BEST DAY.
@#$% IT. SOMEHOW THE UNIVERSE HAS DECIDED THAT I'M THE ONLY GUY LEFT STANDING RIGHT NOW...
AND HELL, IF I GOTTA TAKE A CUE FROM PETE BACK THERE, I WILL.
AHH... EDDDIIEEE...
NO MATTER WHAT HAPPENS NOW.
IF I GO DOWN...
HEY, KID...
...I GO DOWN SWINGING.

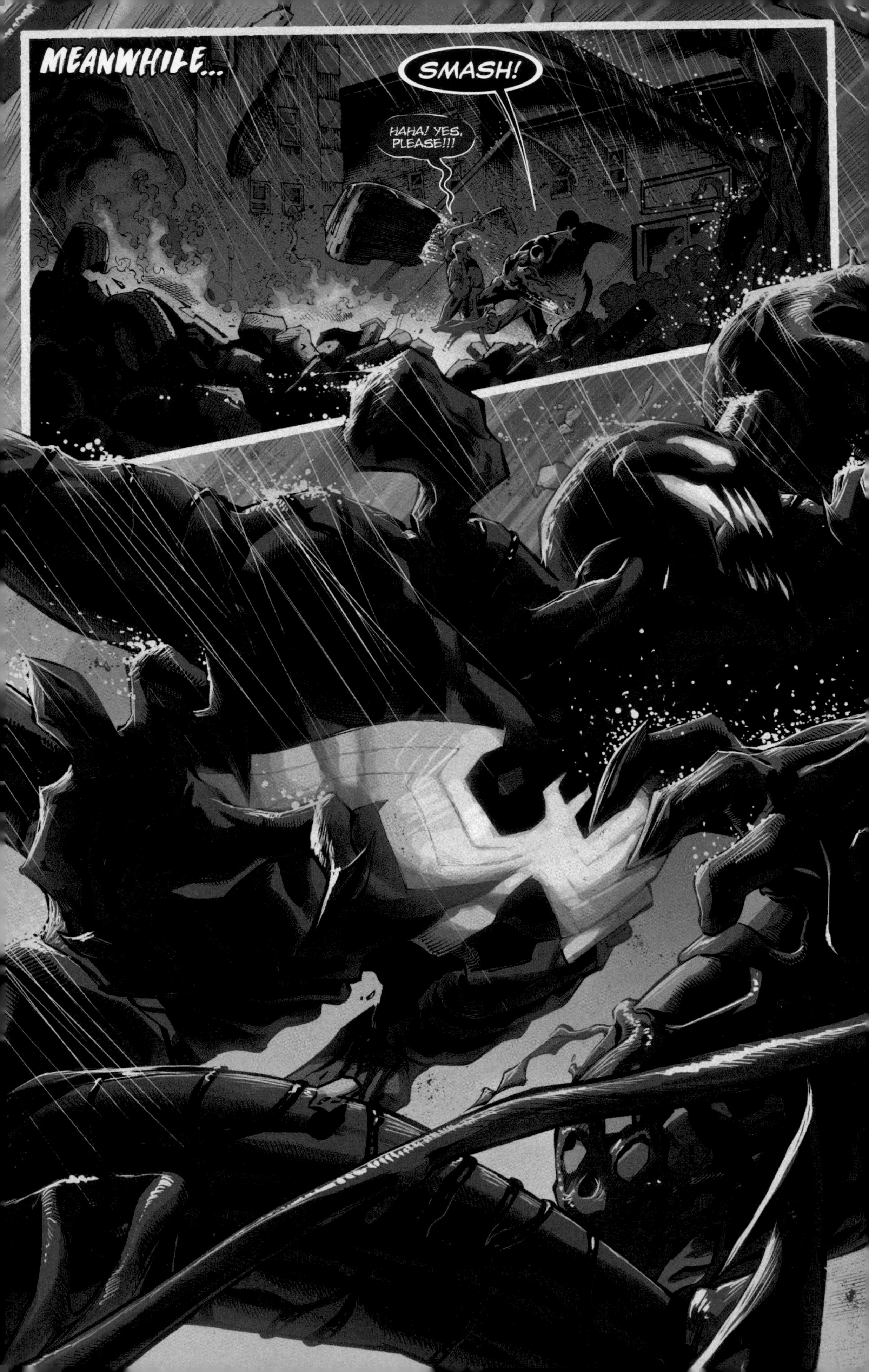
MEANWHILE...
SMASH!
HAHA! YES, PLEASE!!!

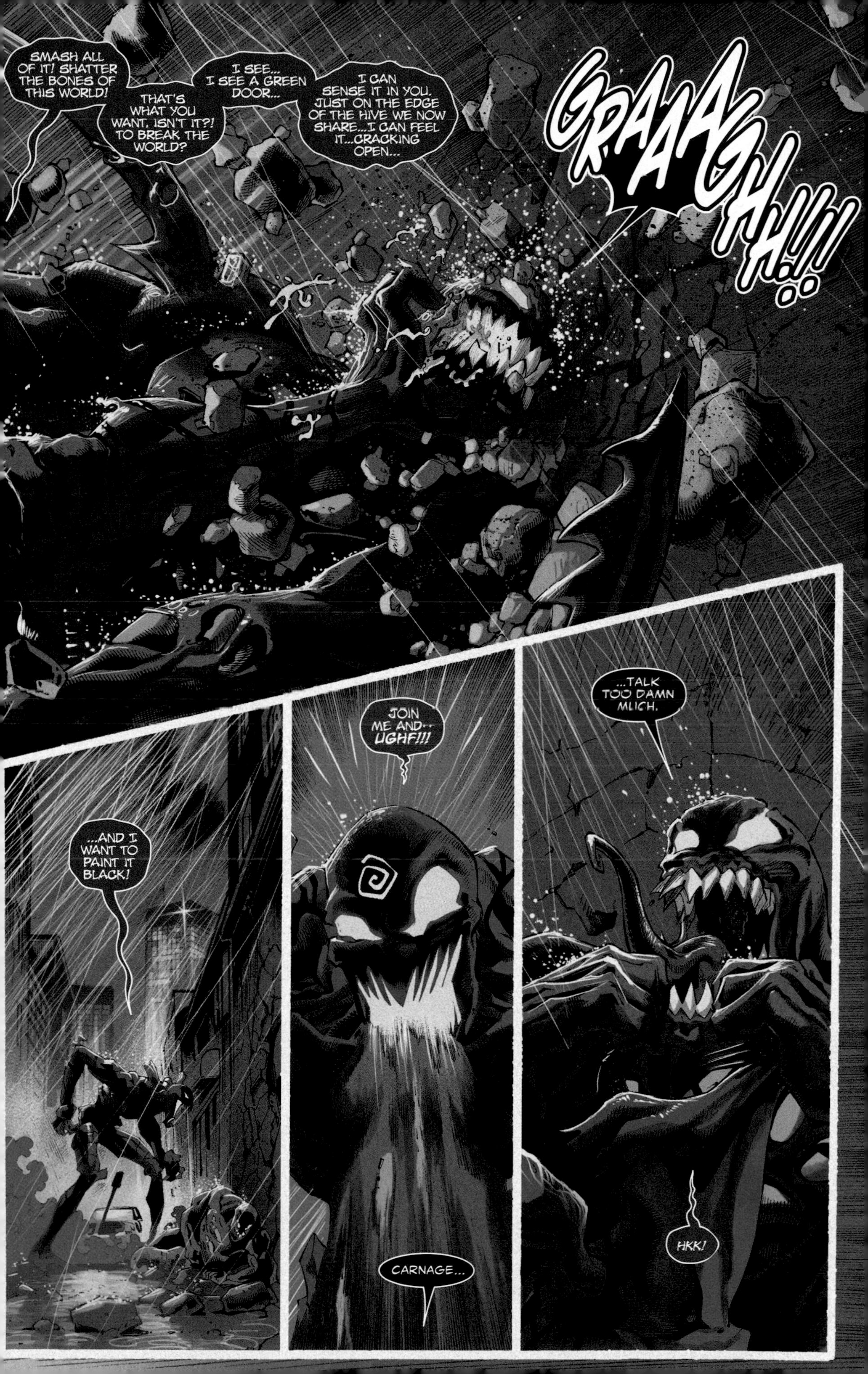
SMASH ALL OF IT! SHATTER THE BONES OF THIS WORLD!
THAT'S WHAT YOU WANT, ISN'T IT?! TO BREAK THE WORLD?
I SEE... I SEE A GREEN DOOR...
I CAN SENSE IT IN YOU. JUST ON THE EDGE OF THE HIVE WE NOW SHARE...I CAN FEEL IT...CRACKING OPEN...
GRAAAGHH!!!
...AND I WANT TO PAINT IT BLACK!
JOIN ME AND-- UGHF!!!
CARNAGE...
...TALK TOO DAMN MUCH.
HKK!

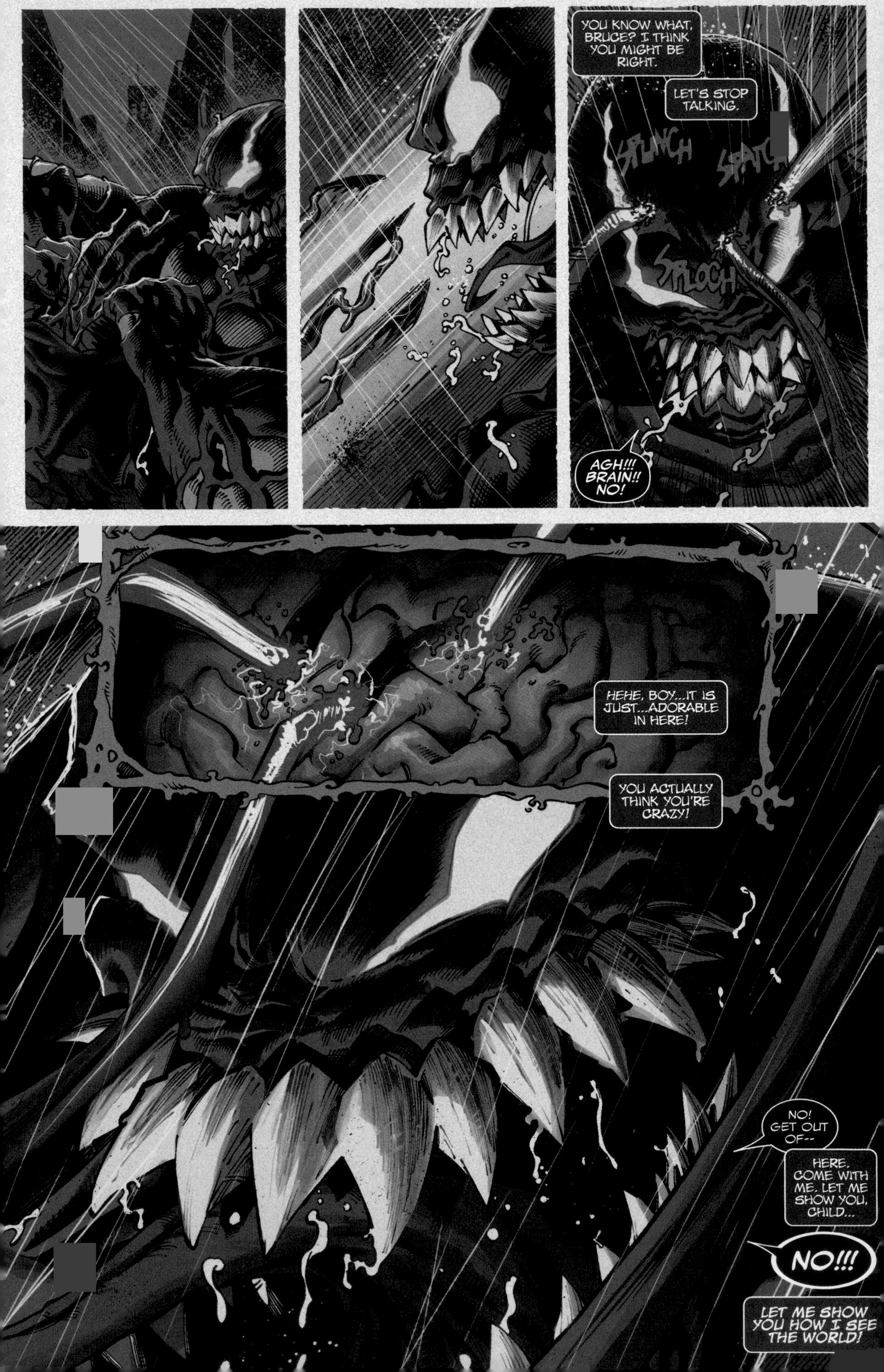

YOU KNOW WHAT, BRUCE? I THINK YOU MIGHT BE RIGHT.
LET'S STOP TALKING.
SPLUNCH
SPATCH
SPLOCH
AGH!!! BRAIN!! NO!
HEHE, BOY...IT IS JUST...ADORABLE IN HERE!
YOU ACTUALLY THINK YOU'RE CRAZY!
NO! GET OUT OF--
HERE. COME WITH ME. LET ME SHOW YOU, CHILD...
NO!!!
LET ME SHOW YOU HOW I SEE THE WORLD!

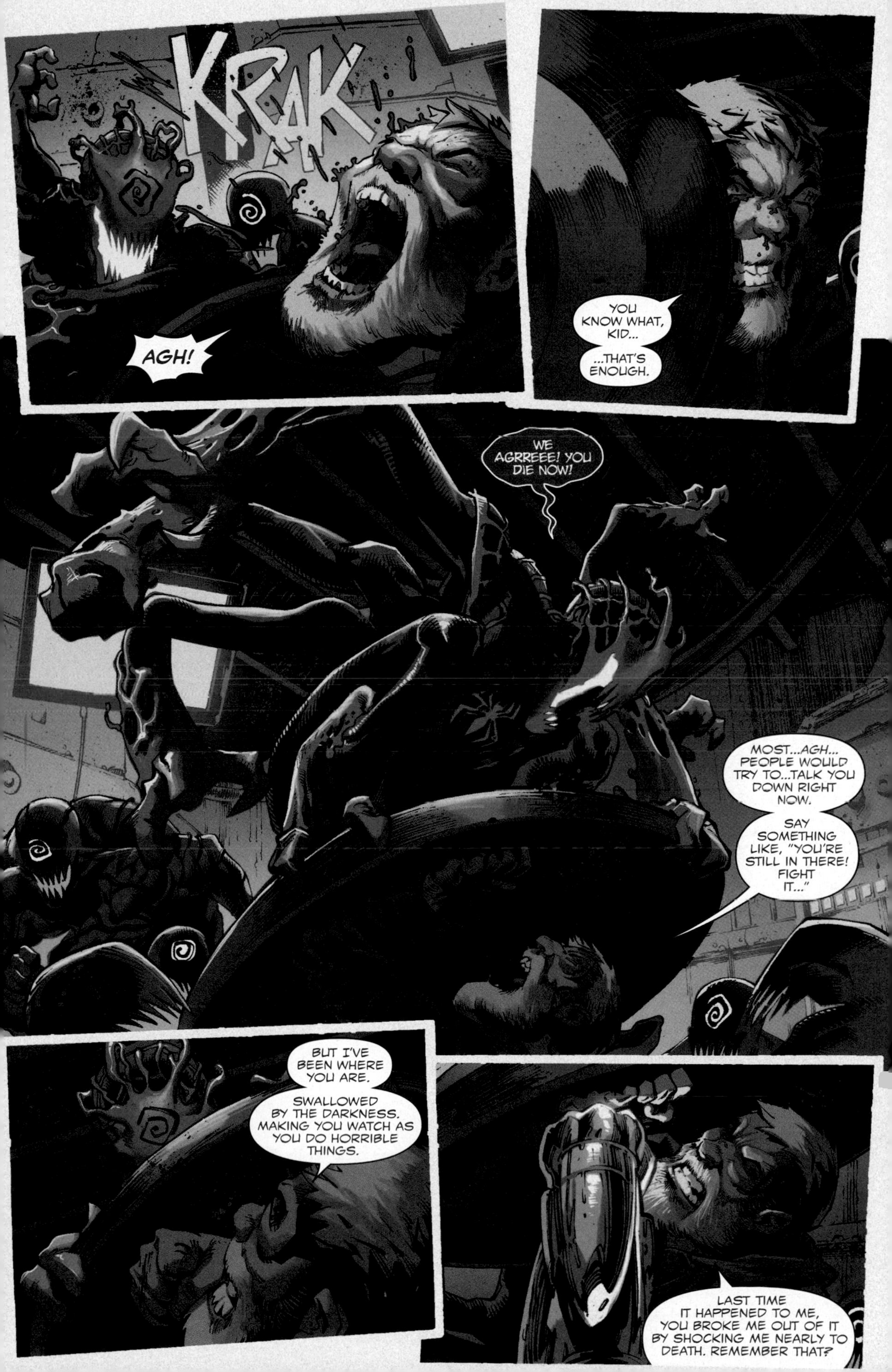
KRAK
AGH!
YOU KNOW WHAT, KID...
...THAT'S ENOUGH.
WE AGRREEE! YOU DIE NOW!
MOST...AGH... PEOPLE WOULD TRY TO...TALK YOU DOWN RIGHT NOW.
SAY SOMETHING LIKE, "YOU'RE STILL IN THERE! FIGHT IT..."
BUT I'VE BEEN WHERE YOU ARE.
SWALLOWED BY THE DARKNESS. MAKING YOU WATCH AS YOU DO HORRIBLE THINGS.
LAST TIME IT HAPPENED TO ME, YOU BROKE ME OUT OF IT BY SHOCKING ME NEARLY TO DEATH. REMEMBER THAT?

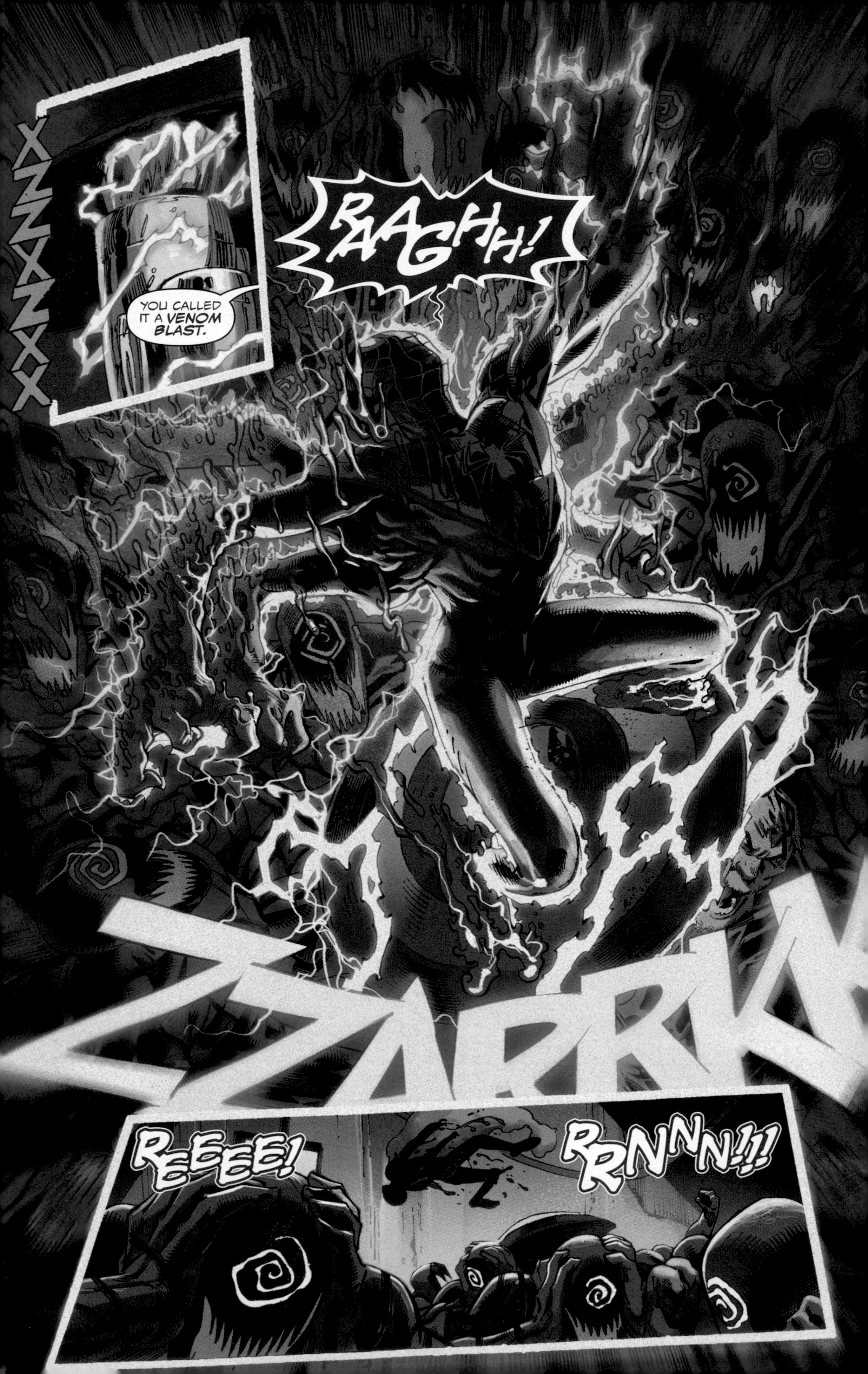
XZZZZXX
YOU CALLED IT A VENOM BLAST.
RAAGHHH!
ZZARK
REEEEE!
RRNNNN!!!

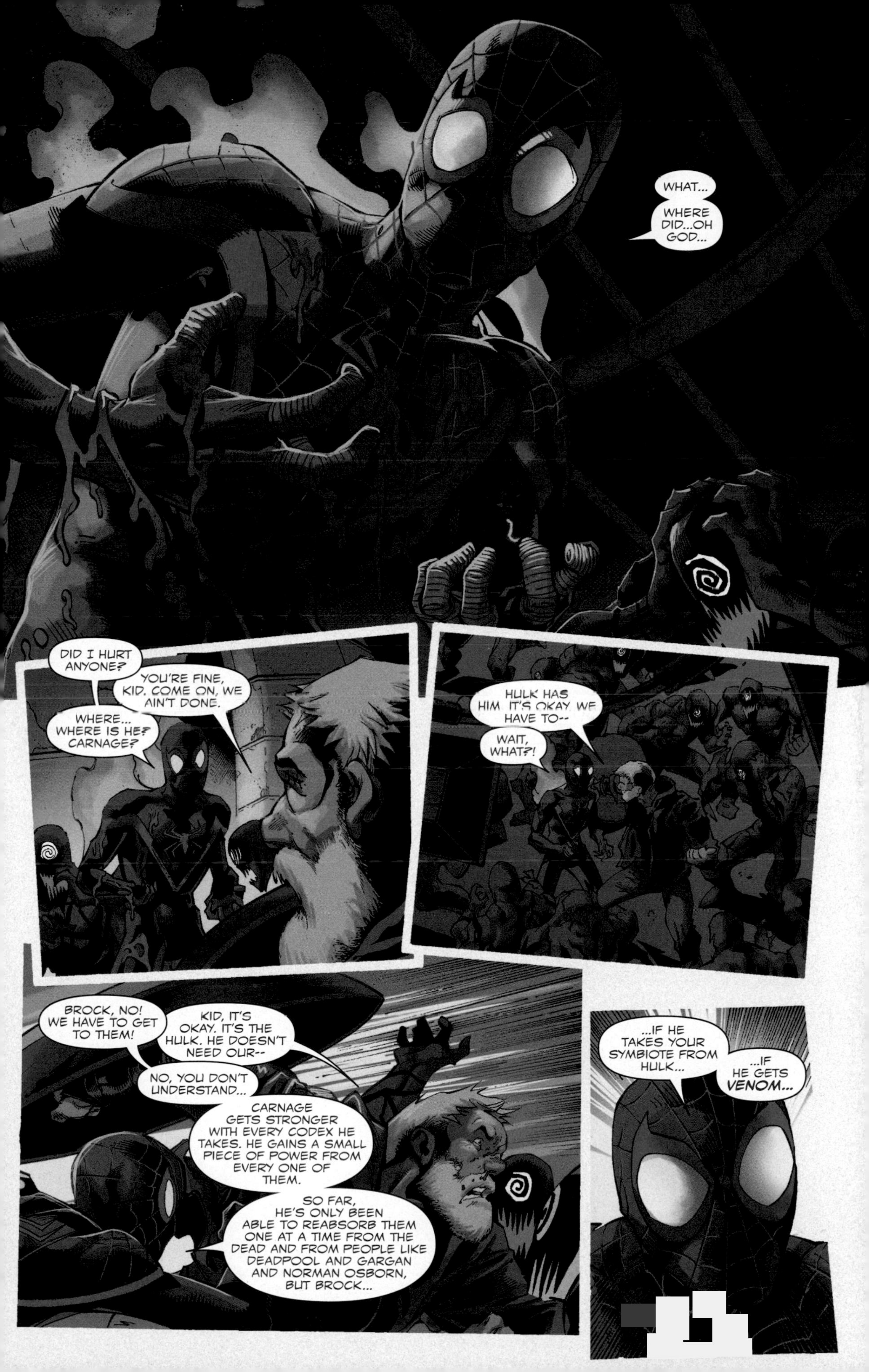
WHAT...
WHERE DID...OH GOD...
DID I HURT ANYONE?
YOU'RE FINE, KID. COME ON, WE AIN'T DONE.
WHERE... WHERE IS HE? CARNAGE?
HULK HAS HIM. IT'S OKAY. WE HAVE TO--
WAIT, WHAT?!
BROCK, NO! WE HAVE TO GET TO THEM!
KID, IT'S OKAY. IT'S THE HULK. HE DOESN'T NEED OUR--
NO, YOU DON'T UNDERSTAND...
CARNAGE GETS STRONGER WITH EVERY CODEX HE TAKES. HE GAINS A SMALL PIECE OF POWER FROM EVERY ONE OF THEM.
SO FAR, HE'S ONLY BEEN ABLE TO REABSORB THEM ONE AT A TIME FROM THE DEAD AND FROM PEOPLE LIKE DEADPOOL AND GARGAN AND NORMAN OSBORN, BUT BROCK...
...IF HE TAKES YOUR SYMBIOTE FROM HULK...
...IF HE GETS *VENOM...*

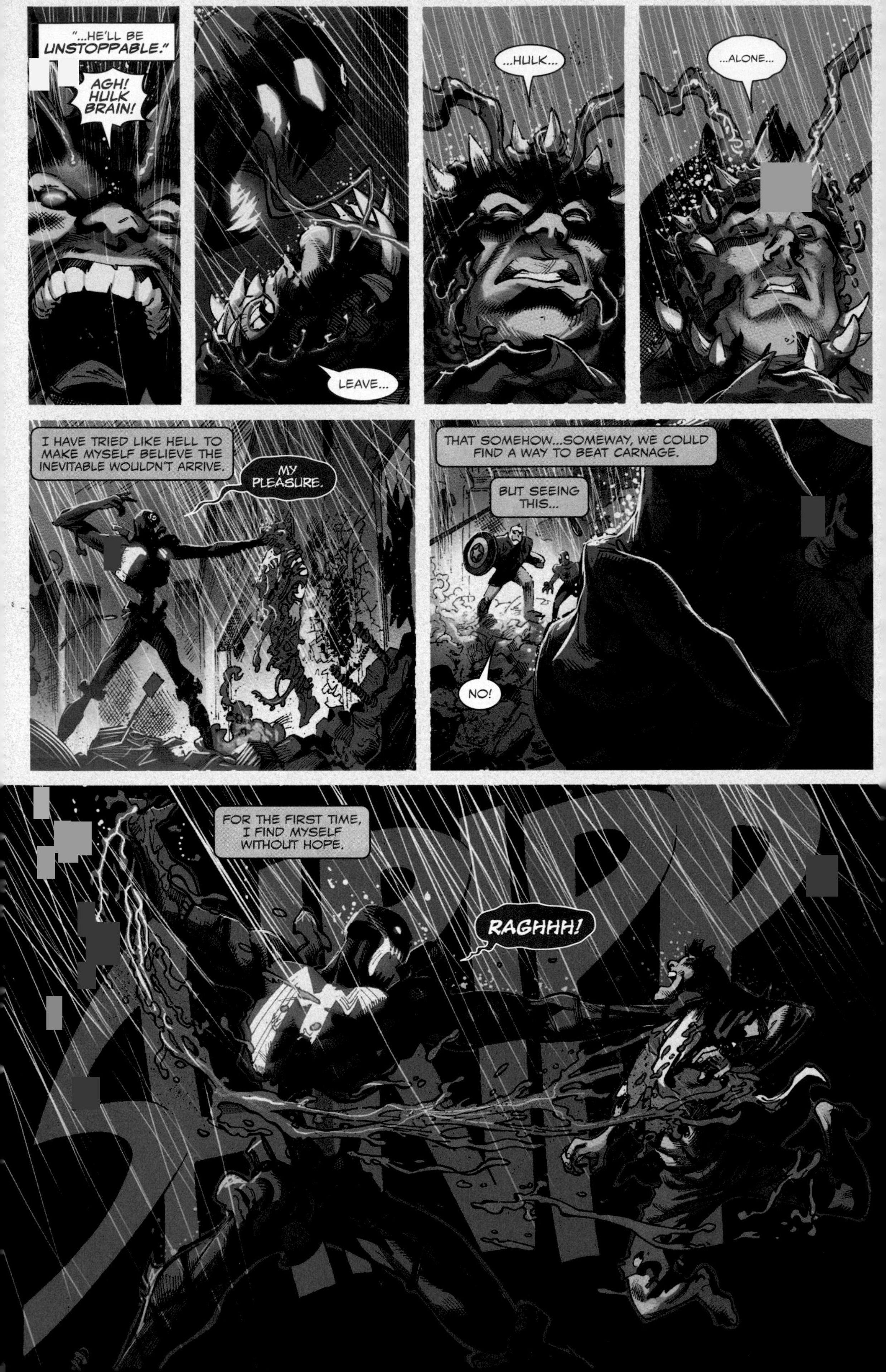
"...HE'LL BE UNSTOPPABLE."
AGH! HULK BRAIN!
LEAVE...
...HULK...
...ALONE...
I HAVE TRIED LIKE HELL TO MAKE MYSELF BELIEVE THE INEVITABLE WOULDN'T ARRIVE.
MY PLEASURE.
THAT SOMEHOW...SOMEWAY, WE COULD FIND A WAY TO BEAT CARNAGE.
BUT SEEING THIS...
NO!
FOR THE FIRST TIME, I FIND MYSELF WITHOUT HOPE.
RAGHHH!

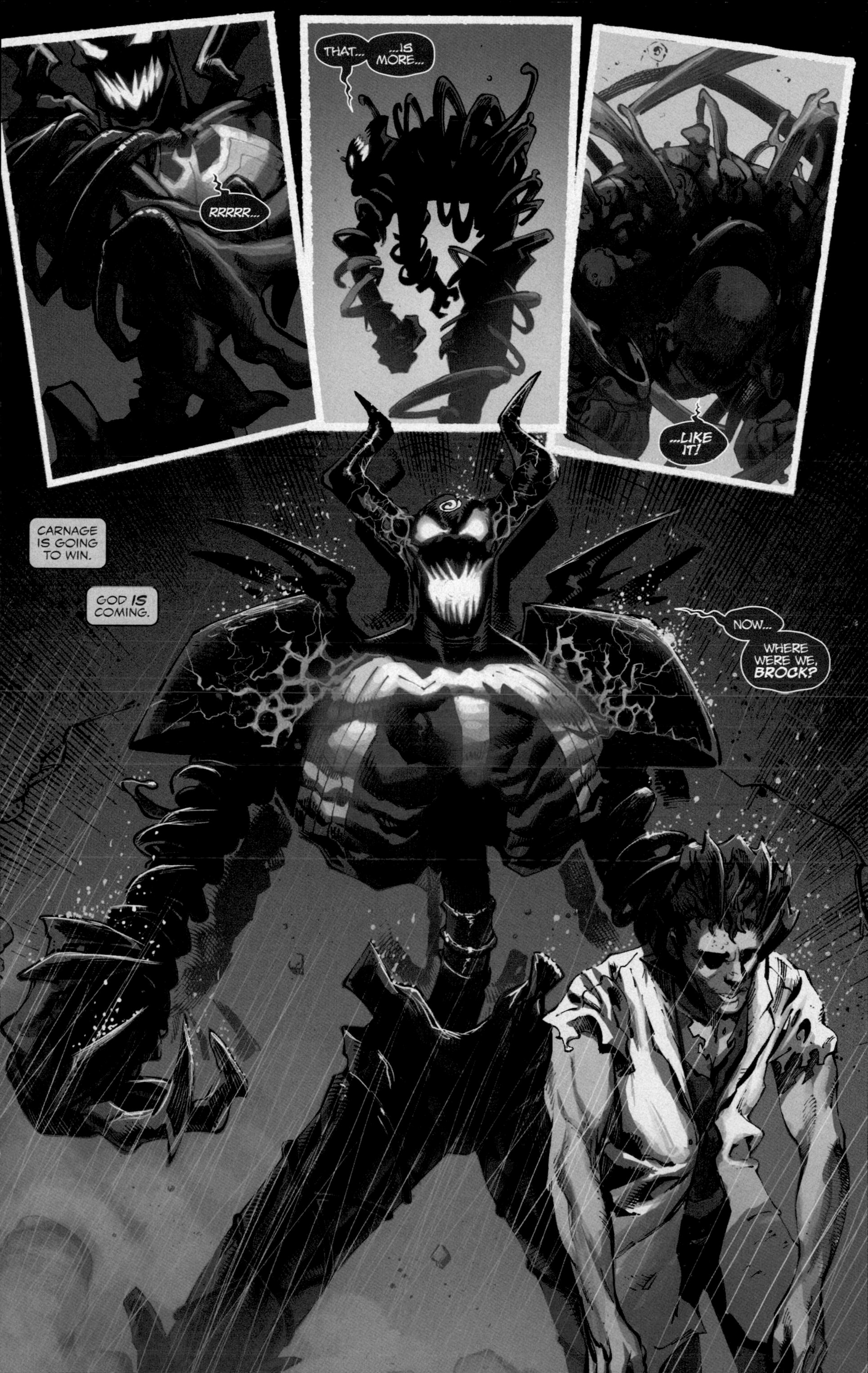
RRRRR...
THAT...
...IS MORE...
...LIKE IT!
CARNAGE IS GOING TO WIN.
GOD IS COMING.
NOW...
WHERE WERE WE, BROCK?

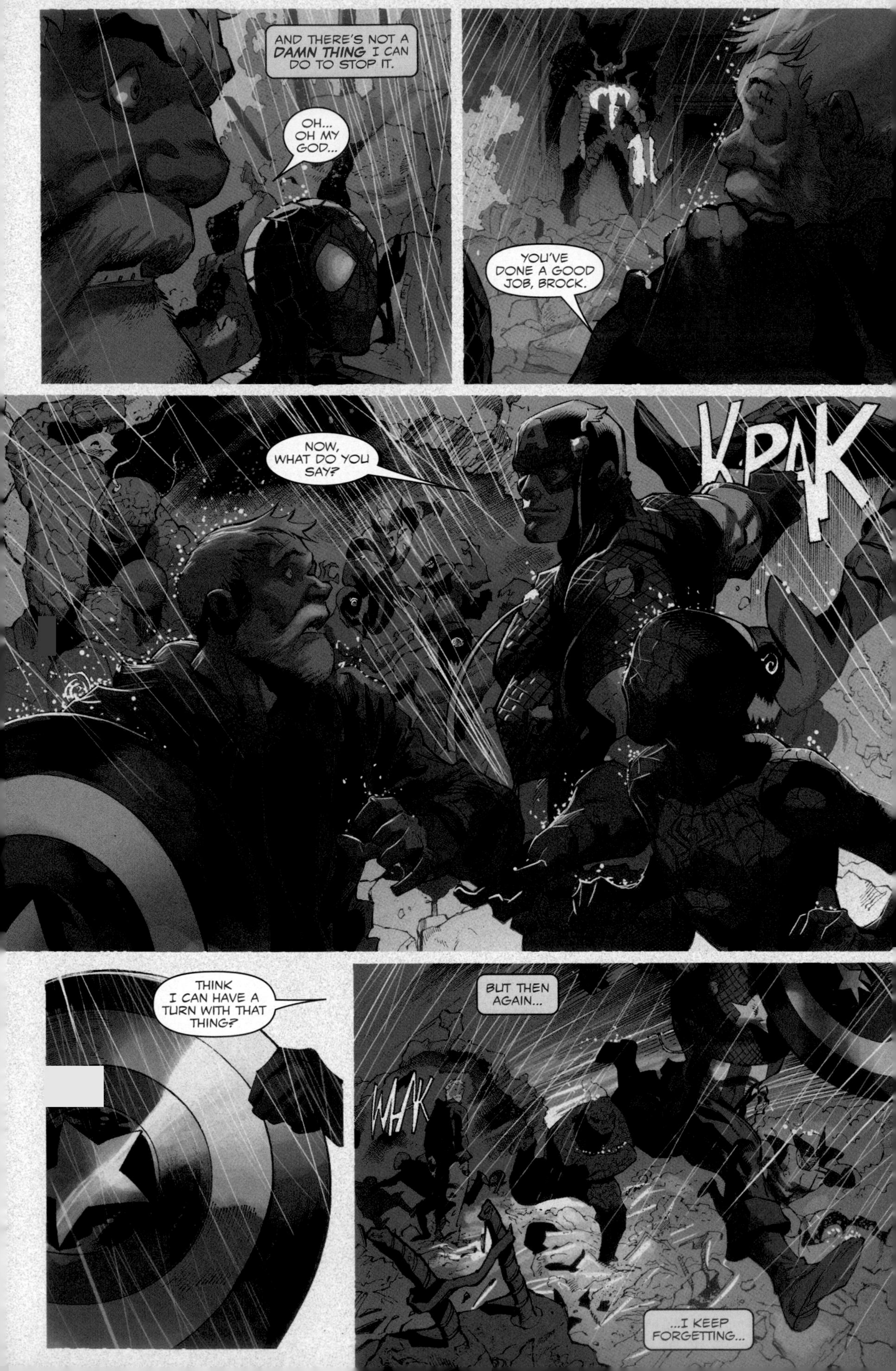
AND THERE'S NOT A DAMN THING I CAN DO TO STOP IT.
OH... OH MY GOD...
YOU'VE DONE A GOOD JOB, BROCK.
NOW, WHAT DO YOU SAY?
KRAK
THINK I CAN HAVE A TURN WITH THAT THING?
BUT THEN AGAIN...
WHAK
...I KEEP FORGETTING...

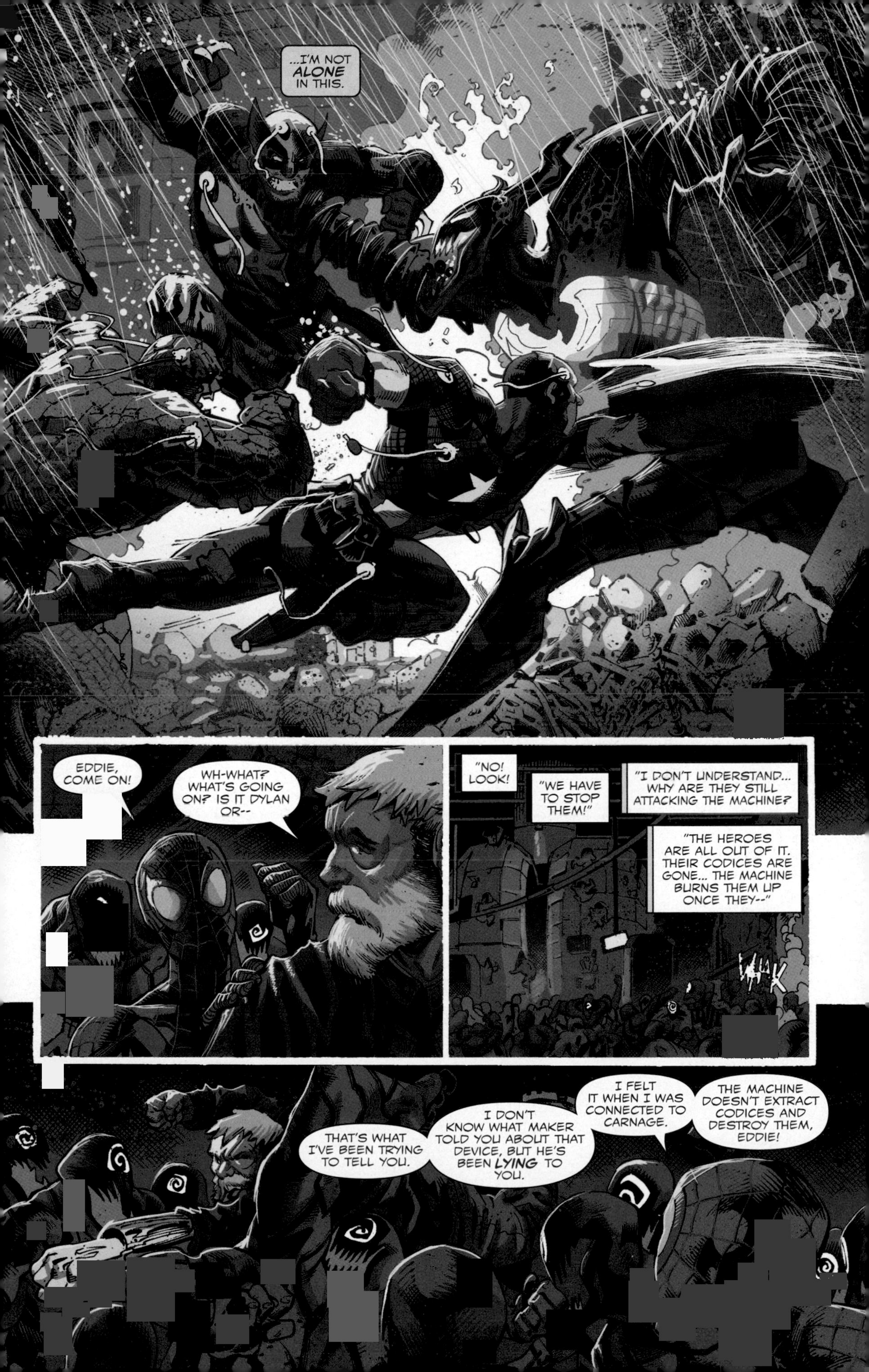
...I'M NOT ALONE IN THIS.
EDDIE, COME ON!
WH-WHAT? WHAT'S GOING ON? IS IT DYLAN OR--
"NO! LOOK!
"WE HAVE TO STOP THEM!"
"I DON'T UNDERSTAND... WHY ARE THEY STILL ATTACKING THE MACHINE?
"THE HEROES ARE ALL OUT OF IT. THEIR CODICES ARE GONE... THE MACHINE BURNS THEM UP ONCE THEY--"
THE MACHINE DOESN'T EXTRACT CODICES AND DESTROY THEM, EDDIE!
I FELT IT WHEN I WAS CONNECTED TO CARNAGE.
I DON'T KNOW WHAT MAKER TOLD YOU ABOUT THAT DEVICE, BUT HE'S BEEN LYING TO YOU.
THAT'S WHAT I'VE BEEN TRYING TO TELL YOU.

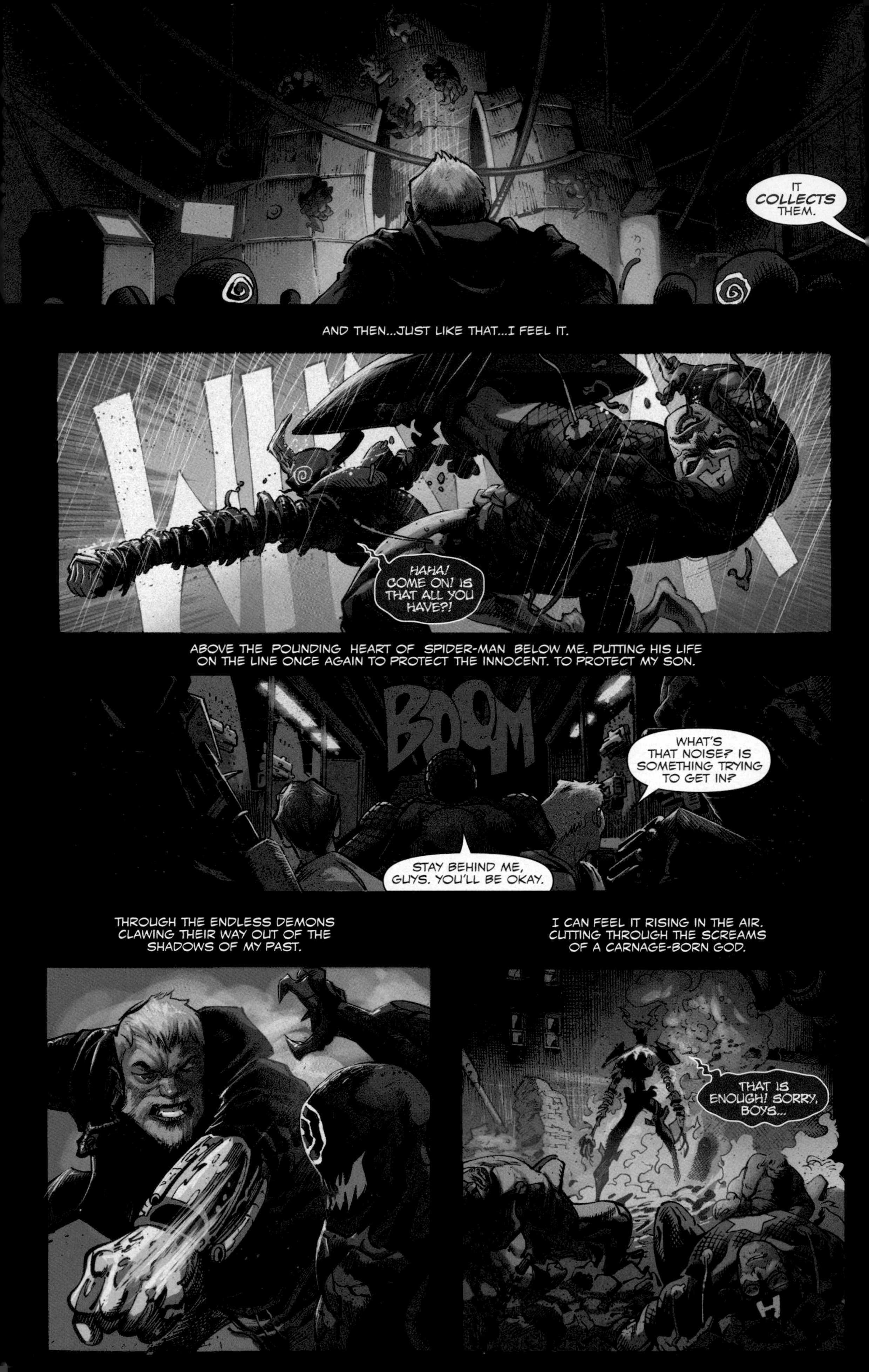
IT COLLECTS THEM.
AND THEN...JUST LIKE THAT...I FEEL IT.
HAHA! COME ON! IS THAT ALL YOU HAVE?!
ABOVE THE POUNDING HEART OF SPIDER-MAN BELOW ME. PUTTING HIS LIFE ON THE LINE ONCE AGAIN TO PROTECT THE INNOCENT. TO PROTECT MY SON.
BOOM
WHAT'S THAT NOISE? IS SOMETHING TRYING TO GET IN?
STAY BEHIND ME, GUYS. YOU'LL BE OKAY.
THROUGH THE ENDLESS DEMONS CLAWING THEIR WAY OUT OF THE SHADOWS OF MY PAST.
I CAN FEEL IT RISING IN THE AIR. CUTTING THROUGH THE SCREAMS OF A CARNAGE-BORN GOD.
THAT IS ENOUGH! SORRY, BOYS...

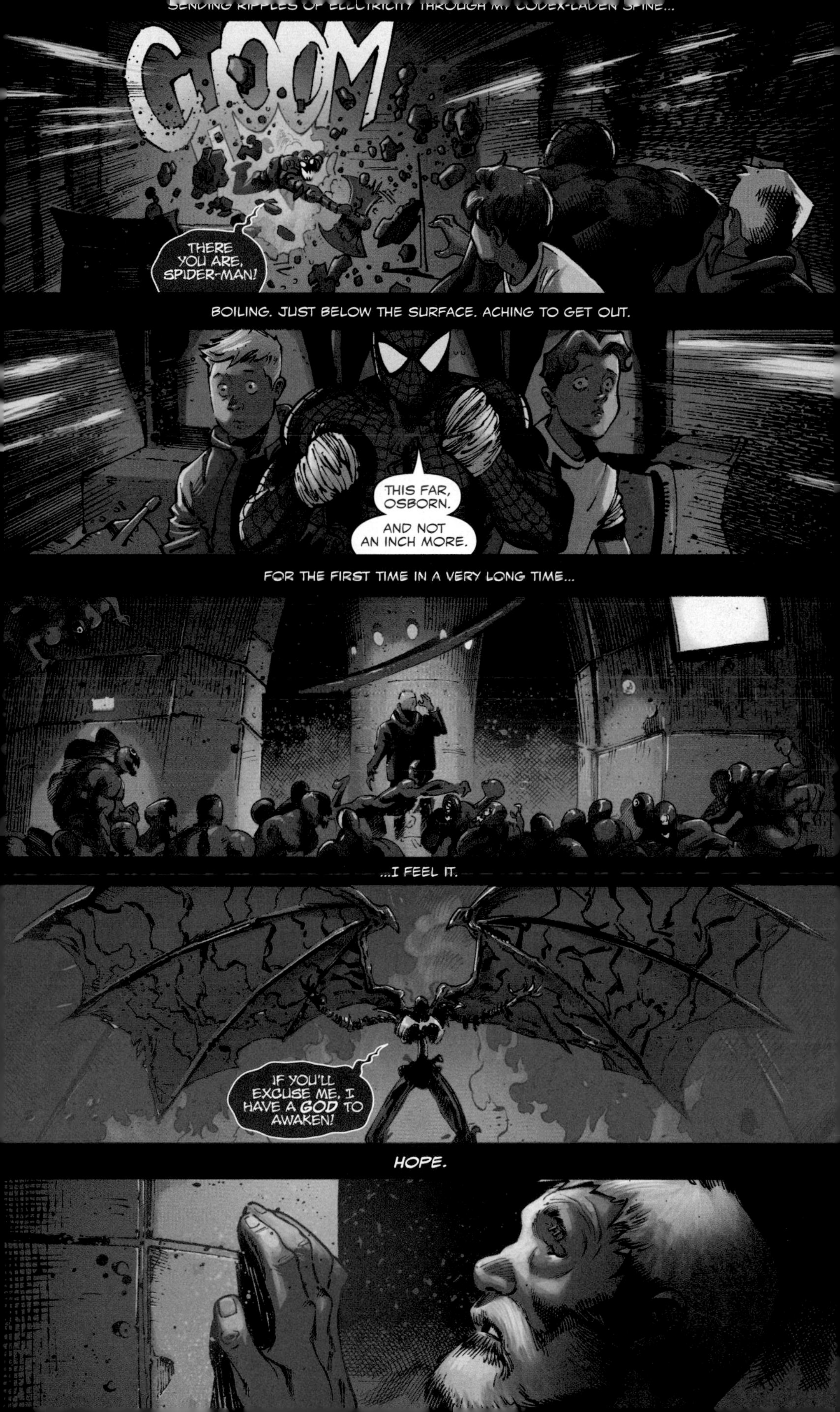
SENDING RIPPLES OF ELECTRICITY THROUGH MY CODEX-LADEN SPINE...
GOOOM
THERE YOU ARE, SPIDER-MAN!
BOILING. JUST BELOW THE SURFACE. ACHING TO GET OUT.
THIS FAR, OSBORN.
AND NOT AN INCH MORE.
FOR THE FIRST TIME IN A VERY LONG TIME...
...I FEEL IT.
IF YOU'LL EXCUSE ME, I HAVE A GOD TO AWAKEN!
HOPE.

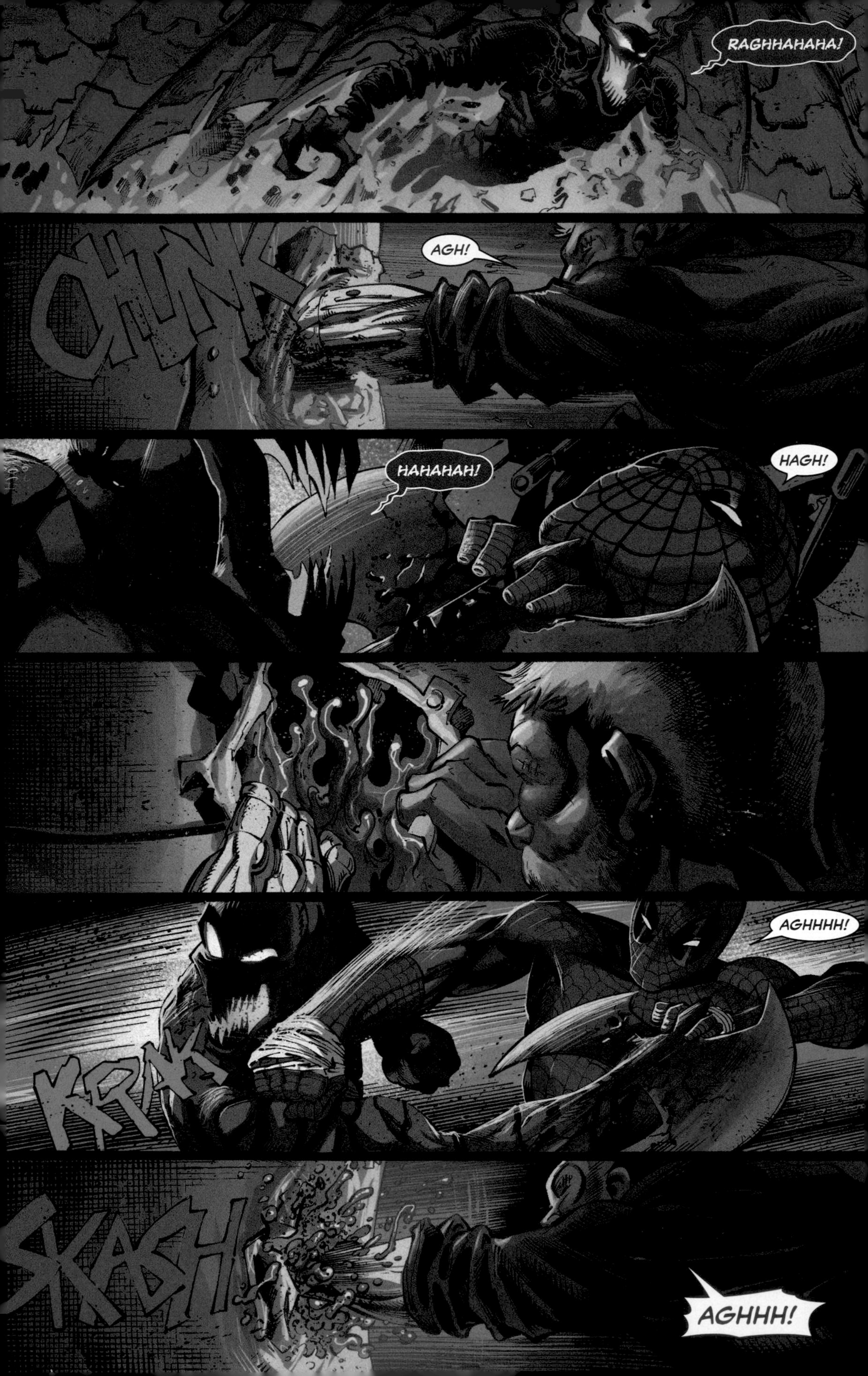
RAGHHAHAHA!
CHUNK
AGH!
HAHAHAH!
HAGH!
AGHHHH!
KRAK
SKASH
AGHHH!

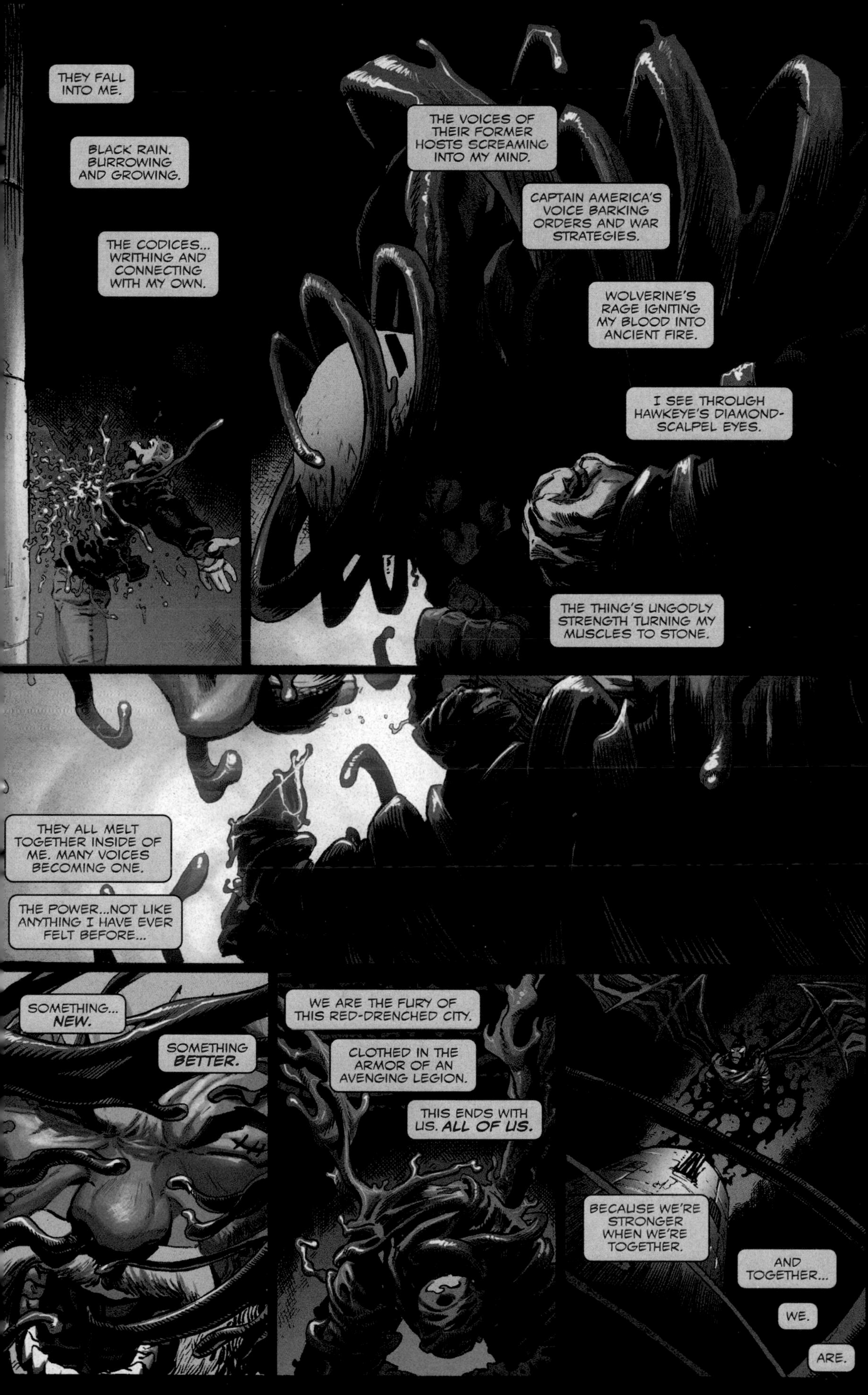
THEY FALL INTO ME.
BLACK RAIN. BURROWING AND GROWING.
THE CODICES... WRITHING AND CONNECTING WITH MY OWN.
THE VOICES OF THEIR FORMER HOSTS SCREAMING INTO MY MIND.
CAPTAIN AMERICA'S VOICE BARKING ORDERS AND WAR STRATEGIES.
WOLVERINE'S RAGE IGNITING MY BLOOD INTO ANCIENT FIRE.
I SEE THROUGH HAWKEYE'S DIAMOND-SCALPEL EYES.
THE THING'S UNGODLY STRENGTH TURNING MY MUSCLES TO STONE.
THEY ALL MELT TOGETHER INSIDE OF ME. MANY VOICES BECOMING ONE.
THE POWER...NOT LIKE ANYTHING I HAVE EVER FELT BEFORE...
SOMETHING... NEW.
SOMETHING BETTER.
WE ARE THE FURY OF THIS RED-DRENCHED CITY.
CLOTHED IN THE ARMOR OF AN AVENGING LEGION.
THIS ENDS WITH US. ALL OF US.
BECAUSE WE'RE STRONGER WHEN WE'RE TOGETHER.
AND TOGETHER...
WE.
ARE.

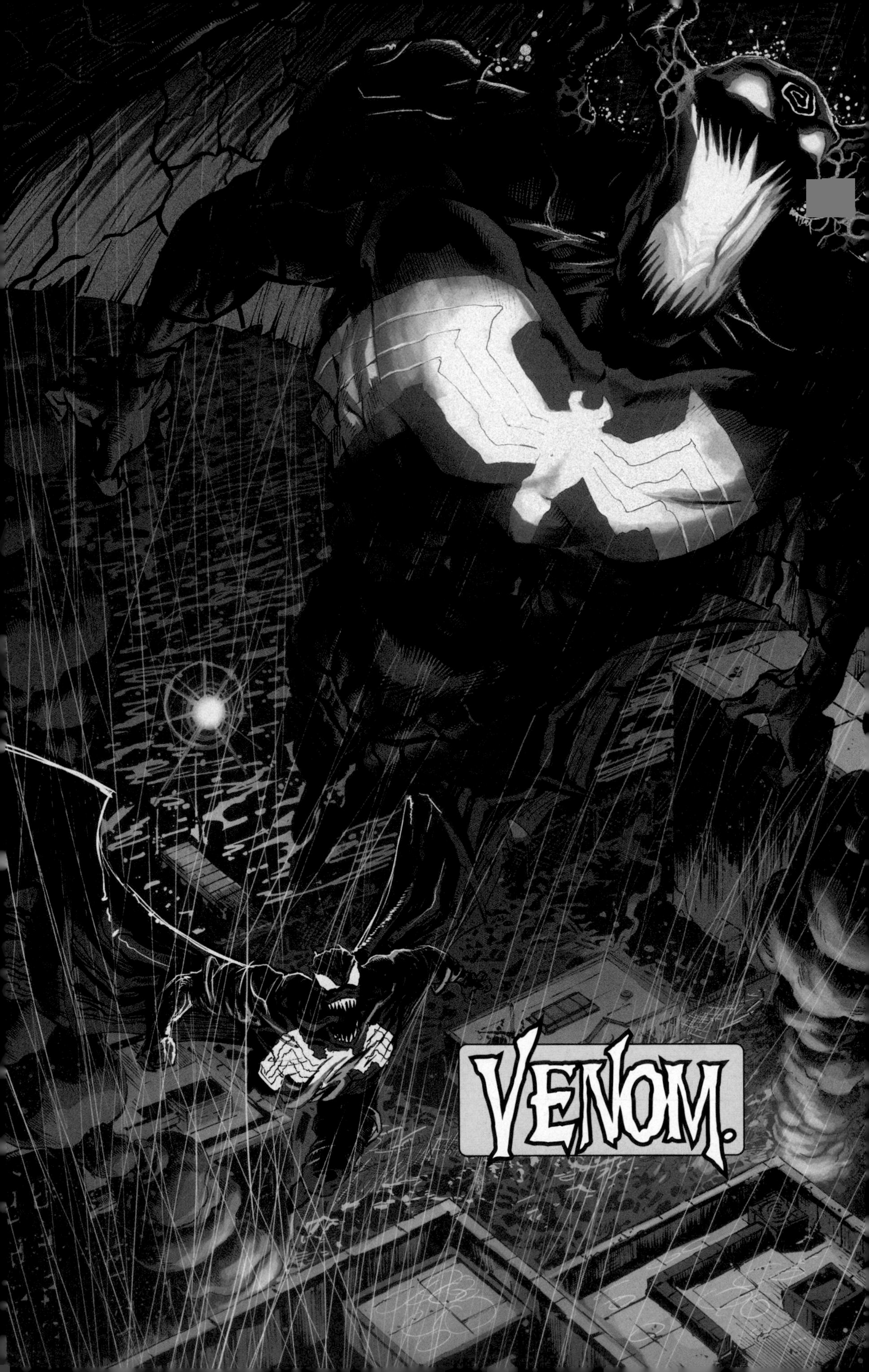
VENOM

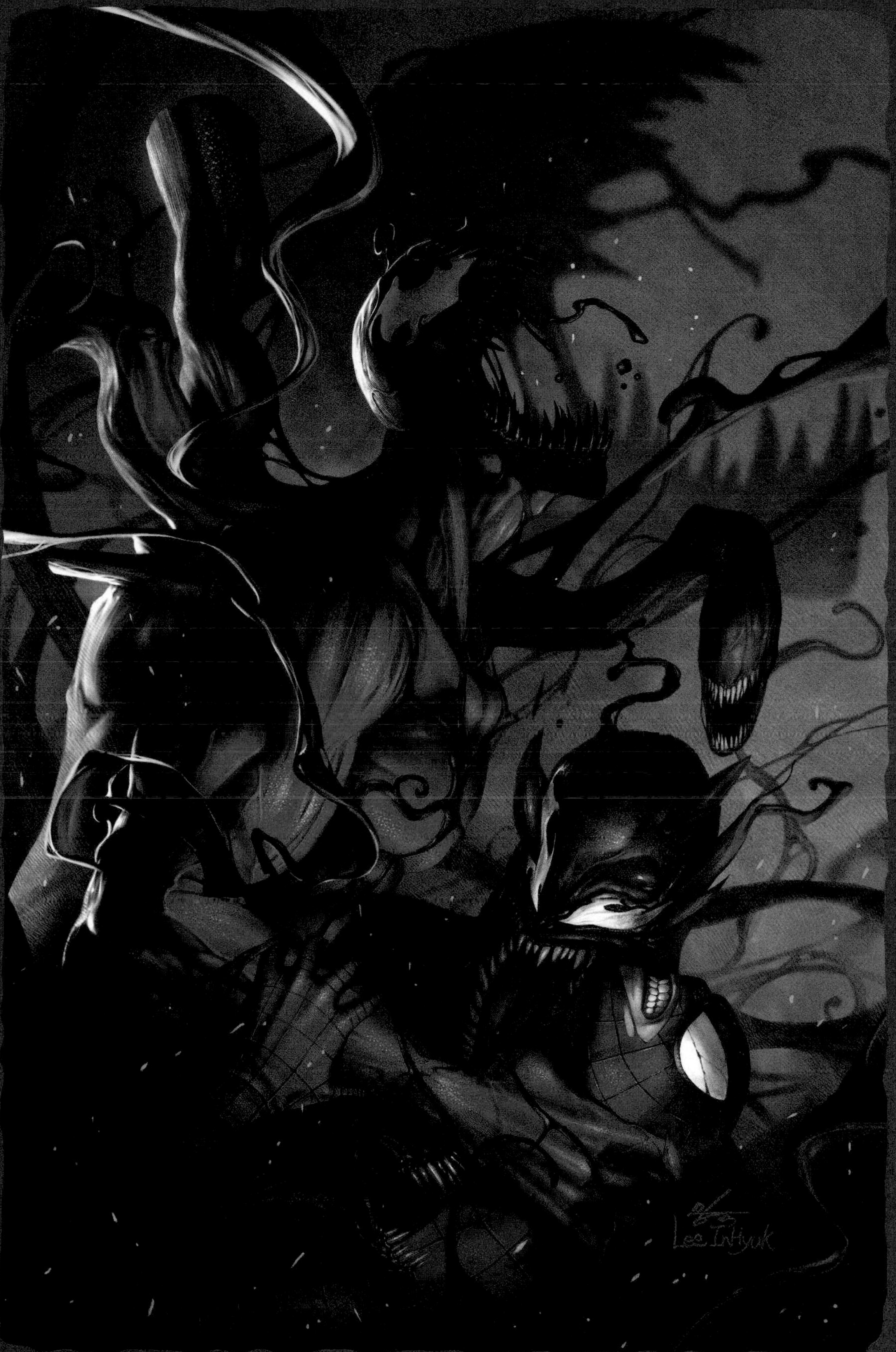
Lee InHyuk

INHYUK LEE

#5 Variant

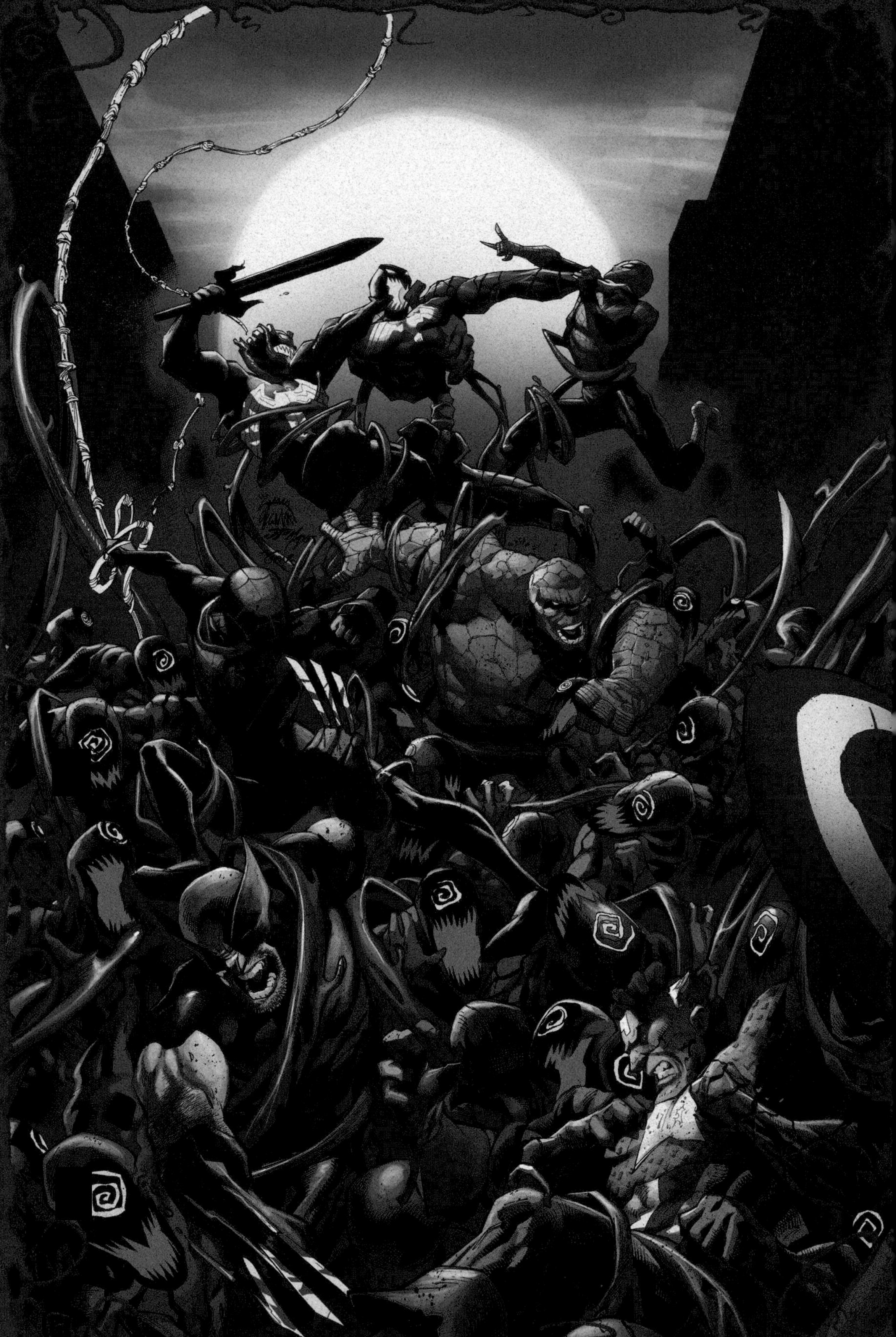

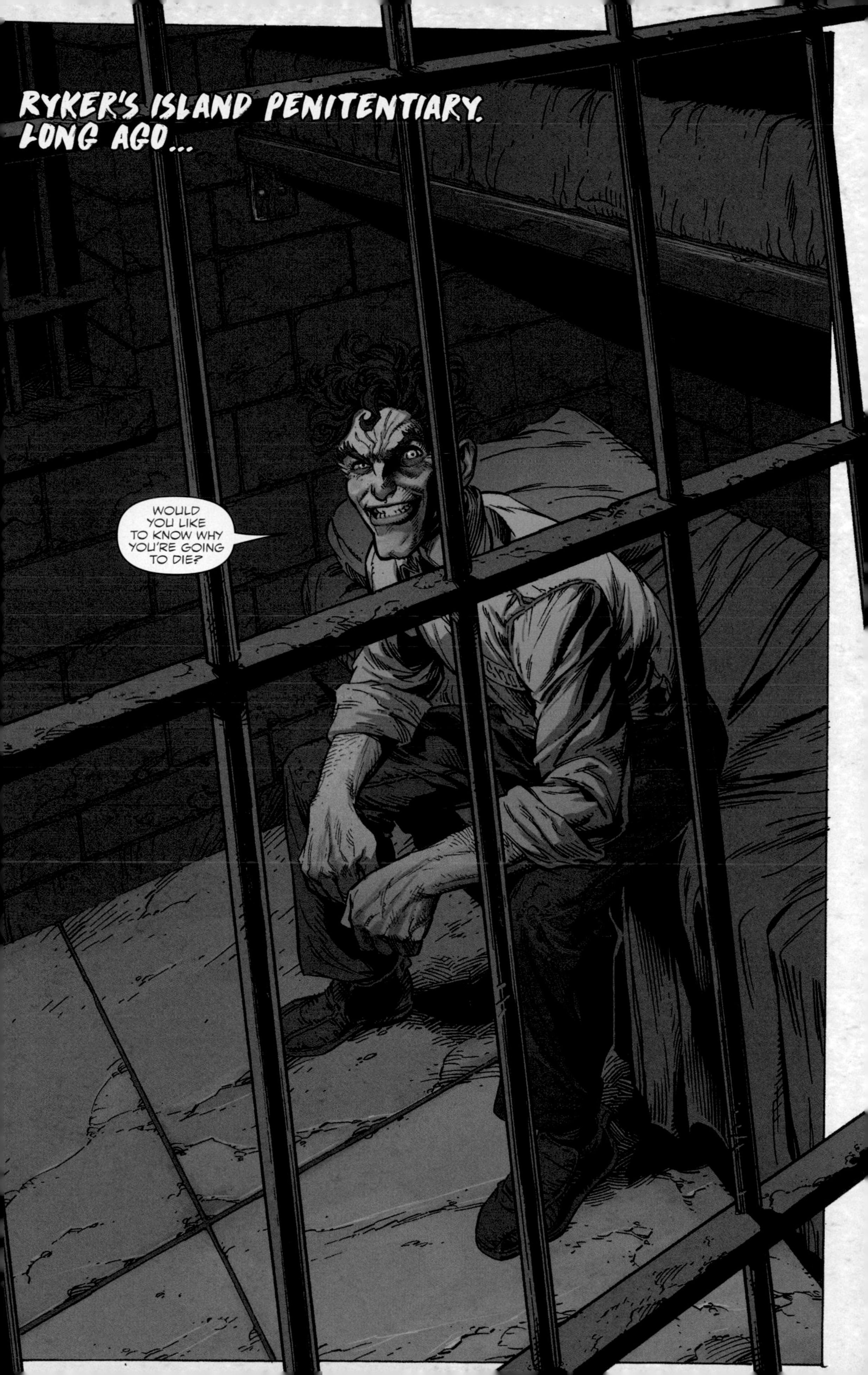
RYKER'S ISLAND PENITENTIARY. LONG AGO...
WOULD YOU LIKE TO KNOW WHY YOU'RE GOING TO DIE?

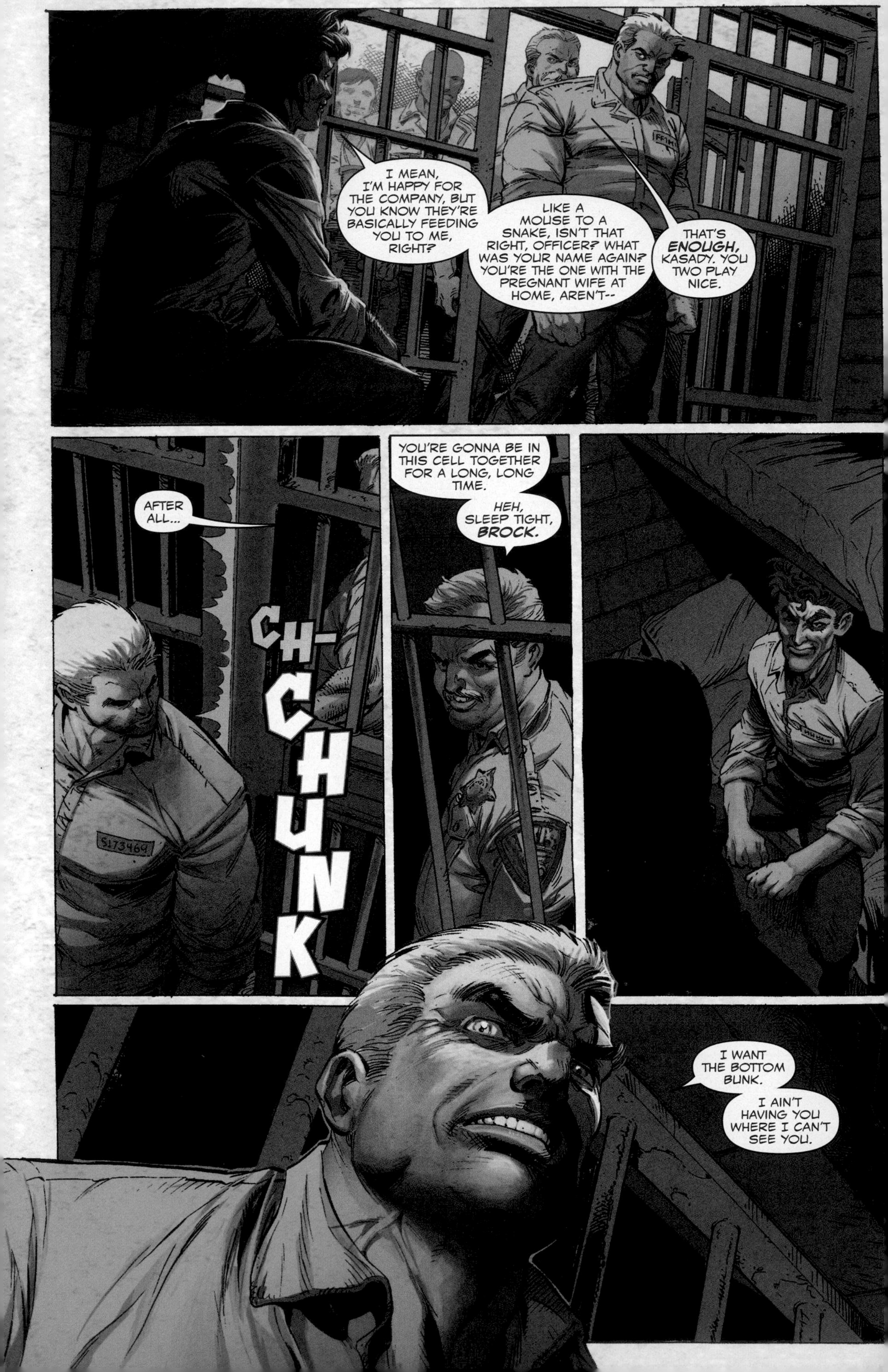

I MEAN, I'M HAPPY FOR THE COMPANY, BUT YOU KNOW THEY'RE BASICALLY FEEDING YOU TO ME, RIGHT?
LIKE A MOUSE TO A SNAKE, ISN'T THAT RIGHT, OFFICER? WHAT WAS YOUR NAME AGAIN? YOU'RE THE ONE WITH THE PREGNANT WIFE AT HOME, AREN'T--
THAT'S ENOUGH, KASADY. YOU TWO PLAY NICE.
AFTER ALL...
YOU'RE GONNA BE IN THIS CELL TOGETHER FOR A LONG, LONG TIME.
HEH, SLEEP TIGHT, BROCK.
CH-CHUNK
I WANT THE BOTTOM BUNK.
I AIN'T HAVING YOU WHERE I CAN'T SEE YOU.

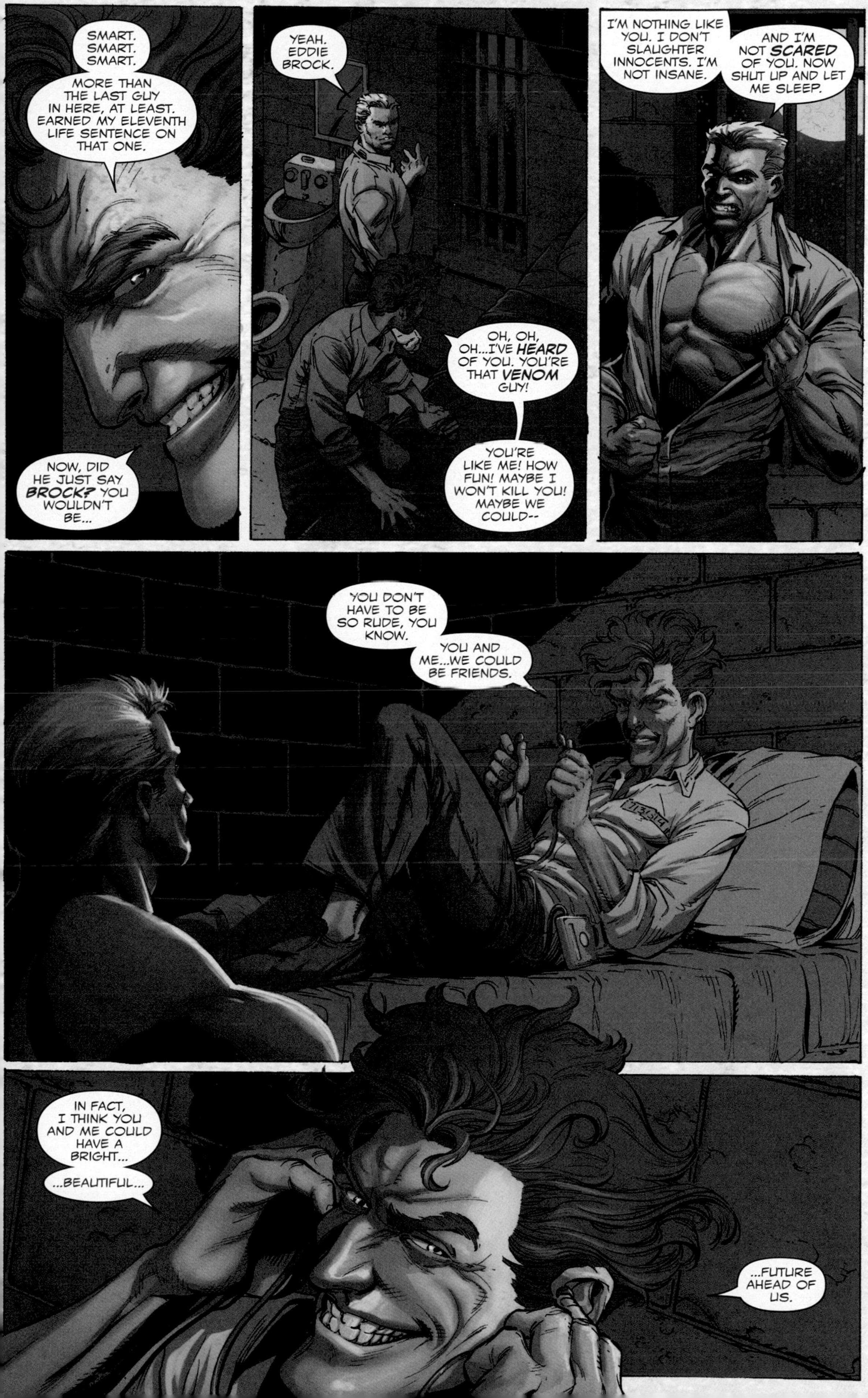
SMART. SMART. SMART.
MORE THAN THE LAST GUY IN HERE, AT LEAST. EARNED MY ELEVENTH LIFE SENTENCE ON THAT ONE.
NOW, DID HE JUST SAY BROCK? YOU WOULDN'T BE...
YEAH. EDDIE BROCK.
OH, OH, OH...I'VE HEARD OF YOU. YOU'RE THAT VENOM GUY!
YOU'RE LIKE ME! HOW FUN! MAYBE I WON'T KILL YOU! MAYBE WE COULD--
I'M NOTHING LIKE YOU. I DON'T SLAUGHTER INNOCENTS. I'M NOT INSANE.
AND I'M NOT SCARED OF YOU. NOW SHUT UP AND LET ME SLEEP.
YOU DON'T HAVE TO BE SO RUDE, YOU KNOW.
YOU AND ME...WE COULD BE FRIENDS.
IN FACT, I THINK YOU AND ME COULD HAVE A BRIGHT...
...BEAUTIFUL...
...FUTURE AHEAD OF US.

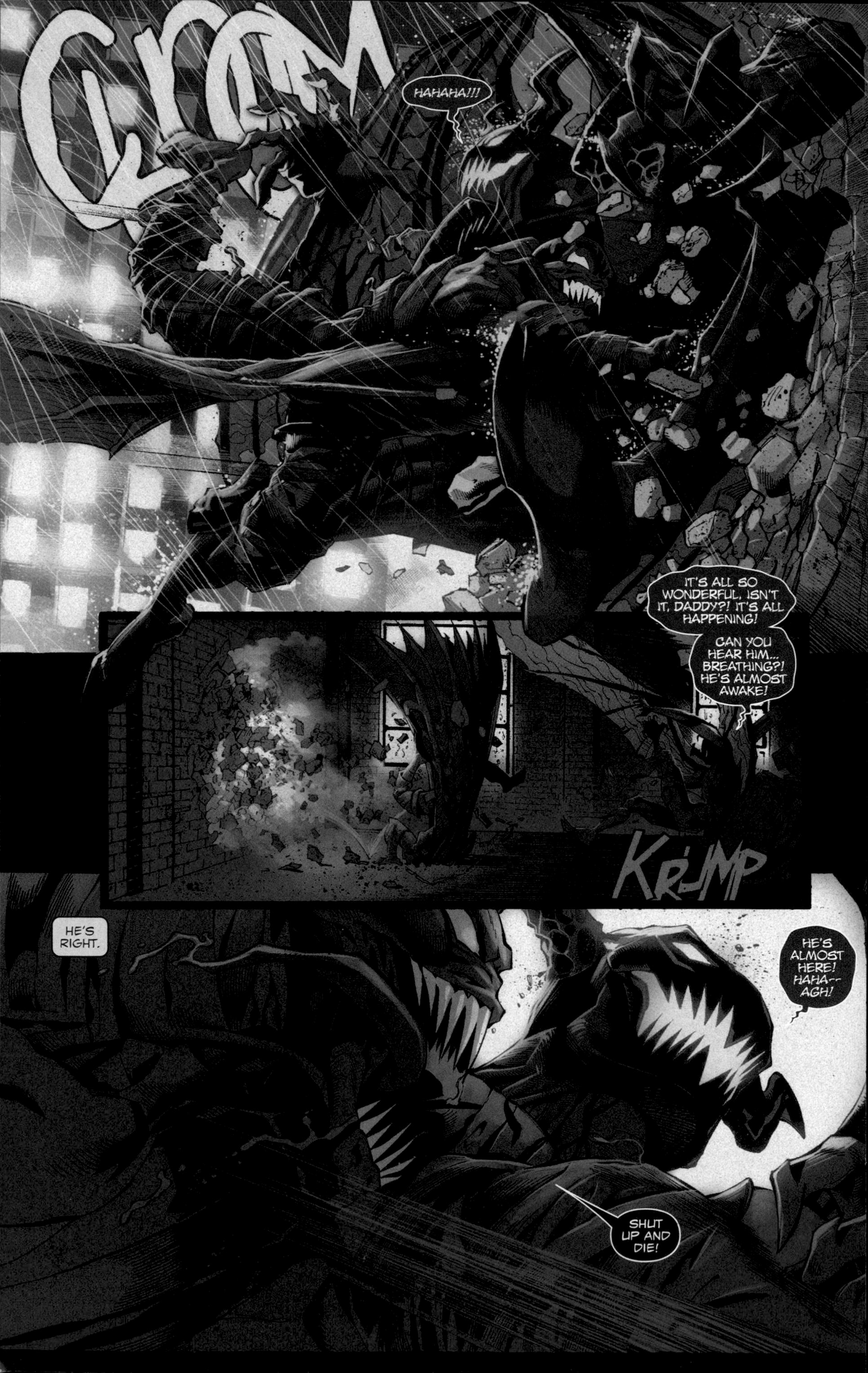
CRAM
HAHAHA!!!
IT'S ALL SO WONDERFUL, ISN'T IT, DADDY?! IT'S ALL HAPPENING!
CAN YOU HEAR HIM... BREATHING?! HE'S ALMOST AWAKE!
KRUMP
HE'S RIGHT.
HE'S ALMOST HERE! HAHA-- AGH!
SHUT UP AND DIE!

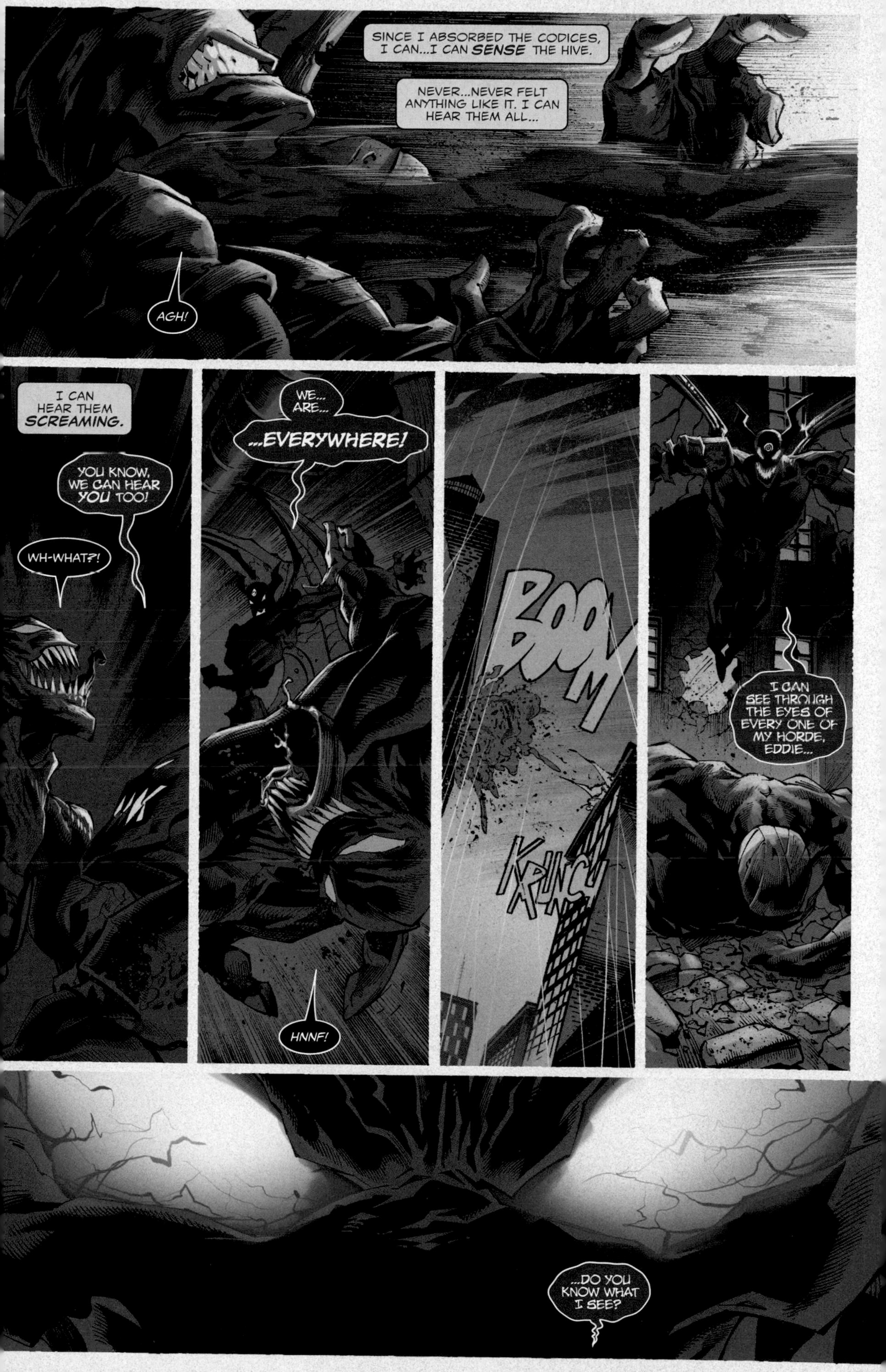

SINCE I ABSORBED THE CODICES, I CAN...I CAN SENSE THE HIVE.
NEVER...NEVER FELT ANYTHING LIKE IT. I CAN HEAR THEM ALL...
AGH!
I CAN HEAR THEM SCREAMING.
YOU KNOW, WE CAN HEAR YOU TOO!
WH-WHAT?!
WE... ARE...
...EVERYWHERE!
HNNF!
BOOM
KRUNCH
I CAN SEE THROUGH THE EYES OF EVERY ONE OF MY HORDE, EDDIE...
...DO YOU KNOW WHAT I SEE?

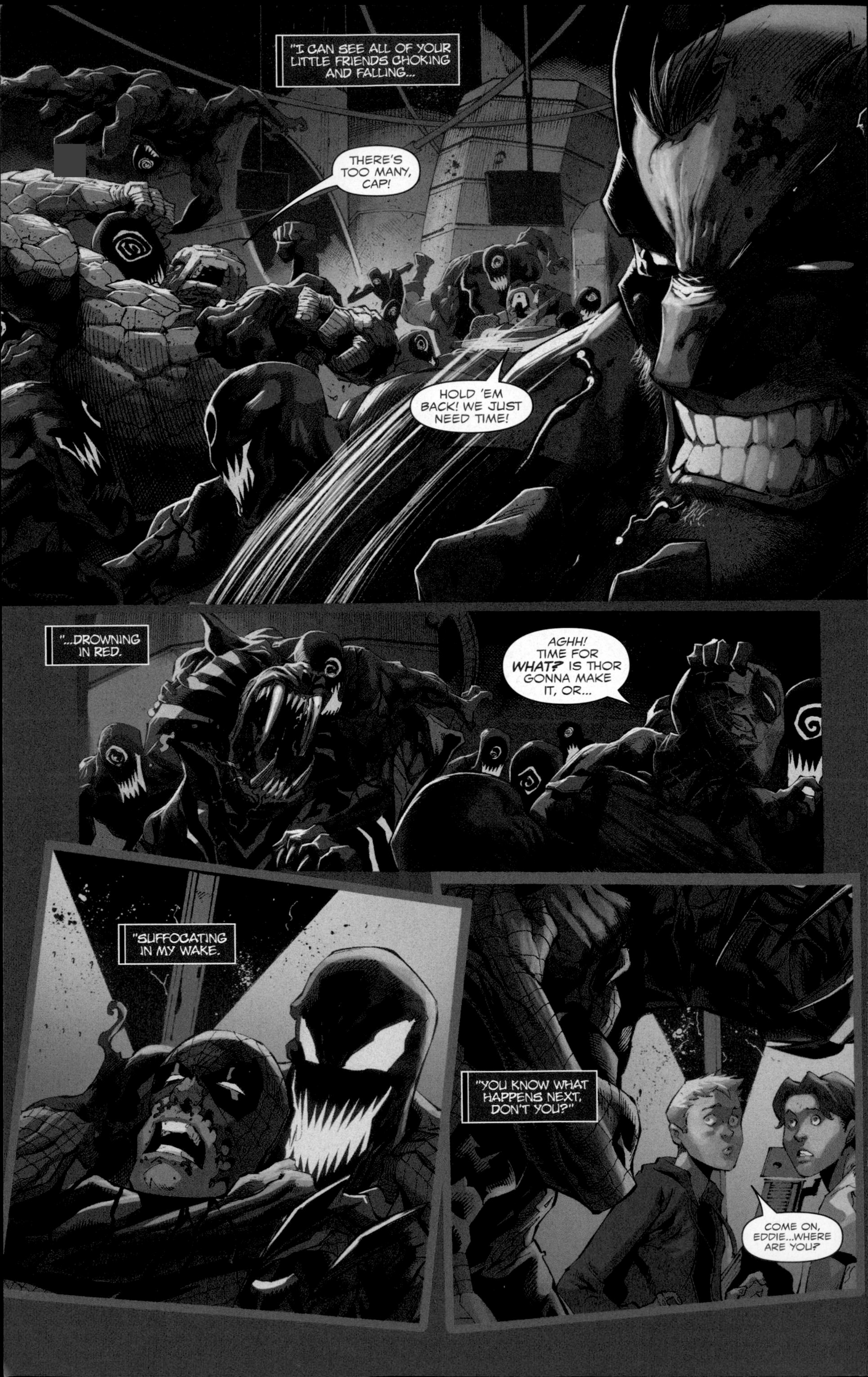
"I CAN SEE ALL OF YOUR LITTLE FRIENDS CHOKING AND FALLING...
THERE'S TOO MANY, CAP!
HOLD 'EM BACK! WE JUST NEED TIME!
"...DROWNING IN RED.
AGHH! TIME FOR WHAT? IS THOR GONNA MAKE IT, OR...
"SUFFOCATING IN MY WAKE.
"YOU KNOW WHAT HAPPENS NEXT, DON'T YOU?"
COME ON, EDDIE...WHERE ARE YOU?

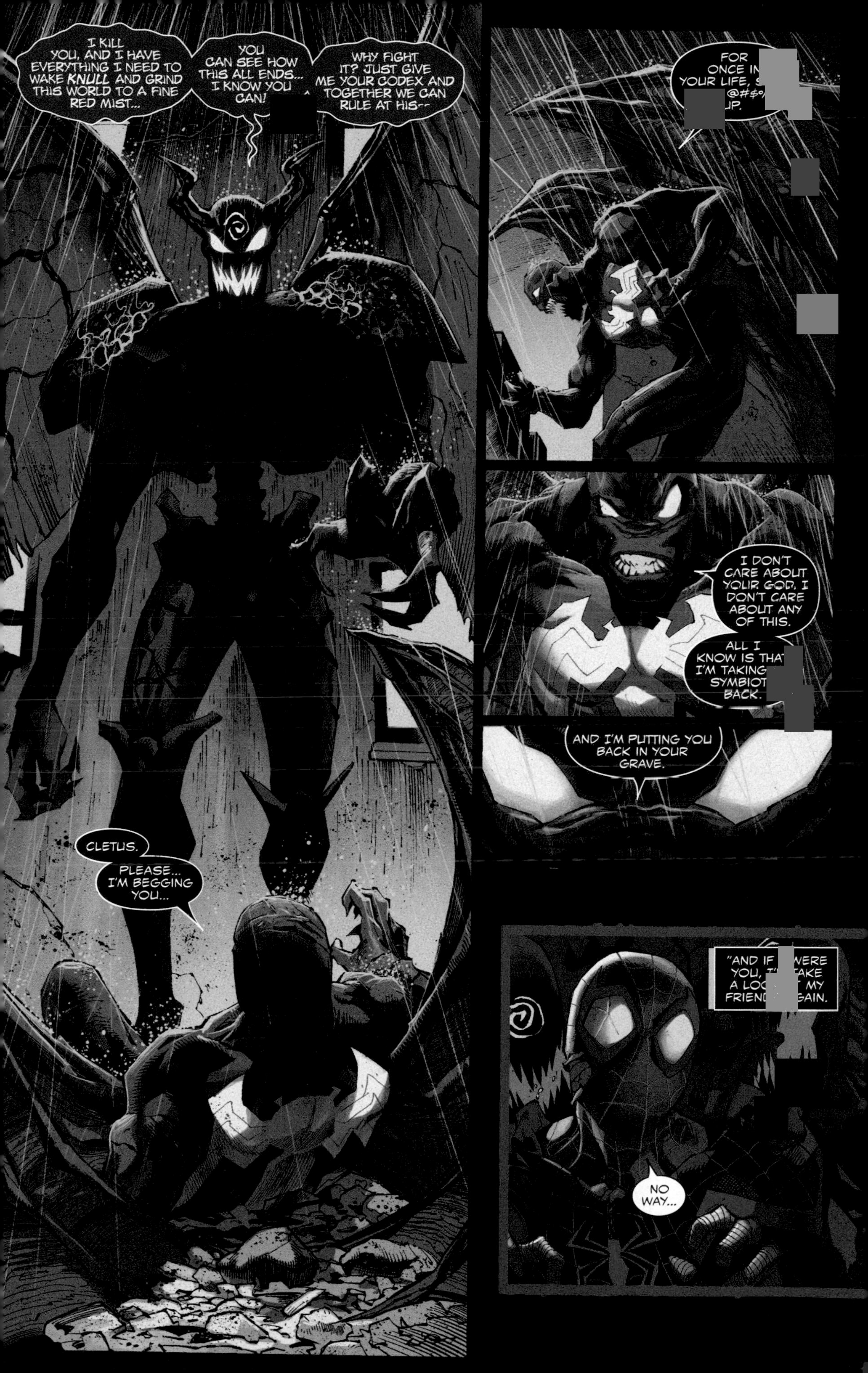

I KILL YOU, AND I HAVE EVERYTHING I NEED TO WAKE KNULL AND GRIND THIS WORLD TO A FINE RED MIST...
YOU CAN SEE HOW THIS ALL ENDS... I KNOW YOU CAN!
WHY FIGHT IT? JUST GIVE ME YOUR CODEX AND TOGETHER WE CAN RULE AT HIS--
CLETUS.
PLEASE... I'M BEGGING YOU...
FOR ONCE IN[redacted] YOUR LIFE, S[redacted] @#$[redacted] UP.
I DON'T CARE ABOUT YOUR GOD, I DON'T CARE ABOUT ANY OF THIS.
ALL I KNOW IS THAT[redacted] I'M TAKING[redacted] SYMBIOT[redacted] BACK.
AND I'M PUTTING YOU BACK IN YOUR GRAVE.
"AND IF [redacted] WERE YOU, I'[redacted]TAKE A LOO[redacted]T MY FRIEND[redacted]GAIN.
NO WAY...

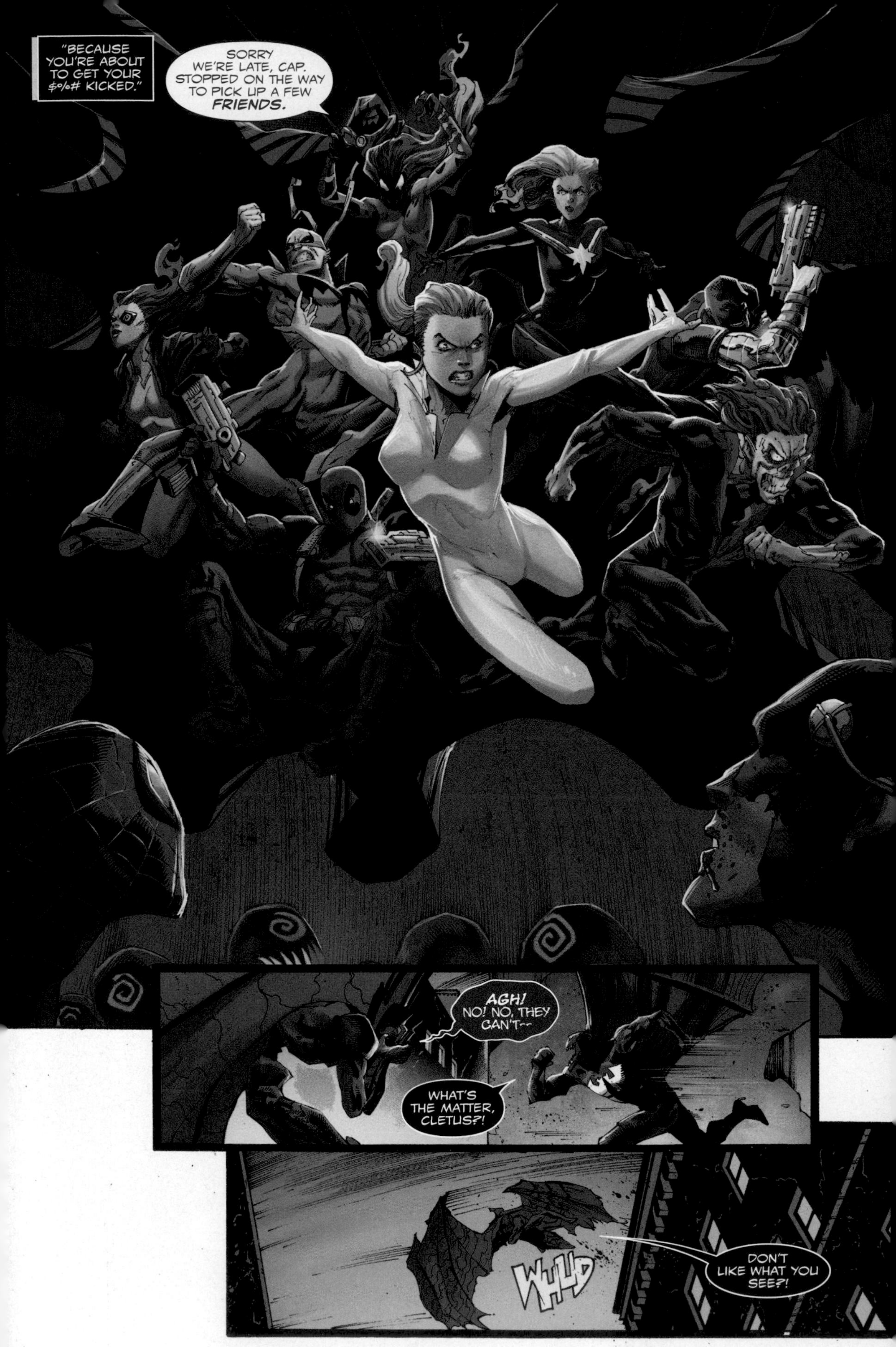
"BECAUSE YOU'RE ABOUT TO GET YOUR $%# KICKED."
SORRY WE'RE LATE, CAP. STOPPED ON THE WAY TO PICK UP A FEW FRIENDS.
AGH! NO! NO, THEY CAN'T--
WHAT'S THE MATTER, CLETUS?!
WHUD
DON'T LIKE WHAT YOU SEE?!

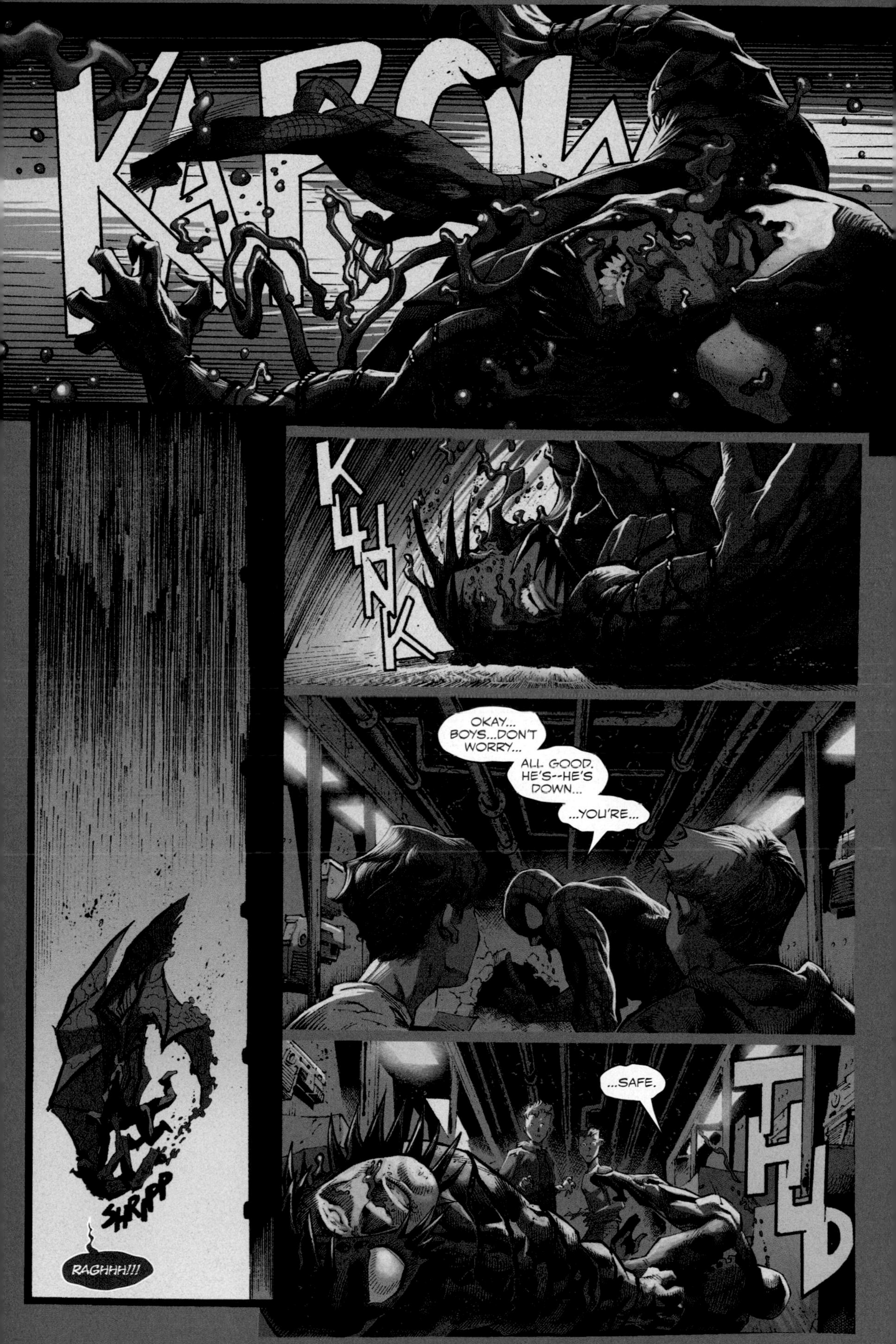
KAPOW
K-THUNK
OKAY... BOYS...DON'T WORRY...
ALL GOOD. HE'S--HE'S DOWN...
...YOU'RE...
SHRAPP
RAGHHH!!!
...SAFE.
THUD

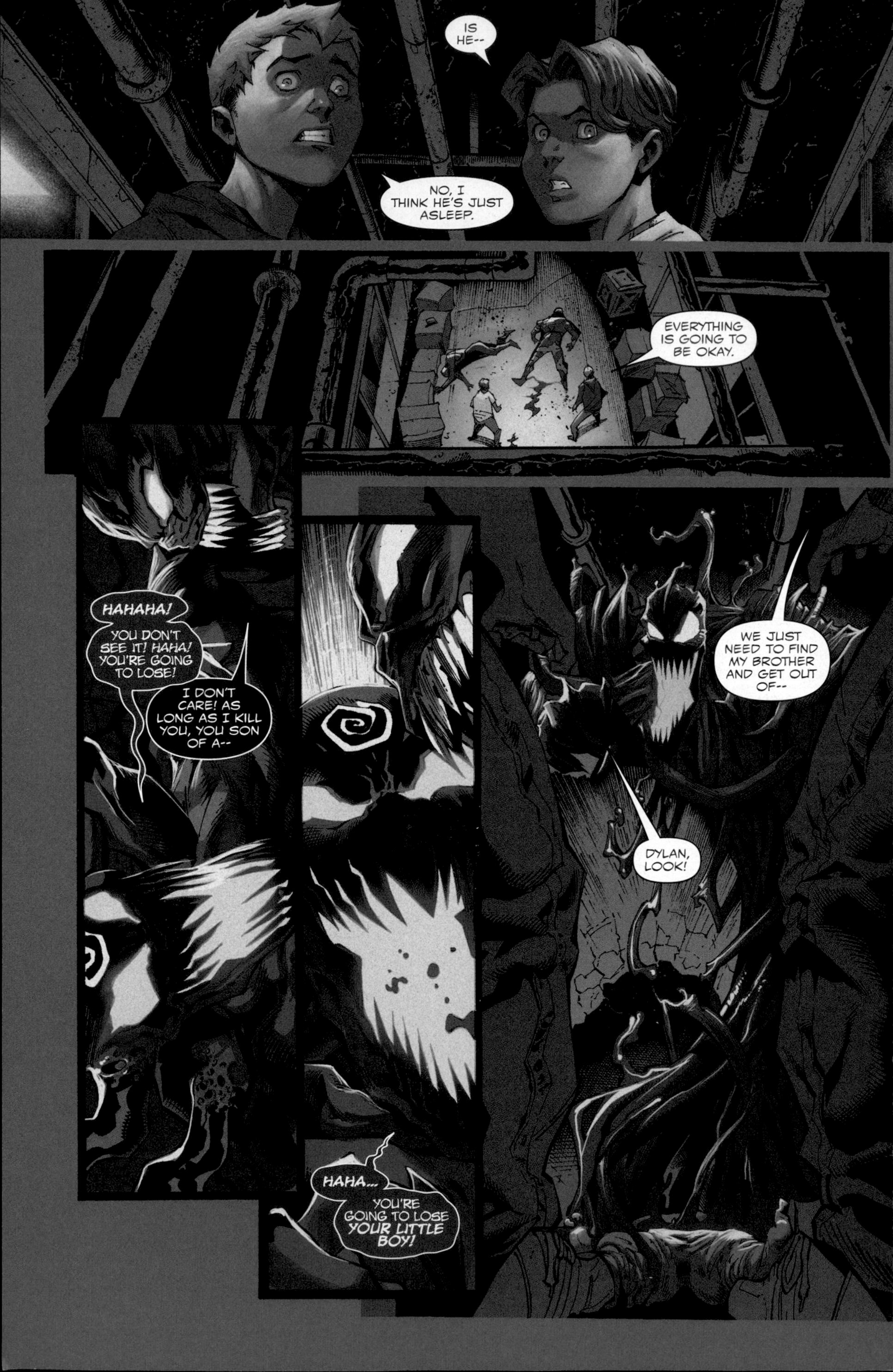
IS HE--
NO, I THINK HE'S JUST ASLEEP.
EVERYTHING IS GOING TO BE OKAY.
HAHAHA!
YOU DON'T SEE IT! HAHA! YOU'RE GOING TO LOSE!
I DON'T CARE! AS LONG AS I KILL YOU, YOU SON OF A--
HAHA...
YOU'RE GOING TO LOSE YOUR LITTLE BOY!
WE JUST NEED TO FIND MY BROTHER AND GET OUT OF--
DYLAN, LOOK!

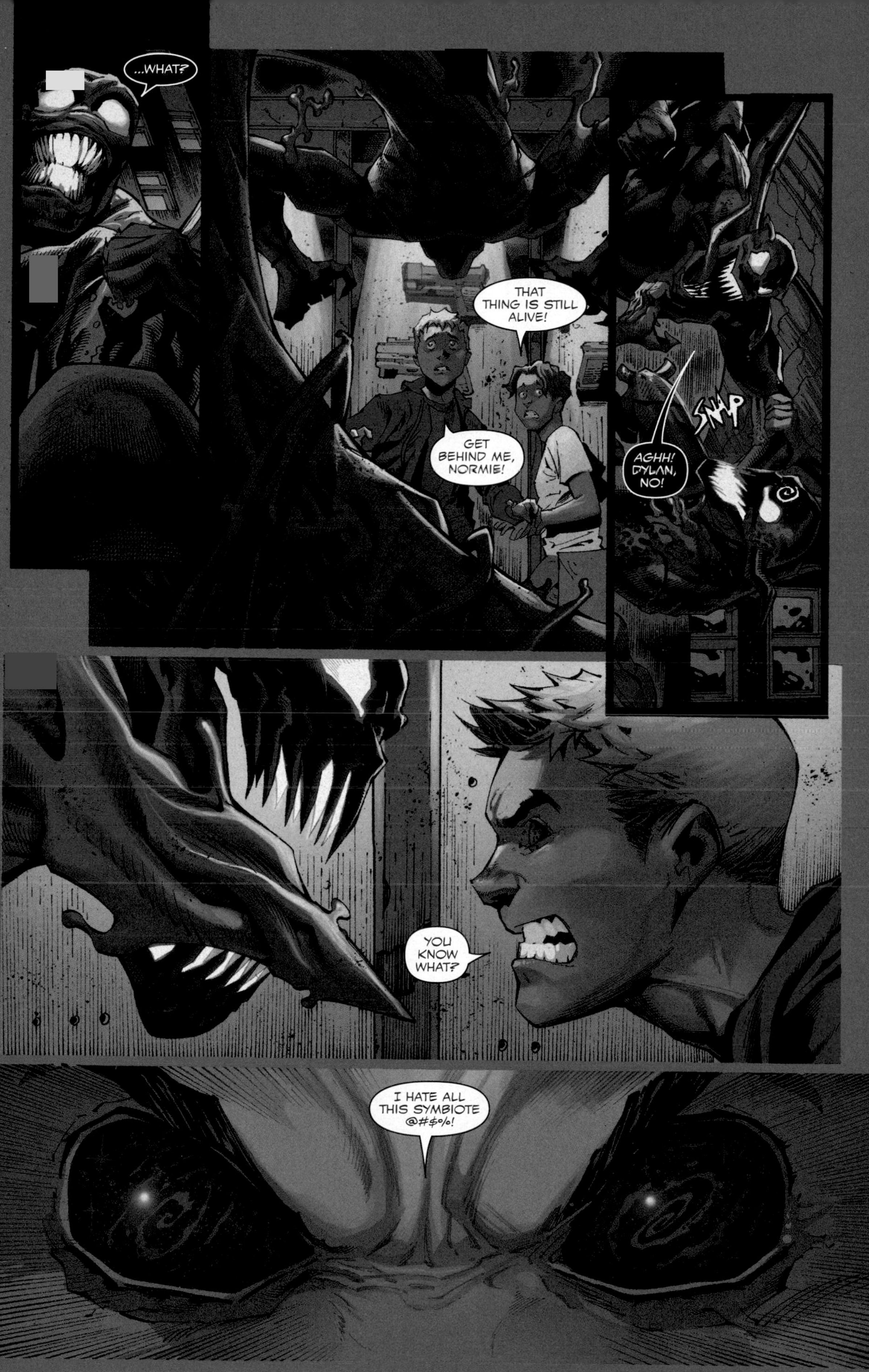
...WHAT?
THAT THING IS STILL ALIVE!
GET BEHIND ME, NORMIE!
SNAP
AGHH! DYLAN, NO!
YOU KNOW WHAT?
I HATE ALL THIS SYMBIOTE @#$%!

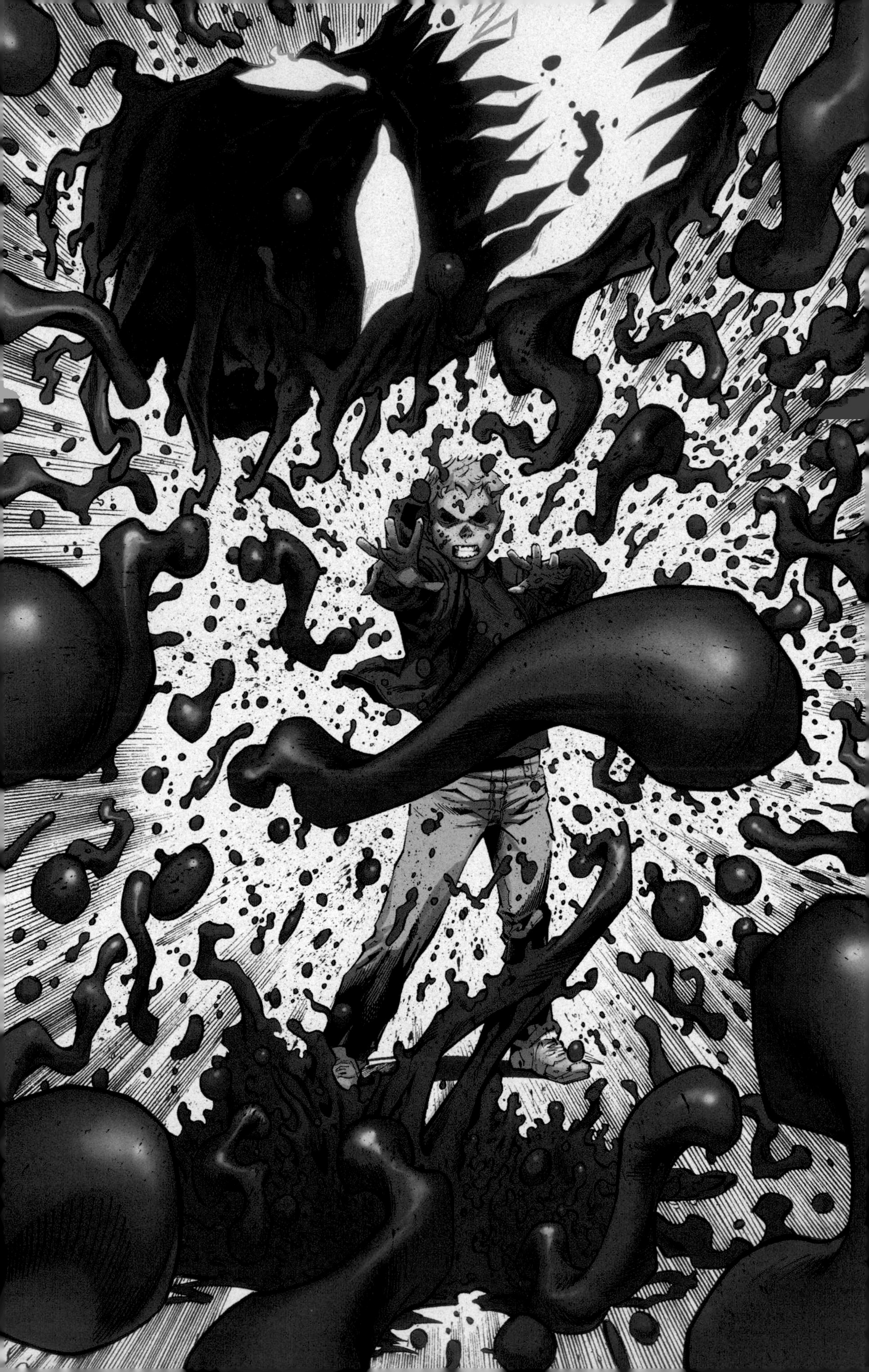

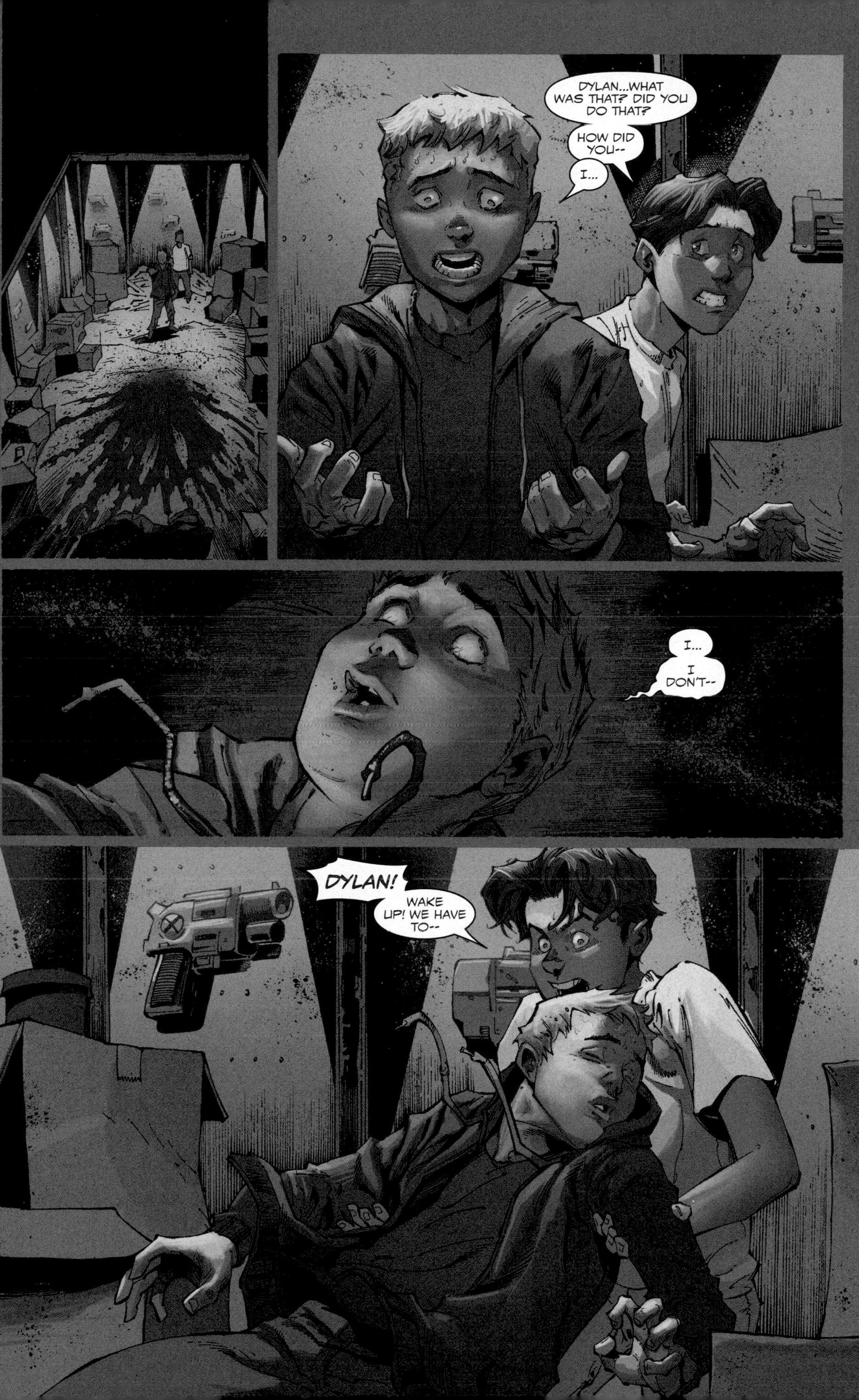
DYLAN...WHAT WAS THAT? DID YOU DO THAT?
HOW DID YOU--
I...
I...
I DON'T--
DYLAN!
WAKE UP! WE HAVE TO--

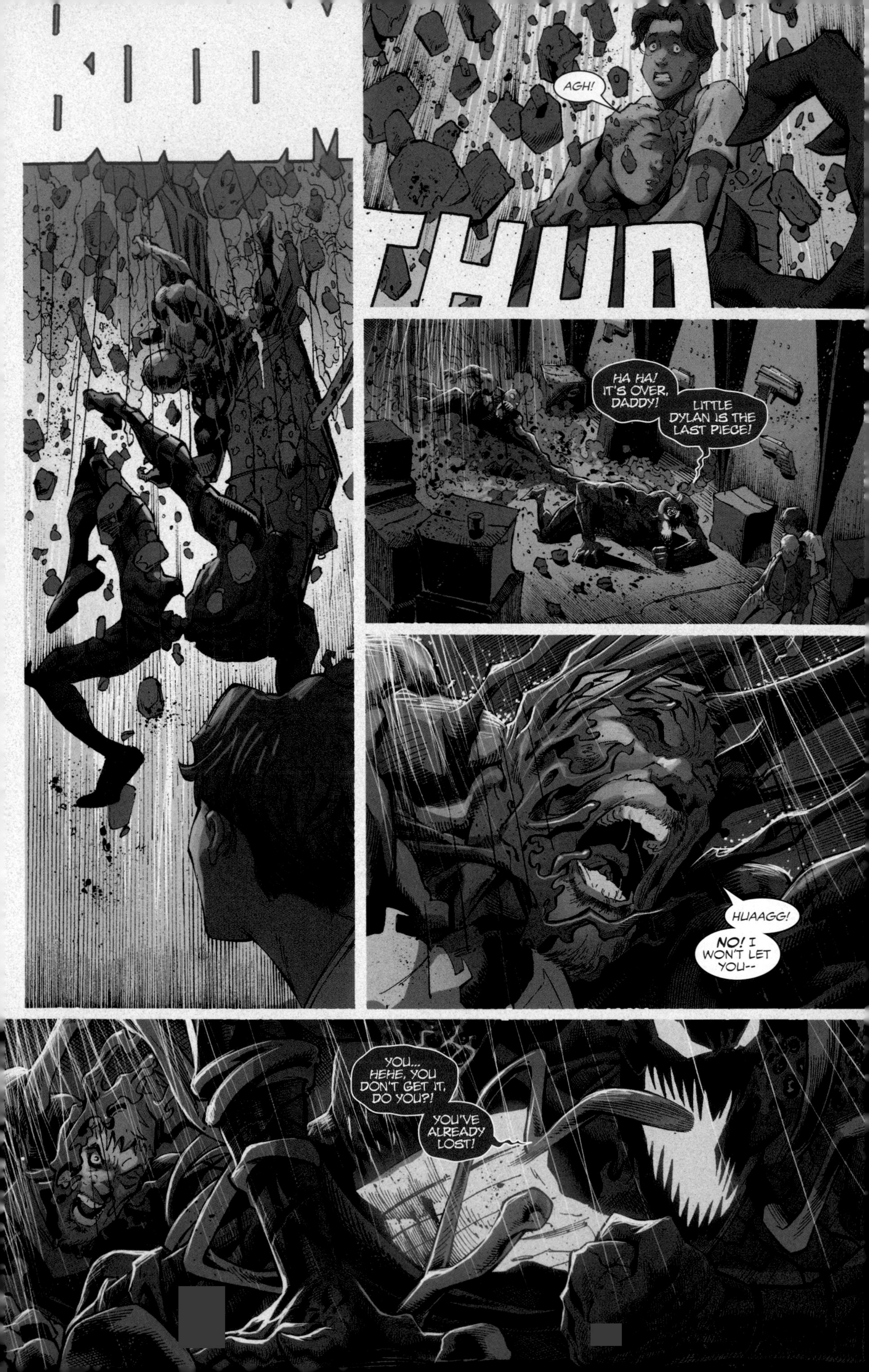
AGH!
HA HA! IT'S OVER, DADDY!
LITTLE DYLAN IS THE LAST PIECE!
HUAAGG!
NO! I WON'T LET YOU--
YOU... HEHE, YOU DON'T GET IT, DO YOU?!
YOU'VE ALREADY LOST!

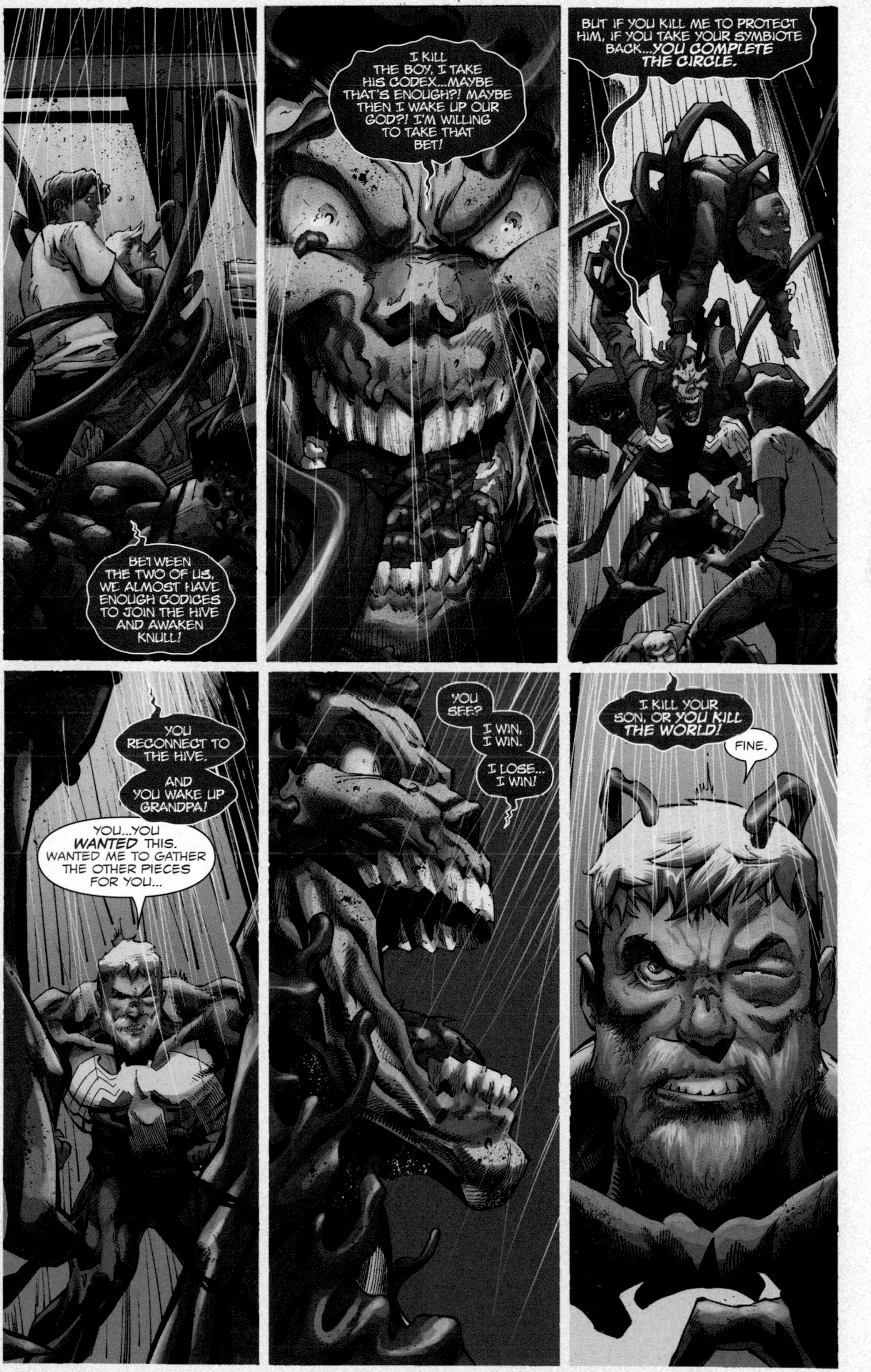
BETWEEN THE TWO OF US, WE ALMOST HAVE ENOUGH CODICES TO JOIN THE HIVE AND AWAKEN KNULL!
I KILL THE BOY, I TAKE HIS CODEX...MAYBE THAT'S ENOUGH?! MAYBE THEN I WAKE UP OUR GOD?! I'M WILLING TO TAKE THAT BET!
BUT IF YOU KILL ME TO PROTECT HIM, IF YOU TAKE YOUR SYMBIOTE BACK...YOU COMPLETE THE CIRCLE.
YOU RECONNECT TO THE HIVE.
AND YOU WAKE UP GRANDPA!
YOU...YOU WANTED THIS. WANTED ME TO GATHER THE OTHER PIECES FOR YOU...
YOU SEE?
I WIN, I WIN.
I LOSE... I WIN!
I KILL YOUR SON, OR YOU KILL THE WORLD!
FINE.

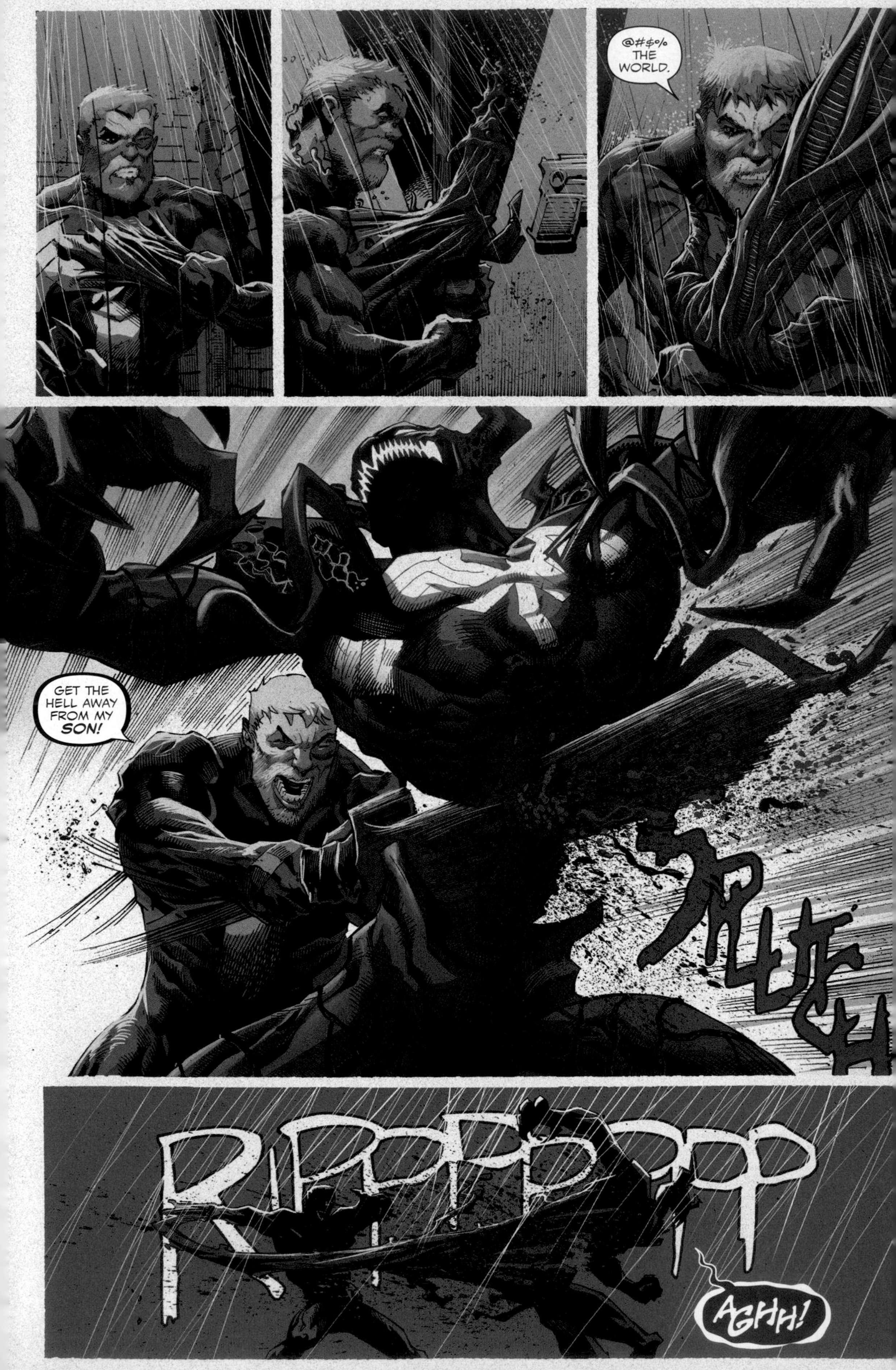

@#$% THE WORLD.
GET THE HELL AWAY FROM MY SON!
SPLUTCH
RIPPPPPPP
AGHH!

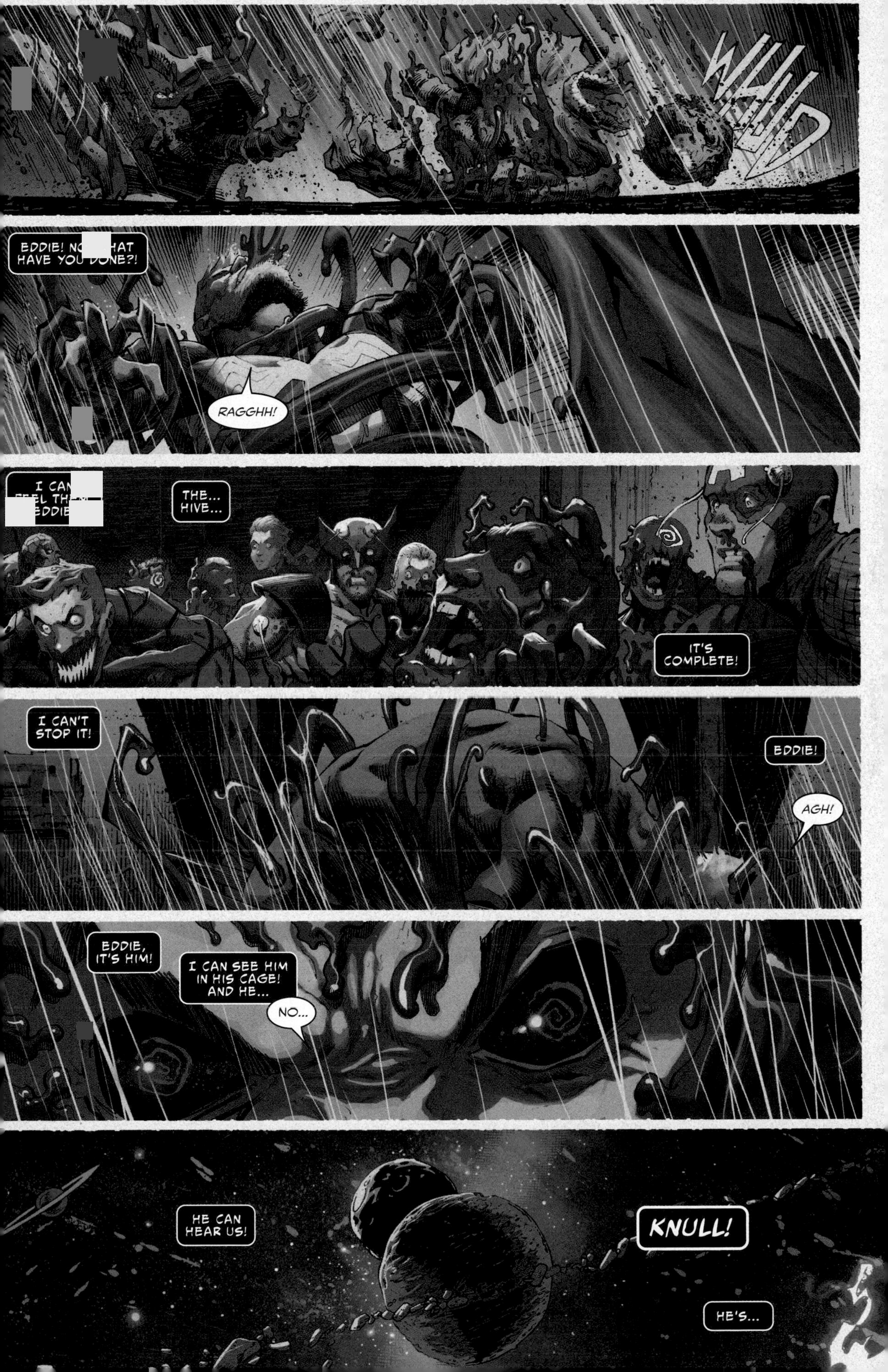
WHUD
EDDIE! NO
HAVE YOU DONE?!
RAGGHH!
I CAN
THE... HIVE...
IT'S COMPLETE!
I CAN'T STOP IT!
EDDIE!
AGH!
EDDIE, IT'S HIM!
I CAN SEE HIM IN HIS CAGE! AND HE...
NO...
HE CAN HEAR US!
KNULL!
HE'S...

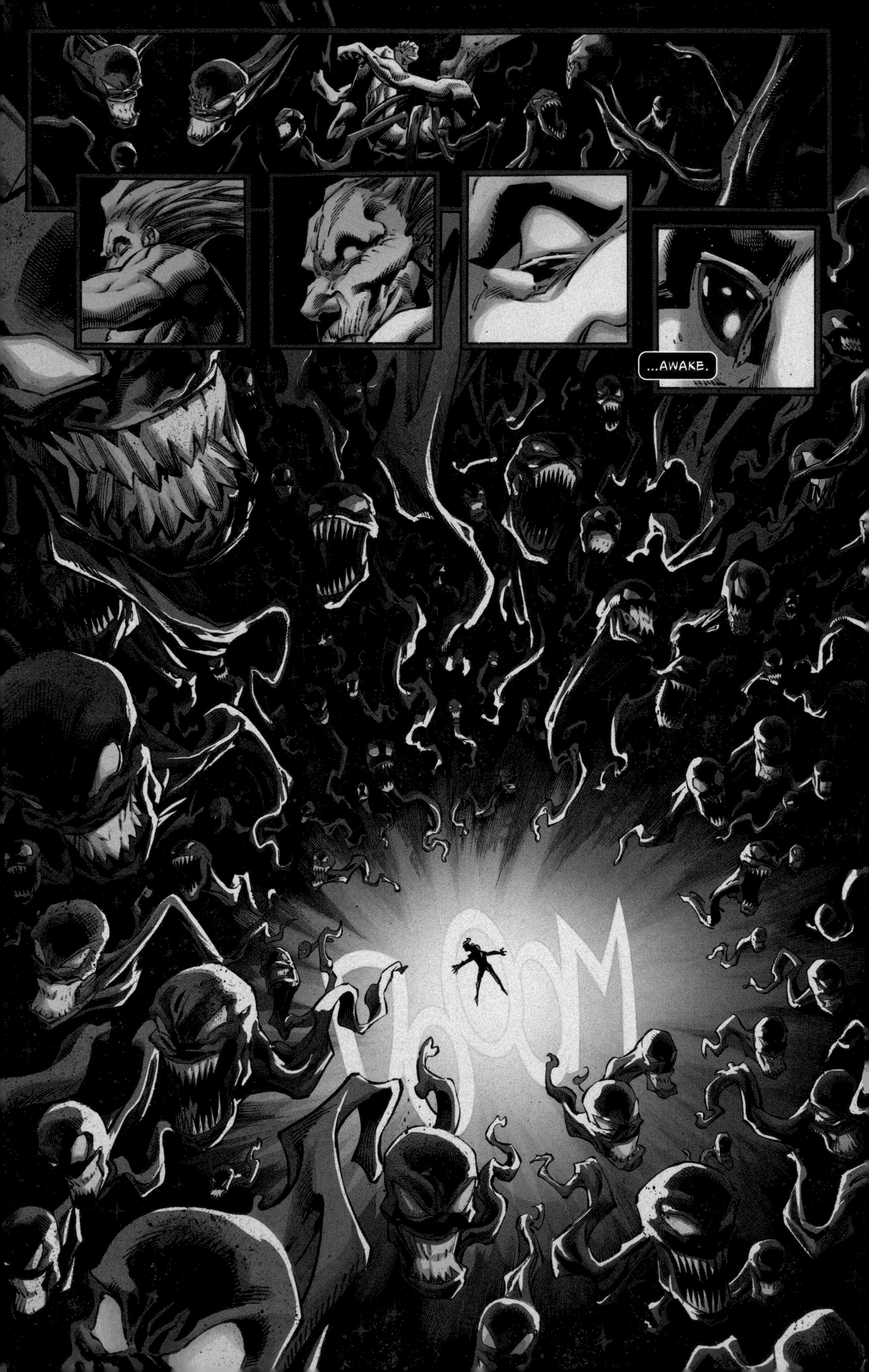
...AWAKE.
CHOOOM

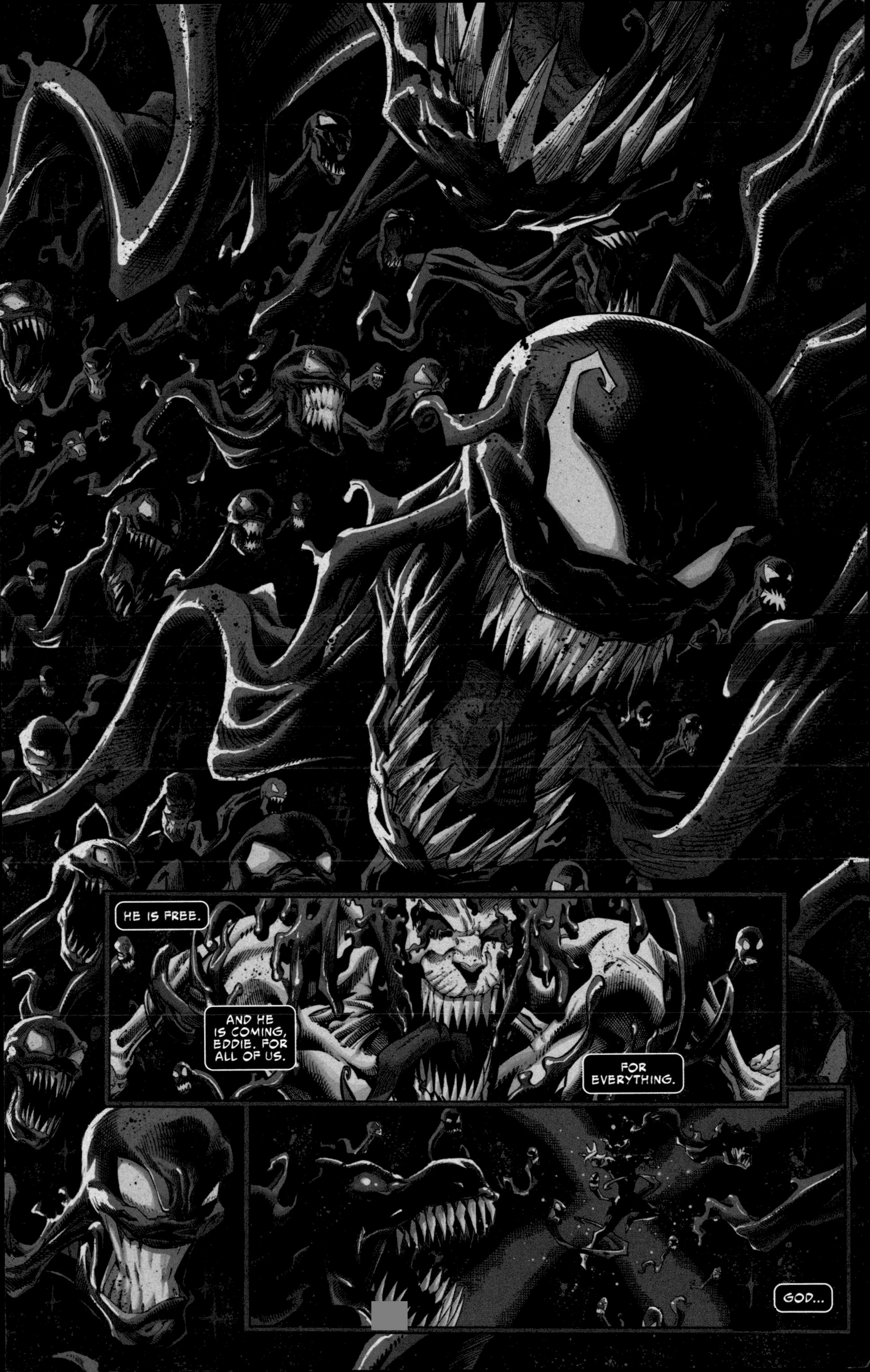
HE IS FREE.
AND HE IS COMING, EDDIE. FOR ALL OF US.
FOR EVERYTHING.
GOD...

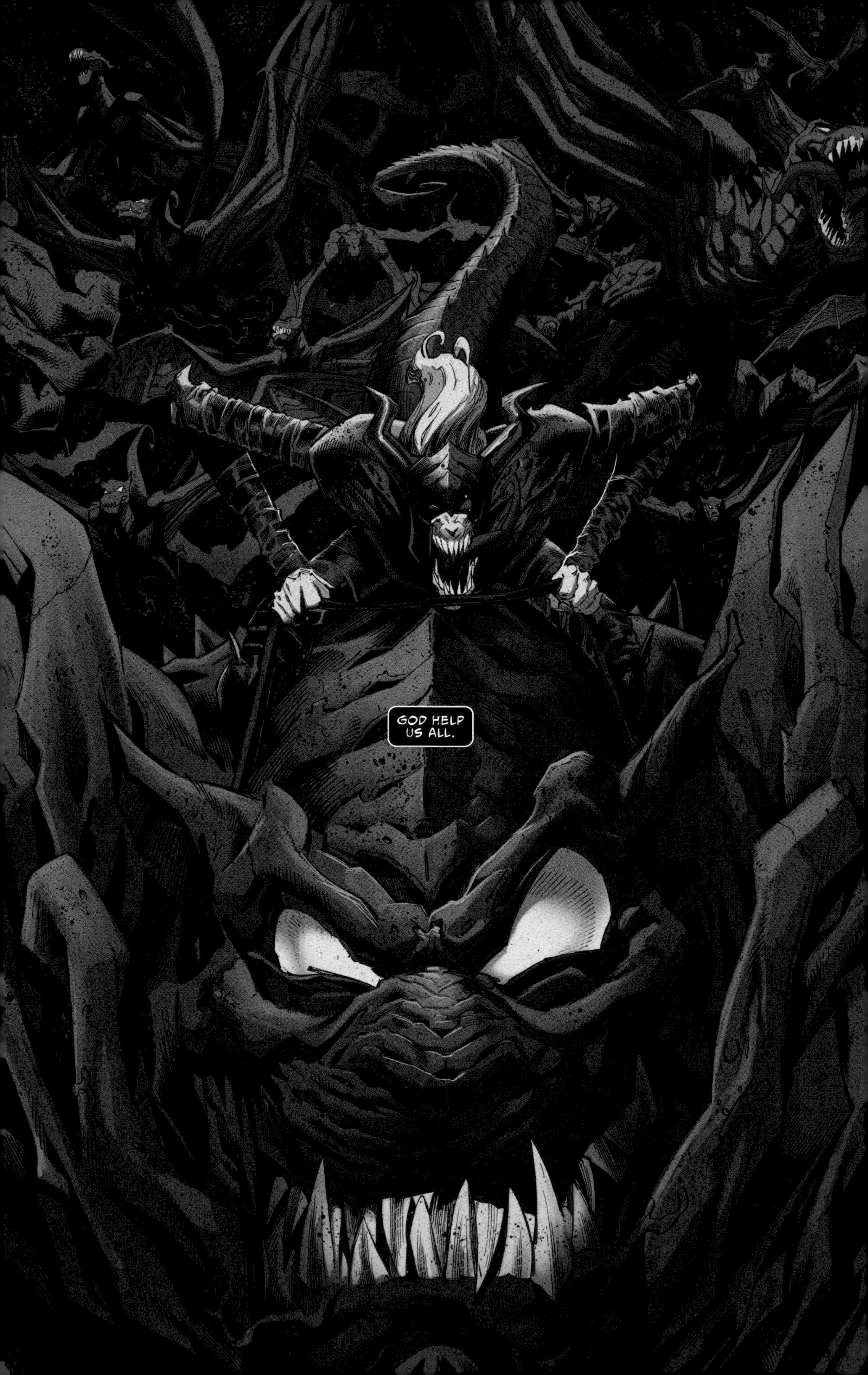
GOD HELP US ALL.

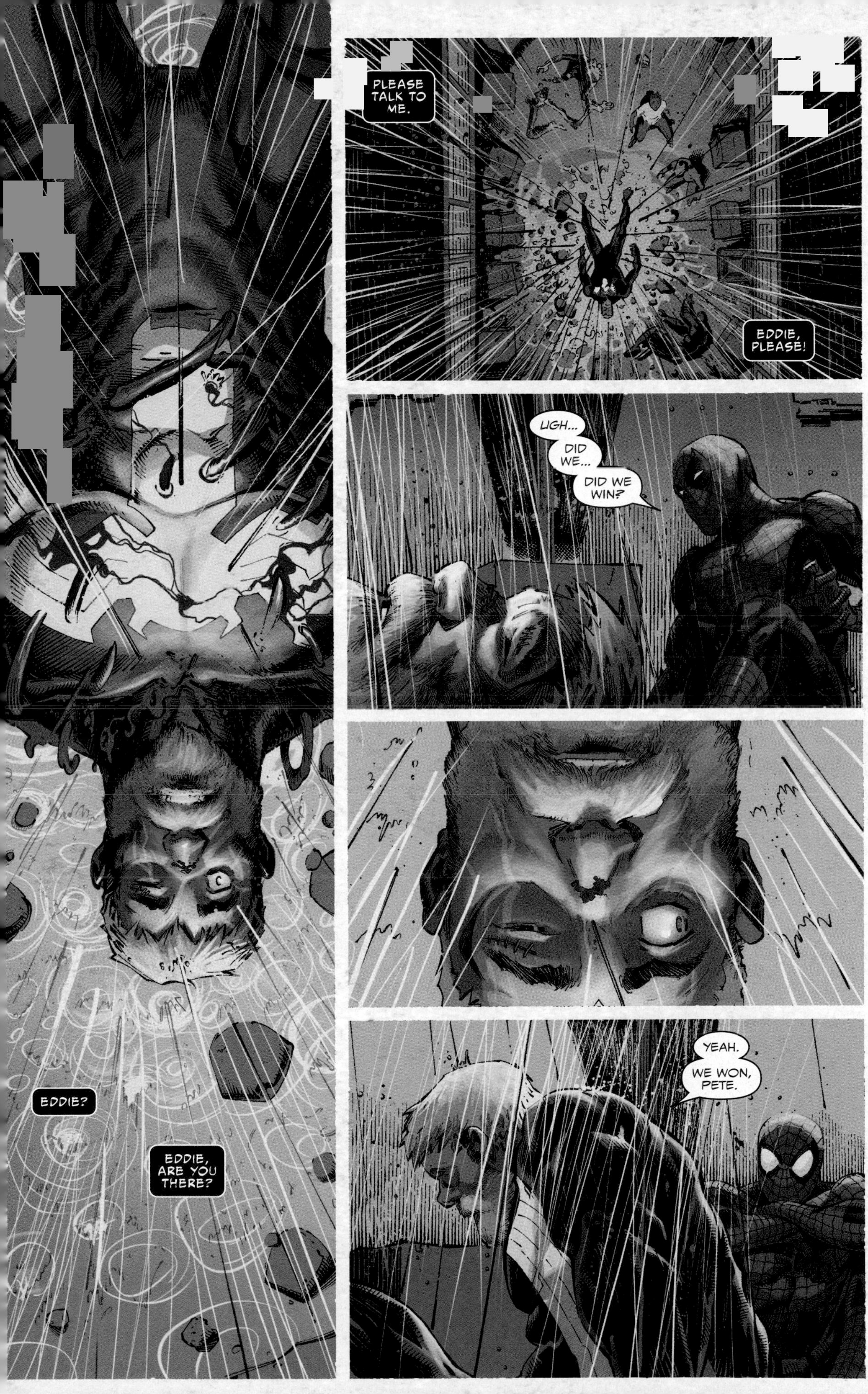
EDDIE?
EDDIE, ARE YOU THERE?
PLEASE TALK TO ME.
EDDIE, PLEASE!
UGH...
DID WE...
DID WE WIN?
YEAH.
WE WON, PETE.

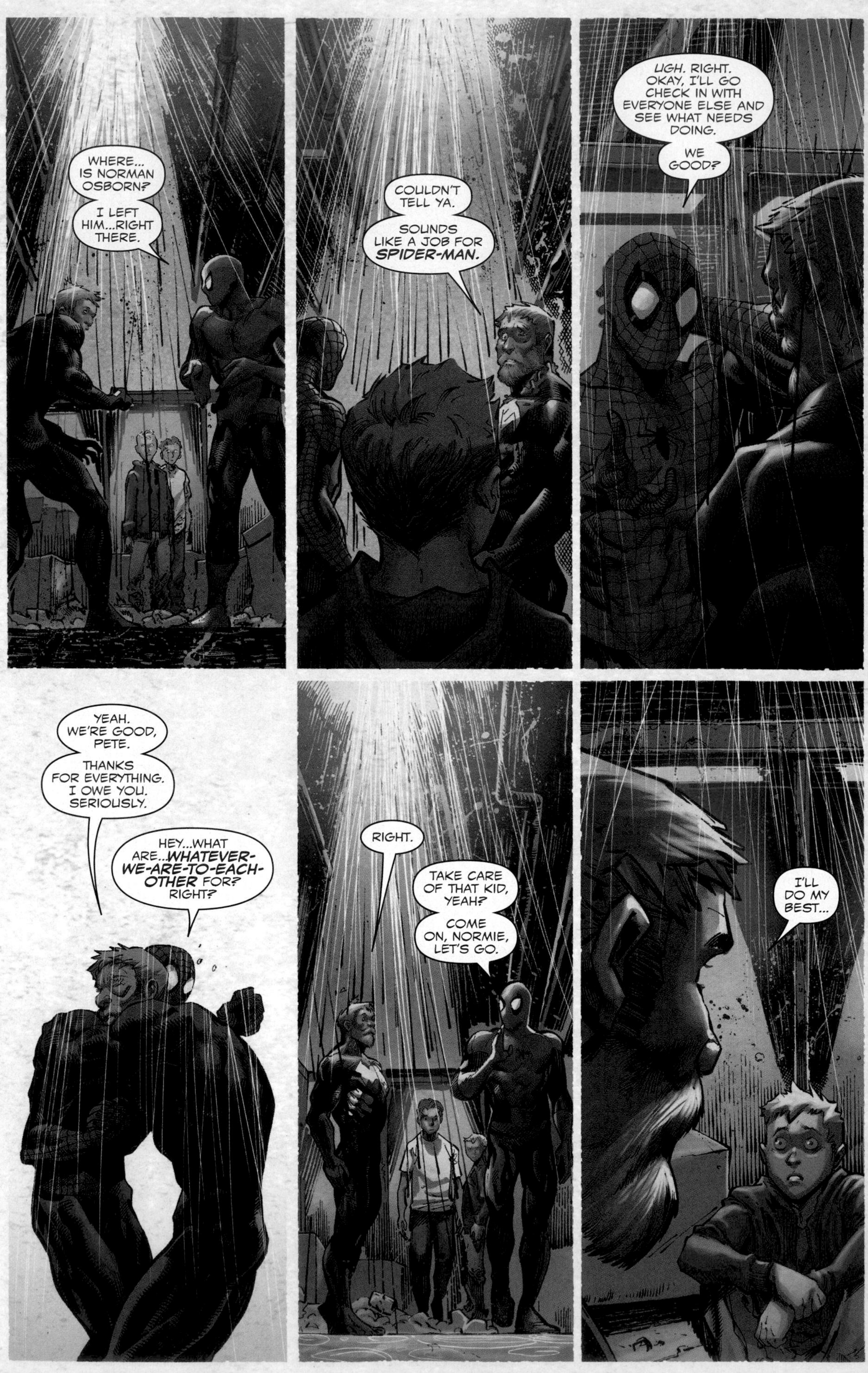
WHERE... IS NORMAN OSBORN?
I LEFT HIM...RIGHT THERE.
COULDN'T TELL YA.
SOUNDS LIKE A JOB FOR SPIDER-MAN.
UGH. RIGHT. OKAY, I'LL GO CHECK IN WITH EVERYONE ELSE AND SEE WHAT NEEDS DOING.
WE GOOD?
YEAH. WE'RE GOOD, PETE.
THANKS FOR EVERYTHING. I OWE YOU. SERIOUSLY.
HEY...WHAT ARE...WHATEVER-WE-ARE-TO-EACH-OTHER FOR? RIGHT?
RIGHT.
TAKE CARE OF THAT KID, YEAH?
COME ON, NORMIE, LET'S GO.
I'LL DO MY BEST...

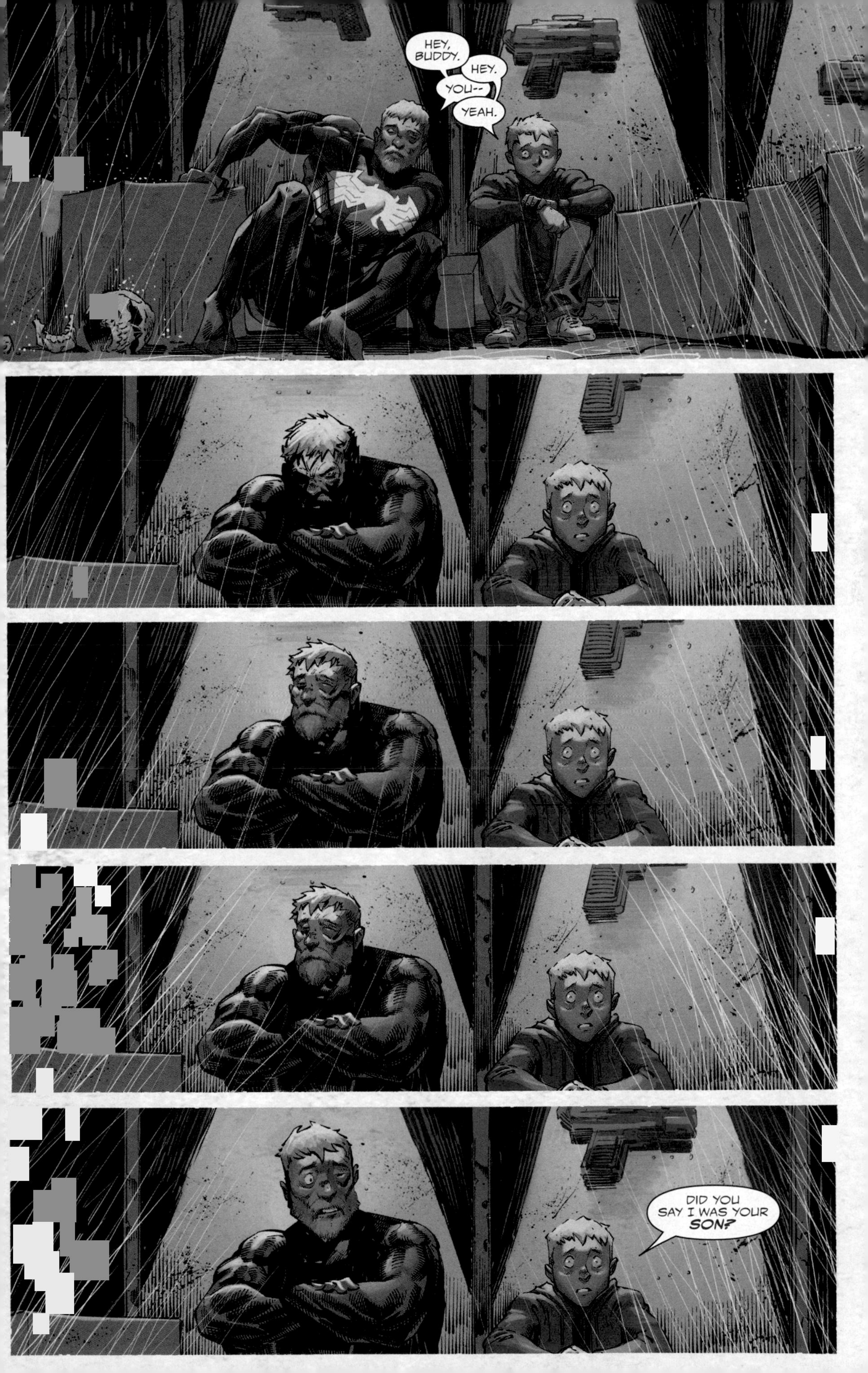
HEY, BUDDY.
HEY.
YOU--
YEAH.
DID YOU SAY I WAS YOUR SON?

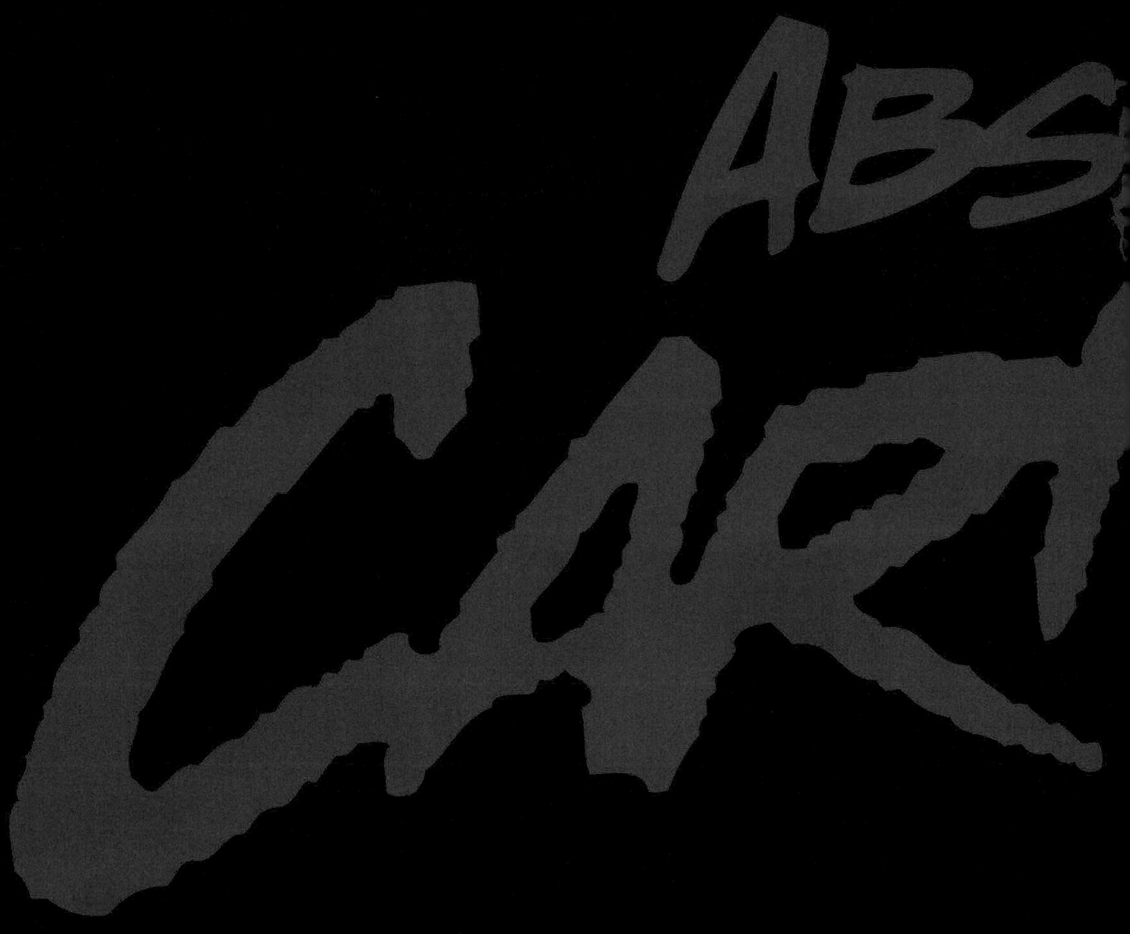
ABS
CAR

LUTE

AGE

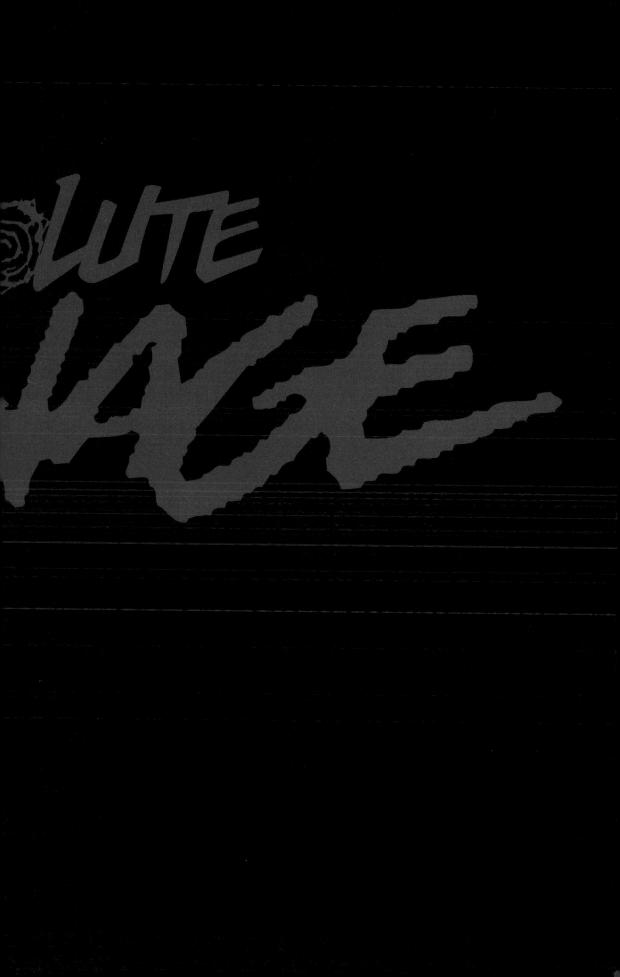

RAVENCROFT
INSTITUTE FOR THE CRIMINALLY INSANE

INITIAL BEHAVIORAL ASSESSMENT

Instructions: *This form is to be completed, signed and dated for all clients who are being referred for psychiatric services.*

Presentation at ED [ ] Self [ ] Family/Friend [X] Police [ ] Provider [ ] Other [ ] N/A

Referral Source/Relationship POLICE (SPIDER-MAN) Date/Time of Referral 6/4

[X] On-site OR [ ] Walk-In AND [X] Scheduled OR [ ] Unscheduled

Assessment Began 3/1 (Date (MM/DD)) and 9 00 (Time (00:00)) a.m. (circled) / p.m. Ended 3/1 (Date (MM/DD)) and 12 00 (Time (00:00)) a.m. / p.m. (circled)

Name of Client CLETUS KASADY (ALIAS: CARNAGE) [X] Male [ ] Female

Street Address ______ City ______ Zip ______ Phone ( ) ______

Date of Birth 0 4 0 7 9 3 (m m d d y y) Patient No. A S M 0 1 0 3 6 1

Employed? [ ] YES [X] NO [ ] Unknown Occupation ______ Veteran? Yes [ ] No [X] Combat? Yes [ ] No [X]

Language [X] English [ ] Spanish [ ] Arabic [ ] Chinese [ ] Other ______ Interpreter Needed [ ] Yes [X] No

[ ] Deaf/Hard of Hearing with [ ] American Sign Language

[ ] Deaf/Hard of Hearing (does not communicate using ASL)

Recent Stressors: [X] Relationship [ ] Family [ ] Job [ ] Housing [ ] Financial [X] Legal [ ] Other ______

Medical History/Treatment/Pertinent injuries: (diagnosis/describe) PATIENT ADMITTED AFTER PHYSICAL CONFLICT W/ Spider-MAN. SUFFERED SHOCK SYMPTOMS AFTER BEING FORCIBLY REMOVED FROM ALIEN/EXTERRESTRIAL SYMBIOTE

Behavioral Health History/Treatment

Substance Use History/Treatment

Is there a family history of substance use issues? [ ] YES [ ] NO [X] Unknown

Does the person currently use mind-altering substances (drugs, alcohol, marijuana, etc.) [ ] YES [ ] NO [X] Unknown

If yes, what substances: Blood Work inconclusive. Prolonged exposure to ALIEN SYMBIOTE APPEAR TO HAVE AFFECTED PATIENT'S BODY CHEMISTRY

Mental Health History/Treatment

Is there a family history of mental health issues? [X] YES [ ] NO [ ] Unknown

(diagnosis/describe) PATIENT'S MOTHER DIAGNOSED W/ PARANOID Scizophrenia / Paternal History Unknown

Is there a family history of suicide attempt(s) or completion(s)? [ ] YES [ ] NO [X] Unknown

(describe) Mother Died During Childbirth / Paternal History Unknown

TRANSCRIPT OF PSYCHICIATRIC EVALUATION
PATIENT NAME: CLETUS KASADY
PATIENT NO.: ASM010361
TRANSCRIBED BY CLAY McLEOD CHAPMAN

INTERVIEWER: Testing. Testing. Dr. Davinia Marcia Pournella initiating intake interview with subject #626, a Mr. Cletus Kasady, at approximately...3:32 PM. Hello, Mr. Kasady.

KASADY: Please. My daddy was the Mr. Kasady around our house. You can call me Cletus, Doc.

INTERVIEWER: I hope you're comfortable, Cletus. The restraints aren't too tight?

KASADY: Snug as a bug in a rug, Doc. You recording this? That what you're doing?

INTERVIEWER: As a matter of fact, yes, I am. Are you uneasy with that?

KASADY: Don't like it. Don't like it one bit. No, sir.

INTERVIEWER: And why's that?

KASADY: You ever had a tape recorder as a kid, Doc? Ever record your own voice for XXXX and giggles? But when you play it back, it don't sound nothing like you? Nothing at all. Matter a fact, it sounds like somebody else's voice altogether... Like it's a different person using your mouth.

INTERVIEWER: Is that how you feel sometimes, Cletus? Like you're a different person?

KASADY: Hell, it's a regular party in my head sometimes. A real rager, you know? I've invited along all my friends and they've cranked the music up so loud, I can't even hear myself think.

INTERVIEWER: I imagine that must be painful.

KASADY: Painful? Doc, have you ever been to one of my brain jamborees? The party don't stop! You should swing by after work. Hop on in.

INTERVIEWER: Thank you for the invite. Now I was wondering if we might talk about why--

KASADY: Turn it off.

INTERVIEWER: Excuse me?

KASADY: I said, turn the tape recorder off. You ain't stealing my voice.

INTERVIEWER: I assure you, Cletus, that's not my intention. This is merely for reference's sake.

KASADY: Ever hear how Native Americans never liked having their picture taken 'cause they thought the photograph captured their soul? I remember hearing that and thinking to myself... That's just silly. But the more I got to thinking about it, the more I kinda liked the idea. Having something to hold onto of somebody special. Somebody you loooved. A little piece of them.

INTERVIEWER: Mr. Kasady--

KASADY: Anybody can take a picture. I wanted more of my special friends. I wanted something reeeal special. Something nobody else could have. I wanted to keep their screams.

INTERVIEWER: That's close enough, Mr. Kasady. Lean back, please--

KASADY: I kept that tape recorder I had when I was a kid. Sometimes I made tapes for my special friends. And just when I was done playing with them, I made sure I brought that itty-bitty built-in microphone right up to their mouths and pressed record right before they breathed their last. I captured that rattle, Doc. That death rattle. Their last exhale is mine, sucked right into the cassette. And I got so many tapes, doc. I play 'em on the car stereo. I make little mixtapes--my Greatest Gasps, I guess you could call it. One rattle after another.

INTERVIEWER: That's enough. I'm concluding this interview--

KASADY: Some of them are move lively than others. Some of them have a husky heft to them, some even say a word, I capture their voices, I listen to them, I play them over and over again, all those sighs, all those squeals, all those screams cut short they're mine all mine I hear them all the time all the time I hear them all I hear them all I hear them all the

(END OF RECORDING.)

RAVENCROFT
INSTITUTE FOR THE CRIMINALLY INSANE

INITIAL BEHAVIORAL ASSESSMENT

Instructions: This form is to be completed, signed, and dated for all clients who are being referred for psychiatric services.

Presentation at ED ☐ Self ☐ Family/Friend ☒ Police ☐ Provider ☐ Other ☐ N/A ☐ CIS

Referral Source/Relationship __POLICE (SPIDER-MAN)__   Date/Time of Referral __5/30__

☒ On site OR ☐ Walk In AND ☐ Scheduled OR ☐ Unscheduled

Assessment Began __8/6__ Date (MM/DD) and __11:02__ a.m. / p.m. Time (00:00) Ended __8/6__ Date (MM/DD) and __11:47__ a.m. / p.m. Time (00:00)

Name of Client __NORMAN VIRGIL OSBORN__   ☒ Male ☐ Female

_____ Street Address   __NEW YORK__ City __10021__ Zip   PHONE

Date of Birth | 0 | 7 | 2 | 2 | 6 | 4 | Patient No. | A | S | M | 0 | ! | 0 | 0 | 1 | 4 |
m m / d d / y y

Employed: ☐ YES ☒ NO ☐ Unknown Occupation __FORMER OWNER + PRESIDENT OF OSCORP__ Veteran Yes ☐ No ☒

Combat? Yes ☐ No ☒

Language ☒ English ☐ Spanish ☐ Arabic ☐ Chinese ☐ Other _____   Interpreter Needed ☐ Yes ☒ No
☐ Deaf/Hard of Hearing with ☐ American Sign Language
☐ Deaf/Hard of Hearing (does not communicate using ASL)

Recent Stressors: ☒ Relationship ☒ Family ☐ Job ☐ Housing ☒ Financial ☒ Legal ☐ Other _____

Medical History/Treatment/Pertinent injuries: (diagnosis/describe) __PATIENT SUSTAINED PHYSICAL AND MENTAL TRAUMA AFTER ALTERCATION WITH SPIDER-MAN; NOW BELIEVES HE IS CLETUS KASADY.__

Behavioral Health History/Treatment
Substance Use History/Treatment
Is there a family history of substance use issues? ☒ YES ☐ NO ☐ Unknown
Does the person currently use mind-altering substances (drugs, alcohol, marijuana, etc.) ☒ YES ☐ NO ☐ Unknown
If yes, what substances: __ALCOHOL, TRACES OF UNDOCUMENTED MIND-ALTERING DRUG__

Mental Health History/Treatment
Is there a family history of mental health issues? ☒ YES ☐ NO ☐ Unknown
(diagnosis/describe) __PATIENT HAS BEEN PREVIOUSLY DIAGNOSED + TREATED FOR MULTIPLE PERSONALITY DISORDERS AND INSANITY__
Is there a family history of suicide attempt(s) or completion(s)? ☐ YES ☐ NO ☒ Unknown
(describe) __PATIENT FILES ON PARENTS WERE HEAVILY REDACTED.__

TRANSCRIPT OF PSYCHICIATRIC EVALUATION
PATIENT NAME: NORMAN OSBORN
TRANSCRIBED BY CLAY McLEOD CHAPMAN

OSBORN: Doctor Treadwell. As I live and breathe… To what do I owe the honor, doc?

TREADWELL: Good morning, Norman. How are we feeling today?

OSBORN: Doc… That ol' saw again? How many times we gonna do this song and dance?

TREADWELL: Pardon?

OSBORN: You tell me I'm that small potato Osborn, I tell you I'm not, you tell me I'm somebody I ain't and I tell you to go **** yourself. Sound about right? We might as well dust off that ol' "Who's on First?" routine we got down. I'll be Abbott, and you be Costello…

TREADWELL: That's quite all right, Norman.

OSBORN: Cletus. Get it through your thick skull before I crush it.

TREADWELL: I wanted to try something different today. Perhaps this might be of interest to you.

OSBORN: What the hell's that? You bringing toys for me? It's playtime now?

TREADWELL: You don't remember this?

OSBORN: Should I?

TREADWELL: It's a doll.

OSBORN: I can see that, Einstein. Why the hell are you bringing it here? You want me to point at the spot on the doll where the bad man touched me? That it?

TREADWELL: This is from your childhood, Norman. As a matter of fact, this doll was given to you by none other than your father. I have been told it was your most cherished possession as a young boy. You wouldn't let it go, no matter how hard your nanny tried. Inseparable.

OSBORN: Hate to break it to you, doc, but I sure as hell didn't play with any dolls when I was a boy… Only toy my daddy gave me growing up was the cherry end of whatever Pal Mal he was smoking.

TREADWELL: I thought you might say something to that effect. Go ahead. Take it. Hold it.

OSBORN: Why?

TREADWELL: Humor me. I've come to believe that when we revisit totems from our past, they can have something of a…cathartic effect. I want to see if this item jogs any memories for you.

OSBORN: Suit yourself, doc. You wanna play with dolls, let's play with dolls… (Takes the item, considers it.) Hold on now. Hold on… You're saying… You're telling me this was mine? When I was still ****ing in my britches?

TREADWELL: That is correct, Norman. What do you remember? What does it make you see?

OSBORN: I see… I see a boy. He's…alone. Crying.

TREADWELL: That's good, Norman. That's wonderful. Tell me more… What else do you see?

OSBORN: Nobody is listening to him. Nobody… Nobody's there to help. Just him and his…his dolly. He's hugging it. Got it pressed so tight against his chest. All he's got… Only friend. He whispers to it.

TREADWELL: What is he saying?

OSBORN: All his pain… All his fear. He puts it into the doll. Lets the doll have it. Dolly says she'll take it. Take it and throw it away for him. She loves the boy.

TREADWELL: Splendid, Norman. Splendid! Can you tell me why the boy is so afraid? Why were you so afraid?

OSBORN: He… He's afraid because…because I've taken him away from his mommy and daddy. The dumb **** didn't listen to his parents when they told him he shouldn't talk to strangers. Now I've brought him home with me. He's my dolly now. And we're gonna play, play, plaaaay till the batteries run out. (Laughs.)

TREADWELL: Very well, Norman. If that's how you—

OSBORN: He's crying, doc. That boy's crying so much, his doll's all soaked through. Nothing but a sponge! All sopping wet... When I was done with that kid, I just brought up that doll to my face and squeeeezed. So refreshing! I decided to keep it. For the life of me, I can't remember where I buried the boy, but let me tell yooou, that dolly was indeed one of my most prized possessions!

TREADWELL: That's enough—

OSBORN: Thanks for bringing it back to me, doc! You got one thing right: It's always fun to jog the ol' memory bank! Can I keep it? Pleeeease? Just for a little while longer? I wanna walk down memory lane with my dollllyyyy…

RAVENCROFT
INSTITUTE FOR THE CRIMINALLY INSANE

INITIAL BEHAVIORAL ASSESSMENT

Instructions: This form is to be completed, signed, and dated for all clients who are being referred for psychiatric services.

Presentation at ED ☐ Self ☐ Family/Friend ☒ Police ☐ Provider ☐ Other ☐ N/A ☐ CIS

Referral Source/Relationship _POLICE_   **Date/Time of Referral** _1/2_

☒ On site OR ☐ Walk In AND ☒ Scheduled OR ☐ Unscheduled

Assessment Began _2/23_ Date (MM/DD) and _4 00_ Time (00:00) ☒ p.m. **Ended** _2/23_ Date (MM/DD) and _4:13_ Time (00:00 ☒ p.m.

Name of Client _FRANCES LOUISE BARRISON_   ☐ Male ☒ Female

_N/A_ ___ City ___ Zip ___ (___)___ PHONE
Street Address

Date of Birth | 0 | 5 | 1 | 2 | 9 | 3 | **Patient No.** | S | M | U | 0 | 1 | 0 | 0 | 0 | 1 |
m m d d y y

Employed ☐ YES ☐ NO ☒ Unknown **Occupation** _____   **Veteran Yes** ☐ **No** ☒   **Combat? Yes** ☐ **No** ☒

Language ☒ English ☐ Spanish ☐ Arabic ☐ Chinese ☐ Other _____   **Interpreter Needed** ☐ Yes ☒ No
☐ Deaf/Hard of Hearing with ☐ **American Sign Language**
☐ Deaf/Hard of Hearing (does not communicate using ASL)

Recent Stressors: ☐ Relationship ☒ Family ☐ Job ☒ Housing ☒ Financial ☒ Legal ☐ Other _____
Medical History/Treatment/Pertinent Injuries: (diagnosis/describe) _GUNSHOT WOUND TO HEAD CAUSED_
MENTAL INSTABILITY

Behavioral Health History/Treatment
Substance Use History/Treatment
Is there a family history of substance use issues? ☒ YES ☐ NO ☐ Unknown
Does the person currently use mind-altering substances (drugs, alcohol, marijuana, etc.) ☒ YES ☐ NO ☐ Unknown
If yes, what substances: _MULTIPLE NARCOTICS_

Mental Health History/Treatment
Is there a family history of mental health issues? ☒ YES ☐ NO ☐ Unknown
(diagnosis/describe) _MENTAL ABUSE BY MOTHER_
Is there a family history of suicide attempt(s) or completion(s)? ☐ YES ☐ NO ☒ Unknown

(describe) _____

TRANSCRIPT OF PSYCHIATRIC EVALUATION
PATIENT NAME: FRANCES LOUISE BARRISON
TRANSCRIBED BY CLAY McLEOD CHAPMAN

POURNELLA: The time is approximately 4:00 P.M. Dr. Davinia Marcia Pournella initiating intake interview. Today's subject is none other than Frances Louise Barrison. Hello, Miss Barrison.

BARRISON: You got pretty eyes, Doc. Anyone ever tell you that? Your eyelashes… They're so...so long.

POURNELLA: Thank you, Miss Barrison. Tell me… How are we feeling today?

BARRISON: Cold.

POURNELLA: Cold? Is the temperature in here too low for you? I can speak with—

BARRISON: No. Not the room. Something underneath my skin. I keep trying and trying to tell the orderlies here that I need my jacket, but they just won't listen…

POURNELLA: Jacket? What jacket?

BARRISON: The jacket I came in here with.

POURNELLA: I'm sorry, I…I don't remember there being anything in your file about a jacket. Personal belongings are usually stored for safekeeping until patients are—

BARRISON: Dead?

POURNELLA: Deemed healthy enough for release.

BARRISON: Come on, Doc… You and I know that ain't happening. So how about you just do me a solid and give me back my jacket, eh? I worked hard on that thing. It's my pride and joy, you hear?

POURNELLA: Tell me about this…this jacket of yours.

BARRISON: What do you wanna know?

POURNELLA: Well, what makes it so special?

BARRISON: It's warm, for one thing. @&%$ing black leather. All shiny. Studs running up the sleeves. Down the back. You know how much heart and soul went into that jacket?

POURNELLA: Tell me. How much?

BARRISON: So much. Like…there was this one guy. Met him at a club in the East Village, I think? They all blur together by now. Anyway. This guy. He comes up to me in the pit, getting all handsy. You ever been in a pit before, Doc?

POURNELLA: Pit?

BARRISON: Geez, Doc… Don't be such an L7! There are rules when you're in the pit. No knuckles and elbows. But this guy, he… Well, he's nothing but knuckles and elbows. Son of a $%\@ had earrings running up and down his lobe. So shiny. This guy, see, he's distracting me. When all I wanted to do was dance. I wanted to shout in that ear of his to mind his own business, so I pulled out my knife and…I guess you could say he was all ears to me after that. Made for a great patch on my jacket.

POURNELLA: I'm sorry… When you say "patch," do you mean—

BARRISON: Punks pride themselves on their jackets. They take time. Your leather has to embody your bands. Your very soul. This is a way of life, you know? A jacket is like, it's like your second skin.

POURNELLA: …Skin.

BARRISON: Folks make patches for their favorite bands and safety-pin them to their jacket. Me, I realized I wanted my jacket to be all about the people in my life.

POURNELLA: I'm sorry, but are you saying you put them on your jacket?

BARRISON: It kept me warm. Kept me alive. I swear, that jacket was just about the only thing keeping me alive sometimes. People saw me walking down the street, wearing that thing—and you know what? None of them would @$%& with me. So…Doc. Please? You guys gotta have it around here somewhere. Don't you? It gets so cold in here. I feel naked without it. So…exposed.

POURNELLA: I'm sorry, but I don't think—

BARRISON: I WANT MY SKIN BACK, DOC. GIVE ME MY SKIN.

POURNELLA: Guards! Guards!

BARRISON: I WANT THOSE EYELASHES! I GOT SOME SPACE ON THE SLEEVES OF MY JACKET! GIVE ME YOUR EYELASHES! GIMME GIMME GIMME—

END OF INTERVIEW

PRISONER:
BROCK, EDWARD

PRISON ID: ASM300

INMATE INTERVIEW: EDWARD "EDDIE" BROCK
Transcribed by Clay McLeod Chapman
RYKER'S ISLAND PRISON INTERVIEW. DETECTIVE LARSEN IN ATTENDANCE.
PRISONER ASM300.

DETECTIVE LARSEN: Smile for the camera, Eddie...everything you do here in Ryker's is being recorded. They got cameras everywhere. You can't wipe your ass without somebody watching.

EDWARD "EDDIE" BROCK: I'll be sure to put on a show the next time I pop a squat.

LARSEN: Don't be modest. You're a star! The warden's already cut together a "Best of Brock's Beatdowns," all starring you. You're leading man material, Eddie...who woulda thought?

BROCK: Talk to my agent. Maybe he can get me out of here. My lawyer sure can't.

LARSEN: *Nah,* I'm serious. You're a celebrity 'round these parts! You haven't even been here for 36 hours and you've already pummeled three prisoners. One of them's in a coma. The doc wasn't able to fix his left eye. Poor guy will be partially blind for the rest of his life 'cause of you.

BROCK: Not my fault he forgot which end of the toothbrush goes in his mouth. I had to teach him. I had to make him see… And my mom always told me: Brush for two whole minutes.

LARSEN: He can't swallow anymore. They got him eating out of a tube now.

BROCK: I needed to reach the back teeth.

LARSEN: That's cold, Brock. Even for a low-life criminal like you.

BROCK: Everything's cold now.

LARSEN: Want me to talk to the warden about adjusting the thermostat for you?

BROCK: You want to break me? You want to take me out? Tell the warden to send tougher thugs next time. None of these low-rent pip-squeaks with shivs. Or better yet, why don't you tell me why you're here--why you're really here--or let me go back to my cell so I can be alone?

LARSEN: What's the matter? You don't seem yourself today… You missing your better half?

BROCK: …

LARSEN: Must've struck a nerve on that one, eh? Lemme guess… You lost your blankie. Your protective blankie. You know the one I'm talking about, right? All black? Got a mind of its own?

BROCK: (Barely audible) Dead now.

LARSEN: What was that?

BROCK: ...

LARSEN: I read the report. When they hauled your ass in... But here's what's bugging me: I don't believe Venom's dead. I don't buy that he just... What was it? Melted or whatever.

BROCK: Slipped through my fingers. Peeled away. Sloughed off...like skin. Meat right off the bones.

LARSEN: ...Come again? You lost me.

BROCK: Nothing but bones now. Everything is so...so exposed. Raw nerves. My whole body.

LARSEN: See...now you're just talking like an addict. I never pinned you for some two-bit junkie, Brock--but this? This just screams withdrawal. Am I gonna need to put you on methadone to get a straight answer out of you?

BROCK: YOU NEED TO PUT IT BACK ON. PUT MY SKIN BACK ON.

LARSEN: Whoa--easy now, fella. Dial it down--

BROCK: So cold. Nothing but cold. I can't feel anything anymore without it--

LARSEN: Sit back down, Brock. Sit down. Now.

BROCK: This? This isn't skin. Not mine. Not anymore.

LARSEN: Hey. What're you--ah. Don't. Don't do that. Stop. I said stop!

BROCK: This...this is just tissue paper. This isn't real. Not flesh. Not me. It all peels away. See? See how easy it peels away?

LARSEN: Oh--oh god. Guards! Hey--guards! Get in here! Get a medic! He's--oh god, he's clawing at himself. Taser him or something! Get somebody who can--

BROCK: GET MY SKIN! I WANT MY SKIN!

(BROCK IS SEDATED.)

LARSEN: What a mess... What a &%&*^& mess. Just, ah... Just bandage him up and take him back to his cell. Let him sleep it off. Maybe his bunkmate can talk some sense into him... What's his name? Kasady something or other?

☆☆☆☆ FINAL

DAILY 🎺 BUGLE

NEW YORK'S FINEST DAILY NEWSPAPER

SINCE 1897
☆☆☆☆
$.25 (in NYC)
$.75 (outside city)

MAXIMUM CARNAGE

DAILY BUGLE EDITORIAL BY J. JONAH JAMESON (Transcribed by Clay McLeod Chapman)

Two days ago, I came face to face with the serial killer called Carnage in the Bugle offices, right here in New York. He demanded that I, in my position of power as the Editor In Chief of this paper, set a trap for the masked menaces Spider-Man and Venom. In that moment, nobody came to rescue me. There was no heroic entrance in the nick of time. Instead, I was face to face with a killer – and one question has been ringing in my mind ever since:

Who are our heroes? The ones in the capes traipsing down Park Avenue? The spandexed rejects reducing our streets to rubble every time they tussle?

Who are the real heroes of New York? I'll tell you who...

Don't look up to the skies.

Look down. Look next to you.

Look at me. Look at you.

Look at the meat-and-potatoes men and women of this city we all call home. It is the common man—the fella (and gal, of course) who wakes up at 5 a.m. Monday through Friday, who hops on the suffocating subway to schlep an hour or more just to get to their job and slog through that soul-crushing, mind-numbing nine-to-five, just to hop back on that same subway and fall asleep for a few hours and do it all over again.

But what truly makes these men and women—such as yours truly—the real heroes of this city is that we all have to do it under the constant barrage of battering breakneckers, nefarious ne'er-do-well and web-slinging psychopaths turning our once peaceful town upside down.

Why are we the heroes? Simple. Because we survive. We live in a constant state of war. A war we didn't ask for. The citizens of New York City are caught in the crossfire of those foul fiends who take to the skies and wreck our way of life while they wreck our homes, all under the guise of serving and protecting the populous at large.

Well, I'm here to tell you this... People of New York: It's time we take back this city. Take it back from the super heroes who aren't so super, who are holding our city hostage while we fight!

Fight for a little peace and quiet. Fight for the right to make a decent wage. Fight to get through the day without death or destruction coming from above or below.

I am calling upon the true heroes of New York. Not Spider-

Man. Not Captain America.

You, dear reader.

YOU.

One need only to look at the last 48 hours of—dare I say it—absolute carnage perpetuated in our streets to understand our city is under siege by the very loons who profess to be protecting us. Your tireless staff of roving reporters, including myself, have risked our necks, putting our own lives on the line to chronicle the carnage that continues to drench the avenues in blood.

Let me paint a morbid portrait for you, dear reader...

This week alone, yours truly witnessed a blistering breakout from Ravencroft Asylum. Those sinister malefactors who were purportedly protected behind lock and key were able to escape, including the likes of Cletus Kasady and Frances Louise Barrison, just to name a small few malfeasants—all thanks to a terrifying team-up that should send shudders down your spine:

SPIDER-MAN and VENOM.

Like chocolate and peanut butter, like Attila the Hun and Mussolini, like Count Dracula and Hitler himself, we now have this petrifying pair to contend with.

But don't think for an instant that it stops there... Oh no, dear reader, this was just the beginning of the week! And like any diligent documenter daring to follow the front line, I was there to cover these scheming miscreants as they continued their reign of terror!

Spider-Man and Venom somehow unleashed a psychic web of psychotic energy over the distressed denizens of our city. What kind of black magic these two terrors had concocted, I shall leave for the scientists or top government brass to detect, but its extrasensory puppeteering played we the people like we were all a bunch of Pinocchios. Don't think for an instant it's a mere coincidence that Spider-Man is always drawing his webs over our heads like he's pulling the strings on a city full of marionettes. Here is proof, living proof, of his master plan! Let me provide a mere taste of the psychic onslaught caused by none other than Spider-Man and his new venomous accomplice...

I watched on in horror as a mother suspended her own two children over a crowded street from the top of her apartment building. Her own flesh and blood. One child could not have been any older than 2; the other was still a newborn. Imagine what decayed state of mind that woman would have had to have been in to do such an awful thing.

I watched on as waiters were tossed out from the windows of the restaurants they worked at, simply because the customers didn't care for the service.

The dance floor at the Deep turned into a meat market. A club bloodbath!

Inmates besieging a police station, taking our city's finest and holding them hostage!

Downtown looting, uptown rioting, wilding in Central Park. Our city was under siege...from itself, held hostage by the psychic web of a certain eight-legged citizen slayer.

What brought this animosity out among the people of our sprawling metropolis? What could have caused such a delirious mob mentality to metastasize over the men and women of New York? What brought this rot to the Big Apple?

I'll tell you what, dear reader... It was a cackling carnival of chaos! Spider-Man in cahoots with Venom! Those foul fiends tried to use my own newspaper—the paper of the people!—as a cudgel against New York! But your brave band of reporters has dealt with the likes of Spider-Man before, and we did not flinch! If our newspaper is the battleground where Spidey and his accomplices wish to do combat, then so be it! They will not win! Do you know why? Because we here at the *Bugle* believe the pen is mightier than the sword! The printed word has always been more powerful than any web slung by that radical and his compatriots.

You don't mess with the *Bugle*, Spider-Man...just like you don't mess with the men and women of New York City. The real heroes of the Big Apple. We don't need a skintight suit to prove it. We don't need to hide behind a mask. We're brave enough to show our faces, like real heroes do. Not like you.

What better way to prove my point than to attest to a bit of journalistic genius on my own part... Just when Spidey and Venom couldn't cut it, unleashing a cutthroat killer like Carnage upon our poor pedestrians, I—J. Jonah Jameson—took the *Bugle* by the horn and blew. That's right, dear reader, I utilized the printed word, our very own nuclear newspaper, and armed it—taking precious page space to set a trap for none other than that creepy Carnage. I was loath to do it, weaponizing words, but sometimes being the editor in chief means you have to make the hardest of hard decisions. The toughest of tough calls.

And I did, dear reader. Heaven help us all, I set the trap that would lure Carnage to his own death...right here in these very pages.

Did I second-guess myself? Not once.

Do I regret it? Not on your life.

Do I look outside my window here at the *Bugle*, look upon the people below as they head off to their jobs, their families, their lives, and believe I made the right call? You bet I do.

It's all for you, New York. For you, dear reader.

So—this goes out to Spider-Man and the rest of his treasonous troop: When you come for the *Bugle*, you come for the people. And the people won't stand for this type of tyranny any longer.

We're taking back our city.

Take *that*, Spider-Man.

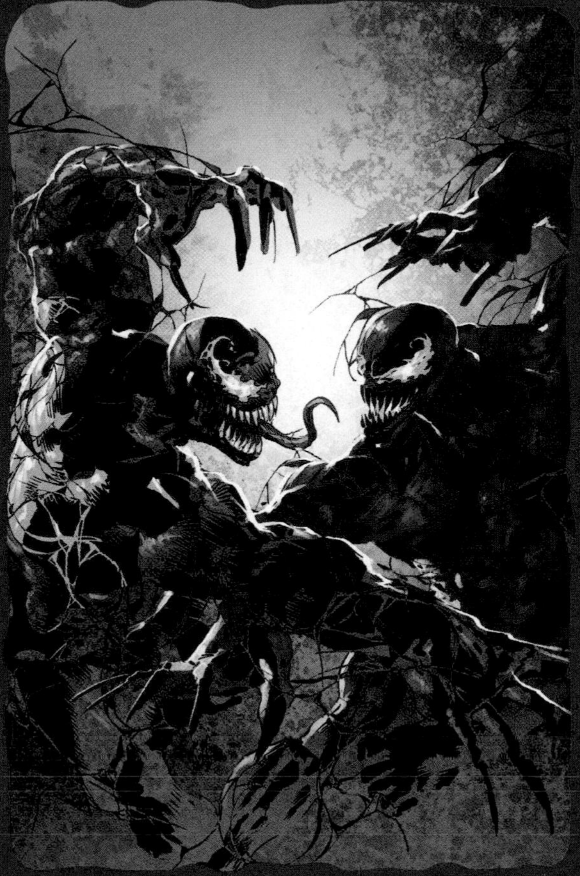

MIKE DEODATO JR. &
RAIN BEREDO
#1 Variant

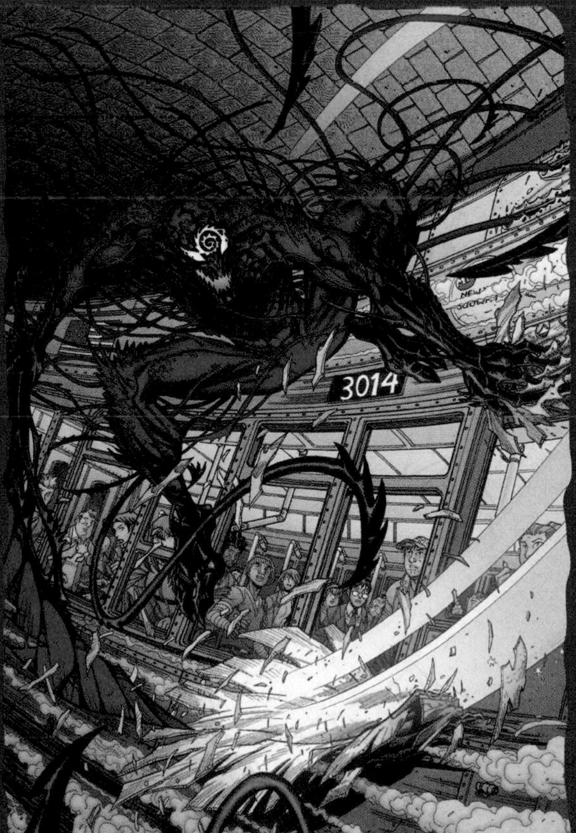
3014

NICK BRADSHAW
& MORRY HOLLOWELL
#1 Variant

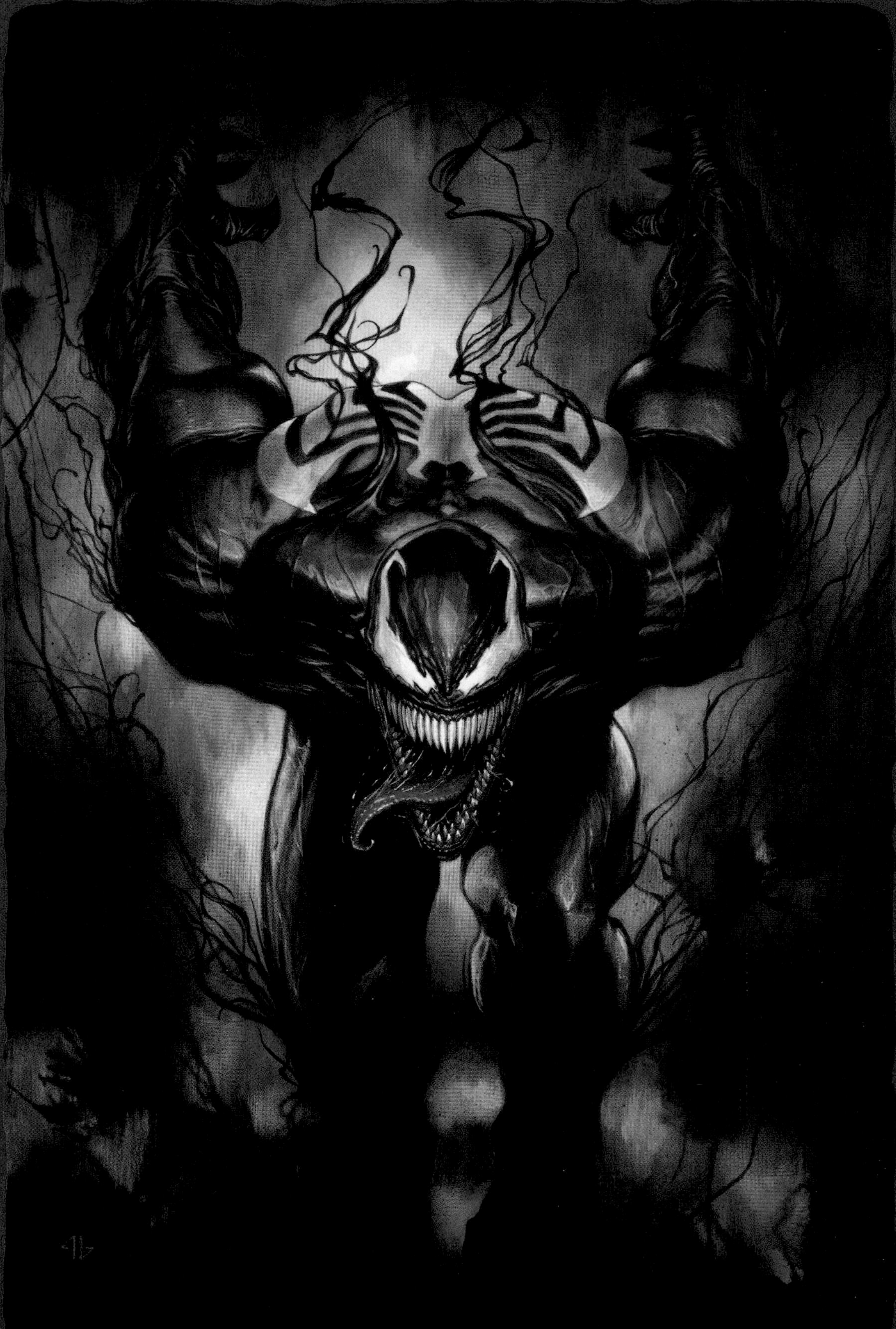

ADI GRANOV
#1 Codex Variant

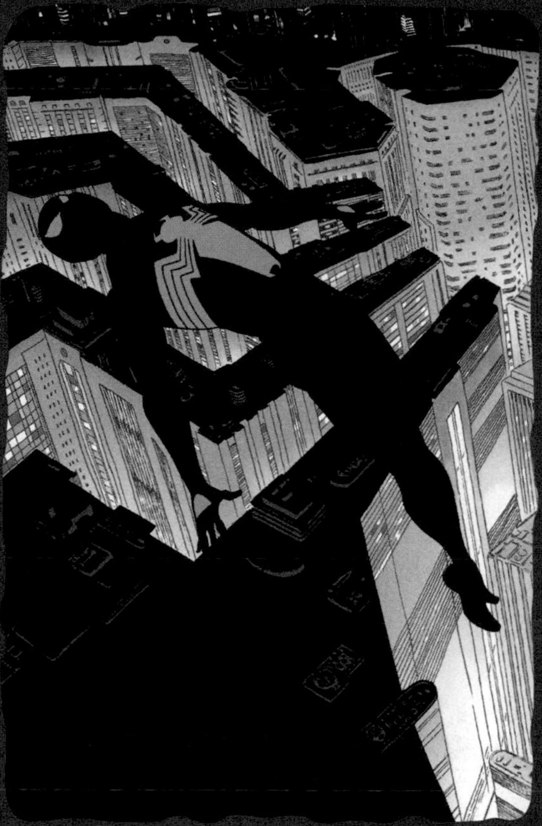

MARCOS MARTIN
#2 Codex Variant

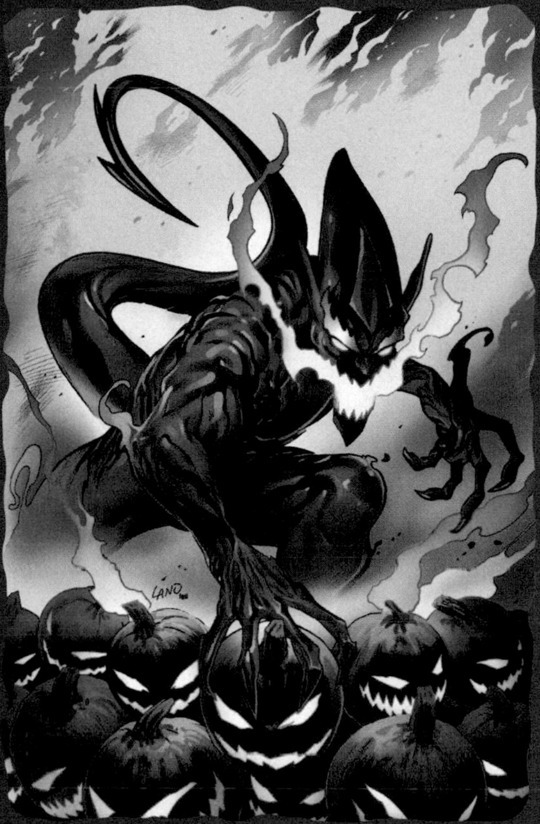

GREG LAND & FRANK D'ARMATA
#3 Codex Variant

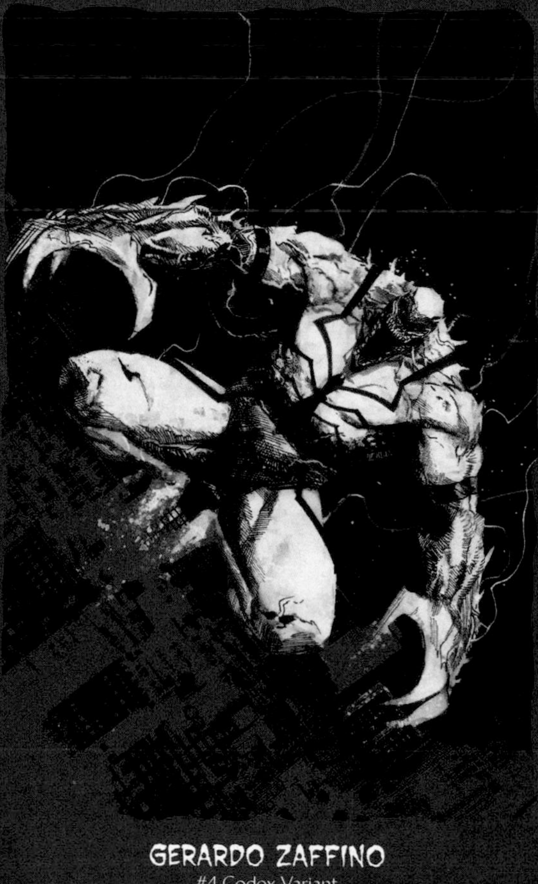

GERARDO ZAFFINO
#4 Codex Variant

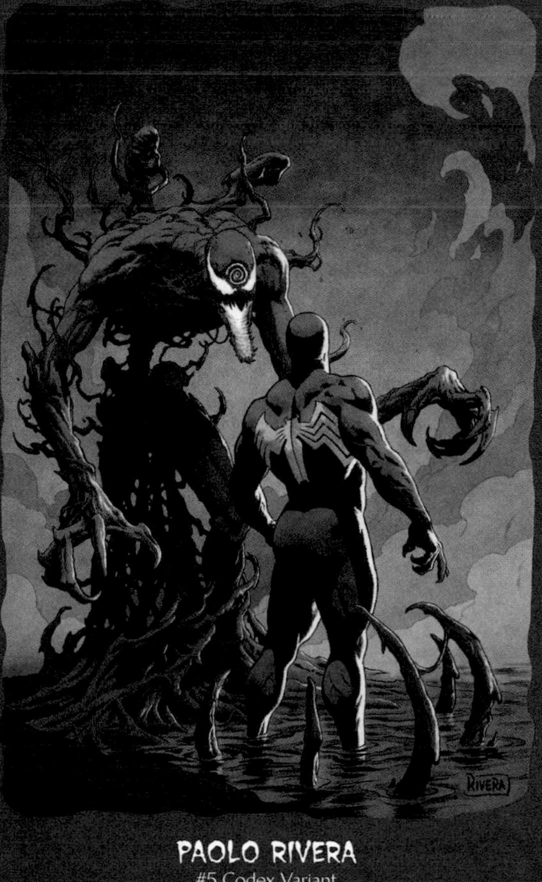
RIVERA

PAOLO RIVERA
#5 Codex Variant

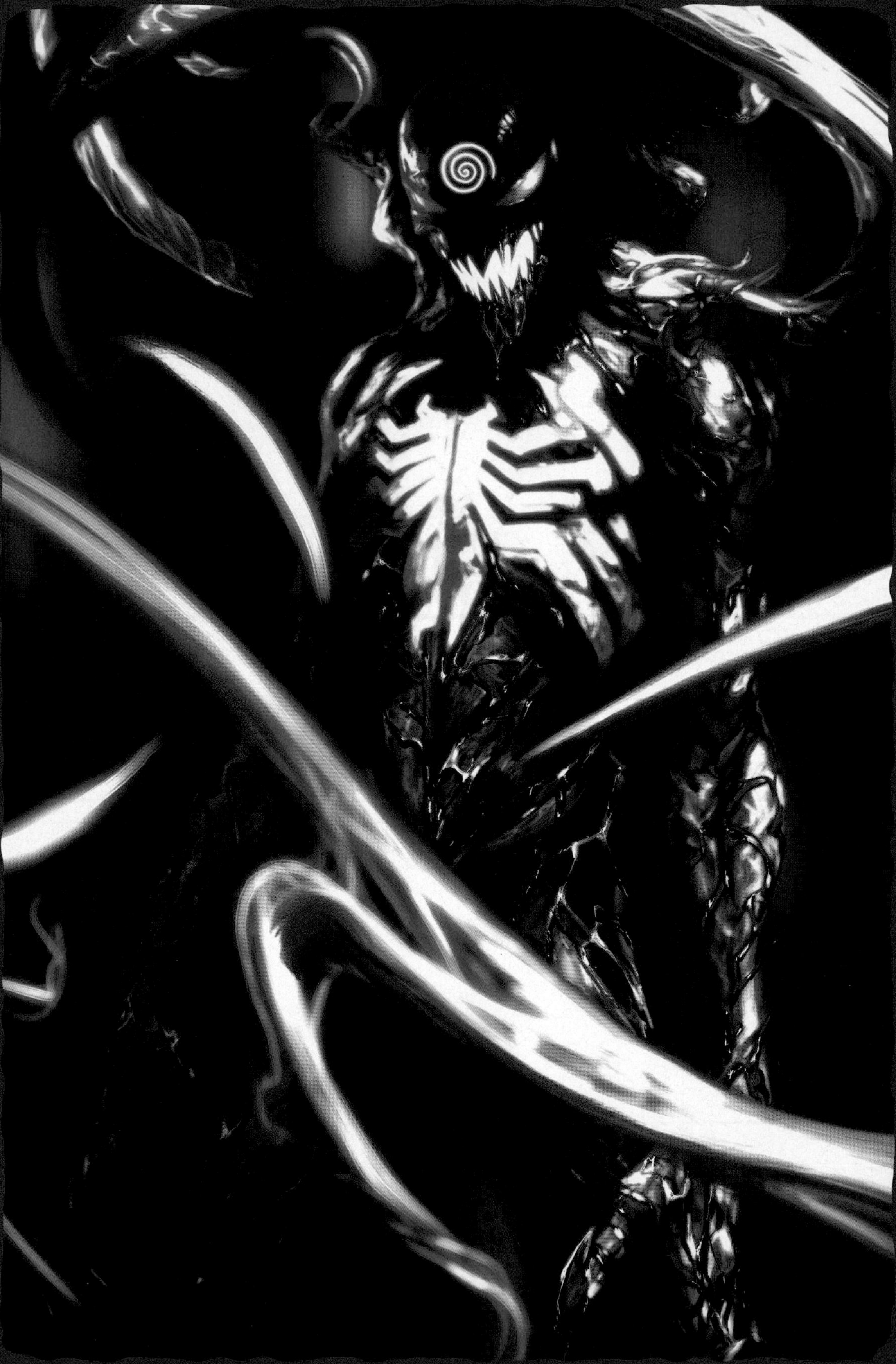

GABRIELE DELL'OTTO

#1 Cult of Carnage Variant

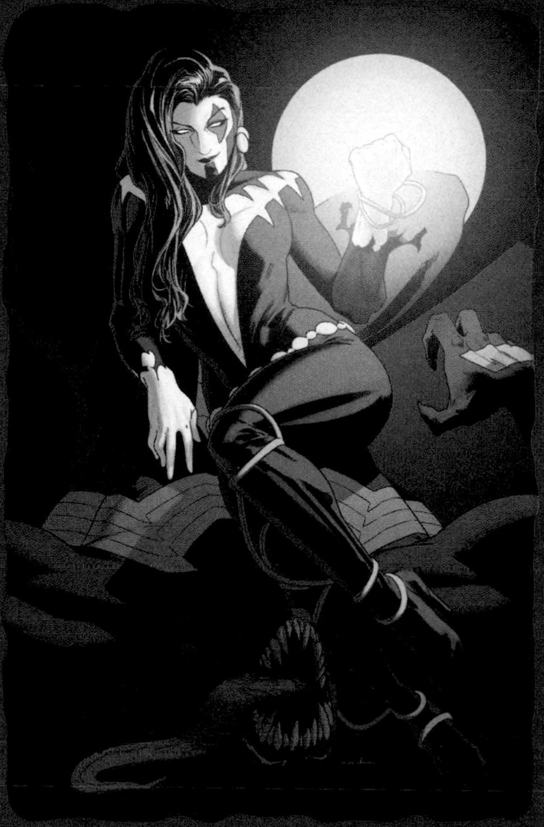

KRIS ANKA
#2 Cult of Carnage Variant

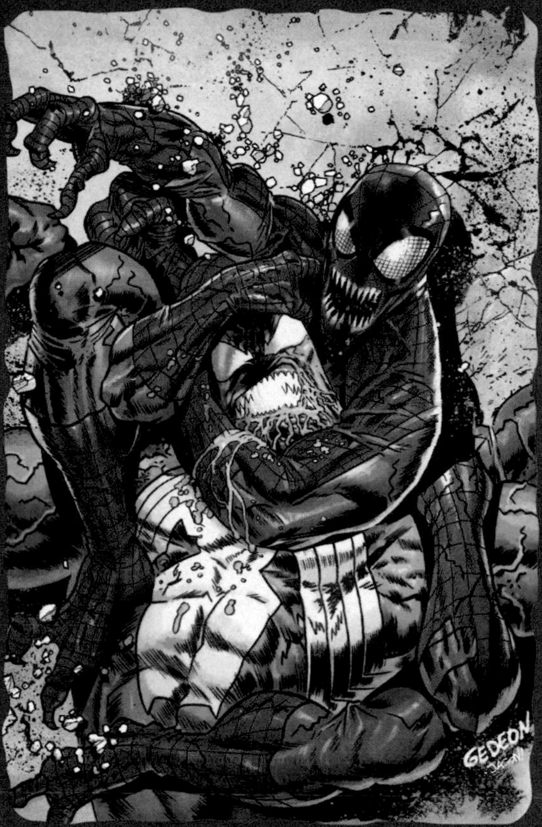
GEDEON

JUAN GEDEON & JASON KEITH
#3 Cult of Carnage Variant

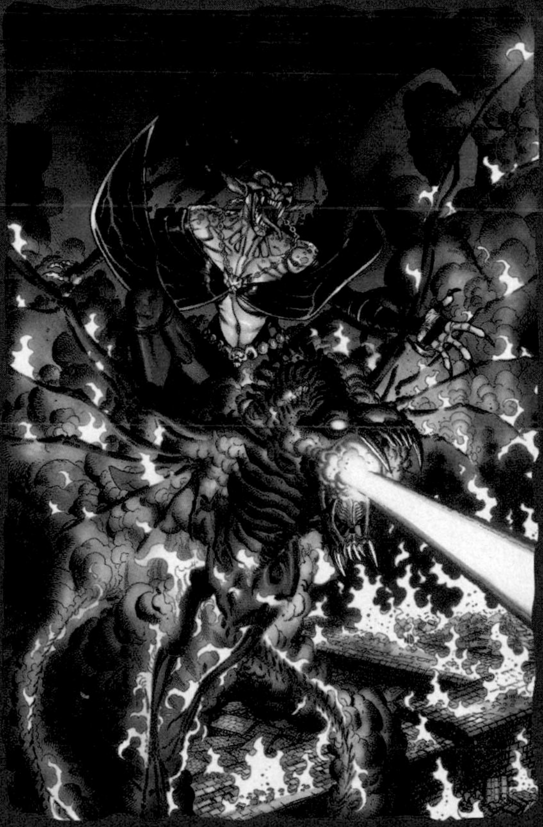

NICK BRADSHAW & JASON KEITH
#4 Cult of Carnage Variant

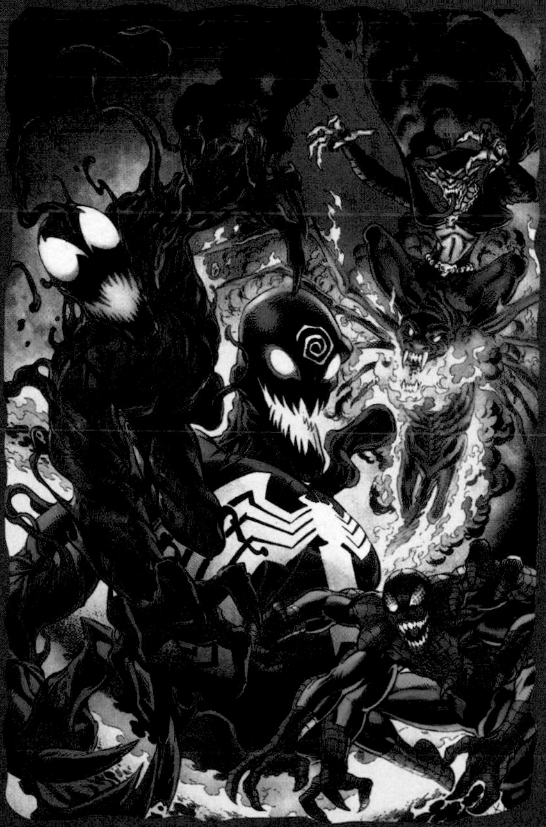

MARK BAGLEY, JOHN DELL & JASON KEITH
#5 Cult of Carnage Variant

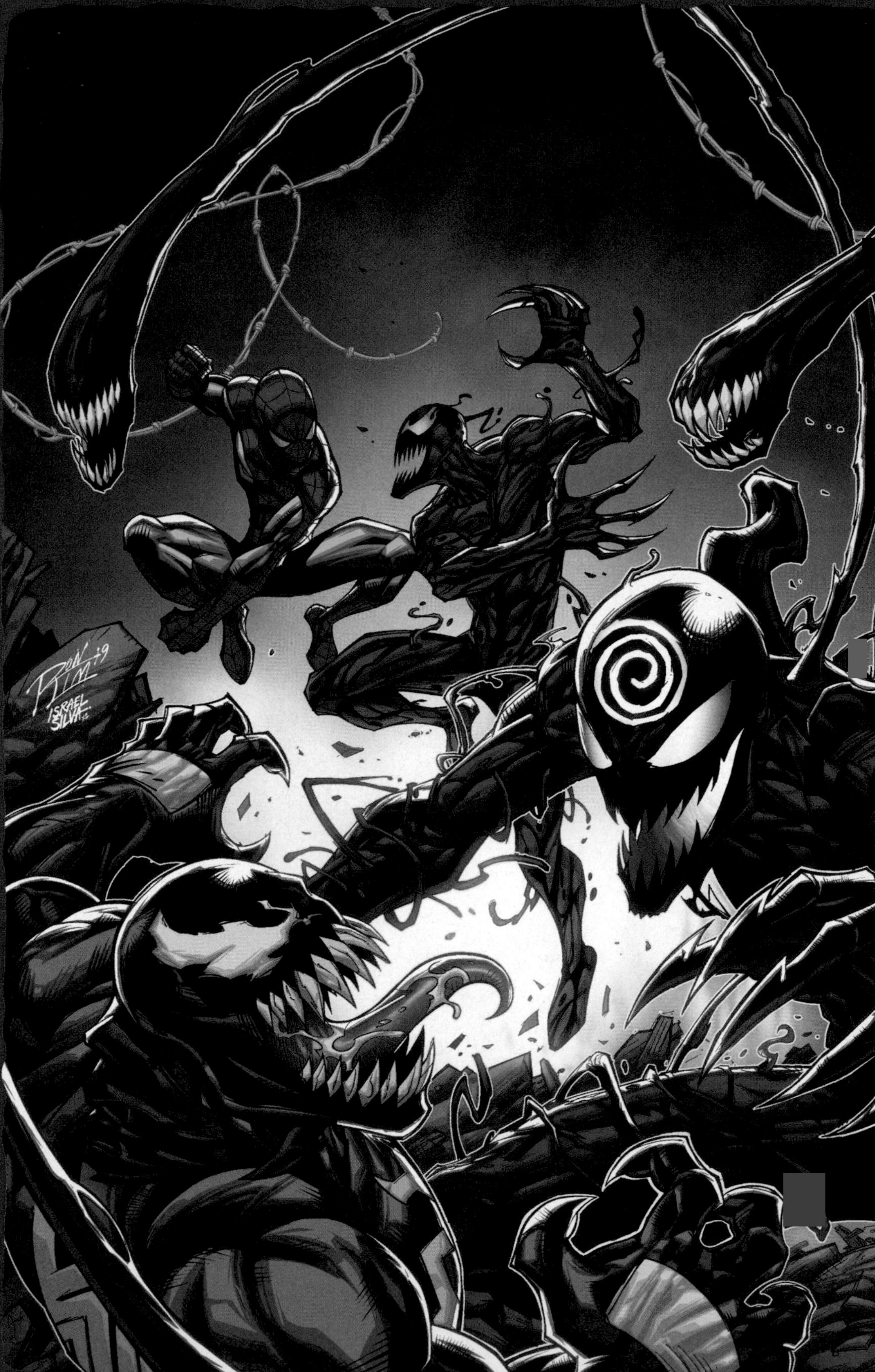

RON LIM '19
ISRAEL SILVA

RON LIM & ISRAEL SILVA

#1 Variant

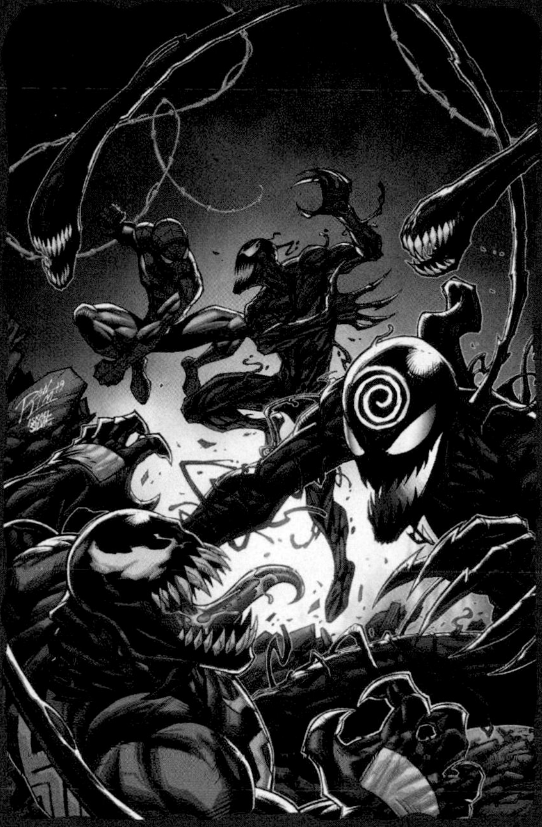
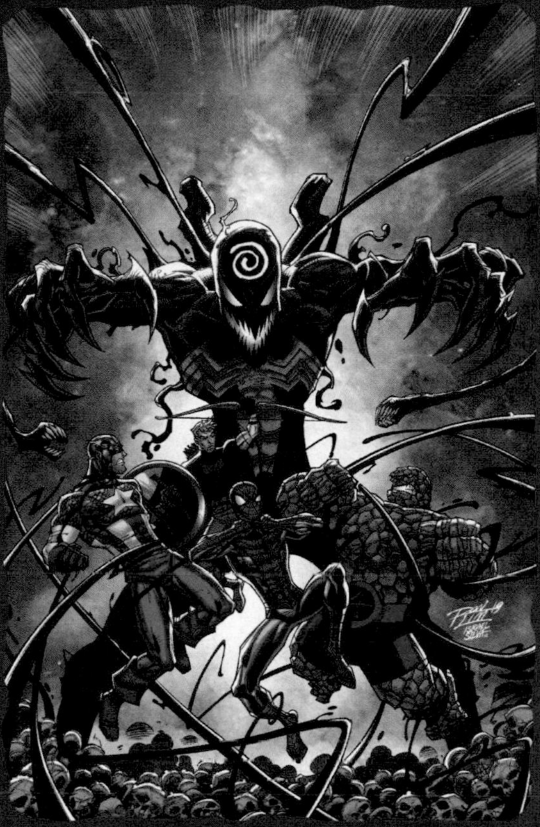
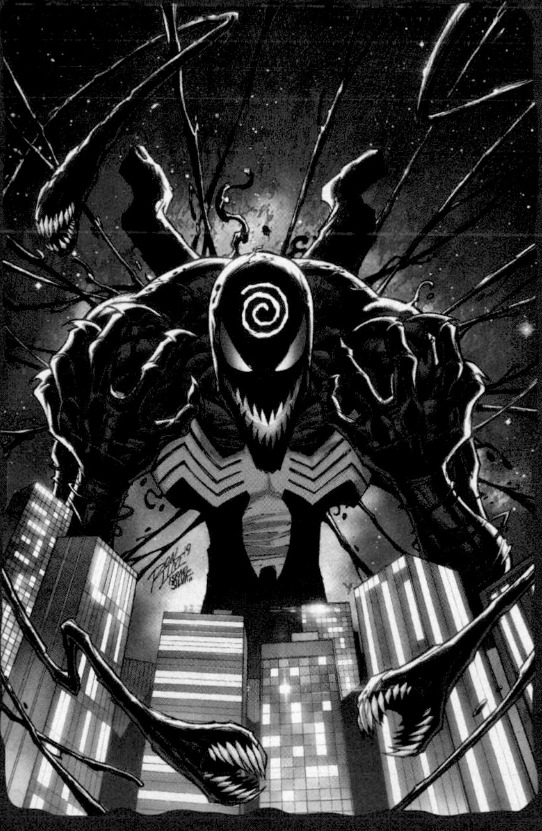
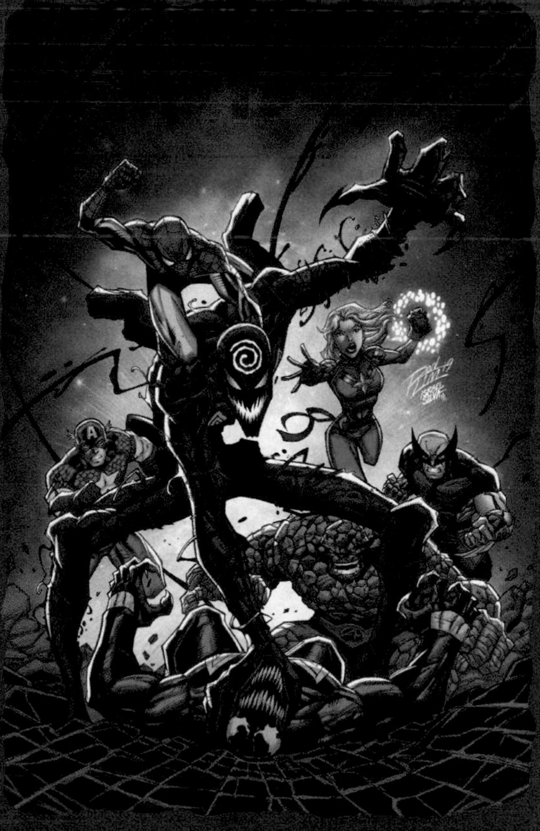

RON LIM & ISRAEL SILVA
#2-5 Variants

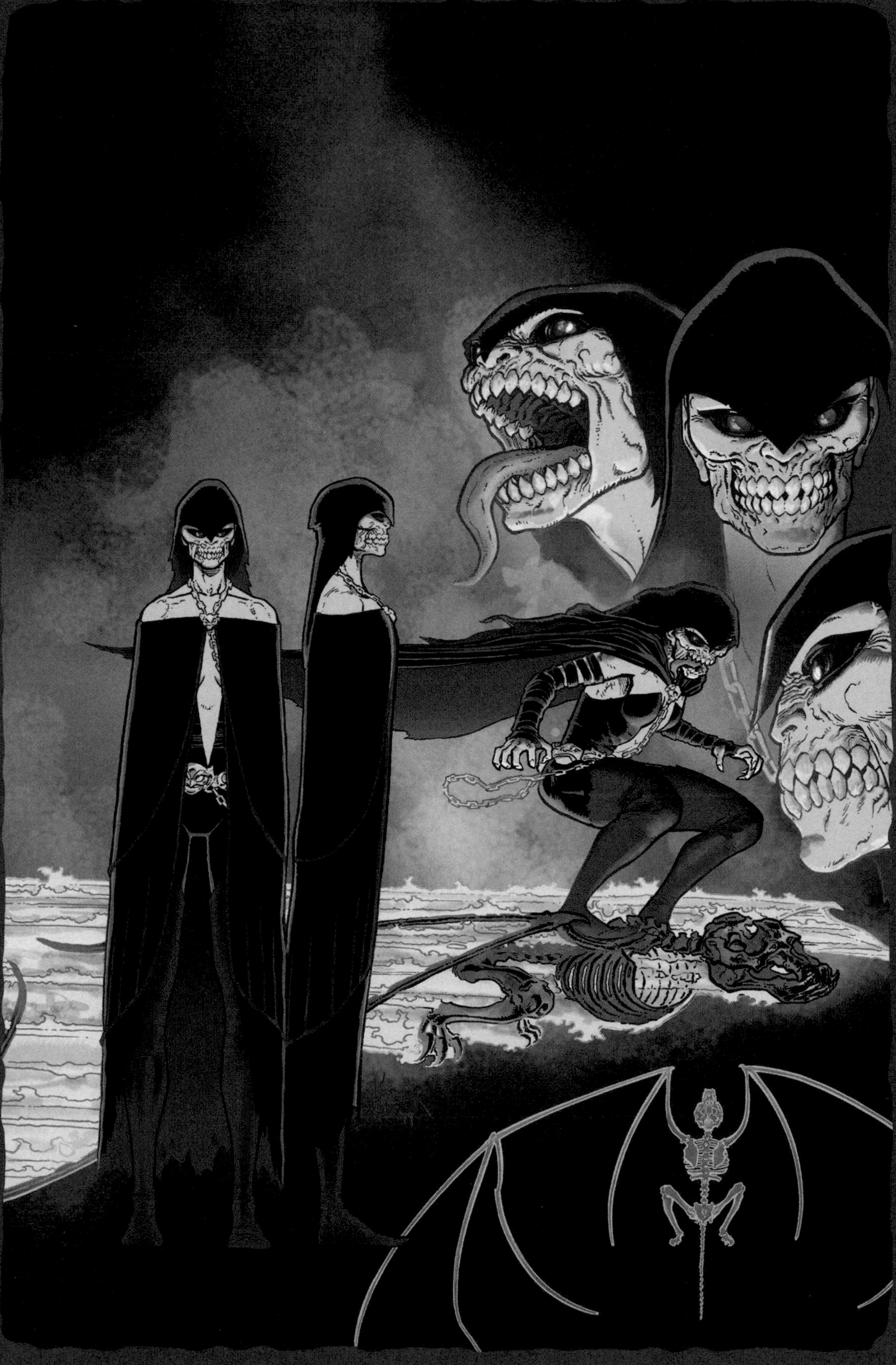

AARON KUDER

#1 Young Guns Variant

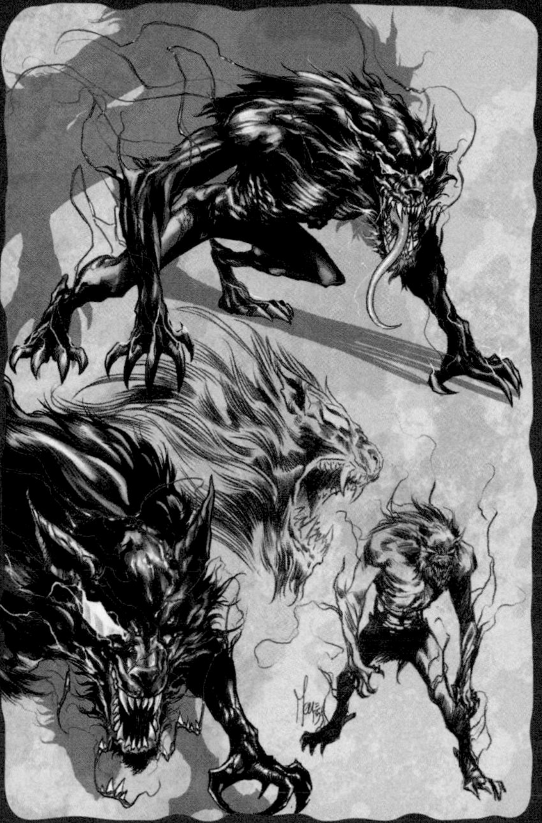

MARCO CHECCHETTO
#2 Young Guns Variant

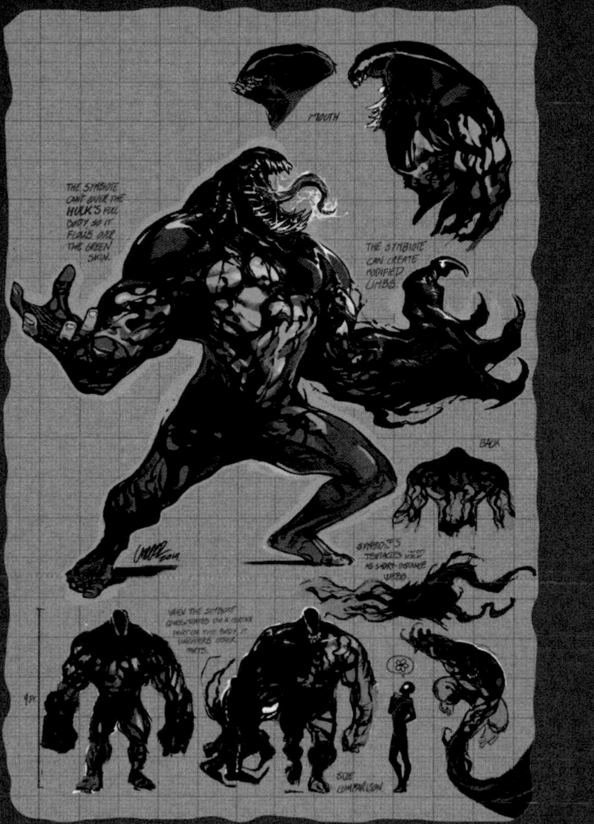
MOUTH
THE SYMBIOTE CAN'T COVER THE HULK'S FULL BODY SO IT FLOWS OVER THE GREEN SKIN.
THE SYMBIOTE CAN CREATE MODIFIED LIMBS
BACK
SIZE COMPARISON

PEPE LARRAZ
#3 Young Guns Variant

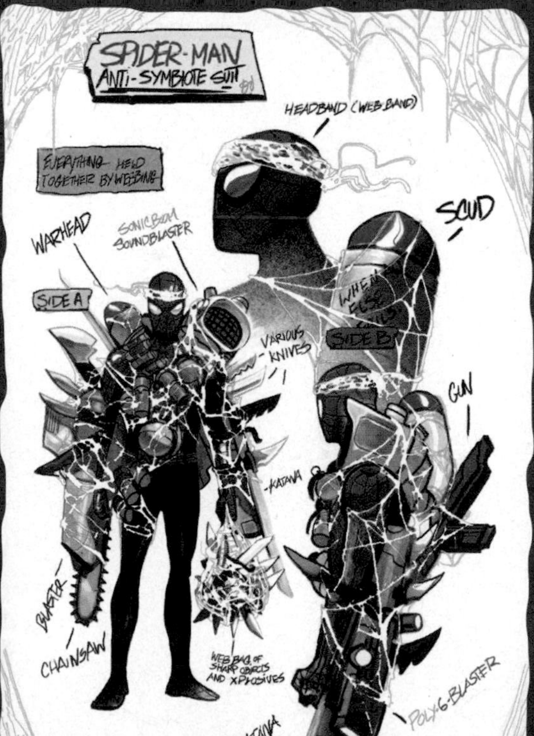
SPIDER-MAN
ANTI-SYMBIOTE SUIT
HEADBAND (WEB BAND)
EVERYTHING HELD TOGETHER BY WEBBING
SCUD
WARHEAD
SONIC BOOM SOUNDBLASTER
SIDE A
VARIOUS KNIVES
SIDE B
GUN
KATANA
BLASTER
CHAINSAW
WEB BAG OF SHARP OBJECTS AND XPLOSIVES
POLY-6-BLASTER
KATANA

MIKE DEL MUNDO
#4 Young Guns Variant

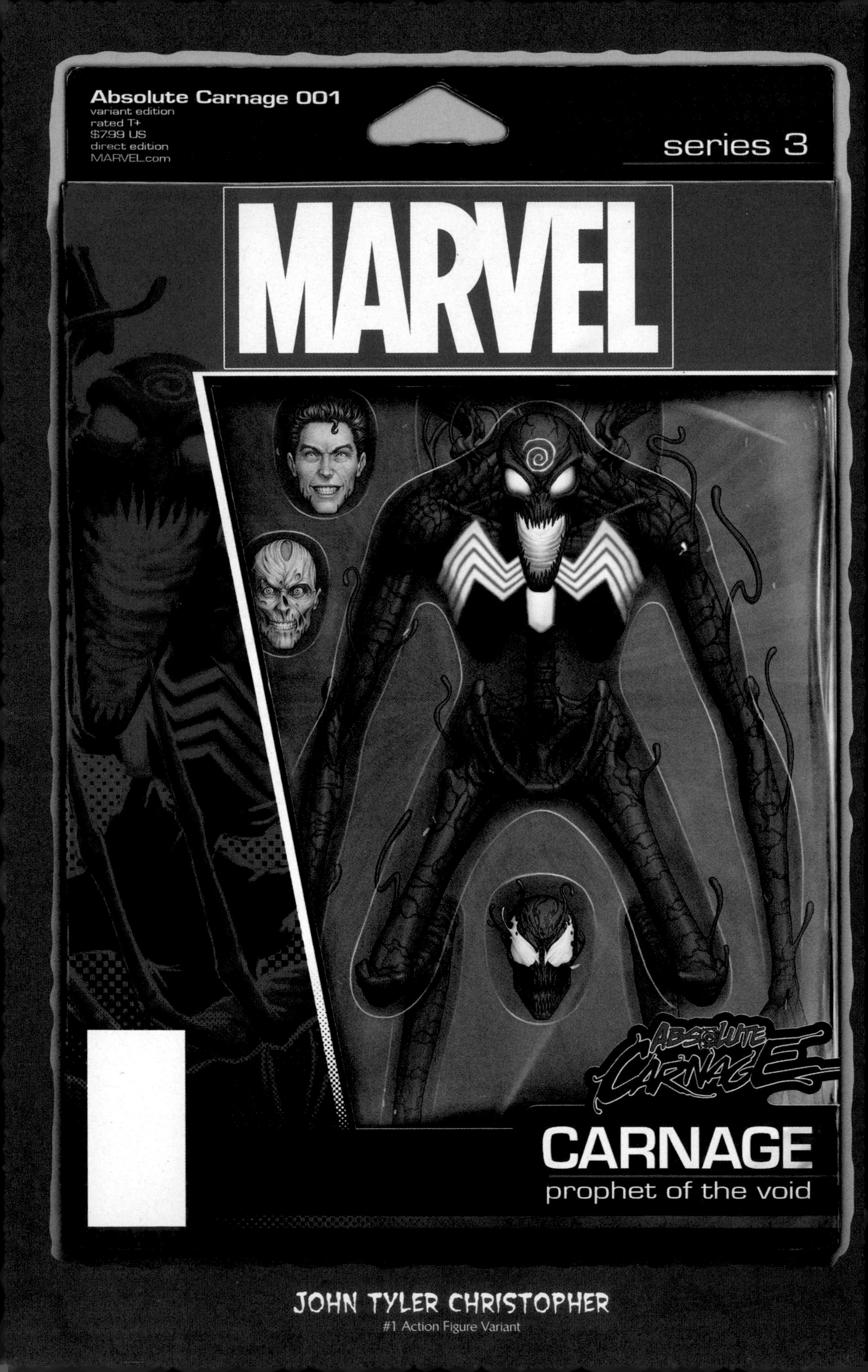

Absolute Carnage 001
variant edition
rated T+
$7.99 US
direct edition
MARVEL.com
series 3
MARVEL
ABSOLUTE CARNAGE
CARNAGE
prophet of the void
JOHN TYLER CHRISTOPHER
#1 Action Figure Variant

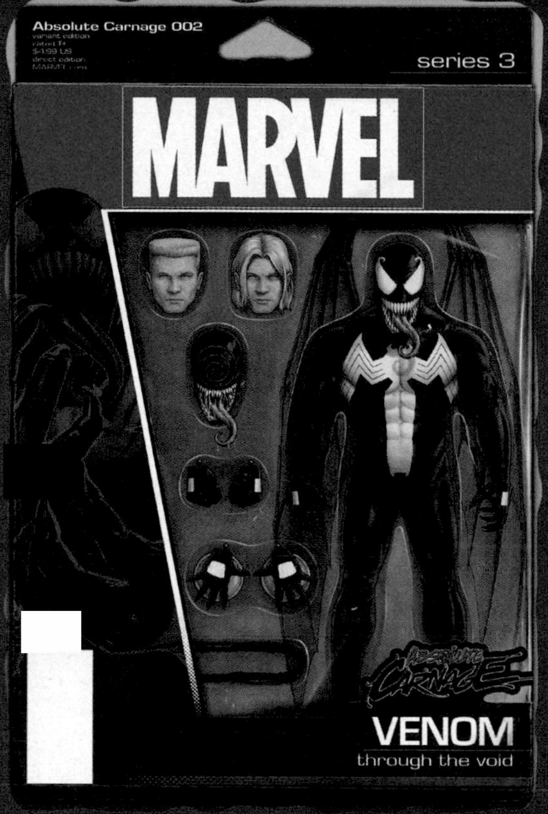
Absolute Carnage 002
series 3
MARVEL
VENOM
through the void

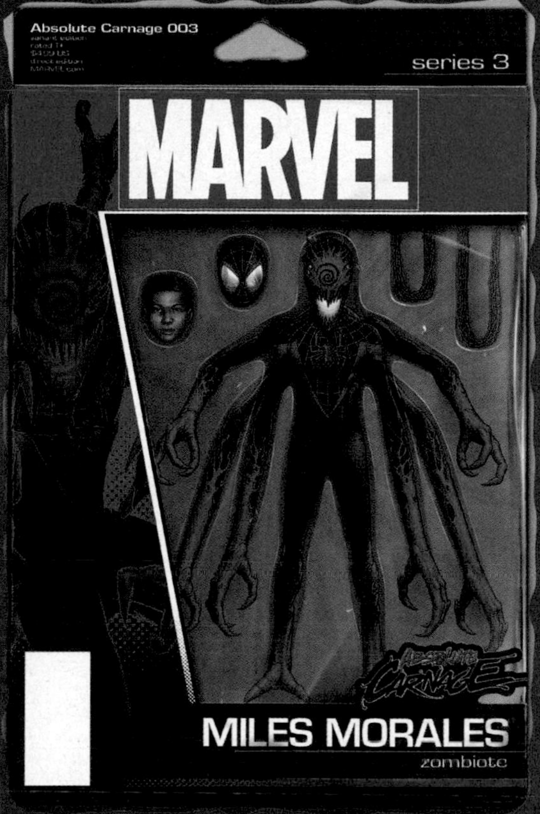
Absolute Carnage 003
series 3
MARVEL
MILES MORALES
zombiote

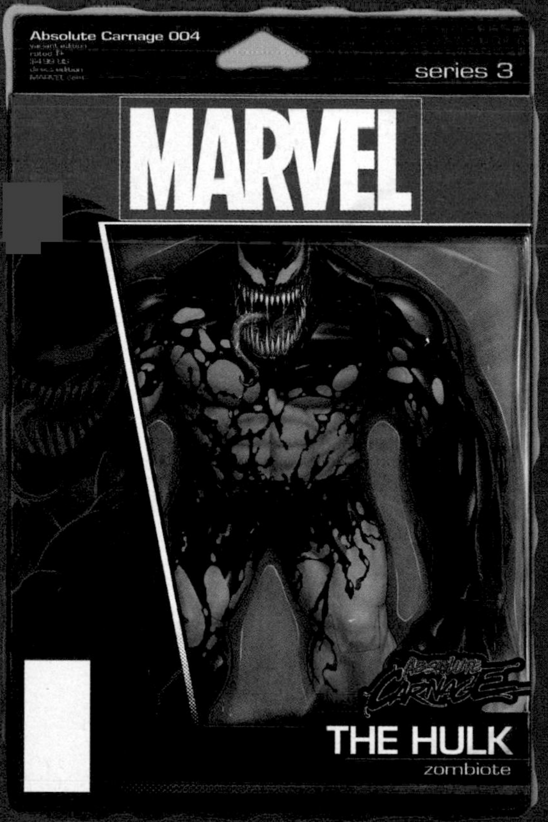
Absolute Carnage 004
series 3
MARVEL
THE HULK
zombiote

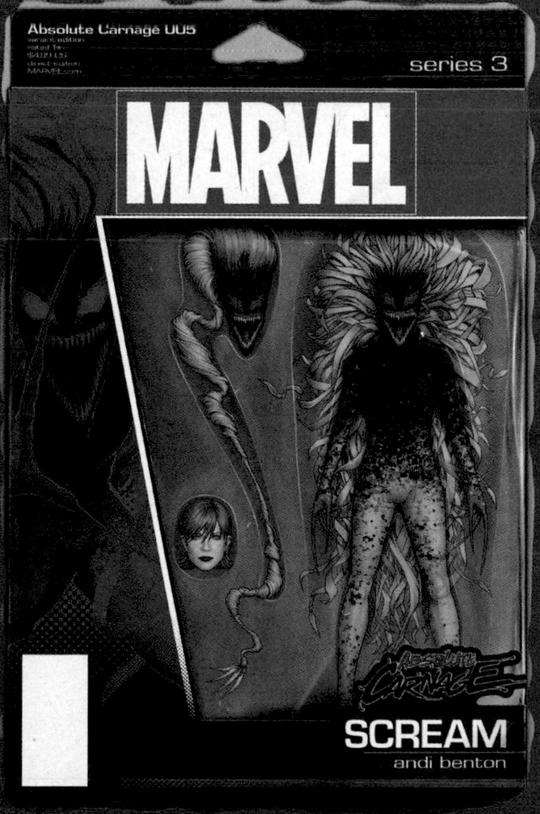
Absolute Carnage 005
series 3
MARVEL
SCREAM
andi benton

JOHN TYLER CHRISTOPHER

#2-5 Action Figure Variants

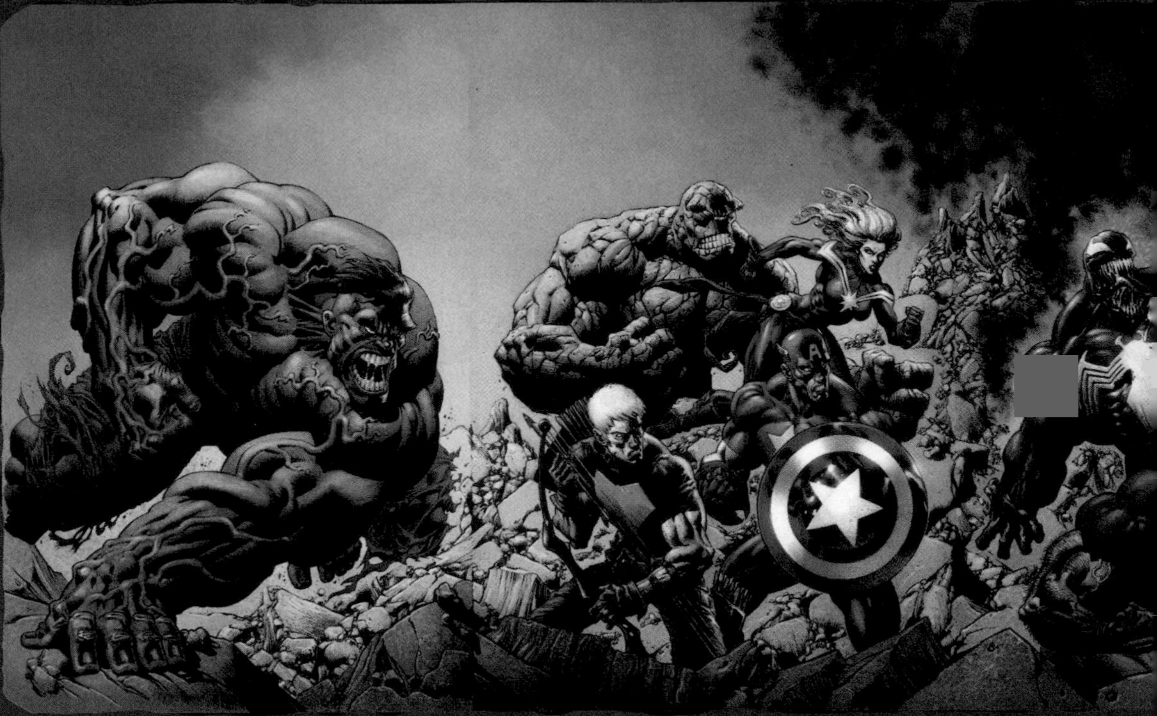

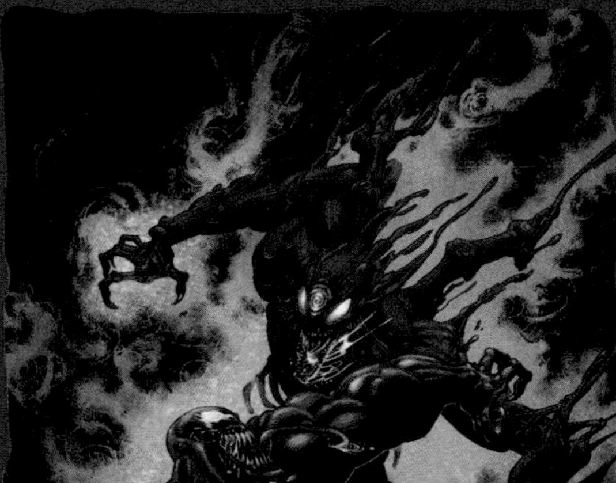

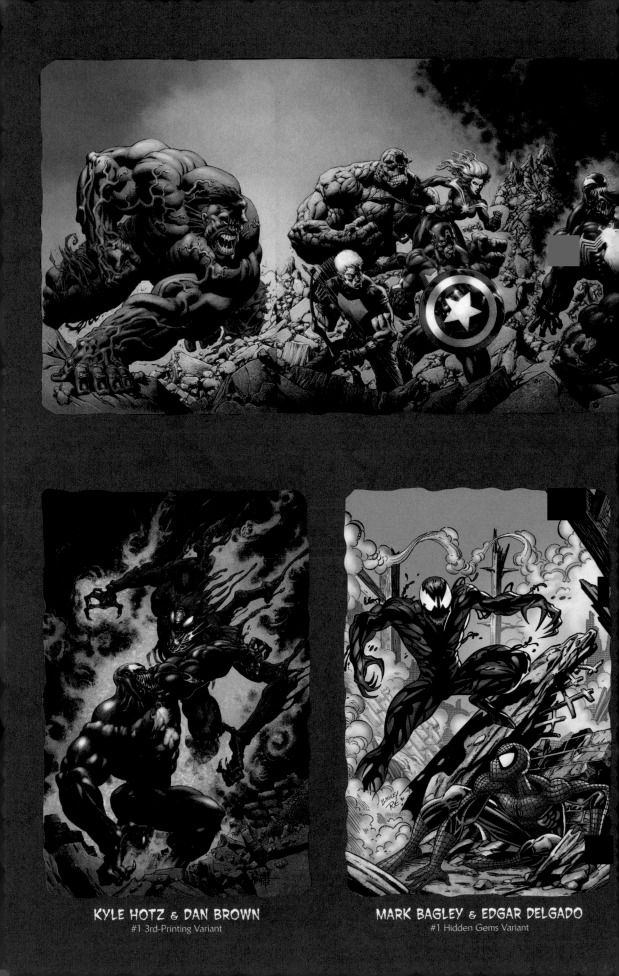

KYLE HOTZ & DAN BROWN
#1 3rd-Printing Variant

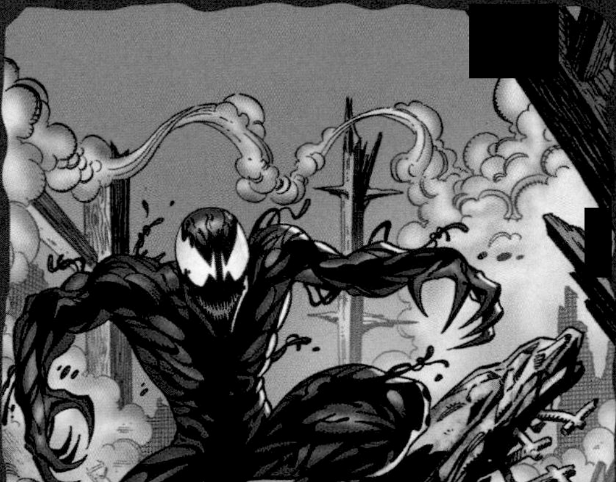

MARK BAGLEY & EDGAR DELGADO
#1 Hidden Gems Variant

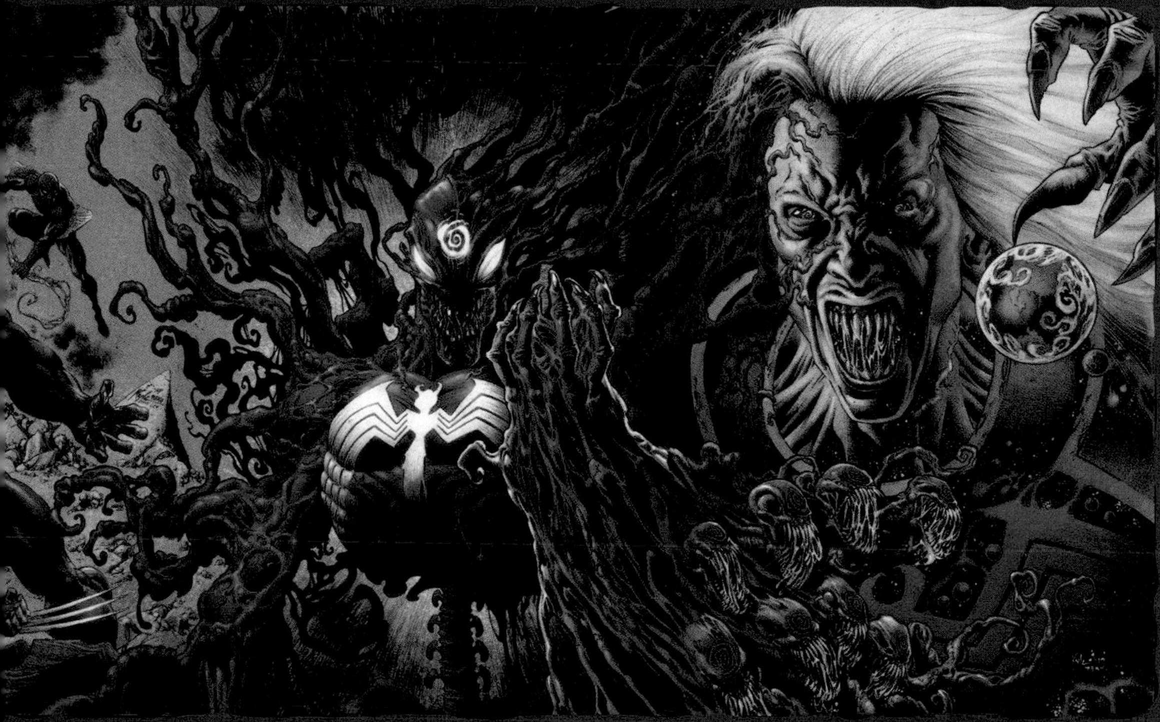

KYLE HOTZ & DAN BROWN
#1-5 Connecting Variants

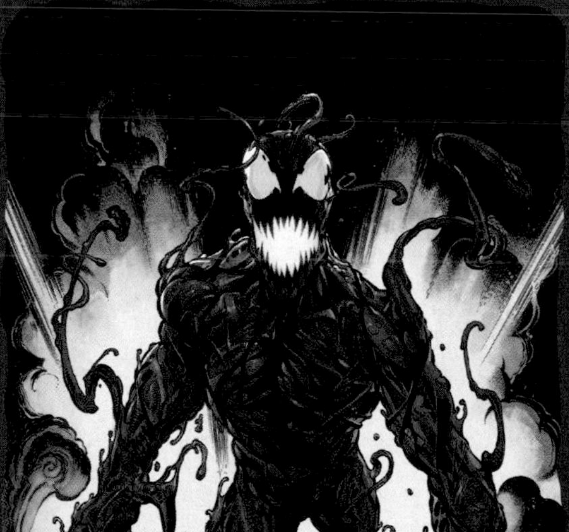

MARK BAGLEY,
ANDREW HENNESSY & JASON KEITH
#1 4th-Printing Variant

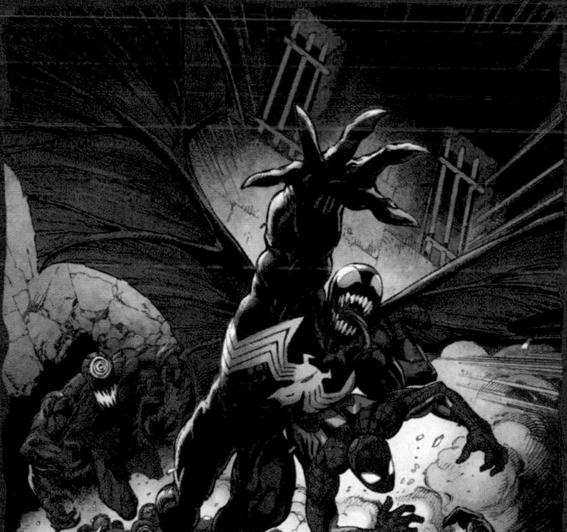

MARK BAGLEY,
JOHN DELL & JASON KEITH
#2 3rd-Printing Variant

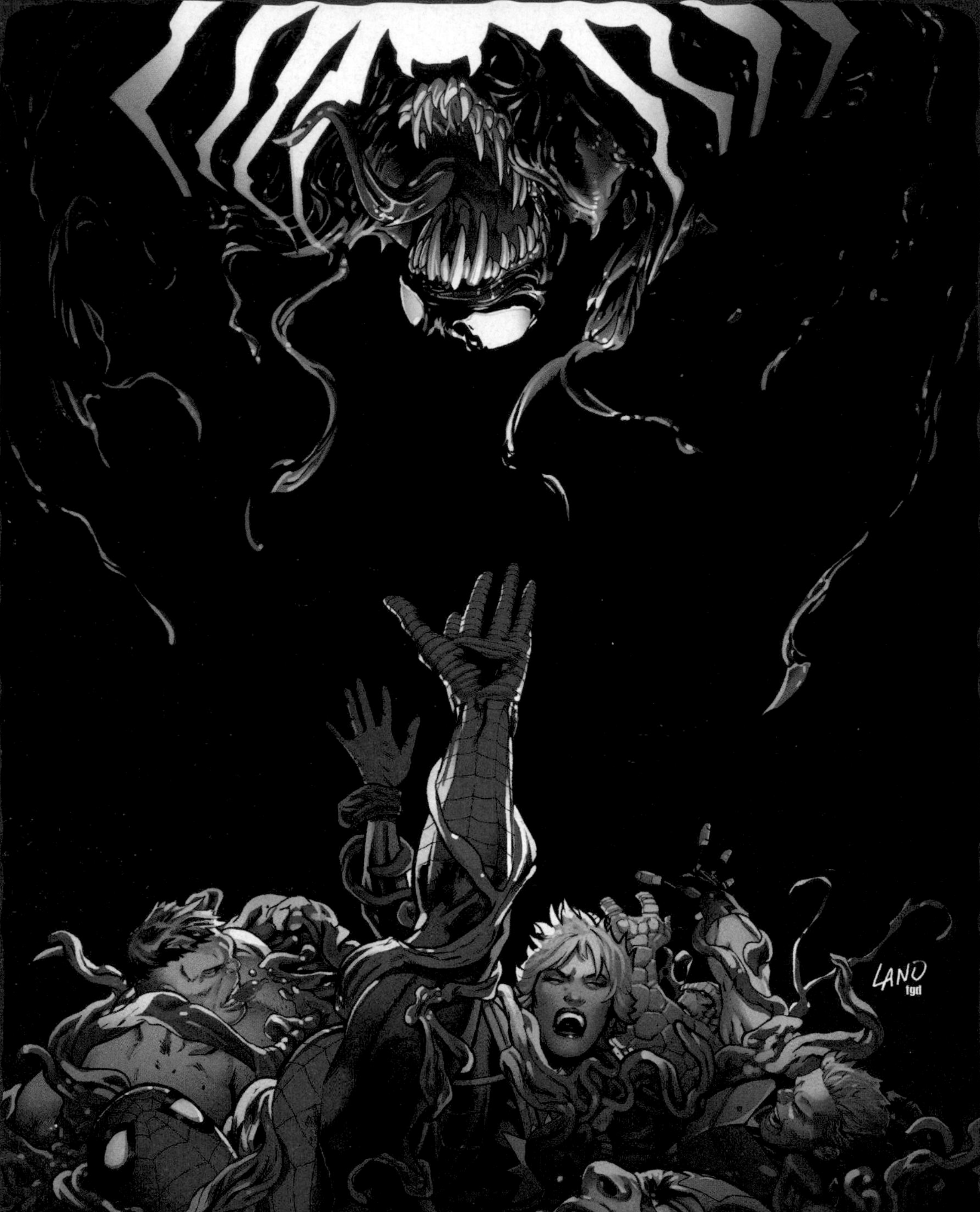
LAND
fgd

GREG LAND, JAY LEISTEN & FRANK D'ARMATA

#5 Variant